Encyclopaedia of

MOUNTAINEERING

Other Sports Encyclopaedias published by Robert Hale & Company

Association Football
BY MAURICE GOLESWORTHY

Athletics
BY MELVYN WATMAN

Boxing
BY MAURICE GOLESWORTHY

Chess
BY ANNE SUNNUCKS

Cricket
BY MAURICE GOLESWORTHY

Flat Racing
BY ROGER MORTIMER

Golf
BY WEBSTER EVANS

Motor Racing
BY ANTHONY PRITCHARD AND KEITH DAVEY

Rugby Football
BY J. R. JONES
   (*Second edition edited by Maurice Golesworthy*)

Rugby League Football
BY A. N. GAULTON

Swimming
BY PAT BESFORD

Encyclopaedia of

MOUNTAINEERING

Compiled by

WALT UNSWORTH

LONDON
ROBERT HALE & COMPANY

NEW YORK
ST. MARTIN'S PRESS, INC.

St. Martin's Press, Inc.
175 Fifth Avenue
New York, N.Y. 10010

Library of Congress Catalog Card Number 74–33913

Robert Hale & Company
Clerkenwell House
Clerkenwell Green
London EC1

ISBN 0 7091 4804 6

Photoset, printed and bound
in Great Britain by
REDWOOD BURN LIMITED
Trowbridge & Esher

Illustrations

Acknowledgements

My thanks are due to the many authors, past and present, upon whose work I have freely drawn in the compilation of this encyclopaedia. Literally hundreds of books have been consulted. I am also indebted to various journals, particularly the *Alpine Journal, Climbers' Club Journal, Les Alpes, La Montagne* and *Mountain*.

Dr P. Hurley and Mr J. Crisp made their libraries freely available, and many climbers gave me information, advice, and encouragement, in particular: Nat Allen, Allan Austin, Mike Banks, Paul Bauer, John Baxter, Barry Bishop, Peter Biven, Alan Blackshaw, Chris Bonington, Mick Burke, John Cleare, John Cunningham, A. D. M. Cox, Peter Crew, Ian McNaught Davis, Henry Day, Nick Estcourt, Dennis Gray, Alfred Gregory, Peter Habeler, Peter Harding, Charles Houston, Tony Howard, Ron James, the late Sir Arnold Lunn, Tony Moulam, Bill Murray, Paul Nunn, Fred Pigott, Doug Scott, Malcolm Slesser, Tony Streather, Jeremy Talbot, Ivan Waller, Mike Ward, Mike Westmacott, Fritz Wiessner, Ken Wilson and Alfred Zurcher. Mrs Diana Penny of the O.A.V. and Mrs Audrey Salkeld also provided useful information and my thanks are due to them.

My thanks are also due to the photographers whose names appear on the list of illustrations and to Brian Evans for his work on the maps and diagrams.

Worsley, 1974   WALT UNSWORTH

"If a man can climb, and in safety, rocks that others will not attempt or cannot scale, he is an exceptional rock-climber; and may be no more. If he can quickly judge the right line and thread his way unerringly and without hesitation through an unknown intricate ice-fall, if he is an unfailing judge of snow and ice, he is a snow craftsman of the first rank; but it may end there. Combine these qualities, add power, resource and courage that rises under the stress of bad weather or in times of difficulty or danger, and he becomes a great mountaineer."

C. T. DENT

Preface

This book is the first attempt to compile a comprehensive encyclopaedia covering the complex sport of mountaineering. Although the entries are strictly alphabetical, the subject matter divides itself into four major areas: 1. Places 2. People 3. Techniques and equipment 4. Miscellanea. A few notes about each of these will not be out of place since they will help the reader to understand the scope and limitations of the book.

An encyclopaedia, while it must be all-embracing, must also have some limits. The chief limitation is that of *depth*: important topics cannot be followed to their ultimate conclusions (some require, and have, books to themselves) yet enough must be given to form a broad picture. This the book does, and where desirable, adds references so that the topic may be pursued further. (See below). More superficial topics receive only a sentence or two. Another limitation is that of *continuity*: mountaineering, like life itself, continues even as the book is being written and produced. There is bound to be a time lag between events and public knowledge of those events, but there is also an imposed time lag while the significance of the events is assessed. The scope of the work itself also imposes limitations on the compiler: whilst every effort has been made to use the best available references it has not been possible to cross-check every detail.

Places.

The entries cover all the important mountain areas of the world and most of the lesser ones. Each area has a comprehensive entry which may be under the country concerned (e.g. Australia) or, if the range is well known, under the range itself (e.g. Alps). These entries give a broad picture. For important ranges, such as the Alps, Himalayas and Andes, there are further entries dealing with each sub-division (e.g. Pennine Alps). Finally, mountains of special significance have their own entries (e.g. Mount Everest). In the case of Britain and the U.S.A. individual crags and outcrops of importance have their own entries. Topographical and historical information is given in all important entries, and there is a note to each regarding the availability of an English language guidebook.

People.

This covers the largest number of entries – some 400 – and was the most difficult to compile. A climber can only be judged in the context of his own time and many of the pioneers who figure in the book would not have gained entry had they lived at a later date. But the matter is further complicated by the fact that many are enshrined in books and climbing lore and for this reason alone require a mention. The nearer we come to modern times the more good climbers there are, but the standard of entry gets tougher! With some of the active experts of the present day, the time lag already mentioned has been brought into play until their achievements can be properly assessed in the light of contemporary standards. The net has been cast fairly wide but in an English language publication it is inevitable that many of the climbers will be British or American – about half in fact. However, it might be noted that where a climber does not have an entry to himself his name will probably occur in connection with various mountains. Wherever possible all entries give full names and dates, except where a climber has preferred to give only his commonly accepted, usually abbreviated, first name.

Techniques and Equipment.

The encyclopaedia is not an instructional textbook, but sufficient information is given to enable the layman or climber to grasp the technique involved or the purpose of any particular piece of equipment. Colloquial expressions have been included where appropriate because climbing does have a special jargon. French, Italian, German and American equivalents are given when appropriate. Due attention has also been given to trends, where these are apparent.

Miscellanea.

Mountaineering has common ground with many broader subjects, such as geography, geology, physics, and so on. In general, phenomena from these subjects are only included where they have a specific bearing on the sport – glaciers being an obvious example. Under this heading, too, comes a host of other fringe topics including ethical and philosophical considerations.

References.

It would double the size of this book to list the thousands of references consulted during compilation. However, books and journals are quoted where it is felt that a fuller explanation would be especially helpful. Climbers' own books are listed with date of publication. Cross references are indicated thus (*qv*) or (*'see'*).

Corrections and Additions

The author would welcome, via the publisher, any factual corrections or suggested additions to the encyclopaedia for possible inclusion in future editions. Such notes should give the exact source: publication and date, author and page number.

ABALAKOV, Vitali Mikhailovich (b. 1906)

An outstanding Soviet mountaineer, often regarded as the 'father' of Russian climbing. Abalakov made some early scrambles on the Krasnojarsk Pillars as a boy (1915) but his serious climbing began in 1931 with the first Soviet ascent of Dykhtau. Then came (Caucasus):

1932 Bezingi ridge traverse Gestola-Shkhara
1947 P. Schurovski, NW Face
Schkhelda, second W Summit by Face
1948 Tomashek–Muller Route, Shkhara followed by traverse to Gestola
1949 Koshtantau–Dychtau traverse
1950 Schkhelda, third W Summit by Face
1951 Chanchahi, N Face
Ullutauchana
1953 P. Schurovski, NE Face
1954 Dychtau, N Face

Important first ascents in the greater ranges are:

Altai – Belukha from N, Iiktu (1933)
Pamirs – P. Lenin from N (1934), P. Trapezia (1935), P.XIX Party Congress (1952), Musdzhilga-Sandal traverse (1955), P. Voroshilov (1959), P. Dserzhinski – P. Lenin – P.XIX Party Congress traverse (1960)
Turkestan – Oloviannaja stena (1934)
Tian Shan – P. Pobeda (1956)

While descending from Khan Tengri in the Tian Shan in 1936 he lost several fingers and toes from frostbite which stopped him climbing for ten years.

Abalakov has been ten times champion of the U.S.S.R. in mountaineering and leader of 12 high-altitude expeditions. He has done considerable work on equipment development both in climbing and other sports, and is a member of the U.I.A.A. Commissions on Safety and Belaying. Honoured Master of Mountaineering, 1935; Honoured Master of Sport, 1943; Honoured Trainer of the U.S.S.R. in Mountaineering, 1957.

Wrote: *The Fundamentals of Mountaineering* (German and Japanese editions amongst others, but no English version).

ABNEY, Sir William de Wiveleslie (1843-1920)

Trained in the Royal Engineers, where he held rank of Captain until he retired in 1881, Abney was one of the foremost pioneers in the development of photographic science, especially the dry plate process. Elected F.R.S. in 1876 and Rumford Medallist for his photographic researches (1883). K.C.B. in 1900. He was for many years science adviser to the Board of Education and was the author of many works on photography.

He seems to have little climbing to his credit but is well known for his magnificent series of portraits of the early Alpine guides published in Cunningham (*qv*) and Abney's *Pioneers of the Alps* (1887).

ABOMINABLE SNOWMAN

The abominable snowman, or *yeti*, is a creature said to live in the high Himalaya and associated ranges such as the Pamirs. One seen on the Fedchenko Glacier in the Pamirs was said to be thick-set with unusually long forearms, walking on its hind legs and bent slightly forwards. It wore no clothing and was covered in thick reddish-grey hair. Several Sherpas claim to have seen yeti, and various expeditions have seen yeti tracks in the snow.

According to the Sherpas there are two types of yeti: the "little yeti" which eats men, and the "big yeti" which eats yaks. Yeti have been seen eating frogs in the Dudh Kosi valley.

There have been at least two yeti-hunting expeditions (one British, one Russian) but both failed to find the creature.

In the Cordillera Real of Bolivia the natives fear a creature known as *Hualapichi* (snow ghost). It has never been seen.

ABRAHAM BROTHERS

George Dixon Abraham (1872-1965) and Ashley Perry Abraham (1876-1951) were two Keswick brothers who played an important part in the establishing of rock-climbing as a sport in Britain. Well known for their association with O. G. Jones (*qv*), they were also innovators in their own right.

They began climbing about 1890 but

their early routes were gullies of little account (Sandbed Ghyll, 1890; Dollywaggon Gully, 1894; Bridge Gully, 1895; Iron Crag Chimney, 1896 – all in the Lake District). At Christmas, 1895, they met Jones and began climbing with him in 1896 (Jones' Direct from Deep Ghyll, 1896; Walker's Gully, 1899 – Ashley did not take part; Pisgah Buttress, 1898 and several famous Welsh climbs, including North Buttress, Terrace Wall Variant and Milestone Buttress, all on Tryfan, 1899). (See below.)

During this period, but without Jones, they visited Skye (1896), climbed Bowfell Links (1897), Mouse Ghyll (1897) and the Keswick Brother's Climb on Scafell (1897). Only the last achieved fame.

After Jones' death in 1899 the brothers continued to make new climbs with other partners, such as Phillipson, Harland, Barton and Puttrell (qv). In the Lakes these were: New West, Pillar (1901), Shamrock Buttress, Pillar (1902) and their eponymous routes on A and B Buttresses, Dow Crag (1903). In Scotland, with Puttrell, they climbed Church Door Buttress, Bidean and the Direct ascent of Crowberry Ridge, where Abraham's Ledge is named in their honour. They made some other minor routes, too, and George returned to Glencoe later the same year on his honeymoon and with his wife climbed Winifred's Pinnacle, Aonach Dubh and Lady's Gully, Buachaille Etive Mor. In 1905 they climbed the celebrated Monolith Crack of the Gribin Facet in Wales.

Ashley visited Skye with H. Harland in 1906 and 1907 making half a dozen new climbs of which Cioch Direct is best known. George revisited Skye as late as 1920 and made a couple of new routes. The brothers climbed extensively in the Alps but seemed content to repeat existing climbs.

The brothers were professional photographers and as such the first to popularize climbing. They agreed to illustrate Jones' book on the Lakes (qv) in return for action shots of the master which they sold in their Keswick shop. A heavy plate camera was their constant companion and many of their climbs were undertaken with photographs in mind, and later, guidebooks (for instance on the Welsh tour of 1899 and Ashley's Skye tour of 1907.) This professionalism aroused considerable antagonism from the older establishment climbers: they were accused of tilting the camera!

After Jones' death they took up writing and publishing guidebooks:

Rock Climbing in the English Lake District, Jones (revised) 2nd and 3rd Ed.
Rock Climbing in North Wales – G. D. and A. P. Abraham
Rock Climbing in Skye, A. P. Abraham
The Complete Mountaineer, G. D. Abraham
British Mountain Climbs, G. D. Abraham
Mountain Adventures at home and Abroad, G. D. Abraham
Swiss Mountain Climbs, G. D. Abraham
On Alpine Heights and British Crags, G. D. Abraham
First Steps to Climbing, G. D. Abraham.

British Mountain Climbs ran to six main editions (1909-48) and was enormously influential in the development of the sport.

George was always the leader on the brothers' climbs together. They have been credited with the invention of belaying (qv).

ABRUZZI, Duke of the (1873-1933)
Luigi Amedeo Giuseppe, grandson of King Victor Emmanuel II of Italy. Abruzzi was in the tradition of wealthy Italian explorer-climbers. Vittorio Sella, the photographer, was another, and he accompanied Abruzzi on several expeditions. The expeditions were large, well organized and equipped with the best Italian guides. They were:

1897   Alaska. The first ascent of Mt St Elias. The expedition was planned after an expedition to Nanga Parbat was prevented by plague in India.

1899   Attempt to reach the North Pole. Abruzzi lost two fingers in an accident and the leadership of the final push devolved upon U. Gagni who reached Lat. 86° 34′ N – the furthest north reached at the time (1900). Several lives were lost and the expedition was an epic of endurance.

1906   Ruwenzori. The expedition climbed all the main peaks (all first ascents) and mapped the area.

1909   Karakorum. An attempt on K2 was foiled at 21,800 ft on the Abruzzi Ridge. Reached 24,600 ft on Chogolisa – the highest point reached at that date.

1928-9 Exploration of the Uebi Shebeli River in Ethiopia-Eritrea.

In the 1914-18 War the Duke was C.I.C. of the Italian Fleet and of the Allied

Adriatic fleets. In 1919 he began work on the Eritrean colony which was to be his final life's work and to which, in the end, he returned to die.

Abruzzi had been a good climber in his early days: he did the Zmutt on the Matterhorn with Mummery and Collie, and made several first ascents. The Pic Luigi Amedeo in the Mt Blanc Range is named in his honour.

ABSEIL (G.) (E.: rope down; Fr.: en rappel; It.: corda doppia)
A rapid method of descent using the rope to slide down. Both the French and German terms are used by British climbers, but the German is more common. Common slang: to 'ab'. Note also "abseiling" (G. *abseilen*).

Abseiling is commonly done using a doubled rope hanging from an abseil point, which may be a tree, rock spike or peg. The climber slides down the rope, using friction to control his descent, until he reaches a stance. When all the party have abseiled to the stance, the rope is pulled down and the next abseil commenced, and so on to the bottom of the climb. On many Continental peaks there are permanent abseil pegs (for example in the Dolomites) to make descent quicker.

Abseiling down ice is also common. It is done from a screw or ice peg. It can also be done from an ice "mushroom" or "bollard" – a substantial pinnacle of ice cut out by the ice axe, but this is not popular.

Abseiling may also be necessary during the course of a climb, especially on a ridge with many gendarmes, e.g. the Jagigrat. On some routes a diagonal abseil is made to change lines, but this only on higher grade climbs. A free abseil is one where the climber does not touch the rock, e.g. from an overhang.

Abseiling is a necessary part of climbing technique but it needs to be learnt on small outcrops first and always with the protection of a safety rope. Done carelessly it is highly dangerous and there have been numerous fatalities. There are several ways of using the rope to gain the necessary friction. The original method, known as the "classic abseil" passes the rope between the legs then across the front of the body and over the opposite shoulder. One hand lightly holds the rope in front, the other hand holds the rope behind – the latter is the controlling hand. The climber leans out from the cliff, backwards, until he is able to walk backwards down the rock, the speed of descent being controlled by the rear hand. By moving this forward, friction is increased and descent slowed. It is possible to stop still if necessary. The climber is actually sitting in the rope and it is this which enables him to leave the rock altogether e.g. at an overhang, yet continue his descent.

The classic method is not comfortable and there are numerous alternatives, of which the "abseil sling and krab" method is best known. The sling is twisted into a figure eight and one leg put through each loop. The krab is clipped onto the front and the doubled rope passed through it and over one shoulder. The rope is held as before and the method of descent is the same.

Other alternatives use twists of rope round karabiners, abseil bars which fit on karabiners, and special devices known as "descendeurs", of which there are several varieties. It is even possible to abseil facing outwards.

Where a lot of abseils are expected, e.g. in the Dolomites, it is usual to carry a special abseil rope. This may be 300 ft in length but it need not be as thick as a climbing rope – no. 3 hawser or 9 mm perlon is quite satisfactory.

The chief dangers of abseiling are: insecure abseil points, e.g. loose pegs; unsatisfactory abseil points, e.g. allowing the rope to ride off; insufficient rope to reach the desired stance; and incorrect or careless technique. Where a lot of overhangs are involved the climber should always carry prusiks (*qv*) so that if the abseil ends away from the rock he can climb back up the rope to safety and try a different abseil. For this reason, too, it is worth putting a knot in the end of the rope.

ABSEIL LOOP
A loop of rope, normally hemp, used as an abseil point. In the Alps especially, it is possible that the abseil rope might jam if it is placed directly round a rock spike. By placing the loop round the spike and then hanging the rope from the loop, this is avoided. Abseil loops are left in place, of course, but old ones should not be used as they may be rotten.

ABSEIL SLING
A sling made of seven to nine feet of nylon rope, spliced, and used in the sling and karabiner method of abseiling. Hawser rope of no. 2, 3 or 4 size is used.

ACCIDENTS

An increase in the number of participants in mountain sports in recent years has led to a serious increase in the number of accidents.

Table 1 Increase in accidents in British Mountains 1957-68

Year	Accidents	Fatalities
1957	57	12
1968	221	30

(skiers not included)

The table shows accidents reported to the Mountain Rescue Committee; there are many minor accidents not reported (and possibly some severe ones). Later figures (1970) for Scotland show the trend continuing: 70 accidents and 22 deaths, though seasonal factors play a larger part in Scottish figures than elsewhere in Britain and 1970 was a bad year.

The risk of accidents in mountaineering does not seem greater than in other sports, but the risk of *serious* accident is much greater:

Table 2 Estimated accidents per 10,000 ascents in 1965

Europe	6.5 (2.5 fatal)
U.S.A.	9.8 (6.0 fatal)

Table 3 Accidents resulting in death (Swiss insurance figures 1967)

Mountaineering	3.12 per cent
Other sports	0.01 per cent

The statistics continually show more accidents and deaths to walkers than to climbers in Britain. In the period 1957-68 accidents to climbers increased by 323 per cent and to walkers by 583 per cent.

The ages of the victims in the British 1968 report are as follows:

Table 4 Ages of victims, where known

Up to 15	24
16-18	28
19-21	44
Over 21	125 approx

There is no analysis of those over 21, but a Swiss analysis for 1967 shows that accidents are most common in the 15-24 age group and are least common in the 35-44 age group, after which the incident increases again.

The majority of Swiss accidents occur during July and August, but there are no figures for Britain. In view of the winter climbing in Britain the analysis might well be different. Both Swiss and British figures show that a high proportion of accidents occur on easy or moderately difficult terrain and a relatively small number on difficult terrain. There is little doubt that many accidents are caused by lapses of concentration on easy ground, especially in the Alps.

There are many types of accident, but the commonest is the simple slip resulting in a fall. Fairly common are accidents due to falling debris, rope burns and exposure. Lightning causes a number of accidents, and there are many accidents due to imperfect technique: poor belays, abseiling etc. Sometimes the victim has inadequate equipment, especially unsuitable footwear and (in snow/ice) no ice axe or crampons. In climbing, a helmet has been shown to be vital in reducing injuries (see below); and braking gloves and an effective sit-harness also reduce the effects of an accident.

F. G. Höflin and U. F. Gruber of Basle University have published a study of the injuries received from various accidents (*Les Alpes*, August 1971). The following is a brief summary in table form:

Table 5 Minor accidents (37 cases)

Injuries to:	Hands	21
	Legs	20
	Arms	6
	Head	6
	Back	2

Table 6 More serious accidents (37 cases)

Injuries to:	Legs	17
	Arms	10
	Back	7
	Pelvis	1
	Head	3

Table 7 Fatal accidents (62 cases)

Principal injury causing death:	Head	53
	Neck	1
	Back	1
	Abdomen	1 (+6 cases of exposure)

Table 8 Falls up to 2 m (23 cases)

Legs	108
Arms	3
Head	7
Pelvis	1 (no deaths)

Table 9 Falls between 2 and 30 m (30 cases)

Head	17 (3 fatal)
Legs	10
Pelvis	4
Back	3 (1 fatal)

**Table 9 Falls between 2 and 30 m
(30 cases)**

Neck	1
Arm	1
Hand	1

**Table 10 Falls of more than 30 m
(44 cases)**

Head	42 (40 fatal)
Neck	2 (2 fatal)

**Table 11 Slips on grass slopes or ice slopes
(sliding or rolling falls)
(35 cases)**

Head	21 (9 fatal)
Back	9 (5 fatal)
Legs	8
Pelvis	3
Arms	3
Neck	1

See also MOUNTAIN RESCUE.

ACCLIMATIZATION

The adaptation of the human body to the rarified air at high altitudes. The process is a slow one, especially for the really big mountains of the Himalaya, where acclimatization can take from four to six weeks. During acclimatization the following physiological changes take place: breathing becomes deeper and faster, and often irregular (Cheyne-Stokes respiration); heartbeat speed and force is increased; blood thickens because the red cells multiply and the plasma becomes less.

Acclimatization can effect climbers even in the Alps and other relatively low mountains: two or three days should be spent on lower peaks before attempting anything high, though acclimatization is a very personal thing and some people are scarcely affected at all. At its worst it produces mountain sickness, manifested by headaches, sleeplessness and sickness.

At higher altitudes, lack of acclimatization can cause pulmonary edema or cerebral edema. Water is not passed at the usual rate and accumulates as fluid on the lungs or the brain. The treatment is oxygen via a face mask and a diuretic drug to make the patient pass water. Evacuation to a lower altitude is urgent and only then will the patient revive – otherwise edema is rapidly fatal.

A CHEVAL

A method of climbing a rib or arête in which the climber places one foot on either side of the arête and grips the crest with his hands. He then moves up in a series of frog-like hops. The Americans call it rib-riding. The technique is not common in Britain, but there is a well-known one at the Black Rocks, Derbyshire.

In the Alps some narrow arêtes are taken by sitting astride them for a few moves and this is also called à cheval.

ACHILLE RATTI (1857–1939)

A Catholic priest later to become Pope Pius XI. As a young man he was an enthusiastic mountaineer, climbing mainly in the Monte Rosa area. The Achille Ratti climbing club is named in his honour.

ACONCAGUA (22,835 ft)

The highest peak in South America and in the western world, Aconcagua dominates the Central Andes of Argentina. There are two summits: North (22,835 ft) and South (22,730 ft). The Ordinary Route (NNE Face) begins at Puente del Inca and rises via the huts at Plaza de Mulas, Plantamura (two huts) and Indepencia, to the summit of N peak. In 1965 there had been over 50 ascents, but no fewer than 36 lives had been lost in attempts. The mountain has sudden severe storms when winds reach 160 m.p.h. and the temperature can drop to –45°C. The name comes from the local native word *Kon-kawa* (snowy mountain).

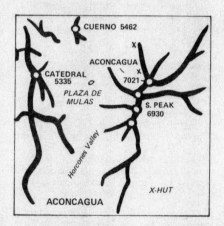

In 1883 P. Gussfeldt (*qv*) attempted the mountain from the N, with only local help – his guide, Burgener (*qv*), being ill. With virtually no equipment he reached a height of about 21,600 ft. Another attempt was less successful. In 1897, the Fitzgerald Expedition attempted the peak. The leader gave up about 1,500 ft short of the top, but the guide Matthias Zurbriggen reached the N summit on 14 January – a first ascent. A month later S. Vines and N. Lanti also reached the summit. 1897 and 1898 saw two incredible attempts by a German party helped by Chilean miners. Using Gussfeldt's route they reached a height of about 21,300 ft. In 1898, M. Conway (*qv*) deliberately stopped some 50 ft short of the summit. He later claimed that he did not wish to embarrass Fitzgerald by doing in a week what it had taken the latter months to achieve! Other notable ascents include

1934 East Face, first ascent – K. Narkie-vicz-Jodko, St. Dazynski, W. Ostrowski, S. Osiecki

1940 First woman's ascent – Adriana Link and party

1947 South summit, first ascent – T. Kopp, L. Herold

1951 Gussfeldt's route completed – W. Foerster, L. Krahl, E. Maier

1953 W Face–S Ridge, first ascent – F. Ibanez, Mr. and Mrs. F. Marmillod, F. Grajales

1953 First winter ascent – E. Huerta, F. Godoy, H. Vasalla

1954 SSE Face, first ascent – R. Ferlet's Expedition

1965 W Face, first ascent – G. Mason, T. Hill, R. Mackey

1966 S Face of S summit, first ascent – F. Moravec's Expedition

Ferlet's expedition of 1954 is reckoned one of the greatest feats in Andean climbing. (See *A. J.* 60.)

Several dogs have been to the top of Aconcagua – almost certainly the canine height record.

ADAMS REILLY, Anthony Miles William (1836–85)

Irish artist noted for making the first reliable map of the Mont Blanc area, begun in 1863 and published two years later. In 1864 he was with Whymper on many of the first ascents in the area, and they had intended to attempt the Matterhorn together but Whymper was recalled to England.

AIGUILLE DU DRU (3,754 m)

An outlier of the Verte massif in the Mont Blanc range, overlooking the Mer de Glace. Seen from Montenvers (*qv*) it presents one of the most startling pictures in the Alps – a gigantic obelisk.

There are two tops, known as the Grand and Petit Dru (3,733 m) and one speaks of "the Drus". The great modern climbs for which the mountain is famous lie on the flanks of the Petit Dru.

The first ascent was that of C. T. Dent and J. Walker with A. Burgener and K. Maurer, 1878 – Dent's 19th attempt on the peak. The Petit Dru was first climbed by the guides J. E. Charlet-Stratton, P. Payot and F. Folliguet, in 1879. The first traverse, Petit-Grand (the usual way), was by E. Giraud with J. Ravanel and A. Comte, 1903 and the first winter ascent and traverse was by the two guides A. Charlet and C. Dévouassoud, in 1928.

The three modern classics are: North Face (P. Allain, R. Leininger 1935) after it had previously been descended by abseil by A. Roch and R. Gréloz (1932); the West Face (L. Berardini, A. Dagory, M. Laine, G. Magnone, 1952) – climbed in two stages separated by 11 days and thus provoking criticism; the Bonatti Pillar, climbed solo by Walter Bonatti in five days 1955; one of the epics of modern climbing (see Bonatti, *On the Heights*). The Americans, Hemming and Robbins, made a direct start to the West Face in 1962 and Harlin and Robbins made another in 1965. Both are very hard.

Guidebook: *Selected Climbs in the Range of Mont Blanc* (Vol II), by R. Collomb and P. Crew.

AINSLIE, Charles (1820–63)

Original Member of the A. C. With Hudson, Kennedy and the Smyths he made the first guideless ascent of Mont Blanc, 1855.

ALASKA, CLIMBING IN (including Yukon)

Alaska contains the highest mountains in North America: Mt McKinley (20,320 ft) and Mt. Logan (19,850 ft) – the latter in the St. Elias Mts of which the best-known peak is Mt St Elias (18,008 ft). Some of the world's largest glaciers are in this region. Difficulty of approach makes climbing in many parts of Alaska expeditionary in nature. The principal ranges and peaks are:

Alaska Range

Mt McKinley, 20,320 ft – H. P. Karstens, H. Stuck, W. Harper, R. Tatum, 1913.

Mt Foraker, 17,395 ft – C. S. Houston, T. G. Brown, C. Waterston, 1934.

Mt St Elias Mountains

Mt Logan, 19,850 ft – MacCarthy and Lambert's party, 1925

Mt St Elias, 18,008 ft – Duke of the Abruzzi's party, 1897

Fairweather Range
Mt Fairweather, 15,318 ft – Carpé, Moore, 1931
Chugach Mountains
Mt Marcus Baker, 13,215 ft – B. Washburn's party, 1938
Wrangell Mountains
Mt Sanford, 16,208 ft – Washburn, Moore, 1938
Coast Mountains (shared with British Columbia)
Kate's Needle, 10,002 ft – F. Beckey, Craig, Schmidtke, 1946
Other good peaks are said to exist in the Brooks Range and Stikine Range. In Alaska today, it is common for parties to fly in, saving long treks. Disadvantages are bad weather and earthquakes. (See also: MT McKINLEY)
Guidebook: *A Tourist's Guide to Mt McKinley*–Washburn.

ALBERT 1er, King of the Belgians (1875–1934)
A noted mountaineer who died as a result of an abseiling accident in the Ardennes. Though the King had climbed a number of the higher Alpine peaks (Matterhorn, Monte Rosa, Eiger), his special interest was in rock climbing and his favourite area was the Dolomites, where he climbed most of the hardest routes of the day. Before his accession to the throne he and his wife, Princess Elisabeth, had climbed together many times and made the first ascent of the NE Ridge of Piz Carale. In the Kaisergebirge he made some of the hardest climbs of the day on the steep faces of the Fleischbank, Predigstuhl and Totenkirchl. Though he climbed with guides, the King was often leader on the climbs.

ALBULA ALPS
The mountains on the N side of the Engadine from the Splügenpass to the Flüela Pass. It is bisected N – S by the Chur-Silvaplana road (Julier Pass). The highest summit is the Piz Kesch (3,418 m). Other peaks of interest are the Piz Vadret (3,229 m) and Alplihorn (3,006 m). These are in the eastern part of the group, but in the centre, above Tinizong, rise the interesting group of the "Bergun Dolomites": Piz Ela (3,338 m) Das Tinzenhorn (3,172 m) and Piz Michel (Mitgel) (3,159 m).
The area is surrounded by famous ski resorts: St Moritz, Davos, Arosa, Lenzerheide. (No English guidebook.)

ALLAIN, Pierre
A French climber, trained on the rocks of Fontainebleau, who became one of the leading guides of the inter-war years. Climbing usually with J and R Leininger, he made numerous routes amongst which are:
1933 SW Ridge of Fou
1935 E Face, Dent du Caimen
       N Face of the Dru
1936 E Ridge of Dent du Crocodil
He later became an equipment designer and manufacturer – the well known P.A. rock boot was a revolutionary addition to climbing gear.

ALLEN, Nat (b.1928)
A founder member of the Rock and Ice Club and the Alpine Climbing Group. In the former, particularly, he played an important role and was partner to Brown and Whillans (both *qv*) on numerous occasions, among which might be mentioned the first ascents of Llithwrig and the East Buttress Girdle of Clogwyn du'r Arddu, and Erosion Grooves, Carreg Wastad.
In the Peak District, Allen made forty new gritstone climbs and two new limestone climbs before 1951, and many more since then. His limestone climbs are mainly in the Manifold Valley and Dovedale and his best known gritstone climbs are at Froggatt (Allen's Slab, etc). He has also made new routes in Pembroke, Swanage and on Cader Idris (Route II, Slanting Gully Grooves). Allen is almost certainly the leading authority on Peak District climbing today: he has inherited the mantle of Eric Byne (*qv*).

ALLGAUER ALPS
Part of the Northern Tyrolese Alps forming the border between Tyrol and Bavaria. There are really two parts: the Allgauer Voralpen and the Allgauer proper, separated by the long valley wherein lies the ski resort of Obersdorf, the principal centre. The very long Lechtal separates the Allgauer and Lechtaler Alps (*qv*).
The highest summit is Grosser Krottenkoff (2,657 m). Other peaks of interest include the Mädelegabel (2,649 m), Höfats (2,258 m) and the Hochvogel (2,594 m), all typically steep limestone. There is an interesting sub-group, the Tannheimer, just south of Fussen (Kellenspitze, or Köllespitze, 2,240 m). (No English guidebook.)

ALMER, Christian (1826–98)
Possibly the greatest of the early Alpine

guides; his only possible equal being Melchior Anderegg (*qv*). Almer took part in the celebrated ascent of the Wetterhorn from Grindelwald by Sir Alfred Wills (*qv*) and thereafter climbed with many of the leading amateurs including Moore (*qv*) Whymper (*qv*) Hornby and Philpott (*qv*) and Coolidge. He climbed with Coolidge almost exclusively from 1868 to 1884, but during a winter ascent of Jungfrau (1864) he lost several toes from frostbite and was incapacititated for a couple of seasons. He seems to have been fully active again by 1890, but his place as Coolidge's chief guide had by then been taken by his son, Christian Almer II.

He made numerous first ascents in the Oberland and was with Whymper during the famous seasons of 1864 and 1865, though he did not take part in the Matterhorn ascent (*qv*). His experience ranged from end to end of the Alps – Dachstein in Austria (1866) to the Maritime Alps (1879). His favourite peak was always the Wetterhorn and he made a Golden Wedding anniversary ascent with his wife in 1896 – he was 70 and his wife, who accompanied him, was 71. He climbed it again in 1897.

Almer was at the centre of two famous climbing controversies. One, known as 'Almer's leap", concerned an illustration by Whymper in *Scrambles* showing Almer making a daring leap across a break in the ridge of the Ecrins: this led to a classic controversy between Whymper and Coolidge over whether the incident took place. The other was the publication by Abney and Cunningham (*qv*) of a facsimile of Almer's *Führerbuch* (1897) which was deeply resented by many climbers.

Almer had five sons: Ulrich (*b*. 1849) Christian (*b*. 1859) Hans (*b*. 1861) Rudolf (*b*. 1864) and Peter (*b*. 1869). They all became first-class guides, Ulrich (who died in 1940) being especially notable. He accompanied his father on many expeditions and he also led Cockin on the first ascent of Ushba in Caucasus, 1888. Unfortunately, he fell on bad times through drink and ended his days impoverished and blind.

ALMSCLIFF

One of the most famous gritstone outcrops, well known to the pioneers. The crag is in Lower Wharfedale about five miles from Harrogate and has climbs of all standards, mostly rather short and numerous boulder problems. The training ground for many famous names – Botterill,

Frankland, Dolphin and Austin among them.

Guidebook: *Yorkshire Gritstone*, by M. Bebbington.

ALP

The grassy pastures below the snowline in the Alps but above the valley and the place where the animals are taken to feed in the summer months. Adopted in error by the early travellers who thought it referred to the whole mountain, hence, the Alps. In the Eastern Alps an alp is known as an *alm*.

ALPENSTOCK

A long wooden pole fitted with a spike at the lower end and used as a sort of "third leg" on glaciers and snow slopes by the pioneers. Frequently seen in early alpine engravings. It was supplanted by the ice axe (*qv*) and had virtually disappeared by the 1870s.

ALPINE CLIMBING GROUP

A British club, founded in the early 1950s, to raise the standard of post-war British alpinism and to provide guidebooks for the major areas of the Alps. In 1957 they published *Selected Climbs in the Range of Mont Blanc*. Their publishing interests were later assumed by the Alpine Club and later the A. C. G. formed an alliance with the older club. It remains an elitist group of young climbers comparable with the French G. H. M.

THE ALPINE CLUB

The idea of a club to cater for Alpine climbers was first mooted by William Mathews in a letter to F. J. A. Hort at the end of 1856 or early 1857. It was revived at a meeting between the Mathews and Kennedy in the Hasli Tal, 4 August 1857 and first seriously discussed at the Mathews' house, The Leasowes, Worcestershire, on 6 November 1857, when a list of prospective members was drawn up. The first meeting was at Ashley's Hotel, Henrietta Street, Covent Garden on 22 December 1857 when only 11 members turned up. An attempt to turn it into an elitist group – by electing only members who had ascended 13,000 ft peaks – was defeated. A second meeting was held in the same hotel on 19 January 1858 when the rules were revised for approval at the next meeting 3 February, when E. S. Kennedy was elected Vice-President and Hinchcliffe, Hon. Secretary. The post of President was not filled until 31 March, when John Ball was elected. All those who had joined the Club on or before 19 January were designated Original Members.

The initial idea was that the Club should be of a social nature, but this soon changed and the first lecture was given by Ormsby (*qv*) in February 1860.

A detailed history of the Club can be gleaned from the numerous volumes of the *Alpine Journal* (*qv*) published since 1863, and a general summary in the centennial volume, 1957. Until the 1920s its influence in world mountaineering was considerable, but it declined somewhat when it failed to take account of changing conditions and attitudes to the sport, as shown by Continental climbers. In recent years it has recovered, and now holds a respected position in world climbing circles.

An applicant for membership must be over 21 and be proposed and seconded by two members. Letters of support may come from other members. He is elected by the Committee. Technical qualifications are not high – roughly several Alpine seasons (or other high ranges) with at least 20 good peaks to the applicant's credit. Candidates need not be British, but until May 1974 only male members were admitted.

ALPINE CLUB, PRESIDENTS OF THE
1858 J. Ball
1861 E. S. Kennedy
1864 A. Wills
1866 L. Stephen
1869 W. Mathews
1872 W. Longman
1875 T. W. Hinchliff
1878 C. E. Mathews
1881 T. G. Bonney
1884 F. C. Grove
1887 C. T. Dent
1890 H. Walker
1893 D. W. Freshfield
1896 C. Pilkington
1899 J. Bryce
1902 W. M. Conway
1905 G. F. Browne
1908 H. Woolley
1911 W. E. Davidson
1914 W. Pickford
1917 J. P. Farrar
1920 J. N. Collie
1923 C. G. Bruce
1926 G. H. Morse
1929 C. Wilson
1932 J. J. Withers
1935 J. L. Strutt
1938 C. Schuster
1941 G. W. Young

1944 L. S. Amery
1947 T. G. Longstaff
1950 C. A. Elliott
1953 E. S. Herbert
1956 H. C. J. Hunt
1959 G. I. Finch
1962 T. H. Somervell
1965 E. E. Shipton
1968 R. C. Evans
1971 A. D. M. Cox

ALPINE CLUBS
Following the formation of the Alpine Club (*qv*), similar institutions sprang up in many parts of the world. On the Continent the principal clubs adopted a wider policy of membership and this is still the case, so that clubs such as the Austrian, Swiss and French, for example, have thousands of members, divided into regional sections. The clubs own and maintain an elaborate system of huts for the use of which members pay reduced fees. Reciprocal rights exist.

Following upon the establishment of the British Alpine Club (1857) came:
1862 Austria
1863 Switzerland, Italy
1868 Norway
1869 Germany
1874 France
1878 Spain
1883 Belgium
1885 Sweden
1891 New Zealand, South Africa
1902 Russia, Holland, United States
1906 Canada, Japan
Note: Not all these clubs began on a national basis, but eventually acquired it. They are not all called "Alpine Club".

The Russian A. C. no longer exists. It is interesting to note that a local Alpine Club was founded in Williamstown, U. S. A., as early as 1863. (See also CLIMBING CLUBS.)

ALPINE FASHION
A term relating to rope management, where the climbers move simultaneously (see SNOW CLIMBING). Used frequently in the Alps. When desirable a direct belay (*qv*) is taken round a rock or an embedded ice axe.

ALPINE JOURNAL
The premier mountaineering journal, published by the Alpine Club (*qv*).

A collection of papers first appeared in volume form in 1859 and was called *Peaks, Passes and Glaciers*. It was edited by John Ball (*qv*) and the idea was to disseminate information about the relatively unknown parts of the Alps. Two further volumes of *Peaks, Passes and Glaciers* were issued in 1862, edited by E. S. Kennedy (*qv*), and regular publication with the title *Alpine Journal*, (quarterly) began in March 1863 under the editorship of H. B. George (*qv*). It is now issued annually in volume form. The journal has always concerned itself with world rather than just Alpine climbing.

There are four Index volumes:
Vols I-XV (includes PPG i – iii) 1859-91
Vols 16-38 1891-1926
Vols 39-58 1927-52
Vols 59-73 1953-68

ALPINE START
In the Alps it is usual to start a climb very early in the morning so as to obtain the best snow conditions. The actual time depends upon the route: 4 a.m. is common, but it may be any time between midnight and 6 a.m.

ALPINISM
Sometimes used to denote climbing which involves snow and ice at fairly high altitudes – as in the Alps. Perhaps a corruption of the French *alpinisme*.

THE ALPS
(Fr.: *Les Alpes*; G.: *Die Alpen*; It.: *Le Alpi*)
The best-known range of high mountains in the world. The Alps stretch from the Mediterranean hinterland near Nice in an immense arc to the environs of Ljubljana in Yugoslavia and Vienna in Austria. In general terms they form a natural border between Italy and her neighbours France, Switzerland, Austria and Yugoslavia and for much of the distance a political border too.

Within this overall picture the internal structure is complex with several important groups of mountains lying off the main watershed, particularly the Bernese Alps. There are, too, important flanking ranges known as the Pre-alps (e.g. the Jura). While the main range tends to be igneous (granite, etc.) the outliers tend to be limestones (including the Bernese Alps). In all of these regions, mountaineering is actively practised.

The accepted classification of the range for mountaineering was put forward by Coolidge (*qv*) though the extension of the sport, particularly in rock-climbing, has led to minor modifications (See below).

Coolidge laid down three principal divisions: I – Western Alps (Col de Tenda to Simplon): II – Central Alps (Simplon to Reschen Scheideck and Stelvio) III – Eastern Alps (Reschen Scheideck to Radstädter Tauern). In common parlance climbers speak of "the Alps", meaning the first two, and "the Eastern Alps" meaning last.

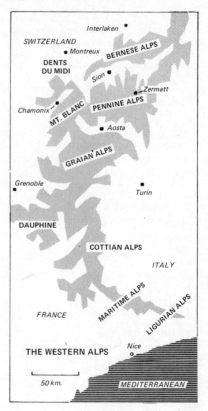

The highest mountain is Mont Blanc (4,807 m) and there are 52 mountains of 4,000 m, 64 counting multiple summits (Collomb, 1971) – but it is not always easy to determine these. All but one – Piz Bernina – are in the Western and Central Alps. There are hundreds of summits between 3,500 m and 4,000 m.

Much of the range is under permanent ice and snow and there are numerous glaciers, the longest being the Great Aletsch, 13.75 miles long. Most glaciers are in retreat and there are marked differences between conditions now and in the pioneering days. (See GLACIERS.)

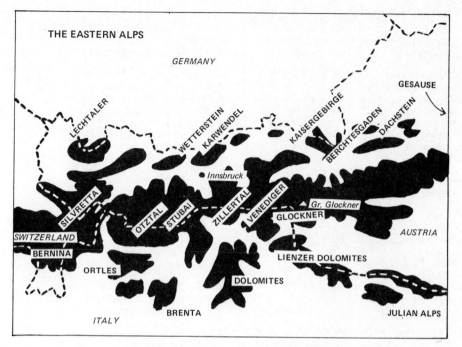

THE EASTERN ALPS

GERMANY

GESAUSE

LECHTALER

WETTERSTEIN
KARWENDEL

KAISERGEBIRGE

BERCHTESGADEN

DACHSTEIN

Innsbruck

SILVRETTA

OTZTAL

STUBAI

ZILLERTAL

VENEDIGER

Gr. Glockner

GLOCKNER

SWITZERLAND

BERNINA

AUSTRIA

ORTLES

LIENZER DOLOMITES

DOLOMITES

ITALY

BRENTA

JULIAN ALPS

The complex variety of the range means that climbing of every kind and every standard is common. There are innumerable hotels, guest houses, mountain huts (*qv*) and bivouac huts (*qv*) throughout, as well as ancillary services such as guides, rescue teams, and mountain transport of all kinds. Many centres today exist primarily for the skiing and tourist industries but it is still possible to find areas which are relatively unknown.

The great peaks and glaciers were of no interest to the native population before visitors arrived. The word "alp" (Eastern Alps: alm) refers to the lower hill pastures and was mistakenly adopted by visitors to refer to the whole mountain. Similarly the word *Mont* or *Monte*, originally meant a pass (e.g. Monte Moro), which was the only feature of high mountains useful to the natives. Some of the famous passes were certainly known to the Romans and possibly earlier.

Wills' ascent of the Wetterhorn in 1854 is often taken to be the start of mountaineering as a sport, but Coolidge lists 132 peaks ascended before that date (including the Wetterhorn itself). Mont Blanc was climbed in 1786 (by M. G. Paccard and J. Balmat). Preceding the ascent of Mont Blanc were:

1358 Rochemelon
1492 Mont Aiguille
before 1654 West Karwendelspitze
before 1694 Mont Tabor
before 1742 Scesaplana
1744 Titlis
c. 1762 Ankogel
1770 Buet
1778 Triglav
1779 Mont Velan
1782 Scopi
1784 Aig. and Dôme du Goûter
      Dent du Midi

These were isolated events. The first real explorers of the high alps were H. B. de Saussure and the monk, Placidus à Spescha, in the late eighteenth century. Considerable exploration (and ascents) took place before 1854, but from then until the ascent of the Matterhorn in 1865 is known as the Golden Age, the conquest of great peaks, though La Meije was not climbed until 1877. From 1865 to 1914 was the Silver Age during which the route rather than the peak became important, with many difficult ridges and "smaller" peaks being climbed (e.g. the Drus). Since the First World War, increasingly difficult routes, especially on the faces, have been followed, and there has been an increase in winter ascents of great difficulty.

The Divisions and Groups of the Alps (based on Coolidge) DIVISIONS: I – Western Alps, II – Central Alps, III – Eastern Alps

GROUPS	SUB-GROUPS
I	
Ligurian Alps	
Maritime Alps	
Cottian Alps	
Dauphiné Alps	Grandes Rousses
Graian Alps	West, Central, East
Mont Blanc Group	Haute Savoie
Pennine Alps	West, East
II	
Bernese Alps	West, Oberland, East
Lepontine Alps	
Tödi Range	
North East Switzerland	
Bernina Alps	Bregaglia, Bernina
Albula Group	
Sivretta-Rhatikon Group	Silvretta, Rhatikon, Verwall
III	
Lombard Alps	Brenta Dolomites
Ortler, Otztal and Stubai Alps	Ortler, Otztal, Stubai
Central Tyrolese Alps	Zillertal, Tuxer, Venediger, Glockner, Radstatter Tauern
Niedere Tauern	
North Tyrolese Alps (Bavarian Alps)	(*) Lechtaler, Wetterstein, Karwendal, Kaiser, Kitzbuhler, Berchtesgadener, Tennen, Dachstein, Totes.
Dolomites	
South Eastern Alps	Carnic, Karawanken, Julian

(*) Principal groups only.

List of Alpine 4,000 m peaks
(Summits and other eminences indicated)
4,807 m Mont Blanc
4,748 m Mont Blanc de Courmayeur
4,634 m Monte Rosa (ten tops)
4,545 m Dom
4,527 m Lyskamm (two tops)
4,505 m Weisshorn
4,491 m Taschhorn
4,477 m Matterhorn (two tops)
4,469 m Picco Luigi Amédeo

4,465 m Mont Maudit
4,357 m Dent Blanche
4,327 m Nadelhorn
4,314 m Grand Combin (four tops)
4,304 m Dôme de Goûter
4,294 m Lenzspitze
4,274 m Finsteraarhorn
4,248 m Mont Blanc de Tacul
4,241 m Stecknadelhorn
4,226 m Castor
4,221 m Zinal Rothorn
4,219 m Hohberghorn
4,208 m Grandes Jorasses (five tops)
4,206 m Alphubel
4,199 m Rimpfischhorn
4,195 m Aletschhorn
4,190 m Strahlhorn
4,171 m Dent d'Hérens
4,165 m Breithorn (three tops)
4,158 m Jungfrau
4,153 m Bishorn
4,122 m Aig. Verte (two tops)
4,114 m Aigs du Diable (two tops)
4,107 m Aig. Blanche de Peuterey
4,102 m Grande Rocheuse
4,101 m Barre des Ecrins
4,099 m Mönch˙
4,091 m Pollux
4,078 m Schreckhorn
4,069 m Mont Brouillard
4,063 m Obergabelhorn
4,061 m Gran Paradiso
4,052 m Aig. de Bionnassay
4,049 m Gr. Fiescherhorn
4,049 m Piz Bernina
4,043 m Gr. Grünhorn
4,042 m Lauteraarhorn
4,035 m Dürrenhorn
4,035 m Aig. du Jardin
4,029 m Allalinhorn
4,025 m Hinter Fiescherhorn
4,023 m Weissmies
4,015 m Dôme de Rochefort
4,013 m Punta Baretti
4,013 m Aig. du Géant
4,010 m Lagginhorn
4,001 m Aig. du Rochefort
4,000 m Les Droites
(Next highest, Fletschhorn, 3,996 m)

By far the largest number of the above are in the Pennine Alps (*qv*).

For further details see: *The Alps in Nature and History*, by W. A. B. Coolidge, and *Mountains of the Alps* (2 vols), by R. Collomb.

See also various groups, individual peaks, villages, etc.

ALTAI MOUNTAINS
A long range of mountains stretching from

the Oirat area of the U. S. S. R. into Mongolia. Belukha (14,784 ft) is the highest-known point. It is within the U. S. S. R. and was first climbed by B. V. and M. V. Tronov in 1914.

AMERY, Leopold Charles Maurice Stennet (1873-1955)
Statesman and Cabinet Minister, and keen mountaineer who climbed in many parts of the world. In 1929 he made the first ascent of the mountain in Canada which bears his name. President of the A. C. 1944-7 during which the A. C. led in the formation of the British Mountaineering Council (*qv*). Wrote two books of his climbing experiences: *Days of Fresh Air* (1939) and *In the Rain and the Sun* (1946).

AMES, Edward Levi (1832-92)
Original Member of the A. C. In 1856 he made the first ascent of the Fletschhorn and Allalinhorn.

ANDEREGG, Jakob (1827-78)
Cousin and contemporary of the great Melchior Anderegg (*qv*), whose reputation long overshadowed him. Much more daring than Melchior, to whom he proved a perfect foil, though they did not always climb together. It was Jakob who led the ice arête of the Old Brenva on the first ascent when Melchior might have retreated.

Jakob took part in many first ascents of famous mountains and climbs:
1864 Balmhorn; Jungfrau by the Rottal; W Peak of Lyskamm; Zinal Rothhorn.
1865 Piz Roseg; Ober Gabelhorn; Pigne d'Arolla; Old Brenva.
1866 Piz Palu (Central and W Peaks)
1869 Gspaltenhorn; Midi by NE Arête
1870 Aig. de Trélatète (N Peak)
1872 Studerhorn (NE arête and W face); Grand Paradis (new route)
1875 Monte della Disgrazia by SE arête
1876 Aig. du Plat; Le Rateau by S and E arêtes; Grd. Flambeau; Finsteraarhorn by SE arête; Aig. Verte from Argentiere Glacier; Les Courtes from Argentiere Glacier
1877 Le Plaret.

Many of his later climbs were done with Henri Cordier (*qv*) who was killed in a foolish accident on the glacier after the Plaret climb. During the Verte ascent Jakob was soaked and this led to recurring illnesses from which he never recovered.

ANDEREGG, Melchior (1828-1912)
Born near Meiringen, Melchior, as he was always known, became one of the greatest of all the early guides – his career only equalled by that of Christian Almer (*qv*). Though he had done some guiding before 1855, the year he was "discovered" by Hinchcliff (*qv*), his principal occupation was wood-carving. He was expert at this; some later work was exhibited in London galleries.

His principal climbs include the first ascents of Rimpfischhorn, Mont Blanc by the Bosses Ridge (1859), Monte Disgrazia (1862), Dent d'Hérens, Parrotspitze of Monte Rosa (1863), Mont Blanc by the Brenva Face (1865), Mont Mallet (1871). He climbed with many of the leading amateurs but especially Stephen (*qv*) and later, the Walkers (*qv*).

A big, genial, intelligent man, Melchior is credited with many famous Alpine quotes, amongst which are: "We must go back – we cannot reach the summit in less than five or six hours" (on seeing a winter Snowdon from Crib Goch. They reached it in 1 hr 5 min.).

On looking out over the rooftops of London, Stephen said, "That is not so fine a view as we have seen together from Mont Blanc." "Ah, sir, it is far finer", Melchior replied.

On observing the Zmutt Ridge from the Dent Blanche: "It goes – but I'm not going."

Melchior was guest of honour at an A. C. Winter Dinner in 1894. He was married and had a large family, of whom Andreas, his second son, became a noted guide. He was one of the few early guides to die comparitively affluent.

ANDERMATTEN, Franz (1823-1883)
One of the earliest of the Saastal guides who made the first ascent of the Strahlhorn (1854), Lagginhorn (1856), and Nadelhorn (1858). His most famous expedition was with Dent, Burgener, Imseng and Passingham on the first ascent of Zinal Rothorn from Zermatt (1872).

ANDERSON, John Stafford (1851-1930)
Brother in law of G. P. Baker (*qv*) with whom he frequently climbed in the Alps. Anderson made several important new climbs among which the following were outstanding; The Viereselgrat of the Dent Blanche (1882) so called after his chief guide, Ulrich Almer, commented "Wir sind vier Esel!" (we are four asses), the

Andersongrat of the Schreckhorn (1883) and the first E-W traverse of the Breithorn (1884).

ANDES, THE

A long mountain system (4,000 miles) running down the western side of the South American continent, from Caracas in Venezuela to Cape Horn. Within this vast range there are peaks of almost every size and shape ranging from the great volcanos such as Cotopaxi and Chimborazo, through the ice-draped peaks of the Cordillera Blanca, to the stark rock obelisks of

Patagonia. Some, even quite high ones, are easy to climb and were certainly ascended by the native Indians before the coming of the white man. Others are extremely difficult and provide some of the hardest rock and ice climbs in the world. The highest peak is Aconcagua, 22,835ft (the highest peak in the western hemisphere). (M. Zurbriggen (qv), solo, 1898).

The earliest attempts on the mountains were made in the north where the peaks are lower. A Conquistadore is credited with the ascent of Pichincha (15,718ft) as early as 1582. This was repeated by Bouguer and

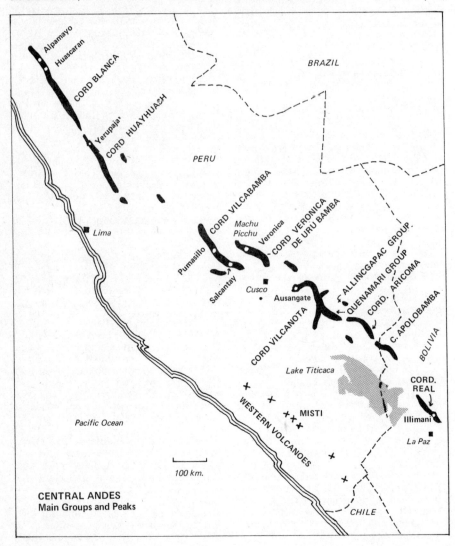

CENTRAL ANDES
Main Groups and Peaks

Condamine between 1736-1744, who also climbed Corazón, a similar peak. Humboldt climbed Pichincha in 1802 and tried Chimborazo, but was defeated. The huge volcanoes were prime targets for the early expeditions: Cotopaxi (19,350 ft) was climbed by A. Escobar and W. Reiss in 1872 and Whymper climbed Chimborazo (20,563 ft) in 1880. Sievers and Engel began climbing in the Sierra Merida of the extreme north in 1885 and 1887, but the big guns were now turned on Aconcagua in the south. Gussfeldt (1882-3) failed twice and it was E. A. Fitzgerald's guide, M. Zurbriggen, who succeeded (1898). Conway's expedition climbed Aconcagua and also Illimani (21,201 ft), though an attempt on Sarmiento in Tierra del Fuego (1898), failed.

A number of expeditions followed, especially German, and built up to a climax in the 1930s. In 1932, P. Borcher's party climbed the South Peak of Huascarán (22,205 ft) and four other peaks of about 20,000 ft. After the war, exploration and climbing in the Andes rivalled that of the Himalayas for intensity. All the larger peaks were ascended: an outstanding feat being that of L. Terray's party on Chacaraju, 1956. Further south, in Patagonia, Terray and G. Magnone climbed FitzRoy (11,066 ft) in 1952, C. Maestri and T. Egger climbed Cerro Torre (9,908 ft) in 1959 and Bonington and Whillans climbed the Central Tower of Paine in 1963. Despite the large number of expeditions, the range of the Andes is so vast that there is still plenty of scope for exploration and new ascents. From north to south the Andes comprise the following Cordillera:

Venezuela	Sierra de Norte
	Sierra de Sarta Domingo
	* Sierra Nevada de Merida
Colombia	* Sierra Nevada de Santa Marta
	Cord. Central
	* Cord. Oriental (Cocuy)
Ecuador	Cord. Oriental
	Cord. Occidental
	Llanganate Range
Peru	* Cord. Blanca
	* Cord. Huayhuash
	Cord. Central
	Raura-Guaco Group
	Cord. Occidental

	Cord. Oriental
	* Cord. Vilcabamba
	* Cord. Vilcanota
	Cord. Carabaya
	* Cord. Veronica de Urubamb..
Bolivia	* Cord. Real
	Cord. Apolobamba
	Cord. Munecas
	Cord. de Quinza Cruz
	Cord. de Santa Vera Cruz
	Cord. de Cocapata
	Cord. Occidental
Chile and Argentina	Northern Cord. de los Andes
	* Central Cord. de los Andes
	* Patagonia
	* Tierra del Fuego

Note: The cordilleras marked with an asterisk will be found separately in the text.

See also ACONCAGUA, CHIMBORAZO, CERRO TORRE.

ANDINISMO

A word used in South America to mean Andean climbing: a local variation on alpinism (*qv*).

ANDREWS, Arthur Westlake (1868-1959)

A. W. Andrews first visited Snowdonia in 1889 or 1890, but it was not until he returned in 1901 that he met J. M. A. Thomson (*qv*) and shared with him, Eckenstein (*qv*) and a few others the early exploration of Lliwedd (*qv*). Central Chimney (1908) is perhaps his best-known route. With Thomson he compiled *The Climbs on Lliwedd* (1909), the first pocket guide to a British crag.

In 1902 he began climbing at Wicca and Bosigran in Cornwall (*qv*) and for over 30 years was alone in the development of Cornish climbing. The early routes on all the major cliffs are his – his sister usually acting as second. With E. C. Pyatt he edited *Cornwall, a climber's guide*, (1950).

Andrews was of independent means, a scholar and notable athlete. He was an international miler and in 1900 reached the semi-finals of the Men's Singles at Wimbledon.

ANNAPURNA (26,504 ft)

The Annapurna Himal lies on the eastern side of the Gandaki Section of the Nepal Himalaya. There are four principal summits:

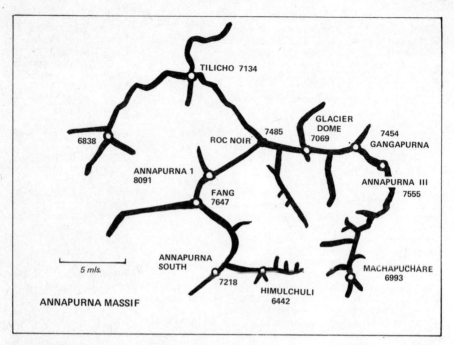

TILICHO 7134

GLACIER
DOME
7069

7485

7454
GANGAPURNA

ROC NOIR

6838

ANNAPURNA 1
8091

ANNAPURNA III
7555

FANG
7647

5 mls.

ANNAPURNA
SOUTH

MACHAPUCHARE
6993

7218

HIMULCHULI
6442

ANNAPURNA MASSIF

Annapurna I	8078 m	26,504 ft	1950
Annapurna II	7937 m	26,041 ft	1960
Annapurna III			
	7577 m	24,860 ft	1961
Annapurna IV			
	7524 m	24,688 ft	1955

Annapurna I was the first 8,000 m peak in the world to be climbed. M. Herzog led a French expedition which first attempted Dhaulagiri then changed to Annapurna almost at the last moment. Herzog and Lachenal reached the summit at 2 p.m., 3 June 1950. Both were badly frost-bitten and the French retreat from the mountain was epic. (See: *Annapurna*, by M. Herzog.)

Annapurna II was climbed by Bonington and Grant; Annapurna III by Kholi, Gyatso and Sonam Girmi; Annapurna IV by Biller, Steinmetz and Wellenkamp.

In 1970, C. J. S. Bonington returned with an expedition to attempt the South Face of the mountain and D. Whillans, D. Haston reached the summit. Though not the first Himalayan face climb it was the most difficult to date and brought Alpine thinking to the Himalaya – a sign of the development of Himalayan climbing. (See *Annapurna South Face*, by C. Bonington.)

ANORAK
An Eskimo word for a wind-proof outer

garment which is pulled on over one's head. A modern anorak has a hood, wind-proof cuffs and a map pocket. There are drawcords to the hood and skirt. The skirt is not usually as long as that of a cagoule (*qv*). The best anoraks are made of ventile cloth, which allows the skin to breathe, though it is less waterproof than poly-urethene. An anorak may be covered by a cagoule as extra protection, though in fact the cagoule is tending to replace the anorak altogether in general usage. An alpine jacket is really an anorak with a full length zip down the front.

ANTARCTICA
The vast Antarctic continent is covered with an ice sheet that attains a maximum depth of 14,000 ft. The principal mountain ranges are in the west, beginning with the Horst chain which stretches across the continent from the Admiralty Range to the coasts of Queen Maud Land, a distance of over 3,000 miles. The highest points are the mountains bordering the Ross Ice Shelf; peaks of 14,000 ft, including the highest, Mt Kirkpatrick, 14,860 ft.

West from the Horst, the continent narrows and tapers away into the Antarctic Peninsula. There are several groups of high mountains, of which the highest is the Sentinal Range, rising above the Filchner Ice Shelf. The highest peak, and the highest of the continent, is Vinson Massif (16,860 ft) – N. B. Clinch's Expedition, 1966. The American A. C. expedition which Clinch led also climbed Mt Tyree (16,290 ft), the second highest summit of the continent, and several peaks of 15,000 ft. The Sentinal Range probably has the most to offer the climber in Antarctica.

Surveyors and scientists have climbed many of the Antarctic peaks, but there are still hundreds unclimbed and even unexplored.

APPENINES, ITALY
The long range which forms the backbone of the country, the highest point being Corno Grande (9,616 ft). There are many climbs, mostly limestone, and the C. A. I. owns huts in the mountains. The Appenines are not popular with foreign climbers.

ARANS, THE
Aran Mawddwy (2,970 ft) is the highest peak in Wales outside Snowdonia and Craig Cowarch near Dinas Mawddwy provides long climbs of all standards.

Guidebook: *Craig Cowarch and Other Mid-Wales Crags*, by Lambe and Knox.

ARDENNES
Wooded limestone hills on the Franco-Belgian border; popular with tourists. The chief centre is Dinant. There are limestone crags of considerable interest, particularly those at Freyr on the Meuse between Dinant and Givet. The crags are about 450 ft in height and have numerous climbs, well pegged.

ARNOLD, Matthew (1822-88)
Well-known author, and son of Arnold of Rugby. Honeymooned in the Alps (1851) and paid several later visits. Crossed various passes but no serious ascents. Briefly, a member of the A.C.

AROLLA
A small hamlet at the head of the Val d'Hérens (Switzerland) which has always been a popular centre with British climbers (see LARDEN etc.). The principal peaks are Dent Blanche, Mont Blanc de Cheilon, Mont Collon, Ruinette, L'Evêque, Grand Cornier and Pigne d'Arolla, but there are many lesser peaks noted for their rock-climbs.

ARRAN
An island in the mouth of the Firth of Clyde, Scotland, and famous for a group of rocky peaks whose ridges almost rival those of the Cuillin (*qv*).

The peaks are in the NE quarter of the island. They form two roughly parallel ridges joined at their mid-point by a low col known as The Saddle. From The Saddle, Glen Sannox drains NE to Sannox Bay and Glen Rosa drains S towards Brodick, the principal village of the island.

The so-called Main Ridge is the western one, extending from Ben Nuis (2597 ft) in the S to Suidhe Fearghas (2081 ft) in the N. A classic traverse, it includes the celebrated A'Chir (The Comb) and Ceum na Caillich (The Witches' Step). Cir Mhor (2618 ft), also part of the ridge, has been called 'The Matterhorn of Scotland'.

The eastern ridge is shorter, linking Goat Fell (2866 ft) to Cioch na h-Oige (2168 ft). The ascent of Goat Fell, the highest summit in Arran, is by a simple track direct from Brodick, but the rest of the ridge is more difficult. Cioch na h-Oige has one of the largest cliffs in Britain.

There are rock-climbs on most of the peaks, though the rock is a peculiar form of granite, not well adapted for climbing. The first ascent of Ben Nuis Chimney in 1901 is one of the classic stories of pioneer days.

Guidebook: *Climbers' Guide to Arran*, by W. M. M. Wallace.

ARTIFICIAL CLIMBING
(PEG CLIMBING) (Am.: Aid Climbing)
Climbing which relies on aids such as pegs, bolts and étriers to overcome a problem. It may be that the rock (or ice) overhangs too much for natural balance, or that there is a deficiency of holds. A climb may have a few artificial moves, or a few pitches, or may be entirely artificial from start to finish. The majority of climbs, of course, have no artificial climbing whatsoever and are known as "free climbs", if a distinction has to be made between the two. A free climb which relies upon one or two pegs for aided moves is not regarded as artificial. A number of originally artificial climbs have later been done free.

On rock, artificial climbing involves the planting of pegs in cracks and moving up on the pegs by means of étriers (*qv*). By using karabiners, the pegs can also serve as runners (*qv*) and thus, if the pegs are well planted, the leader of an artificial climb is well protected. It is possible to belay by sitting in the étriers and belaying to a peg, and even to bivouac using special hammocks slung between pegs (e.g. on some of the long Yosemite routes). Where the rock has no cracks, bolts (*qv*) may be used. Bolts are often left in place and in the Alps pegs are too, though it is considered more ethical for the last man to remove the pegs if possible.

On artificial ice-climbs, ice-pegs or (more usual) ice-screws are used to support the étriers. Artificial ice-climbs are generally fairly short (e.g. overcoming a sérac barrier).

There are single and double rope techniques for artificial climbing. In the former the rope is used only for protection. The climber keeps himself in balance when planting a peg by means of a short loop called a cow's tail (*qv*). In double rope technique he may also use a cow's tail but he can be kept in position by the second man pulling on the rope. Once another peg is placed above, the rope can be passed through a karabiner on this peg and tension gained from above. The climber instructs his second in this and it is useful to have two differently coloured ropes, e.g. "slack on white, pull on red". There are many variations on this, usually aimed at saving time and energy, for artificial climbing is both slow and tiring. A considerable amount of gear may need to be carried on a long route.

Artificial climbing was once held in disfavour but this is no longer the case. The opportunity for its misuse is apparent and still provokes occasional comment. The term "mechanized climbing" is obsolete.

See also SIEGE TACTICS.

ASCHENBRENNER, Peter (b.1902)

A climber from Tyrol who made many fine climbs, particularly on limestone ranges. Best known is the Asche-Lucke Route, E Face of Fleischbank (with H.Lucke, 1930)

In 1932 Aschenbrenner joined Merkl's expedition to Manga Parbat, during which he succeeded in climbing Rakhiot Peak (23,210ft) with Kunigk, and in reaching Camp V (20,330ft) before retiring with frostbite. He returned to the mountain in 1934 and with Schneider reached 25,280ft, the highest point reached by the expedition, before taking part in, and surviving, the terrible retreat (*See*: Nanga Parbat). After the war he was in charge of the climbing on the successful Herrligkoffer Expedition to Nanga Parbat, when H.Buhl reached the summit (1953).

ASSAM HIMALAYA

The most easterly section of the Himalaya, extending from Pauhunri (23,180ft) in the

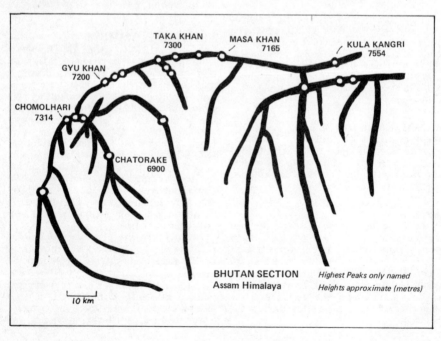

TAKA KHAN
7300

MASA KHAN
7165

KULA KANGRI
7554

GYU KHAN
7200

CHOMOLHARI
7314

CHATORAKE
6900

10 km

BHUTAN SECTION
Assam Himalaya

Highest Peaks only named
Heights approximate (metres)

west to Namche Barwa (25,445 ft) in the east. The western part is in the state of Bhutan, which has a disputed frontier with Tibet and the eastern half is along the Assam-Tibet frontier zone, which is not clearly marked. Though Bhutan has allowed scientific parties to explore the country recently, very little has been done in the way of climbing – though this may change soon as Bhutan abandons an isolationist policy. There seems little chance of climbing in Assam.

The best-known peak is Chomolhari (23,997 ft) climbed by Chapman (*qv*) and Sherpa Pasang in 1937. According to S. Nakao, who made surveys in Bhutan in 1958, there are many peaks of 7,000 m and over, the highest being the four summits of Khula Kangri (the highest of these being 24,784 ft, 7554 m) with the Chutte Kang next at 24,541 ft, though these heights can only be approximate. Virtually nothing is known of the peaks between Bhutan and Namcha Barwa. One outlier, regarded by authorities as not in the Himalaya proper, is Gyala Peri (23,460 ft).

ATLAS MOUNTAINS
A range of high mountains extending along the North African coast from Tunis in the east to Ifni in the west. The highest peak is Toubkal (13,665 ft). Of the various groups, the most important are found in Morocco – the coastal Rif; the Middle Atlas, on the northern slopes of which lie Fez and Meknes: the High Atlas dominating the town of Marrakesh; and the Anti Atlas. Only the High Atlas have been climbed to any large degree and even here, the Toubkal massif has had the major share of attention. There are several huts.

In summer the mountains are arid, but conditions are better in spring, or, as a number of parties have recently found, winter. Long ridge traverses give the best climbing, though there are some face and buttress routes. The rock can be poor.

AUSTIN, John Allan (b. 1934)
A leading British rock climber of the postwar years with several hundred new routes to his credit, especially, but not entirely, in the Pennines and Lake District. For several years he has been the guiding force of Yorkshire and Langdale climbing.

His early gritstone routes (with R. B. Evans) include High Street, Ilkley (1956), the Shelf, Crookrise (1957), Western Front, Almscliff (1958) and the Wall of Horrors, Almscliff (1961). With Evans and

Fuller at this time (1957) he did Nightshade, Poisoned Glen (one of the best of Irish climbs) and in 1960, Astra, Langdale (Metcalfe and Roberts). Later climbs include Hanging Slab, Sgurr Mhic Coinnich and Haste Not Direct, White Ghyll (both 1971).

It is perhaps Austin's development of Yorkshire limestone which has been most significant: and especially the free lead of Scorpio at Malham in 1959. Austin has always been a purist when it comes to aid climbing and his example has done much to make limestone shake off its reputation as being purely for such climbs. At Malham, pegs are strictly taboo except where specifically stated in the guidebook.

Austin edited the Langdale guidebook of 1967 and the new version of 1973 (with R. Valentine). They have not been free from controversy. He played a substantial part in the two guidebooks *Yorkshire Gritstone* and *Yorkshire Limestone*.

AUSTRALIA, CLIMBING IN
The highest mountain in Australia is Mount Kosciusko (7,328 ft) in the Snowy Mountains, New South Wales. Most other peaks are in the 3–5,000 ft range. Rock-climbing has been extensively developed since the 1950s and there are now routes of 1,000 ft or more and all standards of difficulty. Development has mainly centred on those rocks nearest to the big cities of the SE coast such as Glasshouse Mountains, Frog Buttress, Wurrumbungles, Blue Mountains, Booroomba Rocks, Mt Buffalo, Grampians, Mt Arapiles.

Other developments have taken place in Tasmania, especially on Frenchman's Cap and Federation Peak. Frenchman's Cap has a 1,200 ft E Face, reputedly the finest crag in Australia, but access is very difficult. There are sea-stacks, too, off Tasmania, including the remarkable Totem Pole, 200 ft high and 12 ft square. Ball's Pyramid is an 1,800 ft sea stack, 400 miles off the E Coast. Both stacks have been climbed.

AVALANCHE (G.: Lawine; It.: Valanga)
The sliding away of surface material from a mountain, especially snow. One also speaks of ice avalanches, such as are caused by falling séracs (*qv*) and rock avalanches, caused by chutes of stones in a couloir. Earth avalanches, of loose wet soil, are not unknown. In all cases the word implies considerable volume and force.

Given the correct conditions, snow will avalanche at a very shallow angle and presents considerable danger to the climber and skier. The phenomenon is quite common in Britain as well as in greater mountain areas: people have been killed by snow avalanches in the Pennines, Lake District and Scotland within recent years. In Britain it is recommended that no snow climb (especially gully routes) should be done for three days after a heavy fall of new snow. There is no sure way of testing whether a slope will avalanche or not: the old idea of throwing a heavy stone onto the slope seems of doubtful value.

Some areas of the Alps are known to be avalanche prone at certain times of the year or even times of day, and these should be avoided. These are usually indicated in the guidebooks.

The following types of avalanche are common:

Wet snow avalanche – snow and water flow down the hillside in a compact mass. Often thaw conditions.

Powder snow avalanche – loose powder snow, unable to stick to the under-lying snow-ice (because it is too cold), rolls down in great billowing clouds.

Slab avalanche – a surface layer of snow, compacted by wind, cracks off and slides down, unable to stick to loose snow underneath.

Avalanches often push before them a huge mass of air, the avalanche wind, which can do more damage than the snow. The force is incredible and can flatten whole forests.

In the Alps, winter protection against avalanches includes the building of walls and barriers, and the firing of various bombs to precipitate snow masses which are growing too large. There is little an individual can do if caught in an avalanche, though a swimming action is advocated to try and keep near the surface. Some skiers are now equipped with electronic bleepers which will give their location if they are buried by an avalanche. (See *The Avalanche Enigma*, by C. Fraser.)

AVON GORGE

The famous gorge at Bristol provides some of the finest limestone climbs in England, many in the higher grades.

Guidebooks: *Limestone Climbs in South West England*, by J. Nixon, and *Extremely Severe in the Avon Gorge*, by E. Ward-Drummond.

BACKING OFF
Abandoning a climb in the early stages or even before it is properly commenced, either because of the weather or second thoughts.

BACKING UP
A method of climbing a chimney (*qv*) by placing one's back against one side wall and one's feet, or knees (depending on the width of the chimney) against the other. Movement is made by pushing up with the hands against the back wall (it can help to bring one foot back against the same wall) and then moving the feet up. Rather strenuous, but offers good resting positions. Sometimes called "back and foot" (or "knee") or "chimneying" (obsolescent).

BACKHOUSE, John Henry (1844-69)
A companion of Freshfield (*qv*) and Tuckett (*qv*) in 1865, making with them the 1st ascent of the Grosser Mosele and the first crossing of the popular Mittelberg Joch (Otztal).

BACK ROPE
A rope manoeuvre to see a second man across a difficult traverse. A runner (*qv*) is put at the start of the traverse and a second rope run through this. The leader then takes in the normal rope and pays out the back rope as the second advances. At the end of the traverse the second man unties from the back rope and pulls it in. The runner has to be abandoned unless it can be flicked off. If only one rope is available, the second can use it as a back rope and clip himself over it with a karabiner.

BAFFIN ISLAND
A huge island lying between Greenland and the Hudson Bay. In the south it is deeply indented by the Cumberland Sound, the northern edge of which reaches the Arctic Circle. The Cumberland Peninsula, between the Sound and Baffin Bay, contains the highest peaks (Tete Blanche, 7,074 ft, climbed 1953). The most spectacular peak is Mt Asgard (6,598 ft) which has twin plateau tops divided by a breche and surrounded by steep walls (first ascent, Swiss expedition, 1953). Scott's party (1971) climbed a number of new peaks and some big walls – the latter are one of the chief attractions of Baffin Island. The rock is granite.

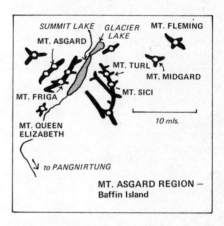

MT. ASGARD REGION –
Baffin Island

BAILLIE-GROHMAN, William Adolf (1851-1921)
A remarkably adventurous Anglo-Austrian who made the first winter ascent of Gross Glockner (1875) and made early explorations of the limestone Alps of Tyrol, especially the Karwendel (1872-4). He opened up the Kootenay River area of British Columbia, where he lived for 11 years and was one of the first to explore the Selkirk Range (1882-93).

Baillie-Grohman's chief interest was game hunting and he wrote many books on the subject. His sporting library of over 4,000 items was bought by the Library of Congress, Washington D. C. in 1919. From 1893 until his death he lived in the Tyrol.

BAKER, George Percival (1856-1951)
Baker is a typical example of those turn-of-the-century climbers who were wealthy enough to make expeditions to the more obscure ranges. He climbed Ararat, and visited Norway, Caucasus, the Canadian Rockies (first ascents Mt Gordon and Mt Sarbach with Collie (*qv*) 1897), Greece and Crete. He also climbed in Skye and was

with Solly (*qv*) on the first ascent of The Eagles Nest Ridge in the Lake District.

BALFOUR, Francis Maitland (1851-82)

A brilliant young biologist who was elected F. R. S. at the age of 26 and for whom a special Chair was created at Cambridge when he was 29. He climbed for two years (1880 and 1881) with his brother, F. W. Balfour, during which time they made the first ascent of the lower summit of the Grépon (Pic Balfour) (1881). In July of 1882 he attempted the unclimbed Aig. Blanche de Peuterey with his guide, J. Petrus and both were killed. The accident was never satisfactorily explained.

Balfour's death was the first of three notable fatalities in the Alps in 1882: the others were W. Penhall with the guide, A. Maurer (killed on the Wetterhorn), and W. E. Gabbett with the guides J. M. Lochmatter and his son (killed on the Dent Blanche). These three accidents caused Queen Victoria to enquire of Gladstone whether she should speak out against mountaineering. He advised against it.

BALL, John (1818-89)

Irish politician and naturalist and first president of the A.C. 1858-60.

Ball first visited the Alps in 1827. From Chamonix he climbed up to Montenvers and he also ascended the Salève: experiences which were to have a profound affect on his whole life. From 1840 until his death, scarcely a year passed without his visiting the Alps. He made the first ascent of Pelmo in 1857; the first major Dolomite peak to be climbed. His other first ascents were minor affairs and he gained his chief satisfaction in exploring the valleys and passes. His knowledge of the whole range resulted in the publication of the famous *Ball's Alpine Guides*, the first real Alpine guidebooks (*The Western Alps*, 1863; *The Central Alps*, 1864; *The Eastern Alps*, 1868).

It was Ball's suggestion to Longman (*qv*) that there should be an annual volume devoted to the interests of Alpine travellers, which resulted in the first volume of *Peaks, Passes and Glaciers* in 1859. Ball was its editor, and the book was the forerunner of the *Alpine Journal* (*qv*).

His travels extended to several other mountain regions besides the Alps: notably the Atlas and Andes. He figured prominently in the great glacier controversies of the mid-nineteenth century.

BALMAT, Auguste (1808-62)

A notable Chamonix guide, renowned for his devotion to duty and high intellectual ability. He was a great nephew of Jacques Balmat (*qv*) but a man of very different character, totally oblivious of wealth or fame.

His career came to prominence in 1842-3 when he was employed by Forbes (*qv*) on glacier work. He was with Wills on the latter's famous ascent of the Wetterhorn in 1854 (*qv*) and with Wills and Tyndall (*qv*) on Mont Blanc in 1858, during which he suffered severe frostbite owing to his burying thermometers in the snow with his bare hands when he realized the digging implement had been forgotten. For his devotion to science on this occasion the Royal Society awarded him a special recognition of 25 guineas, which he took in the form of a camera. In the following year, 1859, he spent 20 hours on the summit with Tyndall.

Wills nursed him through his final painful illness and he died, impoverished in all but spirit, at the Eagle's Nest.

BALMAT, Jacques (1762-1834)

A crystal and chamois hunter of Chamonix who was with Paccard (*qv*) on the first ascent of Mont Blanc in 1786. Earlier in the year Balmat had been with other local men as high as the present position of the Vallot hut, but with Paccard a new route was chosen and it seems certain it was Paccard's choosing. Indeed, evidence suggests that Balmat wished to give up the attempt. It was Bourrit (*qv*), jealous of Paccard, who suggested that Balmat was the prime leader of the ascent, thus starting a controversy which lasted more than 150 years. Bourrit's work was unfortunately given further credence by Alexandre Dumas who interviewed Balmat in 1832 – the story could not be contradicted since Paccard had been dead five years.

Balmat made four further ascents, as a guide, including one with Marie Paradis, a servant from Chamonix, and the first woman to climb the mountain. He gradually gave up climbing and became a gold prospector. He was killed in 1834 while prospecting in the mountains, possibly by foul play. (See *The First Ascent of Mont Blanc* by T. G. Brown and G. R. de Beer).

BANKS, Michael Edward Borg (b. 1922)

Mike Banks began climbing in the Commandos where for many years he was a mountaineering instructor. In 1951, with

1 MOUNTAIN FEATURES

a. glacier
b. moraine
c. ridge
d. gendarme
e. bergschrund
f. névé
g. icefall
h. séracs
i. rognon
j. buttress
k. couloir
l. col
m. crevasses

(The Chamonix Aiguilles)

2 GIMMER CRAG, ENGLISH LAKE DISTRICT. A fine crag with many middle grade climbs and some hard ones. Note the slabs, cracks and overhangs. (right) 3 DINAS Y GROMLECH SNOWDONIA. A cliff with some fine hard climbs. The climbers are on Cemetery Gates.

F. R. Brooke, he made the second British guideless ascent of the Route Major, Mont Blanc. In 1957 he seconded J. H. Deacon on Green Cormorant Face, Cornwall – a major breakthrough in climbing there.

Banks has climbed in many parts of the world but is noted for his expeditions to Rakaposhi and to the Arctic. These are:

1951   Exploration of Queen Louise Land, Greenland

1952-4 British North Greenland Expedition. Probable longest crossing of the ice cap: 800 miles at 78°N. Five new ascents in the Barth Mountains with F. R. Brooke. Awarded Polar Medal

1956   Leader of the British-American Karakorum Expedition. Attained 23,500 ft

1958   Leader of the British-Pakastani Forces Expedition to Rakaposhi. Attained summit with Tom Patey (qv). Awarded M. B. E

1963   Leader, British Joint Services Alaska Expedition. Climbed Mt McKinley and Pt 9860 (latter, first ascent)

1964   Ten new ascents in the Logan Mountains, Canada

1972   Royal Navy Ellesmere Island Expedition. Six new ascents

Banks has also made several winter first ascents in Greenland and crossed the Vatnajokull ice cap of Iceland by snow tractor (1972). He is now a writer and photographer. His books are: *Commando Climber* (1955), *High Arctic* (1957), *Rakaposhi* (1959), *Snow Commando* (1961), *Greenland* (1974).

BARFORD, John Edward Quintus (1914-47)

Best known as the compiler of the Penguin book *Climbing in Britain* (1946) which helped to popularize the sport after the war. He was the first secretary of the B. M. C. (qv). A fine rock-climber, he produced, with J. M. Edwards (qv) the interim guide to Clogwyn du'r Arddu and on his own, to the Three Cliffs. Barford was killed by a stonefall in the Dauphiné.

BARLOW, Frederick Thomas Pratt (1843-93)

Made a number of minor new routes in the Alps including NE arête of Grivola and first English ascent of Grand Paradis from Cogne (1872); Monte Rosa from the Grenzsattel (1874); SE arête of Disgrazia (1875).

BARNARD, George (c. 1807-90)

One of the earliest landscape painters to portray the Alps accurately. Drawing Master at Rugby School, where Adams Reilly (qv) was one of his pupils.

BARTH, Hermann von (1845–1876?)

A Munich lawyer who was one of the founders of German climbing. He made numerous ascents in the Tyrol and Bavaria between 1867 and 1873.

BAR NATIONAL, CHAMONIX

Known as the "Bar Nash", though its proper name is the National Bar. Stands at the corner of the Place Jaques Balmat, near the Post Office. The bar was the favourite meeting place for climbers, especially British and American, during the fifties and sixties and figures in various accounts of that period. A sympathetic owner and relative cheapness were its main attractions. Still patronized by climbers, though less exclusively.

BASE CAMP

The principal depot of an expedition, placed near the foot of their objective. All the materials and men required come to the Base Camp and on a large expedition there may well be a Base Camp Manager to see to the complex arrangements. In certain cases (e.g. Everest SW Face) there may be an Advanced Base Camp, if the first Base Camp cannot be pitched near enough to launch an assault.

BARRINGTON, Richard Manliffe (?-1915)

Well known for his descriptions of St. Kilda, where in 1883 he made the first ascent of Stack na Biorrach by an outsider. He also tried to land on Rockall (1896) but failed. Barrington had a number of Alpine seasons and was an Original Member of the Climbers' Club. His brother, C. Barrington, made the first ascent of the Eiger in 1858.

BAUER, Paul (b. 1896)

German climber of the inter-war years. Made first ascents of the Schönanger Nordwand, Wetterstein and the Kasselerspitze Nordgrat, Zillertal Alps in the 1920s then led an expedition to the Caucasus in 1928 in which he made the first ascents of Tschumurtscherantau (4304 m) Katuintau North Face (4900 m) and Adischtau (4968 m), and took part in the first ascent of Shkhara North Peak, North Face (5184 m), though he did not reach the summit. The expedition was important in that the techniques of the Germans helped the development of the sport in Russia.

In 1929 Bauer led a reconnaisance of Kangchenjunga in which Allwein and Kraus reached 24,250 ft. He returned to the peak in 1931, when Hartmann and Wien reached 25,263 ft, but Schaller was killed.

The terrible disaster of Nanga Parbat in 1934 (*qv*) destroyed the core of experience of Himalayan climbing in Germany, and Bauer was principally responsible for its rebirth. In 1936 he led a party to Sikkim during which expedition Wien and Gottner reached the summit of Siniolchu (22,600 ft). Simvu (21,470 ft) NW peak, was also climbed. The second great Nanga Parbat disaster of 1937 (Wien's expedition) led to Bauer taking command of another attempt in 1938, but without success, though there were no casualties.

In private life Bauer is a notary. English translations of his books are: *Himalayan Campaign* (1937), *Himalayan Quest* (1938) *Kangchenjunga Challenge* (1955) and *The Siege of Nanga Parbat* (1956).

BAUMANN, John (1848-90 or 91)
An enterprising climber who made the first ascent of the Aig. de Talèfre (1879) and a new route on the Lauteraarhorn (1881). He made the second ascents of some of the hardest climbs of his day, including the Dru, the Plan, W ridge of Dent d'Hérens and Zmutt Arête of Matterhorn. He also made unsuccessful attempts on the Mittelegi ridge of Eiger and the N Face of Aig. du Plan. Baumann died in mysterious circumstances in South Africa.

BEACHCROFT, Henry Awdry (1847-1920)
Was with Tucker (*qv*) in 1875 when they made the first English ascent of Hochgall and the first ascent of Saas Maor.

BEARD, Eric (1931-69)
A good all-round climber, but especially known for his record-breaking long distance walks and runs:

Welsh 3,000s – 5 hr. 19 min.
Cuillin Main Ridge – 4 hr. 5 min.
Cairngorm Four Tops – 4 hr. 41 min.
Lakeland Record – 33,000 ft of ascent and descent, 88 miles, 56 tops.
John o'Groats to Lands End (944 mls) – 18 days (plus a few hrs).
"Beardie" did much work for charities.

He was killed in a car accident.

BEETHAM, Bentley (1886-1963)
A schoolmaster from Barnard Castle, noted for his development of climbing in Borrowdale, Lake District. Beetham was, in fact, a good all-round mountaineer and was a member of the 1924 Everest expedition, though illness prevented him going beyond Camp III.

With Frankland (*qv*) Beetham made the second ascent of Central Buttress, Scafell and then, almost accidentally, they together re-opened Borrowdale climbing by first ascents in 1921 of Woden's Face (Bowderstones) and Troutdale Ridge (Black Crag), and finally, in 1922, Brown Slabs Arête (Shepherds Crag).

Beetham investigated the other neglected crags of the valley, at first desultorily, then with more vigour, putting up some 50 new routes. Many of these were of poor quality but the following are notable and popular: Brown Slabs Ordinary (1946), Crack (1947), Direct (1948), Chamonix (1946), Little Chamonix (1946), Crescendo (1948), Shepherds Chimney (1946), Monolith Crack (1947), Devil's Wedge (1948), Donkey's Ears (1947). (All these are on Shepherd's Crag, his most notable "discovery".)

On Raven Crag he made Pedestal Wall (1940), Corvus (1950) Corax (1950) and Summit Route (1951). Again, this opened out the crag considerably.

It was Beetham's idea of stringing individual pitches together to make a climb which helped in the post-war reappraisal of the sport. He himself took the idea to extremes, however, and his later reputation tended to suffer in consequence.

An authority on ornithology, he wrote several books on that subject.

BELAY (Fr.: assurance; G.: sicherheit; It.: sicurezza)
The device and technique employed by a climber to safeguard the party from the effects of a fall by one of its members. Also the verb, "to belay", the act of using a belay. Belays are of four main types: 1. direct belay 2. static belay or anchor 3. dynamic belay 4. running belay or runner (see RUNNER).

Direct belay
On rock, the climber doing the belaying takes a firm stance and simply passes the rope over a convenient spike of rock, or through a piton, and draws it in as the

second man climbs towards him. Used a
lot in Alpine climbing when the going is
fairly easy and speed is desirable, but its
use in steep rock-climbing ended long ago.
It is far from secure. In snow-climbing a
direct belay is often made round an axe
shaft firmly planted into the snow – again,
for speed. On ice slopes, direct belays can
be made round the axe pick driven into the
ice or even round crampons stamped hard
in – both may be regarded as extreme
measures to be avoided if possible.

Static belay

The basic belay normally used in steep
climbing. Its purpose is literally to anchor
the party to the rock face or ice slope. All
members of a party, except the one actually
climbing, should be belayed. A static belay
consists of a loop from the climber's waist-
line or harness passed over a spike, round a
tree, or attached to a piton. Whatever the
anchor point, it should be firm – even large
boulders have been known to move under
shock loading. The loop should not be able
to ride off or be pulled off in the event of a
fall. It is normal practice to use a separate
loop (a belay loop) for static belays. It
should be nylon rope or tape at least equal
in breaking strain to the main rope. In
some cases, where the anchor points are
not good, two or three belays might be
arranged, but this is not common. The
main rope itself can be used to arrange a
belay.

On ice a static belay can be arranged
using an ice peg or ice screw as anchor
point, placed above a stance cut in the ice.
On snow, an axe driven well in can serve as
an anchor or use can be made of a "dead
man" (qv).

Dynamic belay

This refers to the way the rope is handled
when paying out or taking in. The
climber passes the rope around his back
at waist level (waist belay). He pays out
or takes in the active rope with one hand
(i.e. the rope to the other climber) while
the other controls the flow of rope from
the inactive coil. It is usual to take a twist
of rope round this arm to help control.
Should his partner slip, the friction of the
rope round the waist and arm is further
security.

If a second man falls off the leader can
usually hold him by the dynamic belay
alone, without any strain coming onto the
static belay, but if a leader falls the impact is considerable. The rope will run

through the belayer's hands and burn
them severely: belaying gloves should be
worn. Nevertheless, a good dynamic belay
will reduce the worst effects of a fall for the
leader and may arrest him completely,
especially if runners are used (qv). A shoulder belay is not as effective as a waist belay
and is little used today. (See STICHT PLATE)

BELL, Gertrude Lothian (1868-1926)

Noted Arabian explorer and archeologist
who, at the turn of the century, was also a
considerable climber. With Ulrich Fuhrer
as guide she made the first systematic exploration of the Engelhorner in 1901 and
1902. Gertrude's Peak is named after her.
In 1902 she made the first traverse Lauteraarhorn – Schreckhorn. In the same year
she made a dramatic attempt on the NE
Face of Finsteraarhorn, lasting 57 hours,
with retreat in a blizzard.

Miss Bell was an incredibly tough lady:
after interviewing an Arab chief, the latter
is said to have remarked, "And this is one
of their women! Allah, what must their
men be like?"

BENNEN, Johann Joseph (1824-64)

A guide from the upper Rhône valley
whose brief but brilliant career has long
been the subject of controversy amongst
Alpine historians. He came to general
notice after Tyndall hired him for the Finsteraarhorn in 1858, and he it was who led
Tyndall on the first ascent of Weisshorn
(1861). He also made three attempts on the
Matterhorn (see TYNDALL) and it could be
argued that Bennen's lack of consistency
caused Tyndall to lose that great prize. It
may also have contributed to his own
death on the Haut de Cry in February 1864
during a winter ascent of that minor peak.
Against his own expressed judgement he
allowed himself to be talked into crossing a
dangerous couloir and was overwhelmed
by an avalanche.

His correct name was Benet, and it is not
clear why he was universally known as
Bennen.

BEN NEVIS (4406 ft)

The highest mountain in Britain. With
Carn Dearg (3961 ft) and Carn Mor Dearg
(4012 ft) it forms a fine horseshoe enclosing
the Coire Leis and the upper Allt a Mhuillin glen, the entrance to which is to the
NW. The actual summit is a small plateau.

The nearest village is Fort William, at
the entrance to Glen Nevis, but nearer
climbing accommodation includes the

Youth Hostel in Glen Nevis, the Steall Hut (Upper Glen Nevis) and the finely situated Charles Inglis Clark Hut in the Allt a Mhuillin.

The tourist path to the summit begins at Achintee Farm (or the Youth Hostel) in Glen Nevis and follows an old pony track constructed for the former Observatory (1883-1904). It leads easily to the summit without incident. The classic circuit of the horseshoe is airy and dangerous in mists: there have been numerous fatalities here.

The Glen Nevis side of the mountain is grass slopes cut by several deep gullies and various outcrops, of which Polldubh Crags offer the best climbing. The principal climbing, however, is on the N Faces of Carn Dearg and Ben Nevis, overlooking the Allt a Mhuillin where the crags stretch for two miles and reach a height of 2,000 ft (Tower Ridge).

In winter the crags of Carn Dearg and Ben Nevis form one of the major snow and ice-climbing areas of Britain and though there are routes of all standards, they can only be recommended to experienced mountaineers. The mountain has a bad winter record of accidents.

Though the Hopkinsons had visited Ben Nevis in 1892 it was Collie's visit of 1894 which resulted in the first ascent of Tower Ridge that began the mountain's popularity with climbers. A summary of important first ascents is given below:

1892 NE Buttress – Hopkinson brothers.
     Tower Ridge (descent) – Hopkinson brothers.
1894 Tower Ridge – Collie, Solly, Collier.
1895 Castle Ridge – Collie, Naismith, Thomson, Travers.
1897 Gardyloo Gully (winter) – Hastings, Haskett-Smith.
1901 Observatory Ridge – Raeburn (solo).
1902 Observatory Buttress – Raeburn (solo).
     Glover's Chimney – Glover, Dr and Mrs Inglis Clark.
1938 Green Gully (winter) – Bell, Henson, Morsley, Small.
1946 The Crack – Carsten, McGuinness.
1954 Sassenach – Brown, Whillans.
1956 Centurion – Whillans, Downes.
1957 Cresta (winter) – Patey, Lovat, Nicol.
     Zero Gully (winter) – MacInnes, Nicol, Patey.
1959 The Bat – Haston, Smith.
     Point Five Gully (winter) Alexander, Clough, Pipes, Shaw.

Guidebooks: *Climbers' Guide to Ben Nevis*, by J. R. Marshall; *Winter Climbs, Ben Nevis and Glencoe*, by I. S. Clough and H. MacInnes; *The Polldubh Crags*, by K. Schwartz and Blyth Wright.

BEN NEVIS RACE
An annual race from the New Town Park, Claggan to the summit of Ben Nevis and back – approximately nine miles with a vertical interval of 4,400 ft. The winner receives the MacFarlane Trophy, a gold medal and £10, and there are numerous other awards.

The race began in 1895 when it was won by W. Swan of Fort William in 2 hr. 41 min., but only became an annual event in 1951, since when it has attracted leading entries from all over Britain. Though the race is confined to men, the course has been run by women (K. Connochie, aged 16, 3 hr. 2 min., 1955). The usual winners' time is under 2 hr.

From 1951 to 1970 the starting point was the King George V Playing Fields, Fort William. The present starting point makes the run about 1½ miles shorter. The old course record is held by Peter Hall who in 1964 clocked 1 hr. 38 min. 30 sec.

BERCHTESGADENER ALPS
A region of limestone Alps extending south from the famous resort of Berchtesgaden. With the exception of Watzmann (2,713 m) the peaks are fairly undistinguished, though the area is extremely beautiful. The Watzmann is the highest peak entirely in Germany: first ascent – Stanig, Beck and Von Buch, 1801. The mountain has a tremendous E Face above the Königsee, with several routes up it. (No English guidebook.)

BERGSCHRUND (F.: Rimaye)
The crevasse between the glacier proper and the upper snows (*névé*). They may be negligible or formidable and can vary from season to season. Double and triple bergschrunds are quite common. Where the upper lip is much higher than the lower a bergschrund will have to be climbed by ice techniques, even, in extreme conditions, artificial techniques. In descent, in such cases, an abseil is necessary.

BERNESE ALPS
A range of high mountains extending from Lake Geneva to the Lake of Lucerne, bounded in the south, for the most part, by the upper Rhône, and in the north by the

valley of the Aare (Interlaken, etc.). It can be divided naturally into three sections: West Bernese Alps, Central Bernese Alps (the Oberland proper), and East Bernese Alps. The division between the first two is the Gemmi Pass and between the last two, the Grimsel Pass. A good deal of the Bernese Alps are not, paradoxically, in the Canton Berne but in Valais (principally), Vaud, Fribourg, Uri, Unterwalden and Lucerne.

From a mountaineering point of view the Western section is of the least interest. The highest summit is Wildhorn (3,248 m) and two other peaks of note are Wildstrubel (3,242 m) and Les Diablerets (3,210 m). The climbing is generally easy, though the Argentine (2,422 m) offers rock climbs of quality. Various huts.

The Eastern section is both more complex and interesting, and is split into a northern and southern portion by the Susten Pass. N of the pass the principal centre is Engelberg and the highest peak is Titlis (3,239 m). Other peaks of interest include Uri Rotstock (2,928 m) and the little-known Fünffingerstöck – Spannort range. The limestone of the region gives good rock-climbing, Gross Schlossberg etc., and is easily accessible.

South of the Susten Pass rises the Sustenhorn (3,504 m) group which provides easy snow climbs (centre: Stein) and south of that again is the more difficult Dammastock (3,630 m) group offering good rock climbs (centre: Furka Pass). At the extreme east end of the area is the famous Salbitschijen (*qv*).

The central region of the Bernese Alps is known, not altogether accurately, as the Oberland. It is a heavily glaciated region of high peaks (Gr. Aletsch glacier 22 km – the longest in the Alps): nine peaks exceed 4,000 m. The principal centre is Grindelwald (*qv*) but this is not convenient for outlying peaks. Kandersteg (*qv*), Lötschental, the upper Rhône valley and Grimsel are all useful in this respect. There is an important rail-car link between Kandersteg and Lötschental and hence to the Rhône valley.

The climbing is mainly mixed snow/ rock of all standards including some famous ridges and faces. The highest peak is Finsteraarhorn (4,274 m), first climbed in 1812 by A. Volker, J. Bortis and A. Abbühl. The Hangendgletcherhorn (1788), Sparrhorn (1800), Rottalhorn (c1811) and Jungfrau (1811) were climbed earlier. The Wetterhorn (3,701 m) was first climbed in 1844 by M. Bannholzer and J. Jaun, but Wills' famous ascent of 1854 led to the Golden Age of alpinism (see WILLS). The most famous peak of modern times is undoubtedly the Eiger (3,970 m) (*qv*). Notable routes include:

1865 Guggi route, Jungfrau – H. B. George, Sir G. Young, with C. Almer, A. Baumann, U. Almer
1866 Nollen Route, Mönch – E. von Fellenberg with C. Michel, P. Egger
1883 Andersongrat, Gr. Schreckhorn – J. S. Anderson, G. P. Baker with U. Almer, A. Pollinger
1899 Galletgrat, Doldenhorn – J. Gallet, with J. Kalbermatten, A. Muller
1904 NE Face, Finsteraarhorn – G. Hasler with F. Amatter
1909 Unterbächhorn – Nesthorn Traverse – G. W. Young, G. L. Mallory, D. Robertson
1911 NE Ridge, Jungfrau – A. Weber with A. Schlunegger
1914 Rote Zähne Ridge, Gspaltenhorn – G. W. Young, S. W. Herford, with J. Knubel, H. Brantschen
1921 Mönch Nordwand – H. Lauper, M. Liniger
     Mittelegi Ridge, Eiger – Yuko Maki with F. Amatter, F. Steuri, S. Brawand
1925 Aletschhorn Nordwand – E. Blanchet with A. Rübi, K. Mooser
1932 Grosshorn Nordwand – W. Welzenbach, A. Drexel, H. Rudy, E. Schultze
     NW Face, Gletscherhorn – same party
     Lauper Route, Eiger – H. Lauper, A. Zurcher with J. Knübel, A. Graven
1938 Schneehorn Nordwand – I and J. Taguchi with S. Brawand, C. Kaufmann
     Eigerwand – H. Harrer, F. Kasparek, A. Heckmair, W. Vorg
1966 Eigerwand Direct (winter) – J. Lehne, G. Strobel, D. Haston, S. Hupfauer, R. Votteler

As a contrast to the main area the valley of Rosenlaui in the NE of the group offers high-grade rock-climbing on the Engelhörner (*qv*) and there is a famous rock traverse on the Lobhörner, above Lauterbrunnen.

In most of the Bernese Alps the rock is limestone, but there is also some gneiss. There are numerous huts.

Guidebooks: *Bernese Alps West* – Collomb, *Selected Climbs in the Bernese Oberland* – Collomb, *Central Switzerland* –

Talbot, *Engelhörner and Salbitschijen* –
Talbot.

BERNINA ALPS

An important group of mountains on the
Swiss-Italian border rising above the international resorts of St Moritz and Pontre-
sina. It includes Bernina proper and the
adjacent Bregaglia Alps (*qv*). The highest
summit is Piz Bernina (4,049 m) – the only
4,000 m summit outside the Western Alps.
Other well-known peaks are Piz Palu
(3,905 m), Piz Zupo (3,996 m), Piz Argient
(3,945 m), Crast' Aguzza (3,869 m), Piz
Morteratsch (3,751 m), Piz Tschierva
(3,546 m), Piz Scerscen (3,971 m), Piz
Roseg (3,937 m) and Piz Corvatsch
(3,451 m). All are popular and there are
climbs of all grades in the region, both rock
and ice. There are several huts.

The first ascent of Piz Bernina was by J.
Coaz with J and L. R. Tscharner, 1850.
Other notable ascents include:

1866 Spallagrat, Piz Bernina – F. F. Tuckett, F. Brown, C. Almer, F. Andermatten
1872 Gussfeldtsattel – P. Gussfeldt, H.
Grass, P. Jenny, C. Capat (traverse)
1876 Middlemoregrat, Piz Roseg – H.
Cordier, T. Middlemore, J. Jaun, K.
Maurer
1877 Piz Scerscen – P. Gussfeldt, H.
Grass, C. Capat
1878 Biancograt, Piz Bernina – P. Guss-
feldt, H. Grass, J. Gross
1887 Eisnase, Piz Scerscen – P. Gussfeldt,
E. Rey, J. B. Aymonod (in descent)
Bumillergrat, Piz Palu – H. Bumiller,
M. Schocher, J. Gross, C. Schnitzler
1890 NE Wall, Piz Bernina – L. Norman-
Neruda, C. Klucker
Neruda Route, Piz Scerscen – L.
Norman-Neruda, C. Klucker

Christian Klucker was the outstanding
climber of the region and one of the most
famous guides in the Alps (*qv*).

Guidebook: *Bernina Alps*, by Collomb
and Talbot (excludes Bregaglia).

BICKNELL, Algernon Sidney (1832-1911)

Scientist and adventurer. Made ten ascents
of Vesuvius, six during eruptions, in one of
which (1858) he almost lost his life. Made a
winter ascent of Etna and climbed in many
parts of the world. He is said to have
crossed the Andes four times and to have
attempted a crossing of South America
through the Amazon jungle (1894). His
brother, Herman, made one of the early
Matterhorn ascents (1872) and visited

Mecca in disguise.

BINER, Bernard (1900-65)

Prominent Zermatt guide and ski instructor who, with his sister Paula, opened the
disused "Bahnhof Hotel" to provide cheap
accommodation for a party of French
schoolchildren (1951). From this the
"Bahnhof" developed into a climbers'
bunkhouse of international repute.

BIRKBECK, John Sen. (1817-90)

Yorkshire banker who was both climber
and potholer: forerunner of the Slingsby
group in this respect. In 1847 he made the
first descent of Alum Pot with Metcalfe
and in 1872 he made the first attempt on
Gaping Ghyll, reaching a depth of 190 ft
(Birkbeck's Ledge).

In 1855 he was with Hudson, Stevenson
and the Smyths on the first ascent of
Monte Rosa. In 1858 he crossed the
Monchjoch and in 1860 took part in the
first ascent of the Col de Triolet. He was an
Original Member of the A. C.

BIRKBECK, John Jun. (1842-92)

Made one of the earliest attempts on the
Dru and an early ascent of the Weisshorn.
In 1864 made the first traverse of the Dôme
de Goûter with Adams Reilly. His in-
itiation to climbing was unfortunate: he
had a sliding fall of almost 1,800 ft from the
Col de Miage (1861), losing most of the
skin from his back and legs and suffering
severe shock. His remarkable recovery can
be attributed to the speed of his rescue by
his companions: Hudson, Tuckett, Stephen and Anderegg. In 1874 he made the
first double traverse of the Matterhorn –
Breuil back to Breuil in 19 hours.

BIRKETT, R. James

A Lakeland climber active in the immediate pre-war and post-war years, Jim Birkett made 45 new routes, mostly in the
harder grades. He had a fine eye for a line
and most of the routes are now classics.

His activity extended to many crags and
mention might be made of Tophet
Grooves, Gable (1940); F Route, Gimmer
(1941); and Leopard's Crawl, Dow (1947).
His contributions to three crags are outstanding: East Buttress, Scafell; Castle
Rock, Thirlmere; and White Ghyll.

His first big new route was May Day
Climb, East Buttress (1938). Though he
used pegs for protection, it was a very hard
climb for the time. Other East Buttress
routes are the Girdle (1938) and Gremlin

Groove (1945). He also put up Great Central Route on Esk Buttress (1945) among several others.

Birkett's ascent of Overhanging Bastion, Castle Rock (1939) with C. R. Wilson and L. Muscroft created a sensation at the time. It was followed by Zig Zag in the same year, May Day Cracks in 1947 and, finally, Harlot's Face in 1949. This was the first extreme grade climb in Lakeland. A number of his easier climbs on this crag have also become popular.

In 1945 he climbed Hollin Groove in White Ghyll: not the first climb in the Ghyll, but it was Birkett's subsequent climbs that helped make the Ghyll popular: White Ghyll Wall (1946), Slip Knot (1947), Haste Not (1948), Perhaps Not (1948) and Do Not (1949).

Birkett's influence on Lakeland climbing cannot be overestimated.

BISHOP, Barry Chapman (b. 1932)
A leading American mountaineer and geographer who made the first ascent of the West Buttress of Mount McKinley (20,320 ft) in 1951 and the first ascent of Ama Dablam (22,494 ft) in 1961. The latter was a winter ascent.

On 22 May 1963, Bishop, with L. G. Jerstad, became the first American to reach the summit of Mount Everest. They climbed the South Ridge and beat Hornbein and Unsoeld by a few hours – the latter traversing the mountain, West – South. The two parties met on the descent. (See *Everest – The West Ridge*, by T. F. Hornbein.)

As a geographer Bishop has done much research in Nepal and various arctic zones. He works for the National Geographic Society.

BIVEN, Peter Harvey (b. 1935)
An outstanding rock-climber of the postwar years, who, with his partner, Trevor Peck, was one of the few people to match the achievements of the Rock and Ice Club on outcrops. Amongst his early first ascents are:
1953 Original Route, Matlock High Tor
1955 Moyer's Buttress, Gardom's Edge
      Suicide Wall, Bosigran
1956 Phantom, Bosigran
      Congo Corner, Stanage
      Eye of Faith, Gardom's Edge
1958 Central Wall, Malham Cove
In all, Biven made some 300 new ascents. He was one of the earliest practitioners in Britain of artificial climbing. He developed

Millstone Edge as a gritstone peg-climbing quarry, though this was only as practice for the larger peg climbs of the Alps. He later played a considerable part in the development of Chudleigh and the Devon sea cliffs.

In the Alps, Biven made the first ascents of the North Face of Valette and North Face of Aig. de la Vanoise, in the Vanoise, and of the Westwand of Predigstuhl in the Kaisergebirge, all in 1956. He also made the first British ascent of the North Face of Piz Ligoncio in the Bregaglia.

He is the compiler of guidebooks to *Cornwall* (Vol 1), 1968, and *Devon* (with P. Littlejohn), 1970. In private life he is an educational adviser.

BIVOUAC (Fr.) (G.: Biwak)
Spending the night in the open on a mountain. Many long Alpine climbs demand one or more bivouacs for which the climbers go prepared, but climbers are sometimes delayed and forced to bivouac unexpectedly.

In a normal bivouac the climbers will search for some suitable ledge before dark and prepare to sit out the night. It is usual, unless the ledge is extremely wide, to tie off rucksacks and gear to belays such as pegs, and for each person to be similarly belayed. The stove, pots and food are placed accessibly, as constant brewing-up is a feature of bivouacs. All available clothing is usually worn including long johns and duvet gear (*qv*). It may or may not be feasible to lie down, but some sleep is generally possible. In any case, boots are usually removed and put in the rucksack which is then used as a short form of sleeping bag. Some climbers carry pied d'elephants, which are short duvet bags designed for this purpose. The "bivvy sac", once in vogue, is no longer popular and if the night is very cold the protection of a large plastic bag can be employed instead.

Where several bivouacs are intended, or where the weather seems doubtful, a special bivouac tent can be carried. If the bivouac is to be on very steep rock, without ledges, bivouac hammocks can be used slung from pegs.

An involuntary bivouac can be a serious matter if the climbers are unprepared, particularly in bad weather or winter. The main aim is to keep out of the wind and conserve body heat. The emergency plastic bag should be carried at all times. In winter it may be necessary to dig a snow hole or make an igloo.

BLACK ICE

Thin water ice so transparent that the underlying rock shows through, giving it a dark hue. Extremely tough and "rubbery" – very difficult to cut with an ice axe.

BLACK ROCKS OF CROMFORD

One of the earliest developed of the Derbyshire gritstone outcrops; a series of fine buttresses and boulder problems in all grades and longer than usual.

Guidebook: *The Chatsworth Gritstone Area*, by E. Byne.

BLACKSHAW, Alan (b. 1933)

One of the leaders of the post-war British resurgence in Alpine climbing. He visited the Caucasus in 1958 and Greenland in 1960. In 1972 he took part in the British Alpine Ski Traverse and the following year in a ski traverse of Lapland. Elected President of the B. M. C. in 1973.

From 1968 to 1970, Blackshaw was Editor of the Alpine Journal, but is best known for his book, *Mountaineering* (1965) – regarded as the climbers' "bible". A similar book on skiing is planned for 1974. In private life, he is a senior civil servant.

BLANCHET, Emile Robert (1877-1943)

A Swiss climber with a long record of difficult Alpine ascents. Between the wars, often with the guide Kaspar Mooser, Blanchet was responsible for some extraordinary climbs on the big faces, the best known being a variant on the E Face of the Zinal Rothorn (1932). Blanchet and Mooser also reconnoitred the Matterhorn N Face but rejected the route later climbed by the Schmids. Unfortunately, most of Blanchet and Mooser's routes lack the quality of the great face climbs done by other climbers of the period. In private life Blanchet was a pianist.

BLEAKLOW (2,060 ft)

A high moor in the Peak District lying between Longdendale in the north and the Snake Pass in the south. It is crossed by the Pennine Way (*qv*) and the Marsden – Edale Walk (*qv*) and is famous for its groughs (*qv*). There are a few gritstone crags on the edges of the moor, the only one of note being Shining Clough, above Longdendale, which offers fine climbs of considerable length and difficulty.

Guidebook: *Bleaklow Area* (*Rock Climbs in the Peak Vol. 6*).

BLODIG, Karl (1859-1956)

One of the earliest advocates of guideless Alpine climbing and a companion of Purtscheller (*qv*). Climbed often with British climbers: H. O. Jones, Young, Eckenstein, Crompton, etc. He made a number of first ascents but is most notable as being the first to climb all the then known 4,000 m peaks in the Alps (1911). He added to the list as new heights were discovered, including the Gd. Rocheuse and Aig. du Jardin, which he climbed solo at the age of 73. Wrote *Die Viertausender der Alpen*. In private life Blodig was a dentist from Bregenz.

LE BLOND, Mrs. Aubrey (1861–1934)

One of the most skilful of the early women climbers, slightly built but strong. She climbed in every part of the Alps, but particularly the Bernina. Though she employed some of the best guides of the day she made occasional guideless climbs and even "all women" climbs – then almost unheard of. She was one of the founders and first President of the Ladies' Alpine Club.

Mrs Le Blond wrote *High Alps in Winter* (1883), *High Life and Towers of Silence* (1886), *My Home in the Alps* (1892), *Hints on Snow Photography* (1894), *True Tales of Mountain Adventure* (1903), *Story of an Alpine Winter* (novel) (1907), *Mountaineering in the Land of the Midnight Sun* (1908), and *Day in and Day out* (1929).

BOCCALATTE, Gabriele Gallo (1907-38)

A fine Italian climber who made hard new routes in the Mont Blanc massif and the Dolomites. He was in the party that climbed the Aig. du Diable Couloir of Mont Blanc du Tacul in 1930, and he climbed the N Face of Mont Gruetta in 1937. He is best remembered for the climbs done with Mme. Nina Pietrasanta (later his wife): Boccalatte Pillar of Mont Blanc du Tacul (1936) and the West Face of Aig. Noire de Peuterey (1935).

He also paid a visit to the Andes. He was killed attempting the SW Face of the Triolet in 1938.

BOHREN, Peter (1822-82)

One of the early Oberland guides who was with Wills on the Wetterhorn in 1854 (*qv*). He was a very small man, meticulous and intelligent. He figures in many of the early accounts of climbs written by the pioneers and was called "die Gletscher-Wolf". It was Bohren who was responsible for the well-known remark: "Herr, you are master in the valley: I am master here", made when one of his employers questioned his judgement during a climb.

BOILEAU DE CASTELNAU, Henri Emmanuel (1857-1923)

A distinguished French climber noted for his first ascents in the Dauphiné Alps. These include Aig. d'Olan (1876) and all four summits of the Pelvoux traversed for the first time (1877).

After two previous attempts, he finally succeeded in making the first ascent of the Meije (15-17 August 1877). This was the last major summit of the Alps to be climbed.

BOLTS

Sometimes used in artificial climbing to overcome blank stretches of rock. A hole is drilled in the rock and an expansion bolt, holding an angle bracket that will take a karabiner, is inserted and screwed home. Bolting is avoided whenever possible, not only because of the labour involved, but also on ethical grounds: certain climbs have raised considerable controversy. The brackets were sometimes called "golos", but the name seems to have been dropped, in favour of "fishplates" or "hangers".

BOMB

Colloquialism meaning to go quickly e.g. "he bombed up the route".

BONATTI, Walter (b. 1930)

An Italian Alpinist born in Bergamo, who has become one of the world's greatest mountaineers. His Alpine achievements are probably without compare. He became a professional guide in 1954 and has lived at Courmayeur since 1957.

Among many of his new or outstanding climbs in the Alps might be mentioned:

1951 East Face of the Grand Capucin (with L. Ghigo), first ascent
1955 SW Pillar of the Dru (Bonatti Pillar), solo, first ascent
1957 Eckpfeiler Buttress, Mont Blanc (with T. Gobbi), first ascent
1959 Pilastro Rosso, Mont Blanc (with A. Oggioni), first ascent
   Route Major, Mont Blanc, first solo ascent
1965 Matterhorn Nordwand Direct, solo, first ascent

This selection shows Bonatti to be a master of all techniques, from the artificial

climbing on the Capucin to the difficult mixed terrain of the Matterhorn Nordwand. As a solo climber his record is unmatched for difficulty.

In 1954 he was with the Italian party that made the first ascent of K2, the second highest mountain in the world, but not in the summit assault. In 1958 he returned to the Himalaya and with C. Mauri reached the summit of Gasherbrum IV (first ascent).

Earlier in the same year, 1958, he visited Patagonia. Though he failed on Cerro Torre (qv) he made, with Mauri, the first ascent of Cerro Moreno (11,500ft) and then a complete traverse of the Cerro Adela group – five summits in a single push. He returned to S. America in 1961 and climbed Nevado Ninashanca (18,500ft), Cerro Parin Nord (16,950ft) and Rondoy Nord (19,100ft), all first ascents.

Bonatti's career has not been without tragedy and controversy. In the winter of 1956 he and S. Gheser climbed the Brenva Ridge with J. Vincendon and F. Henry. The parties became separated and Vincendon and Henry died in a blizzard. In 1961, only he and P. Mazeaud survived a terrible retreat from the Central Pillar of Freney in a blizzard during which four of their companions died.

His books are *On the Heights* (1964) and *The Great Years* (1974).

BONINGTON, Christian John Storey (b. 1934)

One of the best-known British climbers of the present era, with numerous new ascents in Britain, the Alps and elsewhere to his credit. Bonington first came to prominence with his first winter ascent of Raven's Gully on Buachaille Etive Mor in 1953 (with H. MacInness (qv)) and with some hard first routes on the cliffs of the Avon Gorge in the late fifties. In the sixties he was putting up some hard Lakeland routes, among them: The Medlar (with M. Boysen) and Totalitarian, both on Raven Crag Thirlmere, and The Last Laugh, Castle Rock.

Bonington's first Alpine season was 1957 when, with MacInnes, he made a half-hearted attempt on the Eigerwand. In the following year they made the first British ascent of the Bonatti Pillar of the Dru. In 1959, with Gunn Clark, he made the first British ascent of the Cima Grande Direct. In 1961, with Whillans, he again attempted the Eigerwand, but frustrated by weather they went to Chamonix, where, with Clough (*qv*) and Djuglosz he made the first ascent of the Central Pillar of Freney, then regarded as the greatest unsolved problem in the Alps. In 1962 with Whillans, he took part in the rescue of Nally from the Eigerwand, and later in the same year made the first British ascent of the Eigerwand with Clough. He has made several other first ascents in the Alps, with Brown, Patey and others.

Commissioned into the Army in 1956, Bonington spent five years in the forces before taking up a position as a trainee manager with Unilever, but his increasing involvement with expeditions decided him to resign, and in 1962 he became a full-time writer and photographer. He established himself in this with his photographic coverage of the Eiger Direct climb in 1966. A number of exciting projects followed, including the first descent of the Blue Nile (1968).

Bonington's first Himalayan expedition was in 1960 when he reached the summit of Annapurna II (26,041 ft) with R. Grant. In 1961 he reached the summit of Nuptse (25,700 ft). In 1963, with Whillans, he reached the summit of the Central Tower of Paine in Patagonia. He did not join another expedition for seven years, but in 1970 he organized the immensely successful expedition to climb the S Face of Annapurna: the most important Himalayan face climb to date. In 1972 he organized a post-monsoon attempt on the SW Face of Everest, but this failed.

Bonington is a very popular lecturer. His books are: *I Chose to Climb* (1966), *Annapurna South Face* (1971), *The Next Horizon* (1972) and *Everest South-West Face* (1973).

BONNEY, Rev. Thomas George (1833-1923)

Distinguished geologist and theologian and an indefatigable Alpine traveller, almost rivalling Ball (*qv*). Bonney climbed many of the Alpine giants and made the first English attempt on Pelvoux (1860). Most of his later travels were of a geological nature. Wrote several books on the Alps and geology.

BOOTS

Boots are the most satisfactory footwear for all mountain activities. Shoes, even "walking shoes", are unsuitable because they do not support the ankles and this is necessary over rough terrain. The type of boot depends upon the activities to be undertaken.

Climbing boots

One piece leather uppers, with bellow tongues or overlap, narrow welts, pointed toes, hook fastenings or rings going down almost to the toes, stiffened through-sole, vibram soles. Styles vary but the main point is to have a rigid sole that can be placed firmly on a hold. Used for rock-climbing and alpinism, but not really suitable for mountain walking.

Walking boots

The same qualities as a climbing boot but with a flexible sole that makes walking more comfortable. Can be used for elementary climbing. Cheaper than climbing boots. Lightweight models are made but are usually not as robust or waterproof as the heavier boot. Recently, "Spanish" fell-boots have been adopted for simple walks: canvas boots with cleated rubber soles, not waterproof and unsuitable for rock climbing, but cheap and expendable.

Rock-climbing boots

Specially designed lightweight boots just for rock-climbing. (See KLETTERSCHUHE; P.A.)

High altitude boots or winter boots

"Double boots" consisting of a soft, well-insulated, inner boot, which fits inside a rugged outer boot. Used where extremely cold temperatures are expected. Very heavy and too clumsy and expensive for general use.

Overboots

Canvas boots-cum-leggings used in high altitude climbing to protect the leather boot and add warmth.

It is usual for climbers to wear boots with one pair of wool stockings but some walkers prefer two thicknesses of sock (oversocks). Boots should be a comfortable fit and be worn in before use on the hills. Most boots are now padded at tongue and ankle and do not require the "breaking" that was once common and essential practice. A light polish of silicone wax is the best preservative, and wet boots should be dried by stuffing them with newspaper and leaving in a draught – never in front of a fire because leather tends to bake. (See also NAILS; VIBRAMS.)

BORROWDALE

A long valley, stretching south from Keswick in the Lake District and containing Derwentwater. The villages are: Grange, Rosthwaite, Stonethwaite, Seatoller and Seathwaite – all connected by road. From Seatoller the road goes over Honister Pass to Buttermere (qv). A number of well-known passes (for walkers) leave the valley head: Greenup Edge (for Grasmere), Grains Gill (Langdale), Sty Head (Wasdale). The dominant fell of the valley is Glaramara. Out of the valley, but connected by motor road, is the hamlet of Watendlath.

Since the last war the valley has become one of the premier climbing centres of the Lakes, with a wide variety of climbs in all grades, many hard. The principal crags are: Walla, Lower Falcon, Gowder, Goat, Troutdale Pinnacle, Shepherd's (qv), Great End, Bowderstone, Eagle, Heron, Sergeant's, Raven, Castle and Grey Knotts.

Borrowdale climbing was largely developed by Bentley Beetham (qv).

Guidebook: Borrowdale, by P. Nunn and O. Woolcock.

BOTTERILL, Fred (?-1920)

A Yorkshire gritstone climber who made some outstanding Lake District climbs, notably Botterill's Slab, Scafell (1903) and the Northwest Climb, Pillar Rock (1906). One of the first to bring gritstone standards to other areas, he retired from climbing in 1909 after an accident on Eagle's Nest Ridge, Gable, in which his leader was killed.

BOTTOMING

A term used to mean that a piton has reached the back of a crack before its blade is fully home. Either a shorter piton or a tie-off (qv) is used.

BOULDERING

Climbing boulder problems; a common game amongst climbers. The climbs are usually only a few feet high, but extremely difficult and call for good techniques. The Helyg Boulder, in Wales, is famous.

BOURDILLON, Thomas Duncan (1924-56)

The leading spirit in the British post-war Alpine climbing renaissance whose ascent with Nicol of the N Face of the Dru in 1950 showed the way for others. Was on the expedition to Cho Oyu (1952) and Everest (1951) with Shipton (qv) and took part in the first assault on the summit, with Evans (qv), during the 1953 expedition. He was professionally a physicist and, with his father, developed the oxygen apparatus used on the 1953 expedition. Bourdillon was killed climbing the Jagihorn, Oberland.

BOURRIT, Marc-Théodore (1739-1819)

Precentor of Geneva Cathedral, self-styled "Indefatigable Bourrit". One of the early explorers of the Alps, contemporary and rival of de Saussure (qv). Bourrit was a painter, writer and climber – all of which he did badly. He climbed the Buet in 1775 and explored many of the almost unknown valleys and glaciers of the Central Alps. In 1766 he visited Chamonix and heard about de Saussure's offer of a reward for a first ascent of Mont Blanc. Bourrit changed the apathy with which news of the award had been greeted into enthusiasm, though it took him several years to do it – the first attempt by guides was not until 1775. He made an attempt himself in 1783 with Paccard, but retreated feebly, much to Paccard's disgust. He tried again in 1784 but again withdrew, though his guides reached the Dôme du Goûter. The following year he tried again with de Saussure and failed. When Paccard and Balmat reached the summit in 1786 Bourrit became insanely jealous and published a libellous document about Paccard which was, unfortunately, widely distributed and began the long controversy over the motives and origins of the first ascent (see PACCARD). Bourrit never managed to climb the mountain (see The First Ascent of Mont Blanc, by T. G. Brown and G. R. de Beer.)

BOWDLER, Thomas (1754-1825)

Well known as the man who tried to expurgate Shakespeare and other texts ("to bowdlerize"), Bowdler was also an Alpine traveller who, in 1779, made the first crossing of the Col de la Vanoise (Graians). He was the first Englishman to climb the Buet (also 1779) – he held the height record for an Englishman for eight years until Beaufoy climbed Mont Blanc – and the first Englishman to take an interest in Mont Blanc by offering a reward of five guineas to any guides who succeeded in reaching the summit.

BOWEN, Cecil Hubert (1864-1956)

One of the pioneers of British rock-climbing who, in 1893, took part in the first ascent of the Arrowhead Ridge on Gable, Lake District. His best known ascents were with Jones (*qv*) whom he seconded on the first ascent of Kern Knotts Crack (1897). They also made the first ascent of C Gully on the Screes (1897) and the second of Eagles' Nest Direct, Gable.

Bowen made the first traverse of the Gletcherhorn (1908) and several new climbs in Norway.

BOWFELL (2,960 ft)
A beautiful mountain between Langdale and Eskdale in the Lake District. Usually climbed from the former. There are crags all round the peak: the Bowfell Links on the Eskdale face, though once popular, are loose and little climbed today, but the Langdale face has several crags which are popular. These are: Flat Crag, Cambridge Crag, North Buttress, and the huge Bowfell Buttress, the Ordinary Route of which is regarded as a classic (1902, Shaw, Craig, West, Hargreaves.). Neckband Crag is near the summit of the Band, a spur leading towards the fell. The Sword of Damocles, on North Buttress, is one of the hardest routes in the area.

Guidebook: *Great Langdale*, by J. A. Austin.

BOYSEN, Jan Anders Martin (b. 1941)
An outstanding British climber of recent years. His first ascents include Burma Road at Cheddar Gorge; Skull, Nexus and Nexus Girdle in Wales; Moriarty, Snoopy etc on Fuar Tholl in Scotland, and various others including many on the sandstone outcrops. In the Alps he made the first ascent of the W Face of Pic Sans Nom, Chamonix Face of Aig. Fou. He has been a member of expeditions to Cerro Torre, Annapurna South Face, and the Torre Egger.

BRADBY, Edward Hugh Folkwine (1866-1947)
The third member of a famous trio, Wicks, Wilson and Bradby, who made a number of fine climbs at Chamonix during the turn of the century (see WICKS, WILSON). In private life a solicitor.

BRASSINGTON
Rainster Rocks and Harborough Rocks near Brassington in Derbyshire provide a number of short climbs on dolomite limestone.

Guidebook: *The Chatsworth Gritstone Area*, by E. Byne.

BREGAGLIA
A very popular area of sharp granite peaks on the Swiss-Italian border above the Val Bregaglia between Chiavenna and the Maloja Pass. Promontogno is a popular centre.

Though the total area is fairly small the region divides naturally into three major cirques (on the northern, popular side). From W to E these are: the Sciora Cirque (Val Bondasca), the Albigna Cirque and the Forno Cirque. All contain good climbs, especially in the middle and upper grades of difficulty. Best-known is the Sciora Cirque which contains the famous Piz Badile (3,308 m) (North East Face: Cassin, Esposito, Ratti, Molteni and Valseschi, 1937).

Guidebooks: *Bregaglia East*, by R. Collomb and P. Crew; and *Bregaglia West*, by R. Collomb.

BREUIL (BREUIL-CERVINIA)
Ski resort beneath the Italian slopes of the Matterhorn (*qv*) separated from Zermatt by the Theodule Pass (cable cars etc.). The scene of Whymper's (*qv*) famous attempts on the mountain.

BRIDGE, Alfred William (1902-71)
Alf Bridge was a partner of Kirkus (*qv*) and one of the best-known climbers of the thirties. In 1932 he seconded Kirkus on Curving Crack and the Direct Finish to the East Buttress, Clogwyn du'r Arddu. He was a Manchester man who had done a great deal of Pennine bog trotting and many climbs on gritstone. He perfected a method of controlled falling by which he could drop thirty feet without injury. Bridge was a somewhat controversial personality.

BRIDGING
A method of climbing a wide chimney (*qv*) by using left hand and foot on one side wall and right hand and foot on the other. The term "straddling" is obsolescent.

BRISTOW, Lily
Family friend of Mummery and his wife, Lily Bristow probably began climbing with them sometime between 1883 and 1891, though this is not certain. She sprang to fame in 1892 when, with Miss Pasteur, she accompanied Mummery and his companions on a traverse of the Charmoz, (first ascent by women). In 1893 she accompanied Mummery, Slingsby, Collie and Hastings on the Petit Dru, Zinal

Rothorn, Italian Ridge of the Matterhorn and the traverse of the Grépon. It was only the second time the Grépon had been traversed and Miss Bristow's performance led to Mummery's famous phrase, "an easy day for a lady".

In 1894 she climbed with the guides Pollinger and Zurbriggen and made the first descent ever of the Zmutt Ridge.

Her exact relationship with Mummery remains vague, but she did not climb with him in 1894 and, with Mummery's death in 1895, she seems to have given up climbing altogether.

BRITISH MOUNTAINEERING COUNCIL (B.M.C.)

The advisory body of British mountaineering, composed of elected representatives of member clubs. The Mountaineering Council of Scotland looks after the interests of Scottish clubs, though in fact Scottish clubs may join the B. M. C., and some do.

The Patron is Lord Hunt and there is a Committee of Management, with the usual Officers. Committee members serve a maximum of three years but may be reelected later. There are (1974) three permanent officials, chief of whom is designated General Secretary. There are six Area Committees: Lake District, London and South East, North East, North Wales, Peak District, South West and Southern. There are four Sub-Committees: Equipment, Harrison's Rocks, Hut Management, Professional Guides.

The B. M. C. has wide areas of responsibility. It tests climbing equipment, supervises all aspects of mountain leadership training, including professional guides, runs the Glen Brittle Memorial Hut in Skye, deals with enquiries on mountaineering matters from the public, liaises with numerous organizations of allied interests (e.g. conservation), negotiates over rights of way with landowners and represents Britain on the Union Internationale des Associations d'Alpinisme (U. I. A. A.). It also helps in the publication of books of special importance to climbers.

The B. M. C. was formed in 1944, principally through the work of G. W. Young, and was originally comprised of representatives of 30 clubs, mostly those of long foundation. There are now some 200 clubs and organizations involved.

BROADRICK, Richard Wilfred (1872-1903)

The best known of three Windermere bro-

thers who were pioneer rock-climbers in the Lakes. Broadrick's Crack, Dow Crag, is perhaps the best-known climb (1902). Broadrick was a good alpinist also, making the first traverse of the Aig. Sans Nom and attempting the Mer de Glace face of Charmoz, only failing 200 ft from the summit (1901).

On 21 September 1903, Broadrick, with H. Jupp, A. E. W. Garrett and S. Ridsdale attempted to reach Hopkinson's Cairn from Lord's Rake – an outstanding climbing problem of the day, on Scafell. Broadrick gave up the lead to Garrett who subsequently slipped; the party was pulled from the rock and killed.

BROCKEN SPECTRE

A phenomenon seen in mountains when there is a low cloud base with clear sky above. In the early morning the low-slanting rays of the sun throw a shadow of the peaks, and climbers, upon the clouds below. The shadow is enormously magnified. The name comes from the Brocken Mountains of Germany where the phenomenon is said to be common.

BROOME, Edward Alfred (1846-1920)

One of the most remarkable climbers of his day; a man utterly devoted to the mountains. Though he did not visit the Alps until he was 40, Broome took at once to the sport of climbing, helped by good guides (particularly J. M. Biner) and a strong constitution. He was a formidable walker.

Broome concentrated on the most difficult expeditions of the time, particularly at Zermatt, Chamonix and the Dolomites. He made a number of first ascents including the first complete traverse from the Triftjoch of the Rothorngrat (1903). His most famous expedition was, however, the first ascent of the Schalligrat on Weisshorn (1895).

In his 67th year he traversed the Nordend of Monte Rosa, from Macugnaga (Brioschi Route) and the year before he died, 1919, he traversed the Charmoz. He was then 75.

Broome died at Zermatt in 1920 and is buried there.

BROWN, Joe (b. 1930)

One of the greatest mountaineers Britain has ever produced, whose achievements stretch from the outcrops of Derbyshire to the Himalaya. His influence on rock-climbing, in particular, has been profound.

Brown and his companions from the Valkyrie Club, and later the Rock and Ice Club, played a leading part in the gritstone campaign that swept Stanage and elsewhere from 1949 onwards. In 1952 he formed a partnership with Whillans (*qv*) which for a few years was the strongest ever seen in Britain. Their list of climbs in Derbyshire, Wales and elsewhere is formidable, and all at the highest standards.

Brown's first major new route in Wales was Hangover (Grochan) which he did in 1951 with R. Greenall, M. T. Sorrel, and F. Ashton. Other notable early ascents (among many – see guidebooks for full details) were:

1951 The Boulder (Clogwyn du'r Arddu) (rest unable to follow)
     Cemetary Gates (Cromlech) – D. Whillans
     Cenotaph Corner (Cromlech) – D. Belshaw
     Diglyph (Clogwyn du'r Arddu) – M. T. Sorrel
     Vember (Clogwyn du'r Arddu) – D. Whillans
1952 (All on Clogwyn du'r Arddu)
     Octo – Sorrel and Belshaw
     The Spillikin – Whillans and J. N. Allen
     Pinnacle Flake – Whillans (alt. leads)
     Llithwrig – Allen
     The Corner – Allen and Belshaw
1953 Surplomb (Grochan) – Whillans (alt. leads)
     Subsiduary Groove (Cyrn Las) – Whillans (alt. leads)
     The Grooves (Cyrn Las) – D. Cowan, E. Price.
     East Buttress Girdle (Clogwyn du'r Arddu) – Allen and Whillans.

It must be remembered that at this time and for some time afterwards, Brown was also putting up new routes on gritstone and limestone. In 1953 visits to the Lake District resulted in Laugh Not (White Ghyll) and Dovedale Groove (Dove Crag) and a visit to Ben Nevis in 1954 brought about Sassenach (with Whillans). In the same summer, with Whillans, came the first British ascent of the West Face of the Dru and the Brown-Whillans Route on the Blaitière – easily the hardest British rock climb in the Alps to that date. In 1955, with G. Band, Brown reached the summit of Kangchenjunga, the third highest mountain in the world. In 1956 he reached the summit of the Mustagh Tower in the Karakorum.

This can be taken as the close of the opening phase of Brown's career, and the most remarkable. With Whillans, particularly, he set new standards wherever he went.

In the early sixties Brown investigated the "new" Welsh crags such as Tremadoc and Hylldrem, where mention might be made, respectively, of Vector (1960) and Hardd (1960) (amongst others) but it was not until 1966 that he was persuaded to look at the great sea cliff of Gogarth in Anglesey where he was to create dozens of new routes including the sensational Spider's Web (1968). In 1962 he visited Russia and climbed Mt Communism. He was in the Andes in 1970 and Roraima, Venezuela in 1973.

Brown has appeared in various films and TV climbing broadcasts. He was a property repairer until 1961 when he joined the staff of White Hall Outdoor Pursuits Centre, where he stayed until 1965. In 1965 he opened an equipment shop in Llanberis. His autobiography, *The Hard Years*, was published in 1967.

BROWN, Thomas Graham (1882-1965)
One of the most important British mountaineers of the inter-war years; famous for his work on the Brenva face of Mont Blanc.

Brown began climbing late in life. He was over 30 when he made his first climb (on Pillar, Lake District) and 42 when he first climbed in the Alps. He was primarily a discoverer with a superb eye for a line: the technical climbing, and leading, he left to others.

After a minor route in Eskdale, Brown's first innovation was the opening up of Boat Howe on Kirkfell as a climbing area. In 1925, with Basterfield, he made four routes on this previously neglected crag and four more the next year with Hazard. Convinced that the great face of the Brenva on Mont Blanc had not been exploited to the full he set out to examine its possibilities in 1927. Bad weather delayed matters but late in the season he teamed up with Smythe (*qv*) who wished to do a variant on the Old Brenva Route. Brown wished to do what is now Route Major, and a compromise was reached by making a route between the two lines – Red Sentinel. The following year (1928) they climbed Route Major: one of the most important climbs in the Alps. In 1933 Brown returned with guides Graven and Knubel (*qv*) and climbed the Via della Pera, completing a trio of hard routes which transformed the Brenva Face as a climbing area.

Brown went to the Himalaya twice: Nanda Devi (1936) and Masherbrum (1938) reaching heights in excess of 20,000 ft on each occasion. His other new routes in the Alps are: SSW Buttress of Les Courtes (1927), E Face of Mont Brouillard, traverse of Col Maudit (1932), traverse of summit ridge of l'Ailefroid, N Face of Les Bans (1933), traverse of Dent Blanche from W to E (1935). In 1934 he visited Alaska and climbed Mt Foraker.

His book, *Brenva* (1944) is a modern classic. He was Professor of Physiology, University of Wales, from 1920 to 1947.

BROWNE, Frederic Augustus Yeats (1837-1925)
Made the second ascent of Grandes Jorasses (1868) and a number of new ascents with Tuckett (*qv*). Yeats Browne was on the fringe of the Matterhorn tragedy in 1865: he climbed Mont Blanc the same day as Hudson and Hadow, and after completing the High Level Route to Zermatt, met the first party of guides who were looking for the victims of the disaster. He then made a solo climb of the Rifelhorn, and it was in trying to emulate this that Knyvett Wilson was killed the same day, thus increasing the general outrage which the Matterhorn affair had aroused.

BROWNE, Thomas Lloyd Murray (1838-1900)
Made the first ascents of Dreieckhorn and Ebnefluh in 1868. With his brother, W. R. Browne, he also made the first English ascent of Glittertind, Norway and the first ascent of Uledalstind. The two brothers were amongst the first to draw attention to Scafell Crag (1869) and Lliwedd (1872). They attempted the latter, but failed.

BRUCE, Charles Granville (1866-1939)
One of the great pioneers of Himalayan climbing. His climbing came about through his commission in the 5th Gurkha Rifles: it seemed logical to him that troops stationed in the Himalayan foothills should become proficient mountaineers and his regiment acquitted itself so well in the various border wars that "mountain scouts" became valued. They were even, at Bruce's suggestion, allowed to wear shorts – the first ever in the British Army. Some of the Gurkhas he trained became good climbers, notably Harkabir Thapa, Goman Singh, Raghobir and Karbir. The latter traversed the Alps with Conway in 1894,

Harkabir was loaned to the Col. Stewart for surveys in the Pamirs, whilst Goman Singh and Raghobir perished with Mummery on Nanga Parbat (see MUMMERY).

Apart from the training climbs done with his men, Bruce joined Conway's Karakorum Expedition (*qv*) (1892) and was one of the main reasons for its success. He was with Younghusband (*qv*) in Chitral, and in 1895 with the Mummery party on Nanga Parbat, though he was taken ill and had to leave before the final tragedy. In 1898 he reconnoitred the Nun Kun massif. In 1907 after permission to attempt Everest was refused he joined Longstaff and Mumm (*qv*) in the Nanda Devi area where Longstaff, two Swiss guides and Karbir made the first ascent of Trisul. They also reconnoitred Kamet.

Bruce was wounded during the Great War but was chosen to lead the 1922 and 1924 Everest expeditions (*qv*). It was he who suggested Sherpas as porters.

Bruce was immensely strong and had a legendary sense of humour. He attained General rank, received many honours from geographical and other societies, and was President of the A. C. 1923-26. He wrote four books: *Twenty Years in the Himalaya (1910), Kulu and Lahoul* (1914), *Assault on Mount Everest, 1922* (1923), and *Himalayan Wanderer* (1934).

BRULLE, Henri (1854-1936)
French lawyer noted for his many first ascents in the Pyrenees, particularly around Gavarnie. He made the first traverse of the great Gavarnie Cirque (1881). Brulle climbed in the Alps occasionally: he was the first to climb the Meije in a single day (1883). He visited the Lake District twice, climbing a number of the standard routes.

BRYCE, James (1838-1922)
Distinguished lawyer and politician best known for the Bryce Report on Secondary Education, 1895. In 1884 he introduced the Access to Mountains (Scotland) Bill, but was defeated. Bryce was a keen mountaineer and he never missed an opportunity to climb during his extensive travels. Ambassador to Washington (1907-12); visited every State. President of A. C. 1899-1901. Created Viscount, 1914.

BUACHAILLE ETIVE MOR (STOB DEARG 3,345 ft)
A fine mountain standing at the eastern entrance to Glencoe (*qv*), Scotland. The peak

is invariably called by climbers "the Buachaille".

The N face is a complex series of buttresses and gullies all of which give fine
climbs, summer and winter, of all grades.
Notable ascents include:

1894 Collie's Climb – Collie, Solly, Collier
1900 Crowberry Ridge Direct – Abraham
      brothers, Puttrell, Baker
1910 Crowberry Gully – Greig, Raeburn,
      Cumming, Menzies
      ditto winter 1936 – MacKenzie, Rus-
      sell, Hamilton, Dunn
1929 North Face – Bell, Harrison
1936 Agag's Groove – Hamilton, Ander-
      son, Small
1937 Raven's Gully – Nimlin and party
1953 Raven's Gully (winter) – MacInnes,
      Bonington
1958 Carnivore (Cunningham, Noon)

    Guidebooks: *Climbers' Guide to Glencoe
& Ardgour Vol 1*, by L. S. Lovat and
Winter Climbs: Ben Nevis & Glencoe, by I.
S. Clough.

BUCHAN, John (Lord Tweedsmuir) (1875-1940)

Noted author of the Richard Hannay
stories and others. Climbed extensively in
Scotland and in the Alps around the turn
of the century, as well as South Africa and
Canada. Climbing incidents and mountains are found in many of his stories.

BUHL, Hermann (1924-57)

One of the best-known post-war German
climbers, noted for his winter ascents and
solo ascents of difficult routes in the Dolomites and elsewhere. In 1953 Buhl reached
the summit of Nanga Parbat alone – first
ascent. In 1957 he fell through a cornice
while descending Chogolisa and was
killed. Autobiography: *Nanga Parbat Pilgrimage*, (1956).

BUGABOOS, BRITISH COLUMBIA

A series of granite spires in the Purcell
Range offering some of the finest rock-
climbing in North America. The best approach is via a rough road from Sillama-
cheen, along the Bugaboo creek.

The Bugaboos have a startling aspect,
rising almost sheer from their surrounding
glaciers. The three main peaks are the
Howser Spires, Snowpatch Spire and
Bugaboo Spire. These are all adjacent to
the Warren Glacier in the south of the
range. Other fine peaks lie a little further
north-west, including Mt Conrad, second
highest in the region after the Howser
Spires.

Bugaboo Spire was climbed by Conrad

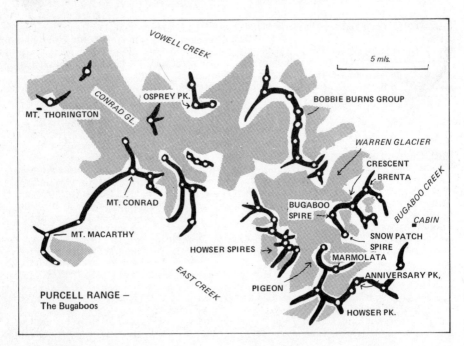

PURCELL RANGE –
The Bugaboos

4 GRITSTONE. Nick Estcourt climbing Moyer's Buttress at Gardom's Edge. One of the famous gritstone edges of the Derwent Valley, Peak District. Note the use of running belays. (*right*) 5 LIMESTONE. Bonington leads 'Coronation Street', a limestone climb at Cheddar, Somerset. His partner (Thompson) has taken a stance in the crack and belays him—a typical expert rope in action.

6 BOSIGRAN, CORNWALL. A popular sea cliff. The climbers are on Doorway, a severe grade route. The leader climbs towards an overhang whilst his second belays him. Note the rock features. (*right*) 7 BUACHAILLE ETIVE MOR, GLENCOE, SCOTLAND. A famous Scottish mountain seen in its winter condition. Notice the snow-filled gullies and the buttresses between them.

Kain (*qv*), with Mr. and Mrs. MacCarthy and J. Vincent by its South Ridge in 1916 – claimed by Kain to be the hardest climb of his career. In the same year Kain also climbed one of the Howser Spires. The East Ridge of Bugaboo was climbed by J. Turner in 1958 and the East Face by Gran and Cooper in 1961.

The South Tower of Howser Spires was climbed in 1941. The West Face of the South Tower by F. Beckey and Y. Chouinard in 1961 and the North Face and traverse of the Howser Spires by Rayson, Lang, Chouinard and Thompkins in 1965.

Snowpatch Spire, climbed in 1940, by the S ridge, is said to be the most difficult of all the Bugaboos to ascend (H. V. S.). The W Face was climbed in 1956 and the NW Ridge in 1958.

Guidebook: *Climbers' Guide to the Interior Ranges of British Columbia*, by W. Putnam.

BULLOCK, Guy Henry (1887-1956)

School companion of Mallory (*qv*) and one of Irving's (*qv*) "recruits". Bullock went on the first Everest expedition (1921) and with Mallory discovered the North Col. (See EVEREST.)

BURGENER, Alexander (1846-1910)

One of the most outstanding guides of the late nineteenth century, noted for his association with great climbers and explorers such as Dent, Mummery, Déchy, Güssfeldt, von Kuffner and others. He came from Eisten in Saas, where the rock peaks of the area gave him a good grounding in rock-climbing – then becoming a necessary art in climbing, since the big snow peaks were all conquered. He began as a chamois hunter – and kept this up all his life. Burgener undoubtedly brought prestige to the Saas valley and was, indirectly, responsible for popularizing the modern resort of Saas Fee.

Amongst his many great climbs might be mentioned:

1870 Lenzspitze, first ascent – Dent, F. Burgener
1871 Portjengrat, first ascent – Dent, F. Burgener
1878 Grand Dru, first ascent – Dent, Walker, Maurer
1879 Matterhorn, Zmutt first ascent – Mummery, Gentinetta, Petrus
1880 Col du Lion, first traverse – Mummery
     Grands Charmoz, first ascent – Mummery, Venetz
1881 Verte, Charpoua Face, first ascent – Mummery
     Grepon. first ascent – Mummery, Venetz
1887 Mont Maudit, Frontier Ridge first ascent – von Kuffner, Furrer, a porter.
     Taschhorn, Teufelsgrat, first ascent – Mummery, Mrs. Mummery, Andermatten

Burgener visited the Caucasus with Déchy (1884) and Dent (1886) and went to S. America with Güssfeldt in 1882.

A big, hearty man with a caustic tongue, Burgener was killed by an avalanche near the Bergli hut in the Oberland.

BURKE, Mick (b. 1941)

Noted British alpinist who made the second ascent of the Robbins – Hemming route on the W Face of the Dru, a new route on the N Face of the Aig. du Midi, winter ascents of the Gervasutti Couloir of Mont Blanc du Tacul, and in 1967, first British winter ascent of the Matterhorn Nordwand. In 1968 he made the first British ascent of the Nose of El Capitan, Yosemite (*qv*) and in 1972 took part in the British ski traverse of the Alps.

Burke has taken part in a number of outstanding expeditions including Cerro Torre (1968), Annapurna South Face (1970) and the SW Face of Everest (1972). He has also visited Baffin Island and, as a cameraman, helped Bonington on the Eiger Direct epic (1966).

BURTON, Sir Richard Francis (1831-90)

One of the foremost explorers of the nineteenth century, particularly famous for his African discoveries in search of the source of the Nile. Mountain climbing was not one of his principal activities but he did make the first ascent of Cameroon Peak (13,129 ft).

BUTTERMERE

Village and lake in the western Lake District. The valley is connected with Borrowdale (*qv*) by Honister Pass and with Keswick by Newlands Hause (both motorable). The principal fells are the High Stile group, Robinson group and Grasmoor group. Buttermere tends to be neglected as a climbing centre but there are several fine crags, especially those of Burtness Combe, dominated by Eagle Crag. Others include Yew Crag and Striddle Crag.

Guidebook: *Buttermere and Newlands Area*, by J. Soper and N. Allison.

BUTTRESS

A rocky protruberance from a mountain side *or* the rock mass between two gullies (but if narrow this may be called a ridge). They are usually named: North Buttress, Central Buttress, Bilberry Buttress, etc. The majority of British rock-climbs are buttress climbs.

BUXTON, Edward North (1840-1924)

A wealthy London brewer whose brief climbing career lasted only six years, after which he turned to big game hunting. Two of his brothers were also climbers for a brief period.

Buxton took part in some important first ascents including that of Nord End (Monte Rosa) in 1861. In 1864 he made the first ascents of Monte Cristallo, Königsspitze and the west summit of Lyskamm.

In his last season, 1865, he made the first ascent of Aig. de Bionnassay. His brother, H. E. Buxton accompanied him on his 1864 climbs.

BYNE, Eric (1911-69)

A Midlands climber who began climbing on gritstone in 1928, and besides taking part in the discoveries of that time, developed a passionate interest in the history of climbing and walking in the Peak District. He accumulated material which formed the basis of the first gritstone series guidebooks, of which he was Editor: (*Climbs on Gritstone, 1948 on; Rock Climbs in the Peak, to date*). Byne compiled some of them himself, and helped with others. He also compiled *A Climbing Guide to Brassington Rocks* (1950), but his best-known work is *High Peak* (1966), which he wrote with G. Sutton.

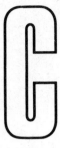

CADER IDRIS (2,927 ft)

A Welsh mountain rising near the coast at Dolgellau, with a long summit ridge and precipitous faces, particularly to the north, O. G. Jones (*qv*) began climbing here but the crags have never been popular.

Guidebook: *British Mountain Climbs*, by G. D. Abraham.

CAGOULE

A long smock of polyurethane used as a windproof outer garment. It is lightweight, hooded and has windproof cuffs like an anorak (*qv*). Though to a certain degree rainproof it tends to trap body condensation.

CAIRN (Fr.: Homme de pierre; G.: Steinmann)

A pile of stones used for marking the summit of a mountain, or even some minor eminence. Can be large and elaborately constructed. Cairns are also used to mark out routes where paths are not obvious – in the Alps, way-marks consisting of splashes of paint, are often used instead.

CAIRNEY, Maud (1893-1939)

A doctor who, with the guide T. Theytaz, made the first descent of the N Face of Lo Besso (1927), the first winter ascent of Obergabelhorn from Mountet (1927) and the first ascent of the N Face of Dent Blanche (1928). The Cairney-Theytaz route on Dent Blanche does not seem to have been repeated.

CAIRNGORMS

The highest part of the Grampian Mountains, between Braemar and the R. Spey, Scotland. Glen Avon penetrates into the heart of the group, whose chief summits are Ben Macdhui (4,296 ft), Braeriach (4,248 ft), Cairn Toul (4,149 ft) and Cairn Gorm (4,084 ft). There are many other summits only slightly less high. The mountains are rounded, but the corries have magnificent crags. The whole area is barren and wild; the largest area of its kind in Britain. It is a nature reserve.

Lochnagar (3,786 ft) is the highest of another group of wild mountains, separated from the Cairngorms by the wide Dee valley. Climbers apply the name "Cairngorms" to the whole region.

Speyside (Aviemore etc.) and Deeside (Braemar etc.) are the best known centres, especially the former, which has Glenmore Lodge and the well-known ski hotels. Perhaps more than in most regions, one's base depends on where one is going to climb. There are huts, bothies and so on, but even so, distances tend to be long.

The whole area is very popular with walkers, climbers and skiers. Conditions in winter can be arctic and every precaution is needed to avoid exhaustion and exposure. The vastness of the area has deceived many.

Popular walks (summer) are the four 4,000 ft peaks (see also SCOTTISH 4,000s) and the long passes of Lairig Ghru and Lairig an Laoigh.

Climbs in the Cairngorms, particularly on Lochnagar, have been known from an early date, but except in winter the area did not achieve popularity until after the last War, when it began to be extensively developed by Aberdeen climbers such as Patey (*qv*) and Brooker. The process is continuing and there are now winter and summer climbs of all standards on numerous crags, best known of which are: Garbh Coire, Coire an Dubh Lochain, Coire na Ciche (all on Beinn a'Bhuird); Coire an t'Sneachda, Coire an Lochain (Cairn Gorm); Hell's Lum Crag, Shelter Stone Crag, Carn Etchachan (all above Loch Avon); Coire Etchachan; Coire Sputan Dearg (Ben Macdhui); Coire Bhrochain, Garbh Choire Dhaidh, Garbh Coire Mor (Braeriach-Carn Toul); Sgoran Dubh; Creag an Dubh Loch, Lochnagar (Lochnagar).

Ben Macdhui is reputedly haunted by Ferlas Mhor (the Great Grey Man) (Collie, Kellas and others).

Guidebooks: *The Cairngorms*, by Sir. H. Alexander; *Climbers' Guide to the Cairngorms Area*, (2 vols) by M. Smith; and *Winter Climbs: Cairngorms and Creag Meaghaidh*, by J. Cunningham.

CALANQUES

A series of sea-cliffs on the French Mediterranean coast, near Marseilles, and popular with climbers. The rock is limestone.

CAMPING MAT (KARRIMAT)
A rectangle of cellular foam plastic, very light and easily carried, invaluable as ground insulation when camping or bivouacking.

THE CANADIAN ROCKIES
The Canadian Rockies extend for a thousand miles NW from the U.S. border. They are bounded by the deep Rocky Mountain Trench on the west and by the prairies on the east. The parts of the range best known to climbers lie in the south, from Mt Joffre (11,316 ft) to Mt Robson (12,972 ft) – the latter the highest peak of the Canadian Rockies. The range (N to S) can be conveniently described thus (major peaks only):

Mt Robson 12,972 ft
(Yellowhead Pass – C. N. R.)

Mt Edith Cavell 11,033 ft
Mt Alberta 11,874 ft
Mt Columbia 12,294 ft
Mt Lyell 11,500 ft
Mt Forbes 11,902 ft
   Some 50 peaks of 11,000+ ft
(Kicking Horse Pass – C. P. R. – Lake Louise)
Mt Assiniboine 11,870 ft
Mt Sir Douglas 11,174 ft
Mt King George 11,228 ft
Mt Joffre 11,316 ft
(Crowsnest Pass – C. P. R.)
(South of Crowsnest Pass the range runs into the Glacier National Park and the Lewis Range of the U.S.)
Note: C. N. R.= Canadian National Railroad
   C.P.R.=Canadian Pacific Railroad
The total length of the above is about 285 miles. There is a motor road across the Vermillion Pass and the mountains are rather more accessible than other Canadian ranges.

The whole of this area is heavily glaciated but the rock is sedimentary, giving rise to the curious stratified appearance of many of the peaks. Snow conditions are often poor.

The first expeditions were those of the Appalachian Club of the U. S. in the 1890s. In 1896, Peter Abbott of the club was killed whilst attempting Mt Lefroy – the first climbing fatality in North America. The ubiquitous W. S. Green had also visited the peaks but made no notable ascents and it was not until the opening of the Kicking Horse Pass and the establishment of a tourist centre at Lake Louise by the Canadian Pacific Railway that climbing flourished. For a decade around the turn of the century, the Canadian Rockies were very much the "in" mountains and were visited by many notable climbers: Whymper, Collie, Woolley, and others. From 1908 the chief goal became Mt Robson and it was finally climbed by C. Kain (*qv*) with MacCarthy (*qv*) and Foster in 1913. It is interesting that Mt Alberta was climbed by the Japanese in 1925; the first overseas expedition by Japanese climbers.

Guidebook: *A Climbers' Guide to the Rocky Mountains of Canada*, 2 vols by Putnam, Boles, Krusyna and Jones.

CANNON STONE
An obsolete name for a rock splinter jammed in a chimney and sticking out like a gun barrel. There is a well-known one in Gwynne's Chimney, Pavey Ark.

CAPSTONE
A chockstone (*qv*) on top of a chimney or gully. Common on gritstone crags.

CARNEDDAU
A mountain group north of the Ogwen Valley, Snowdonia. The principal summits (N–S) are Foel Fras (3,092 ft), Foel Grach (3,196 ft), Yr Elen (3,152 ft), Carnedd Llywelyn (3,484 ft), Carnedd Dafydd (3,426 ft) and Pen yr Olewen (3,211 ft). The principal cliffs are Craig yr Ysfa (*qv*), Ysolglion Duon (Black Ladders), Llech Ddu, Braich Ty Du and Craig Lloer. There are climbs of all standards. The area is somewhat remote.

Guidebook: *Carneddau*, by A. J. J. Moulam.

CARPE, Allen (1894-1932)
An American electrical engineer trained in Germany where he first learned to climb. Explored the Selkirks, Cariboos and Rockies, making several first ascents. In 1925 he took part in the first ascent of Mt Logan; in 1930, with A. M. Taylor and T. Moore, the first ascent of Mt Bona and finally, in 1931, with Moore he reached the summit of Mt Fairweather.

CARR, Ellis (1852-1930)
One of the leaders of the second wave of guideless climbing in Alps which began about 1890. With Morse and Wicks (*qv*) he

made the first ascent of the Pic Sans Nom (Verte) (1890), and with Wilson and the Pasteur family (*qv*) the first ascent of L'Eveque (Verte) (1892).

He seems to have met Mummery in 1891, when they did some climbs together, and he was with Mummery and Slingsby on the dramatic attempt on the North Face of the Plan (1892). Carr's description of this climb, called "Two Days on an Ice Slope" (*A. J.* vol. 16) is one of the great classics of climbing literature.

Carr climbed in many parts of the Alps, the Lake District and Skye. He took part in the second ascent of the North Climb, Pillar Rock, when he is reputed to have invented the Hand Traverse of the Nose Pitch (1891).

Carr had considerable talents as musician and artist. His sketches illustrated Haskett Smith's *Climbing in the British Isles* (*qv*). He was descended from the biscuit-making family of the same name and was a director of Peek Frean.

CARREG WASTAD
One of the Three Cliffs of Llanberis (*qv*) on the N side of Llanberis Pass, Snowdonia. Popular, with routes in the middle and upper grades.

The first climb was Dead Entrance by Edwards and Noyce, 1935 and Edwards took part in all the early climbs, including the popular Crackstone Rib (1935). (See J. M. EDWARDS and THREE CLIFFS.)

Guidebook: *Llanberis North*, by D. T. Roscoe.

CARREL, Jean-Antoine (1829-90)
One of the chief protagonists in the Matterhorn drama which ended with the first ascent of the mountain by Whymper in 1865 (*qv*).

Carrel was a stonemason and one time soldier (hence his nickname, *Bersagliere*) who lived at Breuil, below the Italian slopes of the Matterhorn. Accompanied by other villagers he made his first reconnaissances in 1858-9 reaching a height of a little over 12,500 ft on the Italian Ridge. Between then and 1865 he took part in most of the attempts on the mountain, as guide, with climbers such as Whymper, Tyndall, Hawkins and Macdonald (*qv*). The highest point reached was with Tyndall, Bennen and three others guides or porters in 1862, to a point now called Pic Tyndall, a little below the final summit.

Carrel was an intense patriot, and there is little doubt that he wanted the mountain

climbed by Italians, but whether in that fateful July of 1865 he actually double-crossed Whymper, as the latter implied, is a subject which many mountain historians have tried to unravel. Whymper found that Carrel had set out for the peak with a party of Italian climbers and in a fit of pique he left Breuil for Zermatt, from where the first ascent was made. From the summit of the Matterhorn Whymper was able to see Carrel's party still climbing up the Italian Ridge so he threw down rocks to attract their attention. Carrel at once turned back, but he returned the next day and on the 18 July, he and J. B. Bich made the first ascent of the Italian Ridge and second of the mountain.

Whymper had a strange kinship with Carrel. He forgave him his "treachery" and climbed the Matterhorn with him in 1874. Carrel was also one of Whymper's guides on the Andes expedition of 1879-80.

Carrel died of exhaustion during a retreat from the Italian Ridge in a snowstorm, with the climber Sinigaglia. He left a wife and three children. A memorial marks the place where he died.

CASCADES RANGE
A long range of mountains extending north through Oregon and Washington states to the Canadian border. It includes Mt Rainier (14,410 ft), Mt Adams (12,470 ft), Mt Hood (11,225 ft) and Mt Jeffereson (10,570 ft). Many are volcanic, including Rainier. Rainier has 28 glaciers including the difficult Nisqually ice-fall.

Further north the range has lesser peaks but offers very good climbing, both rock and ice. There is a heavy rainfall, but the summer months are frequently pleasant.

Easier climbing is found in the Olympic Range, across Puget Sound from the Cascades. Plenty of glaciers.

Guidebooks: *Climbers' Guide to the Cascade and Olympic Mts. of Washington* – American A. C.; and *A Climber's Guide to Oregon*, by N. A. Dodge.

CASSIN, Riccardo (b. 1909)
An Italian climber from Lecco; one of the finest mountaineers of the present century. Cassin's career falls into two parts: pre-war and post war.

He began rock-climbing in the Grigna (*qv*) in 1928 with other local youths, and they formed themselves into the "New Italy Climbing Group". He paid his first visit to the Dolomites in 1932 and at once began doing the hardest climbs and making new routes. His greatest Dolomite success was the first ascent of the N Face of Cima Ovest (1935). He followed this in 1937 with the NE Face of Piz Badile – for long regarded as one of the most daring climbs in the Alps, but now one of the most popular of the harder rock climbs. Beset by storms, Cassin, Ratti and Esposito, with two Como climbers, Valsecchi and Molseni, spent three days on the face before reaching the summit. Unfortunately, the two Como men died of exhaustion.

In 1938 came Cassin's finest ascent: the Walker Spur of the Grandes Jorasses which he did with Esposito and Tizzoni, 4 to 6 August. It was Cassin's first visit to the Mont Blanc area and his first sight of the Jorasses! It remains one of the greatest climbs in the Alps; very popular.

Although he holds instructors' certificates in both climbing and skiing, Cassin never became a guide. He worked first as a mechanic and then manager at an electrical engineering works in Lecco. During the war he became a partisan and was wounded. After the War he established a factory making climbing equipment.

Cassin has led a number of successful expeditions:
1958 Gasherbrum IV (Himalaya)

1961 South Face of Mount McKinley (Alaska)
1969 West Face of Jirishanca (Peru)

Cassin still climbs at a high standard. He repeated the NE Face of Badile when he was 62.

CASTLE ROCK OF TRIERMAIN
A bold crag at the southern entrance to St John's in the Vale, Lake District. Extremely popular because it is very accessible and the climbing is of high quality. Most, but not all, the climbs are hard.

The harder routes are on the big North Crag, which impends, whilst the easier angled South Crag contains routes of the middle grade. The North and South Crags are actually faces of one rock bastion.

The first climbs were done by G. G. Macphee and various partners in 1928 (Yew Tree Climb etc.) on the South Crag but the great North Crag was not overcome until 1939 (Overhanging Bastion: Birkett, Wilson, Muscroft). In post-war years the North Crag saw numerous new routes of a high standard.

Guidebook: *Eastern Crags*, by H. Drasdo and J. Soper.

CAUCASUS
A range of high mountains extending between the Black Sea in the west and the

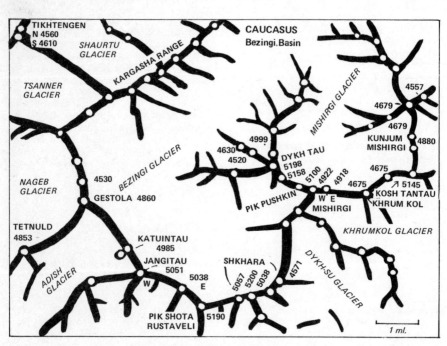

Caspian Sea in the east, some 600 miles in' length. The Caucasus is entirely within the Soviet Union, being bounded by Georgia and Azerbaijan to the south and various small Soviet republics to the north. It is a geographical boundary between Europe and Asia, and as such may be regarded as the highest mountains in Europe. The highest peak is Elbrus (18,481 ft) and the Central Caucasus average some 3,000 ft higher than their Alpine counterparts.

The range is divided into three natural divisions: Western Caucasus, Central Caucasus and Eastern Caucasus. All of these contain high peaks. The weather, which can often be poor, is wetter in the west than the east. The snowline is higher than in the Alps and the glaciers smaller.

Western Caucasus
Reaches as far as the Klukhor Pass. The best climbing is in the eastern part of the section. The highest peak is Dombai-ulgen (13,255 ft) (Schuster and Fischer, 1914) Other important peaks include:
Juguturlyuchat 12,864 ft
Bu-ulgen 12,838 ft
Aksaut 12,828 ft
Kara-kaya 12,782 ft
Ertsog 12,687 ft
Dottakh-kaya 12,677 ft
and several others over 12,000 ft

Central Caucasus
From the Klukhor Pass to the Krestovy Pass. This section contains the highest peaks and is by far the most popular with climbers, especially in the Bezingi valley – a vast cwm of immense, jagged peaks. The so called Bezingi Wall is 6,000 ft high and eight miles long, with many hard climbs. There are many other fine peaks, away from Bezingi, notably Shkhelda (14,173 ft) and Ushba and, of course, the easily climbed extinct volcano of Elbrus (Freshfield, Moore, Tucker, 1868 to the lower E summit – though possibly climbed by surveyors in 1829). The principal peaks are:
Elbrus 18,481 ft
(W Summit – Moore's party 1874)
Dykh-tau* 17,074 ft
Koshtan-tau* 16,880 ft
Jangi-tau* 16,571 ft
Kasbek 16,546 ft
Shkhara* 16,529 ft
Katyn-tau* 16,355 ft
Pik Rustaveli* 16,273 ft
Mishirgi* 16,149 ft
Kunjum-Mishirgi* 16,011 ft
Gestola* 15,945 ft

Tetnuld* 15,922 ft
Jimarai-khokh 15,673 ft
Ushba 15,454 ft
Ullu-auz* 15,352 ft
Khrum-kol* 15,338 ft
Adai-khokh 15,243 ft
Tikhtengen 15,125 ft
* Peaks in the Benzingi region
Note 1. Highest summit of peak only – some have two.
Note 2. Many more peaks of less than 15,000 ft

Eastern Caucasus
East of the Krestovy Pass. Rather drier than the other areas. The peaks tend to be more separated, and are generally of little interest to climbers. The highest peak is Tebulos-mta (14,744 ft) and there are several more over 13,000 ft.

Apart from survey work, climbing in the Caucasus began with the visit of Freshfield, Moore and Tucker in 1868 when they explored the entire range and climbed Elbrus and Kasbek. Moore, with Gardiner, Grove and Walker returned in 1874 and climbed the W (higher) Summit of Elbrus. In 1884, de Dechy paid the first of his seven visits to the range (1884-1902). During this period, too, many British climbers visited the range. There were nine expeditions between 1868 and Mummery's of 1888.

Notable ascents include:
1888 Dhyk-tau – Mummery
       Shkhara, Jangi-tau, Ushba N –
       Cockin
1903 Ushba S – Schultze

Since these pioneer days, ascents have concentrated on the two aspects of climbing for which the Caucasus is admirably suited, that is long ridge traverses, often of several days, and steep face climbs. Foreign parties are frequently invited to join Russian parties in the Caucasus. The first British party to do one of the classic traverses was MacInnes and Ritchie on Shkhelda, 1961. It took nine days. Others have done new face climbs and repeated some of the Russian routes. (See *Exploration of the Caucasus*, by D. W. Freshfield (for pioneer ascents) and *Red Snows*, by C. Brasher.)

CAWOOD, Albert Harold (1835-1913)
Arthur Cust (*qv*), J. B. Colgrove and A. H. Cawood were a trio of teachers from Rossall School who made a number of interesting guideless climbs in the Alps. Their most notable achievement was the

first guideless ascent of the Matterhorn (1876).

CENTRE INTERNATIONALE DE SECOURS ALPINS (CISALP)
Located at Geneva. A bureau supplying information about rescue services in the Alps. It does not initiate or co-ordinate rescues itself.

CENTRIST AND EX-CENTRIST
One of the great feuds of the Alpine Club in the latter years of the nineteenth century was between those who believed in living at a centre such as Zermatt and climbing the peaks round about (a centrist) and those who believed in moving from valley to valley, crossing cols and peaks *en route* (ex-centrist). Davidson (*qv*) was a typical centrist, known as "King of the Rifel" where he stayed season after season, whilst Conway (*qv*) was the archetypal ex centrist. Indeed, his "Alps from end to end", (1894) was done to prove his point.

CERRO TORRE (9,908ft)
A spectacular rock spire in the FitzRoy Group of the Patagonian Andes. In view of the prevailing bad weather, one of the most difficult climbs in the world. Three routes, with some variations, have been attempted: the E and W Faces, and the SE Ridge.

In 1958, W. Bonatti and C. Mauri made an attempt on the W Face and C. Maestri on the E Face. Both failed, but in 1959 Maestri returned with T. Egger and C. Fava and climbed the E Face from the N Col. Maestri and Egger reached the summit but on the descent Egger was killed by an ice avalanche. Maestri's ascent has been disputed.

In 1968 a strong British party attempted the SE Ridge but failed after 2,000ft as did Argentinian and Japanese groups. In 1970 Mauri returned to the W Face but also failed.

During the winter (July) of 1970, Maestri returned for an attack on the SE Ridge, made some progress, then returned a few months later to complete the route (C. Maestri, C. Claus, E. Alimonta). The ascent caused a sensation because Maestri used a compressed air drill for bolting his route. The method has been vigorously attacked as unethical and equally vigorously defended by Maestri.

In 1971-2 two further expeditions, one Spanish, one British, failed to climb the SE Ridge by more conventional methods.

Finally, in 1974 C. Ferrari, D. Chiappa, M. Conti, and G. Negri reached the summit by the W Face and SW Ridge.

CHALET AUSTRIA
A sort of shepherds' hut on the Plan de l'Aiguille to Montenvers track, near Chamonix, frequently used by inpecunious climbers as a base and very famous in this respect, featuring in numerous climbing stories.

CHAMONIX
A valley limiting the northern flanks of the Mont Blanc range, France. It includes the villages of Le Tour, Montroc, Argentière, Les Praz, Les Bossons and Les Houches as well as the principal village of Chamonix-Mont Blanc. There are good road and rail connections with Geneva and, via the Cols Forclaz and Montets, with Martigny. The Mont Blanc Tunnel connects the valley with Italy. The highest cable car in Europe rises from Chamonix to the summit of the Aig. du Midi (3842 m) – it also continues across the Vallée Blanche to Italy.

Chamonix gained early fame as the starting point for ascending Mont Blanc (*qv*) and with the spread of alpinism became a serious rival to Zermatt. It is unquestionably the leading centre for modern alpinism. (See also MONT BLANC: MONT BLANC GROUP: CHAMONIX AIGUILLES.)

CHAMONIX AIGUILLES, THE
A range of shapely peaks (*aiguilles* = needles) on the southern side of the Chamonix valley and separating that valley from the Mer de Glace and the Vallée Blanche. The range extends in an arc from the Aig. du Midi in the SW to the Aig. de L'M in the NE. On the Chamonix side it is bounded by a curious high plateau generally known as the Plan de L'Aiguille, reached by cable car from the village, or from Montenvers, or by various paths. All the climbs on the Chamonix side start from the Plan de l'Aiguille. On the Mer de Glace side climbs are started from Montenvers (*qv*), the Requin Hut, the Envers Hut or the Tour Rouge Bivouac Hut.

The peaks are very popular with rock-climbers because of the excellent granite and there are all standards of climbs. There are also some notable ice climbs, for example the North Face of the Plan. The glaciers, though small, are often steep and can be difficult. The summit of the Aig. du Midi can be reached by cable car from Chamonix or Entreves (Italy). It is the highest cable car station in Europe.

The first complete traverse of all the peaks from Charmoz to Plan was done by Mme d'Albertas with A. Ottoz in 1939. Parts had been done before and it has since been extended from l'M to Mt Blanc.

A list of peaks and their first ascents is given below. Other outstanding climbs include:

1906 Ryan-Lochmatter Route, Plan – V. J. E. Ryan with F. and J. Lochmatter NW Ridge, Blaitière – V. J. E. Ryan with F. and J. Lochmatter

1911 Mer de Glace Face, Grépon – H. O. Jones, R. Todhunter, G. W. Young with J. Knubel, H. Brocherel

1913 Mayer-Dibona Route, Requin – G. Mayer with A. Dibona

1924 North Face, Plan – J. Lagarde, J. de Lépiney, H de Ségogne

1936 East Ridge, Crocodile – P. Allain, J. and R. Leininger

1941 Frendo Spur, Midi – E. Frendo, R. Rionda

1947 North Ridge, Peigne – F. Aubert, J. C. Martin, J. C. Ménégaux, M. Schatz

1954 West Face, Blaitière – J. Brown, D. Whillans

1956 Rébuffat Route, Midi – G. Rébuffat, M. Baquet

1963 South Face, Fou – T. Frost, J. Harlin, G. Hemming, S. Fulton

List of the Aiguilles, Midi-Charmoz, and first ascents

Aig. du Midi (3,842 m) – F. de Bouillé with J. A. Devouassoud, A. and J. Simond, 1856

Aig. du Plan (3,672 m) – J. Eccles with M and A. Payot, 1871

Peigne-Requin branches of Plan:

Aig. du Peigne (3,192 m) – J. Liégard, R. O'Gorman, with J. Ravanel, J. Couttet, 1906

Aig. des Pélerins (3,318 m) – A. Brun, R. O'Gorman with J. Ravanel, E. Charlet, 1905

Aig. des Deux Aigles (3,487 m) – H. E. Beaujard, J. Simond, 1905

Pain de Sucre (3,607 m) – G. Mayer, A. Dibona, 1913

Dent du Requin (3,422 m) – G. Hastings, A. F. Mummery, J. N. Collie, W. C. Slingsby, 1893

Capucin du Requin (3,047 m) – V. Hugonnet with A. Couttet, M. Bozon, E. Ravanel, 1927

Main Chain:

Dent du Crocodile (3,640 m) – E. Fontaine

with J. Ravanel, E. Charlet, 1904

Dent du Caiman (3,554 m) – E. Fontaine with J. Ravanel, L. Tournier, 1905

Pt. de Lépiney (3,249 m) – J and T. de Lépiney, 1920

Aig. du Fou (3,501 m) – E. Fontaine with J and J. Ravanel, 1901

Aig. des Ciseaux (3,497 m) – Mme. Berthelot with J and E. Ravanel, 1906

Aig. de Blaitière (3,522 m) – E. R. Whitwell with C and J. Lauener, 1874

Aig. du Grépon (3,482 m) – A. F. Mummery with A. Burgener, B. Venetz, 1881

Aig. des Grands Charmoz (3,444 m) – H. Dunod, P. Vignon with F. Simond, F. Folliguet, G. Simond, J. Desailloux, 1885

Aig. des Petits Charmoz (2,867 m) – J. A. Hutchinson, 1880

Aig. de l'M (2,844 m)

Pointe Albert (2,816 m)

It should be noted that many other peaks in the area are called Aiguille, but are not part of this particular chain.

Guidebook: *Selected Climbs in the Range of Mont Blanc Vol I*, by R. Collomb and P. Crew.

(See also MONT BLANC GROUP.)

CHANNEL ISLANDS, CLIMBS IN
Some climbs have been done on the sea cliffs of Guernsey but the best prospect appears to be Sark. The island has been almost completely girdled and it was here that Shadbolt in 1912 suggested that limpets might provide portable holds. The idea did not work.

CHAPMAN, Frederick Spencer (1907-71)
Traveller, mountaineer, guerilla leader and writer, Spencer Chapman led a life of adventure seldom equalled in this century. An orphan, Chapman was brought up in the Lake District and at Sedbergh School where he gained a love of the fells. He later came under the influence of men such as Winthrop Young (*qv*) and Wakefield (*qv*).

Helped by the latter he attempted the Lake District Record (*qv*) in 1931 and set the incredible standard of 130 miles and 33,000 ft, but took 25 hours and therefore failed to qualify for the record.

He was in Greenland 1930-1, 1932, and 1934 for which he gained the Polar Medal. 1936 saw him in Sikkim first with Marco Pallis and then Harrison (Fluted Peak, 23,000 ft). From there he joined an official mission tó Lhasa. In the following year (1937) with Crawford and three Sherpas he attempted the unknown mountain Chomolhari (23,997 ft). Chapman and Pasang Dawa Lama reached the summit.

Trained as a Commando during the War he conducted a single-handed campaign against the Japanese in Malaya which lasted three and a half years, during which he was captured and escaped. He recounted these adventures in his best known book, *The Jungle is Neutral*. Other works are: *Northern Lights, Watkins' Last Expedition, Lhasa the Holy City, Living Dangerously* and *Lightest Africa*. His biography, *Helvellyn to Himalaya* was published in 1940.

A schoolmaster by profession, Chapman became first organizing secretary of the Outward Bound Trust after the War. He was later Head of various schools and finally a college warden at Reading, where he died by his own hand.

CHEDDAR GORGE
Famous gorge in the Mendip Hills, Somerset which offers a variety of limestone climbs.

Guidebook: *A Climber's Guide to Cheddar Gorge* by R. Dearman and A. Riley.

CHEE DALE
A Derbyshire dale with many fine limestone climbs. Chee Tor and the Big Plum give climbs of some length and difficulty.

Guidebook: *The Northern Limestone Area*, by P. Nunn.

CHIMBORAZO (20,563 ft)
Famous volcano in the Cordillera Occidental of Ecuador. An attempt was made on it by the explorer Alexander von Humboldt in 1802 who reached a height of about 18,000 ft. It was first climbed by Whymper with the guides J-A. and L. Carrel, 1880 and repeated by Whymper a few months later. From 1745 to 1818, Chimborazo was thought to be the highest mountain in the world.

CHIMNEY (G.: Kamin; Fr.: Cheminée; It.: Camino)
A vertical fissure in a rock face, wider than a crack (*qv*) but narrower than a gully (*qv*). Generally, one can get the body into a chimney but touch the sides easily. Often climbed by back-and-knee (*qv*) or bridging (*qv*) but some are pure squirms. May contain chockstones (*qv*). A "chimney sweep" is an obsolete derogatory term for a rock-climber.

CHINA AND CHINESE ASIA, CLIMBING IN
The two highest mountains in China proper are Minya Konka (24,892 ft) climbed by a remarkable American expedition of T. Moore and R. L. Burdsall in 1932, and Amne Machin (23,491 ft) climbed by an expedition led by Pai Chin Hsiao in 1960. There are certainly other peaks over 20,000 ft in the Amne Machin group.

The other principal mountains are in the provinces of Sinkiang and Tibet. In the former is the Muztagh Ata Range:

Qungur II 25,326 ft
Qungur I 24,918 ft
Muztagh Ata 24,758 ft
Chakragil 22,071 ft

The mountains are really an extension of the Pamirs (*qv*). An extension of the Tien Shan range (*qv*) is Bogdo Ola, whose height is probably less than 20,000 ft. (See *Mountains of Tartary*, by E. Shipton.)

Tibet itself is an immense high plateau from which mountain ranges rise in some confusion. Those bordering the Himalaya are best known: Gosainthan (Shisha Pangma), 26,291 ft (climbed by the Chinese in 1964 and claimed as "the world's last 8,000 m peak")

Namcha Barwa 25,445 ft
Gurla Mandhata 25,355 ft
Gyala Peri 23,460 ft

North of Lake Manasarowar, Kailas rises to 22,028 ft and in the same area other peaks are reported of 23,000 ft or more. Similarly, there are 23,000 ft peaks reported near Lhasa and even higher mountains in the Dupleix Mountains, 300 miles north. At the northern edge of the Tibetan plateau are the Kun Lun and Altyn Tagh where there are known to be peaks of 23,000 ft and possibly one of 25,000 ft. The Kun Lun extend into China proper and north of them are the Nan Shan where there is at least one peak over 20,000 ft.

No western climbers have visited these areas for many years because of political difficulties. Chinese reports of ascents appear from time to time in the *A. J.* and elsewhere, but these are often confusing. Chinese mountaineering is a post-war phenomenon, helped in the first place by the Russians, who supplied the leaders and equipment. One hears only of the massive expeditions to the large peaks – whether climbing is also being developed as a *sport*, is a matter for speculation.

CHOCKSTONE (CHOCK) (Fr: block coincé)

(a) A stone jammed in a crack either naturally or otherwise. Natural chockstones can vary from pebble size to enormous boulders blocking gullies (hence, "chockstone pitch");

(b) Machined metal or nylon shapes, threaded to take runners (qv), and used as artificial chocks.

Natural chockstones can often be used for belays (qv) or runners (qv) and have probably been employed since the earliest use of the rope. Well-known examples are: Central Buttress, Scafell (1914), Pigott's Climb (1927).

Artificial chocks are more recent (1950s) and are really a development of the jammed knot runner. The first metal chocks were simply engineering nuts reamed out to remove the threads. Some chocks are permanently fitted with swaged wire.

CHOSS

Colloqialism to describe a climb which is loose, dirty, covered in herbage etc. "A chossy climb" or "the place is full of choss". Possibly from chaos.

CLASSIC

A much misused and almost indefinable term used to describe certain climbs, both in Britain and abroad. A classic climb need not be particularly difficult (e.g. Bowfell Buttress) but it must have good line and offer stimulating situations at its own level of difficulty. Many are older climbs, but not all; Fool's Paradise in Borrowdale, for example, is one which is not. Neither are all old climbs classics.

A variant is the term, "the route of the crag", meaning the most obvious challenge. Not necessarily classic – some crags have no classic lines.

CLEARE, John (b. 1936)

The outstanding British mountain photographer of the post-war era and a leading climber in his own right. His climbs include a number of new routes (summer and winter) in Scotland and a number of coastal climbs (Traverse of the Gods, Swanage (1963), Magical Mystery Tour, Torbay (1967)). He was with Bonington and Greenbank on the first ascent of Coronation Street, Cheddar (1965) – the first new climb done specifically for T. V. In the Alps he has made a number of British first ascents and first ascents of the W Face Direct, Aig. du Plan (1965), N Face Rib, Cima di Rosso (1969), Right Hand Pillar of the N Face of Pizzo del Ferro (1969). He has also climbed in East Africa and the U. S. A.

As a photographer, Cleare's work has appeared in many international magazines and several books. His own books are: *Rock Climbers in Action in Snowdonia* (with T. Smythe, 1966), *Sea Cliff Climbing in Britain* (with R. Collomb, 1973), *British Sea Stacks* (guide, 1974) and *A Book of Mountains* (1974).

His involvement with T. V. and films began in 1964 when he did the stills coverage for the BBC production of the climbing of Kilnsey Crag. He has worked on most of the other broadcasts including the famous "Coronation Street" (ITV, 1965) and "Old Man of Hoy" (BBC, 1967). He was with the International Everest Expedition, 1971 as film consultant and doing high altitude camera work. His film "The Climbers" won the Trento Prize (35mm) in 1970.

CLIMBING BREECHES

Knee length breeches leave the lower part of the legs unencumbered and are commonly used for all types of climbing. They are usually made of a tough, warm material (e.g. "moleskin") with double thickness at the seat and sometimes, the knees. They fasten at the knee with buckles or velcro and the pockets also have fastenings to prevent things falling out during climbing. A hammer loop or pocket is usually incorporated. In fitting, it is important to ensure there is plenty of freedom for leg movement at the knees and crutch. Braces make the best support, but are currently out of favour.

CLIMBING CLUBS

The term is taken here to mean a club which is not the national "Alpine Club", though it may be national (or international) in membership, and may well have members who are at the top of the sport. Clubs may be based on a geographical area or on some sectional basis, for example, a university. A few clubs are based on elitist principles e.g. G. H. M. (France) A. C. G. (Britain). In Russia, climbing clubs are usually sections of a greater sporting club (e.g. Moscow Locomotive) belonging to a trade union.

Many university clubs are of old foundation. Examples are: Oxford Alpine Club

(1875, later reorganized), Akad. A. C., Zurich (1896) Techniker A. C., Graz (1873), Akad. A. C., Innsbruck (1893).

Local clubs were even earlier, though few of the originals remain: Williamstown Alpine Club, U. S. A., (1863) Society Ramond, France (1865) Leipziger A. V., Germany (1869) Club Jurassien, Switzerland (1865). There were many more.

The earliest U. S. climbing clubs still extant are the Appalachian Mountain Club (1876) and the Sierra Club (1892).

The earliest known "climbing club" in Britain was the Highland Mountain Club of Lochgoilhead (1815) which held a meet every Midsummer Day to climb some local hill and celebrate the fact in true Highland fashion! Other early clubs (all Scottish) were The Gaiter Club (1849), The Cobbler Club (1866), The Dundee Institution Club (1879), Dundee Rambling Club (1886) The Cairngorm Club (1889) and the Scottish Mountaineering Club (1889).

Apart from Scotland and the Oxford Club already mentioned, the earliest British club was the Manchester Zweigverein (1889) – Manchester members of the Austrian A. C. The first club based on a home tradition was the Yorkshire Ramblers Club (1892). This club, the Scottish Mountaineering Club and the Cairngorm Club are still functioning.

The other "senior" clubs are: Climbers' Club (1898), Rucksack Club (1902), Wayfarers' Club, Fell and Rock Climbing Club, and Derbyshire Pennine Club (all 1906).

A number of other clubs were formed before the Second World War and a great many after it: there are now several hundred clubs in Britain. Unlike the "senior" clubs which often have a membership of hundreds and to which entry is by election, many of the newer clubs are small and demand nothing in the way of entry, except a fee. The most famous postwar club is the Rock and Ice Club (*qv*) formed by J. Brown and his companions in the 1950s. In Scotland the best-known club is the Creag Dhu (*qv*), founded in 1930.

Many clubs own one or more mountain huts (*qv*), usually restricted to members, though there are reciprocal rights with other clubs. Some clubs publish guidebooks – specifically, the Fell and Rock for the Lake District, the Climbers Club for Wales, the Scottish Mountaineering Club (by a Trust) for Scotland and Federation of Mountaineering Clubs of Ireland for Ireland. (See also ALPINE CLUBS.)

CLIMBING HELMET

The greatest proportion of serious climbing accidents involve head injuries. Helmets are designed to reduce this risk in two ways: (a) they protect the head in event of a fall; and (b) they protect the head from falling debris. Some of the illustrations show typical climbing helmets. They are made of fibre-glass and have firm chin fastenings – it is essential the latter should not come apart in the event of a fall. The more recent helmets tend to extend some way down the back of the neck and give further protection. Helmets were introduced in the 1950s but only achieved popularity in the 1960s.

CLIMBING WALL

A wall in which bricks have been removed and various projections added in order to simulate a rock face. Often built as one end of a sports hall, for indoor practice in climbing. Useful for teaching techniques. There are several varieties, including outdoor walls, towers, and wooden models known as climbing frames – some of which are semi-portable. (See *Climbing Walls*, by K. Meldrum.)

CLOGWYN DU'R ARDDU

One of the most important climbing crags in Britain; the scene of many of the major post-war climbs.

The crag rises above Lyn Arddu in the Snowdon massif and is very conspicuous from the Snowdon railway (*qv*), the track of which is probably the most convenient approach. Most conspicuous of all are the huge East and West Buttresses. The former is a set of steep walls comprising a triangular face, the upper part of which is known as the Pinnacle, whilst the other is a remarkable series of steeply tilted slabs. They are separated by the Eastern Terrace, a convenient way down from the climbs. To the left of East Buttress is the large somewhat shapeless mass of the Far East Buttress and beyond that again the small Far Far East Buttress. To the right of West Buttress and separated from it by the steep Western Terrace lies The Steep Band and then a considerable area of less formidable rock. The crag is impressively steep, and big.

Though there are a few easier climbs, these are of little importance. The chief routes, the majority, are "Very Severe" or harder. The crag is affectionately known as Cloggy.

The first climb was Deep Chimney by P. S. Thompson in 1905 and there followed a scattering of minor routes in the next few years, though nobody was bold enough to attack the main bastions until 1927 when Pigott's climb was made on the East Buttress (Pigott, Wood, Henshaw, Burton). Longland's climb on the West Buttress came the following year (1928, Longland, Pigott, Smythe, Eversden, Wood). Kirkus (*qv*) then began his campaign (1930-2) to be followed by Brown (*qv*) and Whillans (*qv*) in the 1950s, and Crew and Ingle in the 1960s. These were sustained efforts, but many other climbers played a part in the crag's development.

Almost every climb on Cloggy is of some significance; the following is merely representative of the best and most favoured following Pigott's and Longland's:

1930 Great Slab – Kirkus, Macphee
1931 Pedestal Crack – Kirkus, Macphee
1932 Birthday Crack – Kirkus, Linnell, Pallis
     Curving Crack – Kirkus, Bridge, Linnell, Hargreaves, Dyson
1933 Narrow Slab – Linnell, Piggot, Holliday, Roberts
1941 Bow Shaped Slab – Edwards, Cooper, Parkinson
1945 The Sheaf – Campbell, Cox
1951 Diglyph – Brown, Sorrell
     Vember – Brown, Whillans
     The Boulder – Brown (rest unable to follow)
1952 The Black Cleft – Brown, Whillans
     Pinnacle Flake – Brown, Whillans
     Spillikin – Brown, Whillans
     Bloody Slab (Red Slab) – Streetly (rest unable to follow)
     Llithrig – Brown, Allen
     The Corner – Brown, Allen, Belshaw
1953 East Buttress Girdle – Brown, Allen, Whillans
1955 Slanting Slab – Whilland, Betts
     Woubits – Whillans, Brown
1956 The White Slab – Moseley, J. Smith
1957 The Mostest – J. Brown (rest unable to follow)
     November – Brown, J. Smith
1958 The Shrike – J. Brown, H. Smith, J. Smith
1959 Woubits Left Hand – Brown, Boysen
     The Troach – Banner, Wilson
1961 Pinnacle Girdle – Soper, Crew
1962 The Great Wall – Crew (second did not follow)
     Guidebook: *Clogwyn du'r Arddu*, by H. Banner and P. Crew

CLOGWYN Y GROCHAN
One of the Three Cliffs of Llanberis (*qv*) on the N side of Llanberis Pass, Snowdonia. Invariably called "the Grochan", and very popular. Most routes are in the upper grades.

The first climb was Ledge Way by J. M. Edwards and B. McKenna in 1935 and Edwards took part in all the early ascents, notably Brant and Slape (both 1940). (See EDWARDS, and THREE CLIFFS.)

Guidebook: *Llanberis North*, by D. T. Roscoe.

CLOUGH, Ian Stewart (1937-70)
One of the most popular figures in British post-war climbing; a professional mountaineer of distinction.

Clough began climbing as a youth on his native Yorkshire gritstone. He developed rapidly and under the influence of MacInnes (*qv*) he also became a first-rate snow and ice climber. After National Service in the R. A. F. Mountain Rescue he became a tutor for the Mountaineering Association (*qv*) and later founded (in association with MacInnes) the Glencoe School of Mountaineering.

He made numerous first ascents, especially in the remoter parts of Scotland, but his work on Ben Nevis is perhaps most notable. He opened up the "Little Brenva" face (1958-9), made several rock routes and the first winter ascent of Point Five Gully (1959).

His first visit to the Alps was in 1953 when he climbed Wildstrubel. He later climbed many of the Gr. VI courses and in 1961 traversed the whole of the Chamonix Aiguilles (first British traverse). In the same year with Bonington, Whillans and Dlugosz he made the first ascent of the Central Pillar of Freney. The following summer (1962) with Bonington, he made the first British ascent of the Eigerwand.

He made two expeditions to Patagonia: 1963, first ascent of the Central Tower of Paine; 1967-8, leader of the Fortress expedition, though not himself one of the summit party. He made an unsuccessful attempt on Gauri Shankar in the Himalaya in 1964, and in 1970 returned to the Himalaya as a member of the successful Annapurna South Face expedition. The expedition was virtually over when Clough was unluckily caught by an ice avalanche and killed instantly.

COAST RANGE, BRITISH COLUMBIA
A northerly continuation of the Cascades (*qv*) extending for some 200 miles. The

highest peak is Mt Waddington at 13,260 ft (Wiessner, House, 1936). The Coast Range is difficult of access, except by air which is now the usual way. Despite this, and poor weather, the peaks are among the finest in North America.

Guidebook: *A Climbers' Guide to the Coast Ranges of British Columbia*, by R. Culbert.

THE COBBLER (Ben Arthur) (2,891 ft)

A craggy summit at the head of Loch Long, Arrochar, Scotland. There are three tops: South Peak (also called The Cobbler's Daughter, Jean or The Cobbler's Last); Central Peak (The Cobbler), North Peak (The Cobbler's Wife). There are climbs of all standards and the district is popular with Scottish climbers.

Guidebook: *Climbers' Guide to Arrochar*, by J. R. Houston.

COCKIN, John Garforth (1846-1900)

One of the most active of the early explorers of Caucasus which he visited in 1888, 1890, 1893 and 1896. He made a number of first ascents including the second summits of Janga and Ushba. Most notable, perhaps, was the first ascent of Shkhara (1888).

Cockin was a keen guideless climber. He had made a solo ascent of the Weisshorn in 1889, but was killed on that mountain in 1900 while trying a solo descent when the party he was with were in route-finding difficulties.

COILING A ROPE

Climbing ropes are invariably carried coiled. Unless the coiling is properly done the rope will kink badly and may not uncoil easily when it is required. In Britain the chief coil used is the shoulder coil. In this, one end of the rope is held in the left hand and a length of rope equal to the arms extended is pulled out across the body. The right-hand point is then transferred to the left hand (making a loop) and the process repeated until almost all the rope is coiled. Enough is left to make the shoulder knot. Another popular way of doing this is to coil the rope by boot and knee – but note that a hand must be placed between rope and knee. It is finished with a shoulder knot as before.

A different way of coiling is used for a long rope or abseil rope. The rope is doubled and coiled as before but it is finished by wrapping the two ends round the top of the coils and threading them through to make a "dolly". The rope is tied to the climber's back and waist. Climbing ropes are stored away coiled when not in use.

COL (Fr.) (E.: Saddle; G.: Joch; W.: Bwlch; Ga.: Bealach; It.: Colle)

A dip in a ridge, usually between two peaks. May be deep and wide enough to carry a motor road (e.g. Col de Forclaz) or it may be a mere dip in a high and icy skyline (e.g. Col d' Hérens). The way across a col is known as a pass (*qv*). Narrow cols are known as gaps (F.: breche; G.: scharte).

COLEMAN, Edmund Thomas (c. 1823-92)

Made the first ascent of the Domes de Miage (1858). He later went to America for several years during which he made the first ascent of Mount Baker in the Cascades on his third attempt (1868). He was a companion of General Stevens on the latter's first ascent of Mount Rainier in 1870, but got separated from the main party and did not reach the top.

Coleman was an artist. He was a member of the original committee of the A. C.

COLLIE, John Norman (1859-1942)

One of the greatest mountaineers of the turn of the century, whose activities profoundly affected climbing from Britain to the Himalaya. He began climbing in Skye in 1887 and 1888 with the local guide, John Mackenzie, when they climbed every peak except Sgurr Coire an Lochain. In 1890 they began a systematic survey of the Cuillins (the O. S. maps being unreliable) and each man has a peak named after him – Sgurr MhicCoinnich (Mackenzie's Peak) and Sgurr Thormaid (Norman's Peak). In 1891 they made the first crossing of the Thearlaich-Dubh Gap (with King), thus completing the ridge as a route. They also ascended Sgurr Coire an Lochan, the last summit to be attained in Britain. In 1899 Collie photographed the Cioch, though he and Mackenzie did not visit this popular pinnacle until seven years later. Skye was always Collie's first love; he retired to the island and is buried there, next to Mackenzie, in Struan churchyard.

He was a prolific climber in other areas of Britain. Most famous is his ascent of Moss Ghyll, Scafell, in 1892, when he cut a hold in the rock with an ice axe – the celebrated Collie Step. During the Easter of 1894 with Collier, Solly and Hastings (*qv*) he made the first rock climb on Buachaille Etive Mor and the first ascent of the Tower Ridge, Ben Nevis. This campaign is generally accepted as one which marked the beginning of climbing on the Scottish mainland.

In the Alps he was one of the select band climbing with Mummery (*qv*). His first ascents include: SW Face of the Plan, Grépon traverse (1892), Requin (which he named) (1893) and the first guideless ascent of the Old Brenva Route, Mont Blanc (1894). He accompanied Mummery on the ill-fated Nanga Parbat Expedition (1895).

In 1897 Collie paid his first visit to the Rockies; the first British climber to do so for purely mountaineering purposes. He repeated his visit in 1898, 1900, 1902, 1910, and 1911. He did a great deal of exploration and made first ascents as follows:

1897   Mt Lefroy, Mt Gordon
1898   Survey Peak, Mt Athabasca, Diadem, Mt Thompson
1900   Goat Peak, Mt Edith
1902-11 Mt Murchison, Freshfield, Forbes, Neptuak and Bess

In 1901, 1903 and 1904 Collie visited the Lofoten Islands where he also made a number of first ascents.

Collie related his experiences in numerous articles for climbing journals and in his book, *Climbing on the Himalaya and other Mountain Ranges* (1902).

Collie remained a batchelor all his life. He was an acknowledged aesthete: an expert on oriental art, wine, food and cigars. He was a heavy smoker but this did not seem to impede his fitness – he was a very strong man. His crossing of the Mazeno La in the Himalaya is an epic tale of endurance. He was President of the A. C. in 1920-22 and honorary member of the American and Canadian Alpine Clubs.

By profession Collie was a distinguished organic chemist and a professor at University College, London. He discovered the gas neon and made the first practical applications of X-rays.

COLLIER, Joseph (1855-1905)

A Manchester surgeon and pioneer rock-climber (Collier's Exit, Moss Ghyll, 1892; Collier's Climb, 1893; both on Scafell). He climbed in Scotland, Norway and the Caucasus, but his favourite area was the Dolomites, though he does not appear to have made new routes there. His career is poorly documented, but he is known to have been very popular with other climbers of the period and extremely athletic.

COLORADO ROCKIES

The highest part of the immense Rocky Mountain system outside Mexico. There are 55 named peaks over 14,000 ft and more than a thousand over 10,000 ft. The highest is Mt Elbert, 14,431 ft. The mountains run N–S through the state, but include complex cross ranges. The peaks are known as the "14ers". Many are shapely, but most are easy to climb.

Some of the peaks have cliff faces and arêtes offering climbs of 2,000 ft or so. The best known is the E Face of Longs Peak (14,255 ft), first climbed by the Stettner brothers in 1927. Others include the east side of Crestone Needle and Peak, the N Face of Sierra Blanca, and the NW Face of Capitol Peak.

Some of the most attractive mountains, offering unclimbed ridges and faces are in the San Juan Mountains – Uncompahgre (14,301 ft), Wilson (14,246 ft) and Sneffels (14,150 ft). There are also the sandstone needles of the Garden of the Gods, Colorado Springs, and climbs in the Black Canyon of the Gunnison River.

There are two national parks and several lesser protected areas in the state, and the capital, Denver, is one of the most beautifully sited cities in America.

COMBINED TACTICS

It is occasionally necessary in rock-climbing for one climber to assist another by giving him a "leg up" or "shoulder". The second man should, of course, be secured while he does this. Increasingly rare in use; common in pioneer Alpine literature. It was combined tactics that led to the death of Jones (*qv*).

COMICI; Emilio (1901 – 1940)

A notable climber from Trieste; the leading Italian exponent of peg climbing between the wars. He made some 200 new routes in the Dolomites including the first ascent of the Cima Grande North Face (E. Comici, G. Dimai, A. Dimai, 1933): one of the classic north faces of the Alps and regarded at the time as a great breakthrough. He was a proponent of the *direttissima*: 'I wish some day to make a route and from the summit let fall a drop of water and this is where my route will have gone.' Bolting has made this possible today but it is doubtful whether Comici had this in mind: his ideal has perhaps been usurped by technology.

Comici was at one time a caver, holding the world depth record of his day. He died through a silly accident during a training climb.

COMMANDS

In rock-climbing it is necessary for easily understood communications to pass along the rope. The climbers may be out of each other's sight, wind and weather may make communication difficult, unusual phrases may be misunderstood. To cope with this a series of commands has evolved.

Leader's instructions to second man

L: "Taking in slack!" (pulls in spare rope)
S.M.: "That's me!" (when all rope has been pulled in)
L: "Climb when you're ready!" (S.M. removes his belay and prepares to climb)
SM: "Climbing!"
L: "Aye, Aye!" (not always used)

When climbing

"Take in!" (means pull in more rope, it is too slack)
"Slack!" (means give me more rope, it is too tight)
"Tight rope!" (means take the rope in tightly, I expect to come off)
"Ten feet!" (means you are running out of rope – about ten feet left)
"Hold it!" (means stop taking in, I have met an obstruction – e.g. taking off a runner)
"Take in red (white)" (used in double rope techniques when bi-coloured ropes are employed; similarly, "Slack on red (white)". "Take in both", etc.)

General warnings

If a stone is knocked off a cliff or stone-fall is noticed the general warning shout of "Below!" is given.

If a climber realizes a fall is imminent he should always shout a warning to his belayer; even a split-second warning improves his chances of a good hold.

COMMITTING MOVE

Used somewhat indiscriminately to describe a hard move but it means a move where the climber is forced to commit himself to a technique with the expectation that if he does not succeed he will fall off. Also, a move which is not reversible is a committing move since it commits the climber to finishing the climb – though this is not strictly true since he may be able to abseil off (*qv*). In the Alps, an abseil might itself be committing, if it is not possible to climb back up – as on the S Ridge of the Aig. Noire de Peuterey.

COMPASS

An important navigational aid for mountaineers. The heavy prismatic compasses once favoured are now largely replaced by the Silva type compass developed for orienteering. Local magnetism in the rocks can affect compasses in some areas, for example, Bowfell, Lake District and the Cuillin of Skye.

COMPASS PARTY

A method of navigating in thick mist over dangerous terrain. The party are roped together (or in a large party stood in line) facing the compass direction required. They move off slowly, the rear member being equipped with a compass and shouting directions to keep the others in line. If the front man also has a compass, the technique is easier.

COMPTON, Edward Theodore (1849-1921)

A very active climber who lived in Austria and made numerous first ascents, particularly in the Eastern Alps. Notable are: Torre di Brenta and S Face of Cima di Brenta (both 1882). With Blodig (*qv*) he made the first guideless ascent of Aig. Blanche de Peuterey (1905). His active career spanned over 50 years and he made an ascent of Gross Glockner when he was 70.

Compton was a professional artist; the most famous mountain painter of his day. Exhibited many times at the Royal Academy. His drawings and watercolours illustrate several books and numerous articles written by leading climbers of the time, particularly German climbers (Zsigmondy, Purtscheller etc.). (See D. O. A. V. journals 1883-1912).

CONTOURING

Walking across a hillside so as to keep the same height, that is on an imaginary contour line.

CONWAY, William Martin (1856-1937)

Distinguished art critic, writer and explorer. A romantic, in the manner of Guido Rey (*qv*) or, later, F. S. Smythe (*qv*) in his approach to the hills, and a complete contrast to his contemporary, Mummery, whom he greatly admired. From this outlook stems all his major achievements.

In the Alps he made only a few minor new ascents, and is best remembered for his traverse of the Alps from Monte Viso to Gross Glockner, with two Gurkhas and (for part of the time) E. A. Fitzgerald (*qv*) in 1894. (Wrote *The Alps from End to End*, 1895).

In 1892 Conway organized the first major climbing expedition to visit the Himalaya, choosing the Karakorum region. The expedition was modelled on Whymper's successful Andean expedition of 1879 (*qv*) and received support from the Royal Society and the Royal Geographical Society. It was the prototype for most subsequent major Himalayan expeditions. The members were: Conway, A. D. McCormick (artist), J. H. Roudebush, O. Eckenstein, Lt. C. G. Bruce, Col. Lloyd-Dickin (naturalist), M. Zurbriggen (guide) and four Gurkhas. They achieved valuable mapping work in the Hispar and Baltoro areas and ascended Pioneer Peak (22,600 ft), the highest point climbed at that date. (Wrote *Climbing and Exploration in the Karakorum Himalayas* (2 vols), 1894.)

In 1896 and 1897 Conway visited Spitzbergen, climbing and exploring, using skis for travel. (Wrote *The First Crossing of Spitzbergen*, 1897, and *With Ski and Sledges over Arctic Glaciers*, 1898.)

In 1898 he visited the Andes and made the first ascent of Illimani (20,496 ft) and the third ascent of Aconcagua (23,080 ft). He also tried to climb Mt Sarmiento in Tierra del Fuego, but failed. (Wrote *Climbing and Exploration in the Bolivian Andes* (2 vols), 1901, and *Aconcagua and Tierra del Fuego*, 1902.)

Early in 1881 Conway had published *The Zermatt Pocket Book* which was a guide to the climbs in the Pennine Alps: the first real climbing guide as distinct from travellers' guides (see BALL). He proposed that the A. C. should publish a whole series of such guides (1886) but this did not happen. He therefore revised his own book (1890) calling it *Pennine Climbing Guide* which became the first of a series known as the Conway and Coolidge Climbers' Guides. Conway had no part in them after the first three. (see GUIDEBOOKS.)

The romantic nature of his climbing made Conway the leading ex-centrist in the arguments which raged in the A. C. at that time (*qv*). He gave up climbing in 1901, making his last ascent the Breithorn, as it had also been his first in 1872. He wrote many books and articles on art and climbing, most notably *Mountain Memories* (1920). President of the A. C. 1902-04. Became Lord Conway of Allington, 1931.

COOLIDGE, William Augustus Brevoort (1850-1926)

An outstanding mountaineer and probably the most accomplished Alpine historian of his, or any other, age.

Coolidge was born near New York. His father died shortly afterwards, and his mother, an invalid, went to live with her sister Miss. M. C. Brevoort, to whom fell the task of bringing up the boy. Because he was a delicate child they moved, on doctor's orders, to Paris, and for a short time, to Cannes. In the July of 1865 he climbed the Niesen, the first of his many ascents, and later that year crossed several snow passes.

The part played by Miss Brevoort in Coolidge's career as an Alpinist cannot be over-emphasised. She was herself a mountaineer and encouraged her young nephew to take up the sport. She found a ready disciple: aunt and nephew climbed together until the former's death in 1876. Often, too, they were accompanied by their dog, Tschingel. For the first three seasons they employed as guide Francois Devouassoud, but when he went to the Caucasus with Freshfield in 1868, Coolidge began his life-long association with Christian Almer (*qv*).

Between the Niesen (1865) and his last climb, Ortler (1898), Coolidge did not miss a single Alpine season – 33 years during which he amassed a tremendous practical knowledge of the Alps and made, possibly, more ascents than anyone else (the complete list fills 22 pages of the *Alpine Club Register*). He preferred snow and ice to rock-climbing, and in this respect was a little out of his time, for the Golden Age was ending as he began his career and rock-climbing, as exemplified by Dent (*qv*) and Mummery (*qv*), was definitely in. Nevertheless, he made a number of important first ascents, including Piz Badile (1867) Pic Centrale of La Meije, Ailefroid (1870), Agazzizhorn (1872) and numerous lesser peaks, especially in the Cottian and Maritime Alps, his favourite districts. In 1874 he made the first winter ascent of Wetterhorn and Jungfrau and in 1879, Schreckhorn. He made numerous second or third, ascents of difficult routes done by the pioneers. In all, he visited every part of the Alps except for Tyrol, Carinthia and Bavaria. He did not climb elsewhere – and had little regard for those who did.

Meanwhile he had taken double honours at Oxford and become a Fellow of Magdalen (1875). In 1882 he took Holy Orders, but in 1897 left Oxford to live permanently in Grindelwald. From about 1882 he devoted his time almost exclusively to the study of the Alps and he built up an unique Alpine library.

He put his vast knowledge to use in a long series of articles, books and encyclopaedia contributions; 220 by 1912, on his own count. Notable books are: *Josias Simler et les Origines de l'Alpinisme jusqu'en 1600* (1904), *Swiss Travel and Swiss Guidebooks* (1889), *The Alps in Nature and History* (1908), and *Alpine Studies* (1912). His works are informative rather than readable; vital references for Alpinists.

Coolidge's exactitude made him an ideal guidebook writer and editor. He revised Ball's *Western Alps* (1898) and Murray's *Switzerland* (1891, 1904), but his most famous contributions were to the Conway and Coolidge Climbers' Guides (1881-1910), the first practical pocket-sized guidebooks for mountaineers. (See GUIDE BOOKS.)

From 1880-9 Coolidge was Editor of the *Alpine Journal*.

Coolidge was equally famous for his quarrels and stubborness: he disagreed with almost every climber of note during his lifetime. He resigned from the A. C. in 1899, was elected honorary member in 1904 and resigned from that in 1910. He was re-elected honorary member in 1923. He was called "the Sage of Grindelwald" and, less politely, "the Fiery Lamb". He died at Grindelwald in 1926.

CORDIER, Henri (1855-77)

Began climbing in 1874, but it was in 1876 that he made a series of difficult new climbs in several parts of the Alps including routes on Rateau, Piz Roseg and Finsteraarhorn. Best-known climb, perhaps, is the Cordier Couloir of Aig. Verte. He also made the first ascents of Les Courtes, Les Droites and Pizzo Bianco. The following year he was killed in the Dauphiné in a glissading accident.

CORDILLERA BLANCA

The best-known region of the Peruvian Andes, intensively developed in recent years. The region has everything in its

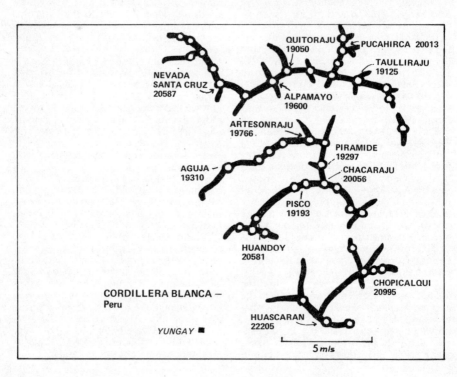

favour: easy access from Lima, good weather from May to mid-August, some of the most beautiful looking peaks in the world, which, at the same time, offer some of the hardest ice climbs known. Unfortunately, the area was subjected to a tremendous earthquake in 1970, which devastated Huaras and other villages, and affected Huascarán (22,205 ft). Fifteen Czech and one Chilean climber were killed in the disaster.

Huascarán is the highest peak, with two summits:
North, 21,834 ft – Miss A. Peck, G. zum Taugwald, R. Taugwalder, 1908
South, 22,205 ft – Borchers' expedition, 1932
Various other routes have since been made on the mountain.

Borchers' Expedition also accounted for many of the other highest peaks of the region including the N Peak of Huandoy (20,981 ft). Three lesser peaks claimed particular attention because of their beauty and difficulty: Chacaraju (20,056 ft), Alpamayo (19,600 ft) and Nevado Cayesh (18,915 ft).
1956 Chacaraju W peak – L. Terray, M. Davaille, C. Gaudin, R. Jenny, M. Martin, R. Sennelier, P. Souriac
1957 Alpamayo – G. Hauser's expedition
1960 Nevado Cayesh – Ryan, Crawford, Stewart.
1963 Chacaraju E peak – L. Terray, G. Magnone, L. Dubost, P. Gendre, J. Soubis

The Cordillera Blanca remains the most popular part of the Andes for expeditions. A guidebook (American) is in preparation. (See *Cordillera Blanca*, by Kinzl and Schreider.)

CORDILLERA CENTRAL (CHILE)
A section of the Andes some 200 miles long and 35 miles wide immediately east of Santiago. The Chile-Argentine frontier runs along the crest line and the highest peak of all, Aconcagua (22,835 ft) (*qv*) is in Argentina. The highest in Chile is Tupungato (21,490 ft) – Vines and Zurbriggen, 1897. Nevado Juncal (20,046 ft) was climbed by F. Reichert, R. Helbing, D. Beiza in 1910. Most of the peaks are somewhat lower than these, 17,000-19,000 ft.

Because the mountains are easily accessible to large concentrations of population, climbing is well developed. There are over 50 climbing clubs in Santiago alone, and several huts have been established in the high valleys. Most popular with the local

climbers are the accessible Cortaderas which rise to about 17,000 ft and are only five hours by car from the city. Ski-ing is equally well developed and there is a five-month season.

The whole area is heavily glaciated and the rock is not generally very good, but in the south are the Parodones (Tall Walls) and Punzones (Piercing Spires) which are said to offer the best rock-climbing in South America.

CORDILLERA HUAYHUASH
South of the Cordillera Blanca, Peru (*qv*). The range has some of the finest and most difficult mountains of the Andes. It is notorious for avalanches, bad cornices and the disease *verruga peruana*. The best base is Chiquian, from which the range can be reached in two days.

The first peak climbed was Nevada Suila (20,841 ft) by E. Schneider and A. Awerzger in 1936. Outstanding climbs include:
Yerupaja, 21,765 ft – Harrah and Maxwell, 1950
Jirishanca, 20,099 ft – T. Egger, S. Jungmeier, 1957
Rondoy, 19,301 ft – V. Walsh, P. Farrell, P. Bebbington, C. Powell, D. Condict, G. Sadler, 1963
Yerupaja has received much attention. It was traversed by Adcock's party in 1968, and the S Face was climbed by Dix and Jones in the same year. The developments within this area have been intense.

CORDILLERA REAL
The Andes of NW Bolivia, stretching 100 miles NW–SE, and quite near La Paz, the capital. The range stretches from Illampu (20,873 ft) in the N to Illimani (21,277 ft) in the S and forms a spectacular background to the high and arid Altiplano (12-15,000 ft), with Lake Titicaca. The range offers some of the best ice-climbing in the Andes. Little in the way of rock-climbing except the striking obelisk of Tiquimani (18,209 ft).

The largest concentration of high peaks and the most glaciers are in the Sorata Group in the N of the range. Notable peaks include:
Ancohuma, 21,082 ft – R. Dienst, A. Schultze, 1919
Illampu, 20,873 ft – E. Hein, A. Horeschowsky, H. Hortnagel, H. Pfann, 1928
Haukǎna, 20,503 ft – Probably the Hein party, 1928.

Pico del Norte, 19,784 ft – Hein party, 1928
Numerous other peaks over 18,000 ft

Between the Sorata Group and Illimani are various groups with many peaks in the 18,000-19,000+ ft range. Notable are:

Chearoco, 20,102 ft – A. Horeschowsky, H. Hortnagel, 1928

Cacca Aca, 19,996 ft – R. Dienst, A. Schultze, 1919

Chachacomani, 19,927 ft – G. Buccholtz party, 1945

Condoriri, 18,548 ft – W. Kuhm, 1941 (probably)

Illimani has three summits. The S and highest summit was climbed by M. Conway, A. Macquignaz and L. Pellisier in 1898. The N Summit, just a few feet lower, by H. Ertl and G. Schröder in 1950.

CORDILLERA VILCABAMBA

An attractive range of mountains attainable from Cuzco, Peru. The peaks are big and icy, often showing the typical flutings of this part of the Andes. All the highest peaks have been climbed but there are many others and some parts of the area are little known. Amongst the highest peaks are:

Salcantay, 19,951 ft – G. I. Bell, F. D. Ayres, D. Michael, W. V. G. Matthews, M de C. Kogan, B. Pierre, 1952

Pumasillo, 19,915 ft – H. Carslake, J. H. Longland, 1957

Sacsarayoc, 19,800 ft – P. Farrell (solo), 1963

The Pumasillo ascent was repeated later by other members of the team. (See *The Puma's Claw*, by S. Clark)

The Cordillera Veronica de Urubamba, on the other side of the Urubamba River, is sometimes taken as part of the Vilcabamba range. The dominating peak is the fine Nevado Veronica, 18,865 ft (Egeler, de Booy, 1956).

CORDILLERA VILCANOTA

A group of mountains some 70 miles from Cuzco, Peru, the highest of which is Ausangate (20,945 ft) climbed by a German party under H. Harrer in 1953. The same party climbed six other high peaks. The peaks are icy, well-shaped, and easy of access. There are no unclimbed summits.

CORNICE (Fr: corniche)

A consolidated snow bank projecting over the edge of a ridge, plateau or corrie, and formed by prevailing winds. They may be temporary, as in Scotland, in which case they are likely to avalanche down a gully or face with the onset of thaw, or they may be permanent as are some in the Alps (e.g. Wildspitze, Mont Blanc de Cheilon). On some ridges double cornices are known, that is, extending out on both sides of the ridge. Cornices can be quite large.

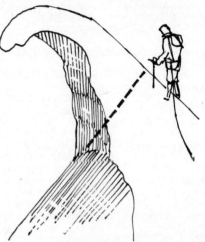

Cornices represent a threat to the climber since he may not be aware of their presence and they may collapse beneath him. If they are suspected then careful prodding with the axe may reveal them. It is safer to traverse well below the edge of the ridge on the other side. If there is a cornice at the head of a gully climb and it cannot be avoided, it may have to be tunnelled through.

CORNWALL

The sea-cliffs of West Penwith have a history of climbing reaching back to 1902 when A. W. Andrews (*qv*) made a number of climbs on the Wicca Pillar and the first ascent of the popular Bosigran Ridge. They have developed steadily since then and now offer a great number of climbs of all grades of difficulty. The rock is mostly good granite and the most popular area is Bosigran where the Climbers' Club have a hut.

Outside West Penwith some other cliffs have been climbed and there is a little inland climbing on tors and quarries, but of minor interest.

Guidebooks: *Cornwall (North Coast of West Penwith)*, by P. H. Biven and M. B. McDermott, and *Cornwall (West and South Coasts of West Penwith,)* by V. N. Stevenson.

CORRIE (Fr.: Cirque; Ga.: Coire; W.: Cwm)

The head of a hanging valley or glacial hollow (armchair hollow) and one of the most noticeable features of glaciated mountains. Corries often have lakes and are usually ringed with crags. In the Lake District corries as sometimes called combs (e.g. Comb Gill, Borrowdale).

CORSICA

A Mediterranean island noted for its fine peaks of which Monte Cinto (8,890 ft) is the highest. Other peaks offering fine climbing on perfect granite include: Monte d'Ore (7,842 ft), Monte Rotondo (8,610 ft), Paglia Orba (8,275 ft) and the cirque of Bonifato. May and June are the best months for climbing in Corsica, the high summer months being rather too hot for most tastes. Camping or bivouacking (there are some fine caves) are popular.

Guidebook: *Corsica-Cinto*, by M. Savrikant.

COTTIAN ALPS

The main range between the Col de l'Argentière and Mont Cenis, and east of the Col du Galibier (west of this is the more important Dauphiné Alps (*qv*)). The area is quite vast but has little to offer to climbers, only Monte Viso (3,841 m), the highest summit, being of any interest. (First ascent: W. Mathews and party, 1861.) (No English guidebook.)

COULOIR (E.: Gully; It.: Canale, Canalone)

The French word is invariably used by British climbers in the Alps, and there is a subtle difference in connotation between couloir and gully, hard to define. It perhaps arises from Alpine couloirs being usually that much bigger. Some couloirs are immense (e.g. on the Brenva face), but most are average size (see photographs). May be snow, ice or rock, depending on the mountains in question. Many are steep, but straightforward, snow slopes.

Couloirs are natural avalanche chutes and are also prone to stonefall, but conditions are local and may be minimal. Where the danger is noticeable, warnings are given in the guidebooks.

COURMAYEUR

The principal mountaineering centre on the Italian side of the Mont Blanc group. It is connected by road to Aosta and there is a rail-head at Pré St Didier, a few minutes' bus drive away. The Mont Blanc road tunnel connects the village with Chamonix (*qv*). At nearbye Entrèves is the start of a cable-car system that also connects with Chamonix.

COWELL, John Jermyn (1838-67)

Explored the Graian Alps in 1860 making the first ascents of Grand Paradis, Levanna Occidentale and Mont Iseran. In the following year he took part in the first ascent of Nord End (Monte Rosa) after which he visited Italy and there contracted an illness from which he never properly recovered.

COW'S TAIL

A short loop of rope attached in front of a harness or waistband for use in artificial climbing (*qv*). The climber, standing in his étrier (*qv*), can clip the cow's tail into the peg and this will support him, allowing him to use both hands for placing the next peg.

COX, Anthony David Machell (b. 1913)

A leading British rock-climber of the immediate pre-war years, Cox began the development of the Dewerstone in Devon with the C. C. Original and Direct Routes (1935-6) and Vixen Tor on Dartmoor. He then added to his list the popular climbs of Sunset Crack, Clogwyn du'r Arddu (1937), the Grimmett and Spiral Route, Craig yr Ysfa (1938) and finally one of the great Cloggy classics, Sheaf (1945).

Cox was on the Machhapuchare expedition of 1957, but failed to reach the top by about 150 ft. President of the A. C. 1971-3.

CRACK (G.: Riss; Fr.: Fissure; It.: Fessura)

A fissure in the rock, not wide enough to be a chimney (*qv*). Cracks may be vertical, horizontal or sloping and they play a very important part in rock-climbing. A crack may form the basis for a whole route, or for a pitch (*qv*). Smaller cracks may provide convenient holds or useful protection (*qv*).

A crack can be climbed using holds on its edge (easiest) but if this is not possible it may be tackled by jamming (*qv*) or layback (*qv*). Cracks are needed for chocks (*qv*) and pitons (*qv*).

CRAG LOUGH

An igneous crag on the Roman Wall, Northumberland, west of Housteads fort. Various routes of all grades. There are several crags developed by climbers along the line of the Wall and many more through-

out Durham and Northumberland, but all
small.

Guidebook: *A Rock Climber's Guide to
Northumberland*, by N. E. Haighton.

CRAIG GOGARTH

A line of sea cliffs in Gogarth Bay, between
North and South Stacks on Holyhead
Island, Anglesey. Discovered as recently as
1964 (Ingle and Boysen), they have already
proved to be the finest sea-cliffs for climbing in Britain and the most outstanding
discovery of post-war years. The climbs are
reasonably long and almost without exception, hard. Since their discovery, development has been intense – 130 routes within
five years, including 50 in 1966 and 52 in
1967. Almost every leading British climber
has made a contribution, but particularly
J. Brown, Crew, Ingle and the Holliwell
brothers.

Guidebook: *Anglesey – Gogarth*, by P.
Crew.

CRAIG YR YSFA

A huge rambling crag in the Carneddau,
Snowdonia, with a fine selection of climbs.
The nearest centre is Ogwen.

Because of its somewhat isolated situation the crag was fairly late in developing,
and Great Gully, one of the finest in
Britain, was not climbed until 1900 (J. M.
A. Thomson, Simey, Clay). Other notable
ascents are:

1905 Ampitheatre Buttress – Abraham
      Brothers, Leighton, Puttrell
1931 Pinnacle Wall – Kirkus (solo)
1938 The Grimmett – Cox, Beaumont
1952 Mur y Niwl – Moulam, Churchill

In Cwm Eigiau, below the crag, the
Rucksack Club established the first climbing hut in Britain (1912).

Guidebook: *Carneddau*, by A. J. J.
Moulam.

CRAMPONS (Fr.) (G.: Steigeisen; It.: Raniponi)

Are used for climbing snow and ice. A
crampon consists of a framework of steel
spikes which fits over the sole of a boot and
is held in place by straps. They are made in
pairs to boot sizes. The French name is universal in Britain and the U. S. – the old
English terms "climbing irons" or "claws"
have long since gone into disuse.

Crampons are of great antiquity: Martin
Conway refers to museum examples in
Vienna dating to 500 B. C. and coming
from Hallstatt. Other early examples have
been found near Bad Reichenhall and in
Carinthia. They were also used by the
Gauls in Roman days (Musée St. Germain
en Laye). Conway believed them to be of
Celtic invention, but the idea seems to have
spread quite widely – they were found to be
in use in Caucasus by early visitors to that
region.

Though these early crampons may have
been used to help in the crossing of icy
passes, they were probably more commonly used as an aid to balance on steep
slopes during haymaking. This use can still
be seen in parts of Tyrol.

Climbing crampons were developed in
Tyrol, being virtually the same as peasant
crampons and made by the local black-
smiths. They were adopted quite readily by
Austro-German mountaineers and were
featured in early German climbing man-
uals. British mountaineers frowned on
crampons as being unsporting and even
dangerous – Ball, Dent and Raeburn
amongst others, wrote condemning them.
A few courageously defended them –
Tuckett, Gilson (who pointed out speed as
a factor in their defence) and Oscar Eckenstein (*qv*) who redesigned them solely for
climbing purposes. Modern crampons are
a development of Eckenstein's work.

Crampons have ten or twelve points, the
front two of which project forward at an
angle. Rings are provided through which
webbing straps can be threaded in a criss-
cross pattern across the top of the boot, the
ends being tied together. This system in
now being superseded by straps which use
quick-release buckles and are permanently
fixed to the rings. Crampons must be well-
fitted or they feel insecure, and because
modern boot design varies so much from
model to model, adjustable crampons
which can be altered at will have been
designed.

Use

There are two basic uses for crampons:
walking over moderately sloping ice or
snow (e.g. on glaciers) and steep ice or
snow climbing.

The trend today is for climbers to wear
crampons whenever they are on snow and
ice, irrespective of conditions. There is
much to be said for this in terms of convenience and speed, but there are also dangers, the chief of which is that soft snow
tends to ball-up under crampons. This can
be overcome by fitting a sheet of polythene
under the crampon so that only the spikes
show through. Snow will not adhere to
polythene.

Crampons allow normal walking on slopes which would otherwise require step cutting (*qv*). With front-point crampons this is particularly easy and the only danger is in catching the spikes on stockings, thus causing the climber to trip. In descent, or walking across a slope, the ankles need to be flexed so that all the points bite into the ice at once.

Where the snow is soft enough for steps to be kicked, many climbers prefer to remove their crampons, since they have no apparent use. It is important to note, however, that a step kicked by a crampon can be more secure than one kicked by a boot, since the front prongs go through to the ice below the snow in many instances and give a more secure footing.

It is on steep ice that the modern crampon comes into its own. Crampons reduce step cutting to a minimum. The climber is armed with two short ice axes, or an axe and an ice dagger (*qv*), one in either hand. The axe is held by its head and used like a dagger for stabbing at the ice. The front prongs of the crampons are likewise stabbed into the ice, thus ensuring four-point contact (two hands, two feet). Each limb is moved in turn, in a steady rhythmical progression. Slopes of 50° or more can be tackled in this way, though most climbers would seek the security of an ice-screw runner (*qv*) at intervals.

On vertical or overhanging ice, where handholds have to be cut, the usefulness of front points is readily apparent.

It is not usual nowadays to remove crampons on mixed ground – quite difficult rock pitches can be climbed in crampons (for example, the gendarmes on the Forbes Arête of the Chardonnet, and the Tower Ridge of Ben Nevis in winter).

CRATCLIFFE TOR
A gritstone crag near Birchover, Derbyshire, known since pioneering days. All standards of climbs. Robin Hood's Stride is a strange group of pinnacles nearby and there are minor rocks at Rowtor and Stanton Moor. The ascent of Suicide Wall, Cratcliffe, by P. J. Harding in 1946, has been hailed as the start of the new era of gritstone climbing which came to fruition at Stanage (*qv*).
Guidebook: *The Chatsworth Gritstone Area*, by E. Byne.

CRAVEN, Alfred Eugene (1848-?)
Made the first English ascent of Gross Lohner and the first ascent of the Zahler-

shorn in 1879. He then joined W. O. Moseley (*qv*), an American, in the first traverse from Gross to Kleine Doldenhorn. A few days later they climbed the Matterhorn and Moseley was killed on the descent at the place now called the Moseley Slab.

CRAWFORD, Colin Grant (1890-1959)
Indian civil servant who climbed in Kashmir 1918 and 1919 and took part in Raeburn's reconnaisance of Kangchenjungs in 1920. Was a member of the Everest expeditions of 1922 and 1933; during the latter he climbed the North Col six times. Made a number of new ascents with Odell and others in the Canadian Selkirks, 1930.

CREAGH DHU MOUNTAINEERING CLUB
Founded in 1930 by A. F. Saunders, the Creagh Dhu had originally 30 members, all from the Glasgow area. Its adventures were chronicled in *Always a little Further* by A. Borthwick, and this gave rise to numerous legends about the club comparable to those about the Rock and Ice Club (*qv*). In the post-war years it was in the forefront of Scottish climbing with members such as MacInnes, Cunningham, and Vigano.

CREAG MEAGHAIDH
N of the Great Glen, near Loch Laggan, Scotland. One of the finest winter climbing areas in Scotland with routes of all standards. The ascent of the Central Pillar by Patey and Smith in 1955 led to its modern development. (See PATEY.)
Guidebook: *Winter Climbs: Cairngorms and Creag Meaghaidh* by J. Cunningham.

CREVASSE (G.: Schrund; It.: Crepaccio)
A crack in the surface of a glacier (*qv*). They can be wide and deep, though this is not always the case. On a dry glacier crevasses can easily be seen and are not usually difficult to avoid. Where this is not the case they can be climbed by the normal ice techniques. Small crevasses are jumped.

Crevasses are much more difficult to detect on a snow-covered glacier. A leader must appraise the general lie of the glacier and estimate the best route. He then probes with his ice axe along the line of march, his companions being constantly alert for a quick belay. The technique is simple but time-consuming and for this reason is too frequently neglected. A good deal depends on the leader's experience.

Some crevasses are spanned by snow

bridges (*qv*). The crevasse between the glacier and the upper snows of a mountain is called the bergschrund (*qv*). F. A. Eschen, a Dane, is the first-known climber to perish in a crevasse (1800, Buet, Switzerland). (See also CREVASSE RESCUE.)

CREVASSE RESCUE
The techniques employed to get a climber out of a crevasse into which he has fallen. In many cases it is simply a matter of hauling him out on the rope or of him pulling himself out since very often the victim goes in with only one leg or to waist depth. This is very common. When the victim goes down below the lip of the crevasse it becomes much more serious.

If the victim is tied with a simple waist loop it is first of all necessary for him to take the strain off his loop or he will black out. To do this he should have a prusik loop (see PRUSIKS). He stands in the prusik loop. Then:

1. *If there is a large party available*: The victim can simply be pulled out.
2. *If the party is smaller*: The middle of a rope is lowered to him, and he passes it through a karabiner at his waist. One end of the rope is secured and the members pull on the other end. The karabiner acts as a pully.
3. *Self-rescue*. Used for a rope of two, possibly three, if the pully method fails. The climber climbs the rope using prusikers. Very tiring.

The active rope is belayed in all the above cases. The belay point should be well back – it has happened that the belayer is also above the crevasse on a snow bridge! Quickness is the essence of good crevasse rescue and the techniques are worth practising.

CREW, Peter (b. 1942)
A leading British rock-climber who, in the early sixties was Brown's natural successor in the exploration of Clogwyn du'r Arddu where he made a number of new climbs, usually with B. Ingle. The Great Wall (1962) when the second did not follow, may be mentioned. His explorations on other crags in Wales were also noteworthy; he made some 70 new routes. With Ingle he also made Hiraeth on Dove Crag in Lakeland (1961).

Crew played a leading part in the exploration of Gogarth, with Ingle, J. Brown and others, including the Main Cliff Girdle, The Rat Race, The Red Wall, Central Park (all 1966) and The Spider's Web

(1968). In addition, he has made some 50 routes on the local outcrops. He was on the Cerro Torre Expedition of 1967-8.

Crew has been a major guidebook contributor: *Clogwyn du'r Arddu* (1963), *Selected Climbs in the Dolomites* (1963), *Llanberis South* (1966), *Craig Gogarth* (1966), *Bregaglia West* (co-author, 1967), *Selected Climbs in the Mont Blanc Range* (2 vols. co-author, 1967), *Anglesey Gogarth* (1969), *Tremadoc* (1970), *Llanberis Area* (1971). He has also produced a *kammkarte* of Snowdonia (1970) and written *Encyclopaedic Dictionary of Mountaineering* (1968) and *The Black Cliff* (co-author, 1970).

CRIB GOCH (13023 ft)
A pinnacled ridge leading up to Crib y Ddysgl in the Snowdon massif. A popular way of climbing Snowdon, but it can be severe in a hard winter. Crib Goch Buttress (Reade and Bartrum, 1908) is a popular rock climb.

Guidebook: *Cwm Glas*, by P. Crew and I. Roper.

CROUX, Laurent (1864-1938)
A notable Courmayeur guide at the turn of the century, employed by many well-known climbers, particularly the Duke of the Abruzzi (*qv*). He made several first ascents, amongst which may be noted:

1897 Mt St Elias (Alaska) with Abruzzi
1898 Aig. de la Brenva, SE Ridge.
1899 Aig. Sans Nom, E Ridge
       Pt Croux (named after him)
1902 Mt Mallet, S Face
       Mt Blanc du Tacul, from S
1903 Guide to Queen Margherita on her Spitzbergen expedition; first ascent of Mt Savoie
1909 Traverse of Aig. Blanche de Peuterey
1911 Dôme de Neige des Ecrins
       Grandes Jorasses, Hirondelles Ridge (in descent)

In 1916 he was seriously injured by an accident in a saw mill which closed his career.

CROWLEY, Edward Alexander ('Aleister') (1875 – 1947)
Aleister Crowley, self-styled Great Beast 666, was a notorious dabbler in black magic and unholy arts during the first part of the present century. At Cefalù Abbey in Sicily and Boleskin House, Foyers, he conducted obscene rituals after the fashion of the eighteenth-century Hellfire Club. A first-class mountebank, many notable people came under his influence.

In earlier years he was a climber of some distinction. He began climbing in 1890. In 1893 he made a new route on Napes Needle and in 1894 climbed on Beachy Head. He visited the Alps each year from 1894-8. Much of his climbing was done with Eckenstein (*qv*), the one friend he never betrayed.

In 1900 he visited Mexico and climbed Popacatapetl with Eckenstein. In 1902 he was second-in-command to the latter in the K2 expedition, when Guillarmod and Wesseley reached 21,400 ft – not exceeded until the U. S. expedition of 1938. Nevertheless, Crowley was a neurotic expedition man and it is difficult to see why Guillarmod invited him to lead a Kangchenjunga expedition in 1905. The outcome was disastrous: three porters and a climber were killed and Crowley refused to help in any rescue. The scandal magnified by a row between Crowley and Guillarmod in the press, and his growing notoriety, ended Crowley's climbing career.

CROZ, Michel (1830-65)
The finest Chamonix guide of his generation, born at Le Tour where he lived all his life. He sprang to prominence when discovered by Wills (*qv*) in 1859 and took part in the most exciting expeditions of the following five years including the great events of 1864 and 1865 with Whymper (*qv*). These include the first ascents of Ecrins, Mont Dolent, Aig. de Trélatête, Aig. d'Argentière and Moming Pass (1864), Dent Blanche and Grand Jorasses (1865) (See also CHRISTIAN ALMER.)

Croz took part in the first ascent of the Matterhorn (1865) and was killed in the accident on the way down (see WHYMPER). He was unmarried.

CRUX
The hardest part of a climb. One speaks of "a crux pitch" or "a crux move". There may well be more than one: "first crux", "second crux".

THE CUILLIN OF SKYE
One of the most important mountain ranges in Britain. In climbing terms "the Cuillin" means the Black Cuillin, a chain of spiky gabbro and basalt peaks stretching from Sligachan (*qv*) in the N to Loch Scavaig and the neighbouring Marsco – Blaven ridge. The adjacent Red Cuillin are comparatively uninteresting.

The chief centres are: Sligachan Hotel, Loch Scavaig (climbing hut), and, above all, Glenbrittle (hut, Youth Hostel, camp site, accommodation). There are roads to Sligachan and Glen Brittle, but not Scavaig.

The main ridge forms a magnificent horseshoe round Loch Coruisk and its traverse is the best expedition of its kind in Britain. (First traverse: Shadbolt and McLaren, 1911; first winter traverse: Patey, MacInnes, Robertson, Crabbe, 1965; first woman's traverse: Mabel Barker with C. D. Frankland, 1926). A so-called Greater Traverse, including Clach Glas and Blaven, has also been done, but is not popular. A time of 12-15 hours is normal for the traverse, but it has been done in much less. The peaks, from S–N (the usual way) are: Gars-bheinn (2,934 ft), Sgurr a Choire Bhig (2,880 ft), Sgurr nan Eag (3,037 ft), Sgurr Dubh na Da Bheinn (3,069 ft), Sgurr Thearlaich (3,201 ft), Sgurr Mhic Coinnich (3,107 ft), An Stac (3,125 ft), Inaccessible Pinnacle (3,226 ft), Sgurr Dearg (3,206 ft), Sgurr na Banachdich (3,167 ft), Sgurr Thormaid (3,040 ft), Sgurr a Ghreadaidh (3,190 ft), Sgurr a Mhadaidh (3,010 ft), Bidean Druim nan Ramh (2,850 ft), An Caisteal (2,730 ft), Sgurr na Bhairnich (2,830 ft), Bruach na Frithe (3,143 ft), Sgurr a Fionn Choire (3,065 ft), Bhasteir Tooth (3,000 ft), Am Bhasteir (3,070 ft), and Sgurr nan Gillean (3,167 ft). (Sgurr Alasdair (3,251 ft) is the highest summit of the island and is often included on the traverse, though it is off the main ridge.)

Off the main ridge lie: Sgurr Sgumain (3,104 ft), Sgurr Dubh Mor (3,089 ft) and various smaller peaks. Sgurr Coire an Lochain (2,480 ft) was the last peak to be climbed in Britain (1896, Collie, Howell, Naismith, Mackenzie.)

Some easy rock-climbing is needed on many parts of the ridge, but the various peaks and corries have many buttresses giving climbs in their own right. Easily most popular are the climbs of Coire Lagan, on the vast crag of Sron na Ciche. Here is the curious pinnacle of The Cioch. There are climbs of all standards.

Skye began to be developed as a climbing area before most other parts of Britain because of its mountaineering qualities as opposed to pure rock-climbing. (See PILKINGTON BROTHERS, COLLIE.) Notable ascents include:

1836 Sgurr nan Gillean – J. D. Forbes, D. MacIntyre

1873 Sgurr Alasdair – A. Nicolson

1874 Sgurr Dubh Mor – A. Nicolson

1870 Sgurr a Ghreadaidh – W. Tribe, J. Mackenzie
1873 Knight's Peak – W. Knight and guide
1880 Inaccessible Pinnacle – C. Pilkington
1883 Bidean Druim nan Ramn – L. Pilkington, Hulton, H. Walker
1887 Sgurr Thearlaich – C. Pilkington, Walker, Heelis
      Sgurr Mhic Coinnich – same party
      Bhasteir Tooth – Collie, King
1891 Thearlaich-Dubh Gap – Collie, King, Mackenzie
1895 Waterpipe Gully – Kelsall, Hallitt
1897 King's Chimney, Mhic Coinnich – King, Naismith, Douglas
1906 The Cioch Ordinary – Collie, Mackenzie
1907 Cioch Direct – A. Abraham, Harland
1918 Crack of Doom – Pye, Shadbolt
1919 Cioch West – Holland, Carr, Miss Pilley
1950 The Fluted Buttress – Dixon, Brooker
1951 The Crack of Dawn – Dixon, Brooker
1960 King Cobra – Bonington, Patey
1962 Trophy Crack – Walsh and party
1968 Purple Haze, Sgumain – Guillard, Irwin

Guidebooks: *The Island of Skye*, by M. Slesser, and *Climbers' Guide to the Cuillin of Skye* (2 vols), by J. W. Simpson.

CULLINAN, Sir Frederick Fitzjames, (1845-1913)
Made the first ascent of the Domgrat of Tächhorn (1878) and first ascent of Aig. de Talèfre (1879). He also made the second ascents of the Dru and the W arête of the Dent d'Hérens.

CUNNINGHAM, Darus Dunlop (1856-96)
A Scottish climber who was an advocate of winter ascents in his own country (with Emile Rey (*qv*) on Ben Nevis, 1884) and who made the second winter ascent of Mont Blanc (1882). He repeated (often second ascent) a number of the harder Chamonix climbs of the day.
Cunningham is best known as Editor with Abney (*qv*) of *The Pioneers of the Alps* (1887).

CUNNINGHAM, John (b. 1927)
One of the leading post-war Scottish climbers; a position he still retains. Amongst his many new routes mention

might be made of Guerdon Grooves (1947), the first big wall climb to be done in Scotland, and Bluebell Groove, one of the hardest climbs in the Glencoe area (1955) – there has only been one repeat so far. His ice-craft was demonstrated when he did Point Five Gully, Ben Nevis in two and a half hours. (First ascent took five days, sieged).
In 1953 Cunningham and MacInnes formed the two-man Creag Dhu expedition to Everest, which, alas, failed through inadequate financial resources! In 1955-6 he was in South Georgia where he ascended many ice peaks of *c*. 7,500ft. In 1958 he was on an expedition to Disteghil Sar and in 1959 to Ama Dablam. Between 1960 and 1965, Cunningham was three times in the Antarctic where he made numerous ascents, including that of Mount Andrew Jackson (11,500ft), the highest peak in British Antarctica. It involved a dog sled journey of 400 miles to base camp.
Cunningham has revolutionized modern ice-climbing (*qv*). The front pointing techniques that were previously used only applied to slopes up to 70 degrees, but Cunningham showed that with special axes the method could be applied to any angle.
In 1973 he wrote *Guide to Winter Climbs: Cairngorms and Creag Meaghaidh*. He is a professional climbing instructor.

CUST, Arthur (1842-1911)
Whilst a schoolmaster at Rossall, he made with his fellow teachers, Cawood and Colgrove, a number of guideless expeditions which culminated in the first guideless ascent of the Matterhorn (1876). His favourite districts were Arolla and the Lepontine Alps. He made the first known ascent of Mont Brulé (1876) and the Mitre de l'Evêque (1879) in the former area, and numerous first ascents in the little-known Lepontine area. He frequently climbed solo.
Cust's Gully, on Great End, has a remarkable rock arch. Cust led a large A. C. party up the gully in winter, 1880 – almost certainly the first climb done on this popular winter climbing crag.

CWELLYN
Name given to an area in Snowdonia around the lake of the same name. It lies immediately W of Snowdon and N of Rhyd-ddu. Numerous crags including the old favourite Llechog, recently revived. The most important is Castell Cidwm, a

fierce crag. The first route was Dwm (Brown, Smith, 1960). The Cidwm Girdle (Clements, Potts, 1965) is one of the hardest of its type.

Guidebook: *Cwm Silyn and Cwellyn*, by M. Yates and J. Perrin.

CWM SILYN

An impressive cwm at the western edge of Snowdonia, just south of Nantlle. The chief crag is Craig yr Ogof with its famous Great Slab (Ordinary Route: Pye, Reade, Elliot, Odell, 1926) but there are several buttresses giving climbs of all standards. Rather remote and so not as popular as it might be. Notable first ascents include:

1931 Kirkus's Route – Kirkus, Macphee
     Outside Edge Route – Edwards, Palmer
     Upper Slab Climb – Kirkus, Hargreaves, Bridge
1952 Ogof Direct – Moulam, Pigott, Bowman
1956 Bourdillon's Climb – Bourdillon, Nicol

1963 Crucible – Ingle, Wilson
     Guidebook: *Cwm Silyn and Cwellyn* by M. Yates and J. Perrin.

CYPRUS, CLIMBING IN

A mountainous island in the Mediterranean. Rock-climbs up to 500 ft have been developed, mostly by Service personnel stationed there. The chief areas are Kornos, Pentadtylos and Kantara in the north. The weather is good.

CYRN LAS

A fine crag on the S side of Llanberis Pass, Snowdonia. The climbs are mostly in the higher grades and many have been notable for their period:

1904 Great Gully – Thomson, Smith
1906 Schoolmasters' Gully – Mitchell, Barker, Drew, Atchison
1935 Main Wall Climb – Roberts, Cooke
1953 The Grooves – Brown, Cowan, Price
1963 The Great Buttress – Ingle, Crew
     Guidebook: *Cwm Glas*, by P. Crew and I. Roper.

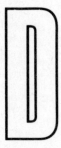

DACHSTEIN GROUP

An important group of limestone mountains south of Bad Ischl in Austria. The highest peak is Dachstein (2,996 m). Other interesting peaks include: Grosser Bischofsmütze (2,455 m) and the Torstein (2,947 m). The northern part of the group is known as the Gosaukamm and is noted for spectacular scenery. There are a number of famous caves in the area. The best centre is Hallstatt. (No English guidebook.)

DAGGER TECHNIQUE

A method of climbing steep ice which does away with the necessity for holds and is therefore quick and less tiring. The climber employs the front prongs (lobster claws) of his crampons, an ice axe in his right hand and an ice dagger in his left. He stabs with the crampons and uses these to progress, maintaining balance by stabbing with the axe and dagger. As in rock-climbing, four-point contact is maintained. He may choose to cut an occasional resting step (the strain on the calves is considerable) and will cut a belay step.

The dagger is a stout steel instrument, with about a four-inch blade, usually with notches and with some device to prevent it being dropped accidentally. In emergency, a piton can be used instead.

Daggers came into use in the late 1950s or early sixties and appear to be a transitional stage in ice-climbing technique. The axe and dagger are now often replaced by two very short axes with steeply inclined blades. The technique is similar, but steeper ice can be tackled due to a better purchase. (See ICE-CLIMBING.)

DANGLE AND WHACK

An obsolete term describing artificial climbing (*qv*); used derogatorily, often about pre-war Continental climbers.

DAUPHINÉ ALPS

A westerly extension of the Cottian Alps, entirely in France, and the most important climbing area between Mont Blanc and the Mediterranean. The principal centres are La Grave, La Bérarde, and Ailefroide.

The landscape of the Dauphiné is starkly barren and the peaks are jagged and rocky. Snow and ice-climbing is relatively unimportant though there are plenty of glaciers and snowfields. The highest summit is the Barre des Ecrins (4,101 m) and the Dôme de Neige des Ecrins is 4,015 m. Many of the peaks show a remarkable uniformity of height between 3,500 m and 3,800 m – 'a forest of peaks', extremely impressive. Other famous peaks, among many, are: La Meije (3,983 m), Ailefroide (3,954 m), Mt Pelvoux (3,946 m), Pic Sans Nom (3,914 m), Le Râteau (3,809 m), Les Bans (3,669 m) and Aigs. d'Arves (3,510 m). The latter is N of the main group, in the Grandes Rousses massif.

One would hesitate to recommend the area to novices though there are climbs of all grades. The traverse of La Meije (Gibson, U. Almer and Boss, 1891) is the traditional classic of the area; one of the finest traverses in the Alps. The South Face Direct of the same peak (Allain, Leininger, Vernet, 1934) is another fine route. The rock of the Dauphiné is not always good.

The area was always one of the most remote and backward regions of the Alps (see WHYMPER, MOORE etc.). Though Mont Pelvoux was climbed as early as 1848 (V. Puiseux), the Ecrins was not climbed until the Moore-Whymper expedition of 1864. The Meije was the last of the really big Alpine peaks to be climbed (E. Boileau de Castelnau with P. Gaspard and son, 1877). Many of the peaks were not climbed until the last quarter of the century, and some minor ones were not climbed until the first quarter of this century. (See Whymper *Scrambles*, Moore *The Alps in 1864* and J. Boell *High Heaven*.) Numerous huts serve the area.

Guidebook: *Selected Climbs in the Dauphiné and Vercors*, by E. Wrangham and J. Brailsford.

DAVIDSON, Sir William Edward (1853-1923)

One of the leading figures of the second generation of Alpine pioneers, and close contemporary of Mummery (*qv*), of whom Davidson had a jealous dislike. Davidson failed on the Grépon and the Charpoua face of the Verte, both expeditions which Mummery accomplished shortly afterwards. There is little doubt that it was Davidson who prevented Mummery's election to the A. C. (1880).

Davidson was a strong climber and his

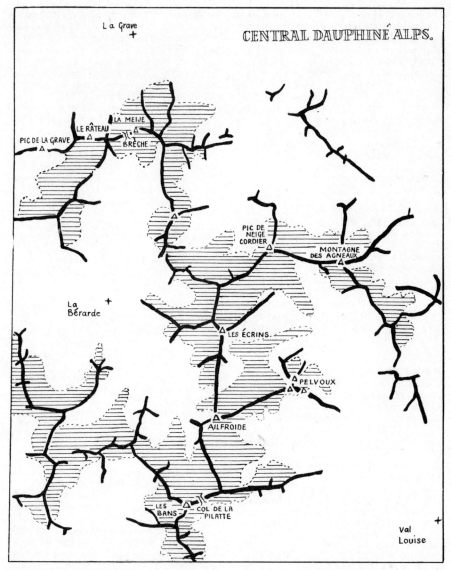

CENTRAL DAUPHINÉ ALPS.

La Grave

PIC DE LA GRAVE
LE RÂTEAU
LA MEIJE
BRÈCHE

La Bérarde

PIC DE NEIGE CORDIER

MONTAGNE DES AGNEAUX

LES ÉCRINS

PELVOUX

AILFROIDE

LES BANS
COL DE LA PILATTE

Val Louise

expeditions included most of the difficult climbs then known. His own first ascents were: Mont Maudit (1878), Aig. du Tacul (1880), Wellenkuppe–Gabelhorn traverse (1895), Le Cardinal (1897). He also made many new routes on the Rifelhorn, a peak he is said to have climbed 250 times.

Davidson always climbed with the best of guides in the best of weather. He was a strong socialite and something of a snob. In private life he was Permanent Legal Adviser to the Foreign Office. K. C. M. G. in 1907, President of the A. C. 1911-13.

DAVIES, Rev. John Llewellyn (1826-1916)
A leading social reformer of his time, particularly in education. Davies made the first ascents of the Dom (1858) and the Täschhorn (1862). He was an Original Member of the A. C.

DAY, Michael William Henry (b. 1942)
An army officer noted for his Himalayan

expeditions. Day began in 1964 with the Cambridge University expedition to Swat Kohistan, making five first ascents and the third ascent of Mankial. He failed on Brahma Peak the following year, but in 1969 made the fourth ascent of Tirich Mir (25,263 ft) and the first ascent of Little Tirich (20,896 ft). In 1970, with G. F. Owens, he made the second ascent of Annapurna (*qv*) using the same route as the French had used on the first ascent. In 1973, he made the first ascent of the East Ridge of Indrasan (20,410 ft).

With Boysen and Burke, Day also made the first ascent of the North Front of the Rock of Gibraltar (1972).

DEAD MAN (SNOW ANCHOR)
A flat alloy plate about six inches square with one edge pointed, and fitted with a wire loop in the centre. Used for belaying in snow. The plate is pushed into the snow at right angles to the surface and a channel cut to take the wire loop, which trails down the slope and to which the climber belays. Some practice is needed in correctly placing dead men, but they are very secure – more so than the traditional axe shaft. There are smaller versions known as 'dead boys'.

DÉCHY, Maurice de (1851-1917)
A Hungarian mountaineer who made a number of first ascents in the Tyrol, but is best known for his exploration of the Caucasus in the years 1884, 1885, 1886, 1887, 1897, 1898 and 1902. In 1905-7 he published his account of these expeditions in a three-volume work entitled *Kaukasus, Reisen und Forschungen im Kaukasischen Hochgebirge*.

In 1879, with the guide Maurer (*qv*), he visited Sikkim on what was intended to be a climbing expedition (the first of its kind in the Himalaya) but he was unfortunately taken ill. See *Exploration of the Caucasus*, by D. W. Freshfield.

DEER BIELD CRAG
A small but important crag in Far Easedale, Lake District. The climbs are only for experts. Deer Bield Chimney (Stables and Turner, 1908), Deer Bield Crack (Hargreaves and Macphee, 1930) and Deer Bield Buttress (Dolphin and A. D. Brown, 1951) are the classic routes of the crag.

Guidebook: *Great Langdale*, by J. A. Austin.

DENT, Clinton Thomas (1850-1912)
One of the most important of the second generation of Alpine pioneers, Dent was a propagandist for the smaller, harder, rock peaks then coming into fashion. In 1870 he began his long association with Alexander Burgener (*qv*) during which they made the first ascents of Lenzspitze (1870) and Portjengrat (1871), and new routes on Ruinette (1872) and Zinal Rothorn (1872). The partnership culminated with the first ascent of the Dru (1878) after 18 previous attempts by Dent.

He later turned his attention to the Caucasus which he visited in 1886, 1888, 1889 and 1895. Made the first ascent of Gestola (1886) and Tsiteli (1895) and crossed several new and difficult passes.

Dent was President of the Alpine Club, 1887-9 and head of the committee which produced the Alpine Distress Signal. He was a first rate photographer and lecturer, His books are *Above the Snowline* and the Badminton volume on mountaineering.

In his professional life Dent was an eminent surgeon.

DERWENT EDGES
The gritstone outcrops flanking the River Derwent in Derbyshire. They stretch for ten miles from the Ladybower Reservoir to Chatsworth Park on the east bank of the river. They have all been quarried to some extent (even Stanage), but there are some exceptional quarries in the area which may be counted as part of the climbing scene there. Climbs are usually less than 100 ft, on excellent Rivelin grit, and are of all standards. The edges are very popular.

From north to south, the principal edges are Stanage (*qv*), Bamford, Burbage, Higgar Tor, Carl's Wark, Millstone, Lawrencefield, Froggatt, Curbar, Baslow, Gardom's, Birchen's and Chatsworth. Millstone and Lawrencefield are heavily quarried but there are other quarries such as Padley, which are worth a visit. Birchen's Edge is one of the finest training grounds for novices in the country.

Sheffield is the natural centre for all these climbs. Other crags in the vicinity are Rivelin, Agden Rocher, Cratcliffe and the Black Rocks (*qv*) though the last two are further south, in the limestone country.

The history of climbing here is a long one, despite keepering by game wardens and water boards in the past. (See *High Peak* by E. Byne.)

Guidebooks: *Rock Climbs in the Peak: Sheffield Stanage, Sheffield Froggatt, Chatsworth Gritstone*.

DESCENDEUR
A metal device intended to make abseiling (*qv*) quicker and more comfortable. There are various patterns. (See ABSEILING.)

DEVON, CLIMBS IN
Considerable climbing has been done in the county, especially in the post-war years. With the exception of Lundy (*qv*) the rocks lie in the southern half of the county and are of various types. The tors of Dartmoor provide short problems similar to gritstone, Hay Tor being the best. On the edge of the moor is the large bastion of the Dewerstone which gives granite climbs of almost 200 ft in various grades, while the limestone of Chudleigh Rocks provides some long and hard routes for experts. Some sea-cliff climbing has been done at Torbay and elsewhere.

Guidebook: *Rock Climbing in Devonshire*, by R. D. Moulton; *South Devon*, by P. Littlejohn.

DIBONA, Angelo (1879-1956)
A guide from the Dolomites famous for his association with Dr Guido Mayer of Vienna. Climbed the Laliderwand in 1911. In their great 1913 season their new climbs included the Mayer–Dibona Route on the Requin, the Coste-Rouge Ridge of the Ailfroide, and the Aiguille du Pain du Sucre in Dauphiné, later renamed Aig. Dibona.

DIEDRE (Fr.) (E.: V-groove)
A large open-book type groove or corner in a crag.

DIEMBERGER, Kurt (b. 1932)
One of the most experienced of the post-war Austrian climbers, with ascents of all the hard Alpine faces (Eigerwand, etc.). In 1956 he made the first ascent of the N Face Direct of Gran Zebru and the North Face Direct of the W summit of Lyskamm. The same year he made a remarkable solo ascent of Piccolo Zebru NE Face by a new route and descended by another new route on the same face.

In 1957 Diemberger reached the summit of Broad Peak (8,047m) and reached 7,150m on Chogolisa in the attempt in which Buhl was killed. In 1960 he climbed Dhaulagiri (8,222m) and Dapa Peak (5,980m). He is thus one of the few men to have climbed two 8,000m peaks. The ascent of Broad Peak (K. Diemberger, H. Buhl, M. Schmuck, F. Wintersteller) was the first 8,000 m peak to be climbed 'Alpine style', that is with no porters or oxygen.

In 1965 and 1967 Diemberger was in the Hindu Kush where, in 1967, he made a new route on the W Face of Tirich Mir, 7,708 m (third ascent) and also the first ascent of Tirich West IV (7,338 m). He made several other ascents of major peaks in the area. He has also climbed in Greenland (1966, 1971), Ethiopia (1969) and the Andes (1973).

In 1971 he published his autobiography, *Summits and Secrets*.

DINAS CROMLECH
One of the Three Cliffs of Llanberis (*qv*). An angular crag, seen clearly on the N side of Llanberis Pass near the Pont y Cromlech. There are climbs of all standards.

Though Castle Gully was climbed in 1892, the cliff, in common with its companions was first developed by Edwards (*qv*). Holly Buttress, (Edwards and Walmsley, 1931) was the first route. The popular Flying Buttress and Spiral Stairs routes also belong to this year and the cliff as a whole was much more developed before the war than the other two. It also played its part in the great post-war developments and mention might be made of Cenotaph Corner (Brown, Belshaw, 1952) and Cemetary Gates (Brown, Whillans, 1951). The reputation of the Corner as a test piece for the elite was unrivalled for a number of years. (See THREE CLIFFS.)

Guidebook: *Llanberis North*, by D. T. Roscoe.

DINAS MOT
A fine crag dominating the S side of Llanberis Pass near the Pont y Cromlech. There are three climbing areas: the Nose, a clean detached "pinnacle", and the East and West Wings on either side of it.

The Black Cleft, on the West Wing, was climbed by J. M. A. Thomson in 1897. Other notable ascents are:

1930 The Cracks – B. L. and H. C. H. Bathurst
The Direct Route – Kirkus, Cooper, Macphee
1931 Western Slabs – Edwards, Edge, D'Aeth
West Rib – Kirkus, Waller
1938 Diagonal Route – Birtwistle, Parkinson
1961 The Mole – Brown, Langmuir
1962 Plexus – Ingle, Crew
Guidebook: *Cwm Glas*, by P. Crew and I. Roper.

DISTRESS SIGNALS
The International Alpine Distress Signal

(commonly used in Britain) consists of six blasts on a whistle (or flashes on a lamp) in a minute, repeated at minute intervals. If no signal equipment is available then any kind of simple signal can be used, for example a red anorak, waved six times. If a flare gun is carried then a red flare indicates distress.

It is immensely comforting to distressed parties to know that their calls have been seen and a reply such as three flashes on the lamp, or a white flare, will suffice. These should not be used in the course of an actual rescue without the team leader's permission in case they confuse the command signals of the rescue party.

In remote country, distress signals are sometimes laid out so that they can be seen by searching aircraft – usually the letters S O S laid out in stones or coloured clothing.

The International Distress Signal was first proposed by a sub-committee of the Alpine Club in 1894 and subsequently universally adopted.

DODERO TEST
The series of tests carried out on climbing ropes to determine their breaking strain, extensibility, weight, construction, stability, material and finish. A rope sample must pass the tests before it is accepted for the U. I. A. A. standard. The test is named after the man who designed it.

DOLOMITE ROCK
Magnesium limestone, the peculiar qualities of which give rise to the towers and pinnacles of the Dolomites. The rock (and area) takes its name from a French geologist, Déodat de Gratet, Marquis de Dolomieu (1750-1801), who visited the Dolomites in 1789 and wrote about the strange quality of the rock. The word 'dolomite' seems to have been established by 1802.

Besides the Dolomites themselves, the rock occurs in several parts of the Alps: Vercors, Royannais, Dévoluy (all near Grenoble) and Pizzo Columbe (near the St Gotthard Pass), whose peaks culminate in the Alperschellihorn near the Splügen Pass (the "Splügen Dolomites"), and the three peaks of the Piz d'Ela group in the Albula Alps. As a dolomite peak, the Piz d'Ela is only exceeded in height by the Marmolata. There are also the Brenta Dolomites, which have the closest affinity with the Dolomites proper.

Dolomite rock is found in England at Brassington (qv), Derbyshire, where it has been well developed for climbing, and in the Cresswell Gorge.

DOLOMITES
A remarkable area of rocky peaks in the NE corner of Italy in what was, until 1918, the Austrian South Tyrol. The political change has meant that most peaks and villages have both German and Italian names. The principal peaks lie south of Brunico and east of the Adige valley (Trento) and do, in fact, cross the border into Austria with the lesser-known Lienzer Dolomites. An important sub-group, the Brenta Dolomites, lies west of the Adige, adjacent to the Adamello-Presanella Alps.

The highest peak of the Dolomites is Marmolata (3,342m) but it is the steep walls and towers, and the unusual rock, which attract climbers and height is of less importance here than almost anywhere else in the Alps. There are rock climbs of all standards, including the highest, and the area is extremely popular.

No one centre is ideal for all the peaks, but for those on the east, Cortina d'Ampezzo offers good communications and for the west, Canazei is a favourite base. For the Brenta group, Pinzolo or Madonna di Campiglio are suitable. There are numerous huts.

The first ascent of a Dolomite peak was that of Monte Pelmo by John Ball in 1857. Of the many hard climbs, most famous is that of the Cima Grande North Face (E. Comici, A. and J. Dimai, 1933).

Guidebooks: *Dolomites East*, by J. Brailsford, and *Dolomites West*, by J. Brailsford.

DOLPHIN, Arthur Rhodes (1924–53)
A Yorkshire man who began climbing as a schoolboy at Almscliff in 1939. He soon showed considerable flair and made the crag very much his own. Notable first ascents are: Great Western (1943) and Birdlime Traverse (1946).

Dolphin turned his talents to the Lake District and in 1948 made the first ascent of Kipling's Groove (with J. B. Lockwood) – for long regarded as the hardest climb in Langdale. Other notable climbs were Kneewrecker Chimney (1949), Rubicon Groove (1951), Sword of Damocles (1952) and Dunmail Cracks (1952), all in the Langdale area. The finest ascent of all was that of Deer Bield Buttress (1951, with A. D. Brown) – one of the Lake District's outstanding problems.

In 1952, having completed his guide-

(*left*) 8 Balance. A young climber demonstrates balance on a gritstone slab. Note how the heels are held down and the hands kept about shoulder height. (*right*) 9 Belay. The usual belay using sling and krab. The route is an easy one with ample ledges and belay spikes. (*below*) 10 Traversing. A traverse goes across a cliff. This is the Black Belt, Craig Ddu, Snowdonia. Note the runner.

11 ABSEILING. A climber makes a roped descent on the Jagigrat, a typical Alpine ridge near Saas Fee, Switzerland.

12 AID CLIMBING (ARTIFICIAL CLIMBING). Using double rope on Twikker, a climb on Millstone Edge, Peak District.

book to Langdale, he turned his attention to the East Buttress of Scafell and put up Hell's Groove and Pegasus.

Though he suffered from mountain sickness at greater heights, he made a solo ascent of the Aig. du Géant in 1953 and was killed in the descent.

DONKIN, William Frederick (1845-88)
Visited the Caucasus with Dent (*qv*) in 1886 and made the first ascent of Gestola. Returned in 1888 with Dent and Fox. After Dent's return, Donkin and Fox continued their tour and were killed in attempting Koshtantau, together with the guides Streich and Fischer.

Donkin was unquestionably one of the finest mountain photographers who ever lived; for his day he was quite outstanding. He was rivalled, but not excelled, by Vittorio Sella (*qv*). For examples of his work see the A. C. Centenary volume, 1957. The A. C. have a complete collection of his photographs.

DOUGLAS, Lord Francis William Bouverie (1847-65)
Second son of the Marquess of Queensberry, who died in the Matterhorn tragedy (see WHYMPER). Douglas had two previous seasons in the Alps and had shown himself a good climber. In 1865 he made the first ascent of the Trifthorn, Unter Gabelhorn and Wellenkuppe and the second ascent of the Gabelhorn (the day after Moore's first ascent).

DOVE CRAG (2,603 ft)
A fell in the Fairfield range of the Lake District which has a bold and difficult crag of the same name. The crag looks down Dovedale and this is the best approach. With few exceptions the climbs are extremely difficult.
Guidebook: *Eastern Crags*, by H. Drasdo and J. Soper.

DOVEDALE (DERBYSHIRE)
Famous beauty spot on Derbyshire–Staffordshire boundary with a number of limestone pinnacles, all yielding climbs. Ilam Rock is best known. In the nearby Manifold Valley are Beeston Tor and Thor's Cave; crags giving long, hard climbs.
Guidebook: *The Southern Limestone Area*, by P. Nunn.

DOVESTONES
A long edge of gritstone overlooking Greenfield, near Oldham, with many climbs of all standards. On the right of the edge are the two famous Dovestones Quarries where the climbs are mostly long and hard. The development of these quarries, especially Main Quarry, by Brown, West and others, gave impetus to quarry climbing in the 1950s. The Greenfield area has a number of other quarries where climbing takes place, notably Den Lane Quarry near Uppermill.
Guidebook: *Chew Valley Area* (Rock Climbs in the Peak Vol. 2).

DOW CRAG
A large crag in the Coniston Fells, Lake District, with many fine climbs, especially in the middle and upper grades. There are five main buttresses (A to E) separated by fine gullies.

The crag was a favourite with the pioneers, and the climbs done by the Hopkinsons, Broadricks, Abrahams and Woodhouses, for example, were outstanding for their day. The crag has had a recent revival and a number of hard new routes have been done.
Guidebook: *Dow Crag Area*, by D. Miller.

DUFF, Donald (1893-1968)
Inventor of the Duff Stretcher for mountain rescue and first Chairman of the Mountain Rescue Committee for Scotland.

DUHAMEL, Henri (1853-1917)
French climber noted for his Alpine topographical work, especially in the Dauphiné, where he made a number of first ascents. The Pyramide Duhamel on the Meije is named after him.

DÜLFER, Hans (1893–1915)
A brilliant young rock-climber famous for his ascents in the Kaisergebirge and Dolomites and, like Mummery, a legend in his own lifetime. The lay-back (*qv*) is known as "à la Dulfer", and it was he who first proposed the form of gradings later perfected by Welzenbach (*qv*). Dülfer was killed at Arras while serving in the Bavarian army. Among his many new climbs two of the best known are: East Face, Fleischbank, 1912 (with W. Schaarschmidt), West Face, Cima Grande, Dolomites, 1913 (with Wa. von Bernuth).

DUNOD, Francois Henri
A Captain in the French army who made

the second ascents of the Charmoz and Grépon, and whose use of three ladders on the latter provoked a sly comment from Mummery. Dunod also made the first traverse of the Drus (1887).

DUVET (E: Eiderdown)

Jackets, trousers, waistcoats and socks made of duvet material are available to mountaineers, but the word by itself when used by climbers refers to the duvet jacket. Duvets are basically heavily quilted anoraks which open down the front like a jacket. They form the best practical insulation against extreme cold. Some are waterproof, but they are usually worn with a cagoule (*qv*) over the top.

DYHRENFURTH, Gunter Oscar (b. 1886)

A geologist and leader of international expeditions to Kangchenjunga, 1930 and to the Baltoro region, 1934. On the former a number of peaks were climbed, notably Jongsong (24,344 ft). Dyhrenfurth was awarded the Olympic Gold Medal, 1936. He has written a number of books about the Alps and Himalayas.

DYHRENFURTH, Norman

A Swiss-American who took part in the second Swiss attempt on Everest in the post-monsoon period of 1952, and organized the great American expedition of 1963. He also took part in an expedition to Lhotse in 1955. In 1971 he organized the large international expedition to attempt the South-West Face of Everest. The expedition received massive publicity but failed amidst considerable acrimony on the part of the participants. Son of G. O. Dyhrenfurth (*qv*).

ECCLES, James (1838–1915)

A fine climber of the second generation of pioneers, responsible for the first ascents of several peaks and cols in the Mont Blanc area, including Cols Infranchissible, de Toule and des Flambeaux (1870), Aig. du Plan (1871), Aig. de Rochefort (1873), Mont Blanc de Courmayeur (1877), Aig. du Tacul (1880) and Dome de Rochefort (1881).

Eccles always had as guides the Payot brothers and it was with them that he made his most famous expedition, the ascent of the Peuterey Ridge from near the Col Peuterey to Mont Blanc de Courmayeur (1877). They approached via the Brouillard Glacier and camped below what is now Pic Eccles, site of the Eccles bivouac hut. Next day they crossed a col to the upper Freney Glacier (Col Eccles) and so to the ridge. It was a remarkable expedition, long unrepeated, the first to be done on this difficult face of Mont Blanc.

In 1878 Eccles and Michel Payot visited the Rocky Mountains of Colorado and Utah where they climbed Wind River Peak and Fremont's Peak. Eccles was an outstanding photographer.

ECKENSTEIN; Oscar Johannes Ludwig (1859-1921)

Born in London of a German father and English mother. Eckenstein was an Original Member of the Climbers' Club and played a part in the exploration of Lliwedd with J. M. A. Thomson (*qv*). His Alpine career seems to have begun in 1886 when he climbed with Lorria (*qv*). He later made new routes on the Dom and Dent Blanche, neither of great importance.

In 1892 he was with Conway (*qv*) in the Karakoram but soon left the party after disagreements with his leader. In 1900 he visited Mexico and climbed Popacatapetl with Crowley (*qv*). He organized his own expedition to K2 in 1902, making Crowley second-in-command. Despite numerous troubles (see CROWLEY), two members of the team, Guillarmot and Wesseley, reached 21,400 ft.

Eckenstein's greatest contribution to climbing was his application of engineering principles to the sport and its equipment. He redesigned crampons (*qv*), introduced the short ice axe, established which knots were strongest and above all, preached the virtues of balance climbing.

Eckenstein was an individualist and though he had many friends in the climbing world, his revolutionary outlook and his acquaintance with Crowley made him unpopular with the Establishment.

EDWARDS, John Menlove (1910-58)

A Liverpool climber noted for daring escapades and for his exploration of Welsh cliffs which earlier climbers had ignored. Edwards's acceptance of "bad rock" was a significant breakthrough in British climbing and is best represented by his exploration of the Three Cliffs of Llanberis Pass, Dinas Cromlech, Carreg Wastad and Clogwyn y Grochan, now great favourites with climbers. His most popular routes include: Spiral Stairs (1931), Crackstone Rib, Hazel Groove (1935), Brant and Slape (1940).

His exploration of the Devil's Kitchen cliffs (15 new routes) led to his compiling the Cwm Idwal guidebook for the Climbers' club (1933). In 1937 he compiled (with Noyce) the guidebook to Tryfan, for which they solved the problem of Soapgut (1936), and made the second (first unaided) ascent of Munich Climb. His last guidebook was Lliwedd (1939), for which he made the first ascent of Central Gully Direct (1938).

Other notable climbs include: first unaided ascent of Flake Crack, Scafell (in nails, 1931), Chimney Route, Clogwyn du'r Arddu (1931), Western Slabs, Dinas Mot (1931), Bow Shaped Slab, Clogwyn du'r Arddu (1941).

Increasing disappointment over his work as a psychiatrist led to his suicide in 1958. (See *Samson*, by G. Sutton and W. Noyce.)

EIGER (3,970 m)

A mountain in the Bernese Alps overlooking Grindelwald (*qv*) and easily accessible from K1. Scheidegg (*qv*). One of the most publicized mountains in the world, due to the various attempts on its great North Face (actually North West), the Eigerwand.

The mountain has three principal ridges and faces. The W Ridge and Face, in combination, is fairly easy and was used in the first ascent. (C. Barrington with C. Almer and P. Bohren, 1858). It descends directly to Kl. Scheidegg. The S Ridge connects with the Mönch via the Eigerjoch, and the S Face (a difficult climb about which little seems known) overlooks the Fieschergletscher. Running NE from the summit is the long Mittelegi Ridge, descended by M. Kuffner with Burgener, Biener and Kalbermatten in 1885 but not climbed until 1921 by Y. Maki with F. Amatter, F. Steuri and S. Brawand. The N Face proper is on the Grindelwald side of this ridge and is separated from the Eigerwand by a rib (The Lauper Route – H. Lauper, A. Zürcher with J. Knubel and A. Graven. 1932). The Eigerwand itself is a vast triangular concave face.

The first serious attempt at the Eigerwand was in 1935 by M. Seldmayer and K. Mehringer, who were killed by a storm at Death Bivouac. In 1936 came the tragedy of E. Rainer, W. Angerer, A. Hinterstoisser and T. Kurz who died on the face despite dramatic rescue attempts. It was finally climbed by A. Heckmair, W. Vorg, H. Harrer and F. Kasparek in 1938. This is now known as the Original or 1938 Route and has been climbed many times, including solo. Many climbers have also been killed attempting it. Two more direct routes were made by an international party (Harlin Route, 1966) and a Japanese party (1969) and two routes on the North Pillar (Polish Route, 1968 and Scottish Route, 1970).

The rock of the Eigerwand is limestone and though there are no pitches technically more difficult than V.S., there is always the danger of stonefall. Almost every part of the 1938 Route has a name: well-known features are: the Difficult Crack, Hinterstoisser Traverse, Swallow's Nest, First Icefield, Ice Hose, Second Ice Field, Flatiron, Death Bivouac, Third Icefield, The Ramp, the Ice Bulge, Brittle Ledge, Traverse of the Gods, the Spider and the Exit Cracks. These names give some indication of the route and the problems involved. (See *The White Spider*, by H. Harrer and *Eiger Direct*, by P. Gillman and D. Haston.)

ELAN VALLEY

In Radnorshire, Wales. The valley, well known for its reservoirs, has a number of crags offering climbs up to 200 ft. The chief ones are: Careg Dhu, Craig y Foel and Cerig Gwynion.

EL CAPITAN (7,564 ft)

A peak in the Yosemite, California, which throws down immense walls to the valley and Merced River below. It stands on the true right bank of the river about two miles below Yosemite village, and thus, in driving up the valley, it is one of the first cliffs to be encountered. Its startling appearance is more than equalled by the climbing on it: 'El Cap' provides the epitome of Yosemite climbing. All the routes mentioned below are hard; they rank with the most difficult rock climbs in the world.

The impressive profile of the cliff, rising sheer for some 3,000 ft, is formed by the Nose, where the SW and SE Faces meet. Beyond the SW Face is the West Buttress and beyond the SE Face a long wall terminating in the East Buttress. The rock is granite: immense smooth walls and difficult cracks, with many overhangs. Pegging and bolting is essential, though there is hard free climbing too. The routes are multi-day (grade VI) and some bivouacs require hammocks. As in all big Yosemite climbs, water shortage (dehydration) is a major problem. The pegs are removed on each ascent, and this has led to bad scarring of the cracks. Nuts are now being used when possible.

In 1952, A. Steck, W. Siri, W. Dunmire and R. Swift climbed up the east wall to a pine tree some 400 ft above the ground (El Cap Tree Route), but the first complete ascent of the cliff took place the following year when Steck and Siri, with W. Unsoeld and W. Long climbed East Buttress in three days. The first big frontal attack took place in 1957-8 with Warren Harding's 18-month seige of the Nose, begun because another party had snatched the NW Face of Half Dome, which he had contemplated climbing himself. With various partners, Harding spent a total of 47 days on the rock, employing 3,000 ft of fixed rope, 675 pegs and 125 bolts. In 1960 the ascent was repeated by J. Fitschen, T. Frost, C. Pratt, R. Robbins in a single seven-day push. The Nose has become the most popular of the El Capitan climbs. It was soloed in 1969 by T. Bauman in six days.

Siege tactics were employed on the first ascent of Dihedral Wall in 1962 by E. Cooper, J. Baldwin and G. Denny, and semi-seige tactics on a few other routes, but generally Royal Robbins's view that seige tactics are unethical has prevailed.

The first breach of the SE Face was North America Wall, climbed in 1964 by Y. Chouinard, T. Frost, R. Robbins and C. Pratt in ten days. Not repeated for four years, it was regarded at the time as a breakthrough in climbing, but has since received less acclaim. More controversial was the ascent by Warren Harding and Dean Caldwell of the Wall of Early Morning Light (Dawn Wall) in 1970 which took 27 days and 300 bolts. It is the longest (time) of any rock-climb in the world. Repeated by Robbins and D. Lauria in 1971 in six days, and soloed by C. Porter (with a variant start) in 1972 in ten days.

The first solo 1st ascent was of Cosmos by J. Dunn in 1972. The first foreign ascent of any route was the Nose, by two French climbers, J. DuPont and A. Gauci, 1966. The first British ascent was the Nose, by M. Burke, R. Wood, 1968. First woman's ascent was the Nose, by Joanna Marte 1971, led by Robbins.

Important first ascents
(W = SW face or W buttress; E = SE face or E buttress; d = days taken)
1953 East Buttress (E) (3d) – A. Steck, W. Siri, W. Unsoeld, W. Long
1958 The Nose (47d) – W. Harding, W. Merry, G. Whitmore
1961 Salathé Wall (W) (9d) – T. Frost, R. Robbins, C. Pratt
1962 Dihedral Wall (W) (40d) – E. Cooper, J. Baldwin, G. Denny
1963 West Buttress (W) (8d) – L. Kor, S. Roper
1964 North America Wall (E) (10d) – Y. Chouinard, T. Frost, R. Robbins, C. Pratt
1965 Muir Wall (W) (8d) – Y. Chouinard, T. M. Herbert
1967 West Face (W) (5d) – R. Robbins, T. M. Herbert
1970 Heart Route (W) (9d) – S. Davis, C. Kroger
       Wall of Early Morning Light (E) (27d) – W. Harding. D. Caldwell
1971 Aquarius (W) (3d) – K. Schmitz, J. Bridwell
       Son of Heart (W) (10d) – R. Sylvester, C. Wreford-Brown
1972 Magic Mushroom (W) (8d) – H. Burton, S. Sutton
       Cosmos (W) (9d) – J. Dunn (solo)
       The Shield ((7d) – C. Porter, G. Bocarde
       Zodiac (E) (7d) – C. Porter (solo)
       New start to WEML–C. Porter (solo)

Guidebook: *A Climbers' Guide to Yosemite Valley*, by S. Roper.

ELIMINATE
A name sometimes given to a direct line up a crag and always of a high standard. The three Eliminates of Dow Crag, Lake District, are well known: Eliminate A, Eliminate B and Eliminate C, up A Buttress, B Buttress and C Buttress respectively. With the modern high standards of climbing, the term is somewhat archaic.

ELLIOT, Julius Marshall (1841–69)
The Rev. J. M. Elliot was the first man to climb the Matterhorn from Zermatt after the accident of 1865 (1868). His guides were J. M. Lochmatter and P. Knubel. Tyndall (*qv*) traversed the mountain next day.

In the Lake District, Elliot took part in the first ascent of the Slab and Notch Route on Pillar (1863) and made one of the earliest "record" fell-walks, the Head of Wasdale, in eight and a half hours (1864).

Elliot was killed while climbing the Schreckhorn unroped.

EMERY, John Arthur Gillah (1933-63)
A talented climber and a survivor of the Haramosh expedition (1957) from which he received severe frostbite injuries. He overcame his handicaps and began climbing again, but was killed on the Weisshorn. Emery was a doctor.

ENGELHORNER
A small range of sharply pointed limestone peaks rising above the hamlet of Rosenlaui in the Bernese Oberland. The nearest town is Meiringen. The Engelhorner peaks are much favoured by rock-climbers. The highest summit is Gross Gstellihorn (2,854 m) but the favourite area is the Semilistock – Kingspitze area. Most climbs are medium to hard in grade. The Engelhorner Hut serves the group.

Guidebook: *Engelhorner and Salbitschijen*, by J. Talbot.

ESTCOURT, Nicholas John (b. 1942)
A computer programmer from Cheshire. Estcourt made a number of fine Alpine climbs, including the first British ascent of the Gervasutti Pillar, Mont Blanc de Tacul (1967) and the first ascent of the NW Face of the Pic Sans Nom (1967). In 1971, with Bonington, he made the first ascent of the White Wizard, one of the hardest routes on Scafell.

Estcourt's first expedition was to East Greenland in 1963, where he made eight first ascents. He took part in the 1970 Annapurna South Face expedition and the 1972 Everest SW Face expedition. In 1973, with Bonington, he reached the summit of Brammah Peak (Kishtwar Himal), a major breakthrough in approaching fairly big Himalayan peaks in an Alpine manner, rather than with a large expedition.

ETHICS OF CLIMBING

Because climbing is a sport which has no rules or laws laid down by a governing body (indeed, has no governing body), the *way* in which an ascent is made is left entirely to the climber. To take extreme cases, there is nothing to stop a man bolting his way to the top of Napes Needle and using every protective device known to science, or, on the other hand, attempting Everest naked in winter. In neither case would he get far, of course – in the first instance he would probably be lynched by irate climbers and in the second he would die of exposure. Between these extremes, the right tactics become less certain, and the discussion of these is called the ethics of climbing.

Ethics have concerned climbers since the early days of the sport – take the examples of Dunod's ladders on the Grépon and the hacking of Collie's step on Scafell – but they have become more serious since the introduction of modern equipment, particularly the peg, the bolt and the chock. When should these be used for aid, and when merely for protection? Until the 1950s it was generally believed in Britain that no aid should be used at all; if the climb was too difficult for one climber, it should be left until a better man came along. But this policy would deny such climbs as the Kilnsey overhang. Anyway, is not the ancient craft of cutting steps in ice making aids? The trend among the best climbers is to *reduce* the aid used on a route, whether it be bolts or step-cutting.

Another major field of ethics is the employment of seige tactics (*qv*). Some of these have aroused great controversy, for instance, Harding's ascent of the Nose on El Capitan, Yosemite, and Maestri's ascent of Cerro Torre.

There is also the question of what constitutes a genuine winter ascent of a route; obviously there are winters when, apart from it being colder, a route may be no different than in summer. Is it a winter ascent, with all that that implies?

It says much for the quality of the sport that despite the many problems and paradoxes, a highly ethical attitude is taken by the vast majority of climbers.

ETHIOPIA, CLIMBING IN

A mountainous kingdom in East Africa. There are nine major ranges, some, like the Batu, with summits up to 14,000 ft and scarcely known. The highest mountain in Ethiopia is Ras Dashan (Dejen) (15,159 ft), first ascended by Ferret and Galinier in 1841. The peak stands in the Simien Range near Gondar. There are a number of others over 14,000 ft but they are mostly easy to climb, with the exception of some notable pinnacles. Travel is difficult and it is doubtful whether any real climbing has been done.

ETIVE SLABS (TRILLEACHAN SLABS)

Unique smooth slabs giving some long and hard climbs on the S Face of Beinn Trilleachan, Glen Etive, Scotland. The first route was by E. Langmuir and party (Sickle, 1954). The climbs had a great vogue in the early sixties.

Guidebook: *Climbers' Guide to Glencoe and Ardgour* Vol 2, by L.S. Lovat.

ÉTRIERS (Fr.) (G.: Steigleiter; It.: Staffa; Am.: Stirrups, Tapes)

Small portable steps used in artificial climbing (*qv*). The two main types are metal étriers and webbing étriers.

Metal étriers have alloy steps about 15 cm long by 3 cm wide, drilled and eyeleted near each end to take 5 mm perlon rope. The étrier will have two or three such steps (individual preference), rarely more. The steps are about 50 cm apart, held in place by a knot *below* the step (it is essential that the step can slide *up* the étrier when needed). There is a loop above the top step for attaching the étrier to a karabiner or fifi hook (*qv*) and below the bottom step because it is useful to be able to connect one étrier to another, by karabiner. Climbers usually buy the steps and make up their own étriers to suit themselves – a two-step étrier needs about 3 m of rope.

Tape or webbing étriers are simply long lengths of nylon tape, 1½ inches or 2 inches wide, tied off into loops with a tape knot (see KNOTS). The loops are then divided off into steps by overhand knots, with a small loop at the top for the karabiner. Alternatively, they can be purchased ready-made with the steps stitched in place. The advantages of tape étriers are that they do not tangle, are lighter and more comfortable. Their chief disadvantage is that they

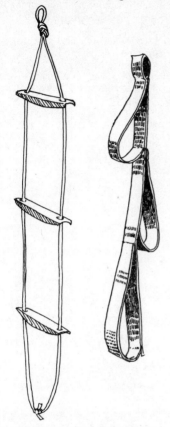

can be difficult to get one's feet into.

EVANS, Sir Robert Charles (b. 1918)
Charles Evans was one of a small group of promising climbers in the immediate post-war years that Tilman was persuaded to take on his Nepal journey of 1950. They attempted Annapurna IV (24,688 ft), and Evans, in the first assault, reached a height of about 24,000 ft. In 1951 he was in the party which attempted Deo Tibba in Kulu, and in 1952 was with Shipton on Cho Oyu. In 1953 he was Deputy Leader of the successful Everest expedition, and was with Hillary and others in an expedition to the Barun Glacier the following year. In 1955 he was leader of the successful Kangchenjunga expedition.

In 1957 Evans married Nea Morin, who is also a considerable mountaineer. President of the Alpine Club, 1967–70. Principal of the University College of North Wales. His books are: *Eye on Everest* (1955), *On Climbing* (1956) and *Kangchenjunga – The Untrodden Peak* (1956).

EXPEDITION
A journey to attempt some specific objective such as climbing a mountain or surveying a mountain area. The word is used also to refer to the corpus of people involved. In early climbing literature the word was used to describe almost any journey above the snowline, but nowadays it is reserved for journeys to remote areas. Even so, the definition is blurred and vague: with increasing ease of transport it frequently happens today that two or three friends visit some remote area for a climbing holiday, and may even ascend a new peak. One thinks particularly of Greenland, Arctic Canada and the Hindu Kush. Is such a journey an expedition in the modern accepted sense?

Expeditions take a name for themselves usually descriptive of their aims or composition, for example the British-Pakistani Karakorum expedition. There is a Leader and usually, Deputy Leader. On a small expedition the rest are known simply as members, though each will have some job allotted to him besides climbing. On large expeditions these jobs usually carry titles, Transport Officer, etc. On a large expedition the Leader may or may not take an actual part in the climbing. Sometimes Himalayan expeditions make the senior Sherpas full members of the expedition, for example, Tenzing on Everest. The actual number of members can vary – on a very large expedition it can run to dozens, though many will be specialists, and include surveyors, botanists, and so on.

The number of people involved depends largely on the objective, though there are divergent philosophies about even large objectives. The vast expeditions such as those of Conway, the Duke of the Abruzzi, and the earlier Everest expeditions, have been challenged in concept by climbers like Tilman (*qv*). Both large and small expeditions have an equal record of success and failure. On the whole, however, when the objective is a major one, the large expedition has been the norm.

The organization of an expedition, especially a large one, takes time and money. Sponsorship is necessary, from the media and other sources – the 1972 Everest SW Face Expedition, for example, cost £60,000. In Britain, financial aid may be granted by the Mount Everest Foundation (*qv*).

Details showing the organization of a modern expedition can be read in the appendices to Bonington's books: *Annapurna South Face*, and *Everest, SW Face*.

EXPOSURE

1. An exposed climb is one where a sense of space predominates: the "fly on the wall" syndrome. It is compounded from the steepness and sheerness of the rock and the height above ground level. Difficulty does not enter into it, though the more difficult climbs tend also to be the more exposed climbs. Similarly, one can speak of "an exposed move".

2. Hypothermia. A common but serious condition brought on by a loss of deep body heat due to excessive chilling of the skin. Usually caused by bad weather: wind, rain, snowstorms, especially when associated with hard physical effort which itself leads to exhaustion. The symptoms are: unreasonableness, tiredness and coldness, lethargy, failure of vision, slurred speech, excessive shivering, collapsing. Severe cases can lead to death. The treatment is to protect the victim *immediately* from further effort and to insulate the whole body with a sleeping bag to prevent further heat loss. Hot glucose drinks help, but not alcohol. The mountain rescue service should be called out and the victim examined by a doctor as soon as possible.

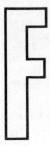

FARMER, Sir John Bretland (1867–1944)
One of the pioneers of Lliwedd in Wales, along with Andrews, Eckenstein, Thomson, etc. His best-known climb is probably Central Chimney, 1908. He was a distinguished botanist.

FARRAR, John Percy (1857-1929)
Farrar was one of the strongest climbers in the Alps at the turn of the century. Though his first ascents were minor he completed almost every difficult climb known, often making the second or third ascent. He also climbed in S. Africa, Canada and Japan. He was President of the A. C. 1917-19. Farrar is little heard of today, but his record is outstanding, and during his lifetime he was rightly regarded as one of the greatest living alpinists. He was elected an honorary member of almost every national Alpine club.

FAY, Charles Ernest (1846-1931)
Though he did not begin mountaineering until he was 50 years old, Fay was one of the pioneers of Canadian and American climbing. Between 1895 and 1903 he made twelve first ascents in the Canadian Rockies. It was he who persuaded the Appalachian Club to visit the Rockies and thus spread the idea of greater mountaineering in the U. S. He helped to found the American Alpine Club and was its first president. Fay was a professor of Modern Languages at Boston.

FELLENBERG, Edmund von (1838-1902)
A distinguished archeologist and mineralogist from Bern. With the exception of a visit to the Tatra in 1860, his climbing was confined to the Bernese Alps which he visited for geological purposes. His first ascents include: Doldenhorn and Kleine Doldenhorn (1862), Silberhorn (1863), Ochs (1864), Lauterbrunnen Breithorn, Gross Grünhorn (1865), Wellhorn (1866),

Bietschorn traverse (1867) and Birghorn (1872). He also made many second and third ascents of famous peaks and crossed many cols.
A member of the A.C. and an Original Member of the S.A.C., of which he was the first secretary.

FIELD, Alfred Ernest (1864-1949)
Pioneer rock-climber who made the first ascents of Walker's Gully, Pillar Rock with Jones and G. D. Abraham (1898) and Route II, Lliwedd with Abraham and Nettleton (1905). He made a number of good Alpine climbs, including the first traverse of the Sans Nom Ridge to the Verte (1902).

FIFI HOOK
A metal hook fitted to the top of an étrier (*qv*) so that the latter can be clipped directly into a peg. The fifi has a thin cord attaching it to the climber's harness so that as he steps up, the étrier below him is automatically pulled up too. It makes artificial climbing (*qv*) much quicker and also eliminates the chance of dropping an étrier. A griff fifi incorporates a handle and is easier to use.

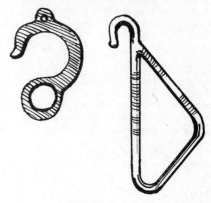

FILIPPI, Filippo de (1869-1938)
A surgeon and noted mountaineer who joined the Duke of the Abruzzi's expedition to Alaska in 1897 and to the Karakorum in 1909. In 1913-14 he conducted his own scientific expedition to the Karakorum: one of the most detailed and painstaking ever carried out. He wrote detailed books about the Duke's expeditions and his own. (See ABRUZZI.)

FINCH, George Ingle (1888-1970)
A climber noted for his icemanship and his

advocacy of oxygen equipment for high altitudes.

His notable Alpine routes were: N Face of Castor (1909), SSW Ridge of the Midi (1911), W Ridge of the Bifertenstock (1913), N Face of the Dent d'Herens (1923). He was chosen for the Everest expedition of 1921, but failed on medical grounds. He was a member of the 1922 team and made a valiant attempt on the summit with G. Bruce, reaching a record height for the time of 27,300 ft. He used primitive oxygen apparatus and was always expounding the advantages it gave him. Critical of the route chosen on Everest, his relationship with the Everest Committee became strained and he took no further part in expeditions.

His active climbing career virtually ended after 1931 when he was involved in an accident on the Jungfrau in which one of his partners was killed. His book, *The Making of a Mountaineer*, was published in 1924. He was President of the A.C. 1959-61.

In private life, Finch was a distinguished scientist.

FIRMIN, Arthur Herbert (1912-55)

Kenyan mountaineer and photographer of distinction. Firmin made ten expeditions each to Mt Kenya and Kilimanjaro and three to Ruwenzori. Notable ascents include first ascent of the N Face of Batian (1944), first ascent of S Face and SW Ridge of Batian (1946), first descent of the N Face of Batian (1948) and first ascent of the W Face of Nelion (1949). His wife was the first woman to reach the main summit of Mt Kenya and of Alexandra Peak, Ruwenzori. As a professional photographer, Firmin's work was known throughout the world.

FIRST AID

Because of the remoteness of their environment it is essential that climbers should have a good working knowledge of first aid, and the equipment to apply it. They may be required to treat: simple cuts and sprains or other minor illnesses; more serious injuries due to an accident; exposure; frostbite. In certain areas other special hazards may need to be taken into account, snakebites for example. An ability to recognize the seriousness of an injury and its nature is perhaps even more vital than the treatment, especially if rescue is fairly simple.

The steps involved are more complicated than in normal conditions: it may be difficult to reach the patient and the patient may need to be secured against further injury, either by belaying him to the cliff or removing him from a dangerous area, perhaps away from a possible stonefall.

Each climber should carry a small personal first-aid pack to deal with simple emergencies (of all kinds). A typical kit contains elastoplast strips, wound dressing, burn dressing, triangular bandage, aspirin, insect repellant, poly bag, toilet paper, matches and emergency food. In addition, each party should carry between them extra items such as inflatable splints, flares, small stove and pan, emergency sleeping bag. In both cases, the items will vary according to the conditions and what is being attempted; the time of year, weather, and the difficulties of retreat/rescue should be taken into account.

A comprehensive account of treatments is given in *First Aid*, the official manual of the British Red Cross Society, St John Ambulance Brigade and St Andrew's Ambulance Association. (See also ACCIDENTS, MOUNTAIN RESCUE, EXPOSURE, FROSTBITE)

FIRST ASCENTS

The recognized ultimate in achievement on any mountain or climb, and the chief goal of many climbers. Any first ascent counts in this respect, though obviously, the harder the climb the greater the achievement. First ascents are usually recorded in the appropriate journal for the district involved, and ultimately, in the guidebooks. Failure to report first ascents invariably leads to later confusion and inaccuracy: climbing history is littered with claims and counter claims. The phrase 'first known ascent' is sometimes used to denote that a climb is suspected of having a previous ascent. There are many instances where first ascents are known to have taken place but where details are lacking.

The historical details of a first ascent usually include the full names of the participants, the exact date of ascent, and in the case of long climbs (e.g. the Alps), the time taken and aid used. A convention is generally employed in guidebooks when noting the names of participants:

A. Smith and B. Jones – means that Smith led the climb

A. Smith and B. Jones (alt. leads) – means that the leading was shared

A. Smith and B. Jones with C. Kaufmann and K. Schmidt – means that Kaufmann and Schmidt were professional guides, Kaufmann being senior

A. Smith and B. Jones, C. Kaufmann and K. Schmidt – means that two ascents were made simultaneously

A. Smith (solo) – means that Smith climbed it alone

The honours attached to a first ascent can be extended considerably, particularly to hard climbs or difficult peaks. The following is a list of ascents usually considered noteworthy:

first ascent of a peak
first traverse of a peak
first ascents of alternate routes
first unaided ascent of pegged routes
first solo ascent
first winter ascents of the foregoing
first ascent on skis (or descent in certain cases)
first national ascent (e.g. first British ascent)
first unguided ascent (obsolete)

FITZGERALD, Edward A. (1871-1932)

Perhaps the greatest dilettante of the mountain world. A wealthy man who accompanied Conway (intermittantly) on the "Alps from end to end tour" (see CONWAY) and who, in the same year (1894) visited New Zealand with the objective of climbing Mt Cook, at that time unclimbed. He was beaten to it by local climbers (see NEW ZEALAND ALPS). Nevertheless he and his guide Zurbriggen made several important ascents.

He led a large and expensively equipped expedition to the Andes in 1897 and attempted Aconcagua (qv). He failed 1,500 ft from the summit, but his guide, Zurbriggen, continued to the top. (first ascent). The expedition climbed several other peaks.

On his return, he gave up mountaineering. There was a certain cool rivalry between Fitzgerald and Conway, exemplified in the latter's writings.

Fitzgerald wrote *Climbs in the New Zealand Alps* (1896) and *The Highest Andes* (1899).

FITZGERALD, Gerald (1849-1925)

Irish barrister who made the first ascent of Taschhorn from the Domjoch (1878) and of Aig. de Talefre (1879). He later climbed extensively with Davidson (qv).

FIXED ROPES

Are of two kinds: (1) permanent ropes, chains or hawsers fixed to the popular routes of some Alpine peaks, and (2) ropes fixed by climbers during the course of an expedition lasting several weeks, enabling them to pass up and down the mountain quickly.

Fixed ropes appear on a number of peaks in the Eastern Alps but are relatively rare in the Western Alps. The best-known examples are probably those on the Hörnli and Italian ridges of the Matterhorn and on the Aig. de Géant in the Mont Blanc range. They make easier what would otherwise be fairly difficult pitches and were originally instituted to help guides get their clients to the summit. Though deprecated by modern climbers there seems little chance that the well-known fixed rope pitches will ever disappear from the climbing scene. There are also fixed ropes of a handrail nature on some of the more hazardous Alpine paths.

In the Himalaya fixed ropes are placed between the various camps where necessary to enable porters and climbers to move freely up and down the mountain. On modern Himalayan face climbs this may involve long prusiking pitches using jumars (qv), but it does enable climbers to retreat to Base Camp for rest periods. The same technique has been used occasionally on hard winter Alpine routes, for example, the Eiger Direct, Harlin Route.

Fixed ropes of all types have been known to break and have been the cause of several notorious accidents.

For fixed rope technique on expeditions see *Eiger Direct*, by D. Haston and P. Gillman and *Annapurna South Face*, by C. Bonington.

FLAKE (Fr.: Éccuille, Feuillet)

A leaf of rock adhering to a crag. There is an immense one on Scafell Crag giving rise to the famous Flake Crack. Small flakes give rise to "flake holds" – sometimes brittle.

FONTAINEBLEAU

The woods around this French town contain sandstone outcrops which are great favourites with Parisian climbers. Known as the "Bleau", and *habitués* as "Bleausards".

FORSTER, William Edward (1818-86)

Eminent politician famous for his introduction of elementary education in England (The Forster Act, 1870). Forster was related to the Buxtons (*qv*) and Arnold (*qv*) and was a friend of John Ball (*qv*). He was an enthusiastic mountaineer and, with Ball, made the third ascent of Cima Tosa in the Dolomites (1865).

FOSTER, George Edward (1839/40-1906)
Foster's career is interesting because he made the first ascent of two peaks which subsequently became popular among discerning alpinists: Mont Collon (1866) and Gspaltenhorn (1869). He is also credited with Mont Pleureur and La Singla, but there is serious doubt about the latter. Foster's greatest achievements, however, were in the new routes he put up on established peaks – Midi, Strahlhorn, Dom etc. – thus helping to point the way for future generations. In some respects his career has been seriously overlooked by historians.

In private life Foster was a wealthy banker from Cambridge.

FOWLER, Robert (1824-97)
Irish barrister who made the first ascent of the popular Aig. du Chardonnet (1865) and the Triftjigrat of the Breithorn (1869).

FOX, Joseph Hoyland (1833-1915)
Brother-in-law of F. F. Tuckett (*qv*), whom he accompanied on many of his expeditions, especially in the Eastern Alps. A cousin, C. H. Fox, made the first crossing of the Alphubeljoch with Tuckett in 1861.

FRANCIS, Godfrey Herbert (1927-60)
A geologist who played a leading part in the British Alpine revival after the last war. In 1951 made the first British ascent of the SW Face of the Aig. Mummery and the following year the first British ascents of the S Ridge of the Aig. Noire de Peuterey and Pillars of Freney. An original member of the A. C. G. Wrote a textbook, *Mountain Climbing* (1958). Killed by lightning on Pillar Rock, Lake District.

FREE CLIMBING
As opposed to artificial climbing (*qv*). In Britain a climb is "free" when it is climbed without artificial aids such as pegs and étriers, though chockstone runners are allowed. A few climbs (very few) allow for an aided move such as lassoing a pinnacle or pulling on a jammed chock runner, but these are always mentioned in the guidebooks. The majority of climbs in Britain are free. On the Continent a free climb is one which does not involve étriers.

FRESHFIELD, William Douglas (1845-1934)
One of the greatest of all mountain explorers, Freshfield travelled and climbed in almost every part of the world, from the Alps to Japan, from the Pyrenees to the Himalayas. He is particularly noted for his exploration of the Caucasus (1868, 1887, 1889), and for his tour round Kangchenjunga (1899). He was President of the A.C. 1893-5, and of the Royal Geographical Society 1914-17, and recipient of many honours from Alpine and geographical societies throughout the world.

His mother had been a keen mountain traveller and Freshfield as a boy accompanied her on some of these journeys, which she described in two books: *Alpine Byways* (1861) and *A Summer Tour in the Grisons and Italian Valleys of the Bernina* (1862).

His first major ascent was Mont Blanc in 1863. Thereafter he climbed regularly until 1920 – a career of almost 60 years, spanning every stage in the development of climbing, except the most recent. His companions included almost every great mountaineer of the times.

Freshfield's first ascents in the Alps were mostly in the east and included Presanella, Grosser Mösele, Piz Cengalo, Cima di Brenta and the first traverse of Piz Palu. In the west he made the first ascent of Tour Ronde and Tour du Grand St Pierre.

His visit to the Caucasus in 1868 was the first exploration of that region. He climbed Kasbek and Elbruz (East Peak). In 1887 he climbed Gulba, Tetnuld and Skoda. His visit of 1889 was to search for Donkin (*qv*) and Fox who had mysteriously disappeared, and he found traces of their last bivouac.

With Professor Garwood and the Sella brothers (*qv*) he made an arduous circuit of Kangchenjunga in 1899, the first time it had been attempted, and brought back a detailed description and map of the area.

Freshfield was a considerable author, with an output almost rivalling that of Coolidge (*qv*). Unlike the latter, he was a brilliant descriptive writer and his books were very popular. They are: *From Thonon to Trent* (1865), *Travels in the Central Caucasus and Bashan* (1869), *Italian Alps* (1875), *The Exploration of the Caucasus* (1896), *Round Kangchenjunga* (1903), *Hannibal once more* (1914), *The Life of Horace-Benedict de Saussure* (1920) and *Below the*

Snow Line (1923). He also published two books of verse: *Unto the Hills* (1914) and *Quips for Cranks* (1923). He was Editor of the *A. J.* 1872-80 and twice Chairman of the Society of Authors.

FROSTBITE

Is caused by extreme cold, cold winds, or, in the feet, by tight boots being worn for long periods in snow and ice. It affects the extremities: fingers, toes, ears, nose, lips – the affected part turns putty-coloured and goes numb. Frostbite is caused by ice crystals forming between the cells, allied to a constriction of the minor blood vessels – all of which cuts down the supply of oxygen to the cells and leads to their deterioration and infection.

The only effective treatment is to increase the supply of oxygen, and high altitude oxygen has been used for this on some expeditions. Full treatment can only be given in hospitals with a hyperbaric oxygen tank. The old remedies of rubbing with snow, lashing with ropes and dipping into alternate hot and cold water do not seem effective even as temporary measures. The best emergency treatment is to warm the affected part. The recovery from frostbite is very painful.

FÜHRERBUCH (Fr.: Livret)

An official notebook issued to Alpine guides in which their patrons can write comments on the guide's performance. It is inspected annually. Führerbuchen are of little consequence today, but those of the early guides were highly thought of. There is a collection of early Führerbuchen in the Alpine Club Library and one or two have been printed in facsimile.

FYFE, Thomas C. (d. 1947)

One of the self-taught pioneer guides of the New Zealand Alps, and companion of G. Graham and J. Clark on the first ascent of Mt Cook (1894). Fyfe made first ascents of Footstool, De la Beche, Darby, Montgomery, Graham's Saddle, Fyfe's Pass, Minarets, Haidinger N Peak, and first crossing of Lendenfeld Saddle. An injury sustained during the last climb kept him inactive for about ten years but he made a remarkable return to climbing when, in 1906, he joined Peter Graham to guide Turner and Ross on the transverse of Mt. Cook.

GABBRO
An extremely rough rock offering good friction grip and the principal rock of the Skye Cuillins (*qv*). Gabbro is found in smaller amounts in other British mountain areas and in the Alps.

GAITERS
In winter climbing or Alpine climbing canvas or proofed nylon gaiters are worn to prevent snow entering the boots. Also prevents small stones from moraines, etc., and gives extra warmth to the lower legs. The gaiters hook onto the front bootlace and are zipped up the back. A strap or cord passes under the sole to prevent the gaiter riding up. A small anklet gaiter (stop tou) was once a popular alternative but is now largely out of favour. Puttees were popular with the pioneers (long bandages of cloth wound round the lower legs) but are not seen now.

GALLET, Julien (1858-1934)
Swiss climber noted for his first ascents, particularly in the Oberland. Among his best-known routes are the Galletgrat of the Doldenhorn (1899), the ENE Ridge of Lauterbrunnen Breithorn (1896) and the Gallet Arête of Mont Blanc de Cheilon (1896). Gallet wrote: *Dans l'Alpe ignoré: Explorations et Souvenirs* (1910) and *Derniers Souvenirs de l'Alpe* (1927).

GALTON, Sir Francis (1822-1911)
One of the most distinguished scientists of his age, Galton's interests ranged over a wide field. He was largely responsible for the invention of weather maps and stereometric maps, and also for the discovery of finger-printing as a means of identification. Climbed in the Pyrenees with Packe (*qv*) and ascended Monte Rosa in 1861.

GANGWAY
An inclined ledge on a rock face. A frequent feature of rock-climbs.

GARBH BHEINN OF ARDGOUR
A remote mountain, seven miles west of Corran Ferry, Loch Linnhe, Scotland, giving some long, fine climbs.
Guidebook: *Climbers' Guide to Glencoe and Ardgour* Vol. 2, by L. S. Lovat.

GARDENING
The removal of turf, plants and shrubs from a rock-climb to make the climb cleaner. Gardening often reveals new holds. The process only takes place on first ascents, or on climbs which are fairly new.

GARDINER, Frederick (1850-1919)
A Liverpool shipowner, cousin of the Pilkington brothers (*qv*). Like the Pilkingtons, he was a keen advocate of guideless climbing and of climbing in Britain (he was with R. Pendlebury (*qv*) on Pendlebury's Traverse, Pillar, 1872). In the Alps his first ascents were not notable, though he made the first traverse of the Rothorn in 1873 and the first ascent of Elbruz, Caucasus, in 1874.
It was his guideless first ascents, often with the Pilkingtons and Hulton (*qv*), which were outstanding for the time. They included Ecrins (1878), Meije (1879), Jungfrau from Wengern Alp (1881) and Finsteraarhorn (1881). Coolidge wrote an account of Gardiner's career which was published privately in 1920.

GARWOOD, Edmund Johnstone (1864-1949)
Geologist and explorer who was with Conway (*qv*) in Spitzbergen 1896-7 and with Freshfield (*qv*) during the tour of Kangchenjunga (1899). His map of the latter formed the basis for all subsequent expeditions.

GENDARME (Fr.) (E.: Pinnacle; G.: Turme; It.: Torre)
A free-standing pinnacle on an Alpine ridge. Gendarmes may be quite small or immense. Depending on the route, they are climbed over or avoided by a traverse.

GEORGE, Rev. Hereford Brooke (1838-1910)
With Stephen, Moore and others, played a considerable part in the exploration of the high Alps. Made a number of difficult passes including the first crossings of the

Jungfraujoch and Mischabeljoch (1862) and the Col du Tour Noir (1863, not repeated for 27 years). Took part in the first ascents of Gross Fiescherhorn (1862) and Jungfrau from Wengern Alp (1865).

George was an Original Member of the Climbers' Club. His views on equipment were advanced for the day: he advocated rucksacks instead of knapsacks and an ice axe in preference to the then common alpenstock. Of the latter he said, "personally, I would prefer an umbrella."

He was the founder of the Oxford Alpine Club and the first married don at Oxford. He wrote several books on history.

GERVASUTTI, Giusto (1909–1946)
An outstanding Italian climber of the immediate pre-war years. With Rene Chabod he attempted the Croz Spur of the Grandes Jorasses in 1934, and might well have made the first ascent of the face had they not retreated in threatening weather – a decision they always later regretted. Both men were very modern in outlook, quoting Mummery (qv) as their mentor (Alpinismo, Chabod and Gervasutti, 1935).

Amongst his outstanding first ascents were:

1934   E Face of Tacul
1935   SE Ridge of Pic Gaspard
1936   NW Wall of Ailefroide
       SW Face of Pt. Gugliermina
1940   Right Hand Pillar of Freney

He was killed on the Mont Blanc du Tacul in 1946 attempting what is now called the Gervasutti Pillar.

GHIGLIONE, Piero (1883-1960)
Distinguished Italian climber who is said to have ascended more mountains than anyone else, and in every part of the world. He was in the tradition of Italian climber-writers, fairly wealthy, and absolutely devoted to the mountain world. Made first ascents in the Andes at the age of 70 and led a successful expedition to Api (Himalaya) at 71. He was killed in a car crash.

GIBRALTAR, CLIMBS IN
A number of routes have been done on this famous rock (limestone), though permission is needed to climb there. The spectacular North Front was climbed by M. Boysen, H. Day and M. Burke in 1971.

GIBSON, John Henry (1862-98)
A fine and daring rock-climber who made a number of guideless Alpine climbs and some of the first climbs in Scotland. These include the first guideless traverse of Grépon and the first ascent of the Black Shoot of Stob Maol (1892).

GILBERT AND CHURCHILL
Josiah Gilbert (1814-92) and George Cheetham Churchill (1822-1906) were two friends who "discovered" the Dolomites. They first saw these mountains in 1856, and explored them between 1860 and 1863. Their actual mountaineering experience was slight, but their book, The Dolomite Mountains (1864), became an Alpine classic. Gilbert (a professional artist) wrote most of the narrative and illustrated the work; Churchill contributed scientific notes (he was a leading expert on Alpine flora). The scope of the book is rather wider than a modern interpretation of the title would suggest. The two men later wrote Knapsack Guide to Tirol (1867).

GIMMER CRAG
A crag in Langdale (qv), noted for its steep, clean lines in the middle and upper grades. Haskett Smith climbed the North West Gully in 1882. Other famous routes are B Route (1907, Lyon, Stables, Thomson), which contains the celebrated Amen Corner, The Crack (1928, Reynolds and Macphee) and Kipling Groove (1948, Dolphin and Lockwood).

Guidebook: Great Langdale, by J. A. Austin.

GIRDLESTONE, Arthur Gilbert (1842-1908)
The Rev. A. G. Girdlestone was one of the earliest guideless climbers, making a guideless ascent of the Wetterhorn in 1867 (but see HUDSON). His experiences, which he related in The High Alps Without Guides (1870), caused great controversy and the book probably did much to put back the proper development of guideless ascents. Girdlestone was the sick Englishman that Whymper visited just before the Matterhorn tragedy (qv). He accompanied Whymper and Lord Francis Douglas to Zermatt and had he been in better health might well have taken part in the Matterhorn ascent.

GITE
An obsolete term for a bivouac (qv). Frequently referred to in early climbing books, such as Whymper's Scrambles.

GLACIER (G.: Gletscher, Ferner; It.: Ghiacciaio)
The permanent ice associated with high or

arctic mountain regions. Glaciers occupy 10 per cent of the earth's surface, but 96 per cent of this is in Antarctica or Greenland. If they all melted they would raise the sea level by 200 ft – enough to drown all the major coastal towns of the world.

There are three types of glacier:

Ice-cap or ice-field type

Easily in the majority by bulk. Antarctica is virtually one huge ice cap of five million sq. miles and 8,000 ft thick, and Greenland has an ice-cap of 650,000 sq. miles and 11,000 ft thick. There are others in Norway, Iceland and Spitzbergen. The well-known Jostedalsbre of Norway (500 sq. miles) is of this type.

Valley glaciers

The type with which most climbers are best acquainted. Virtually a river of ice trapped between mountain spurs, these are found in the Alps, Andes, Himalaya etc. Large glaciers are known to attain a thickness of 1,000-3,000 ft. The largest of all is the Beardmore Glacier in Antarctica, which is 120 miles long and 75 miles wide. The Hubbard Glacier of Alaska is 75 miles long, and the Hispar-Biafo of the Karakorum is 76 miles long. The Karakorum contains the greatest concentration of large glaciers in the world outside the Antarctic, for example Batura 36 miles, Baltoro 36 miles, Siachen 45 miles. The longest glacier of the Alps is the Great Aletsch, 13.75 miles long.

Valley glaciers flow down from the upper snows or névé which help to "feed" them. Fresh powder snow becomes granular ice (firn) which extends to a depth of 100–200 ft, gradually losing air as it becomes deeper. The pure ice below this becomes plastic due to the weight of material above, and flows under gravity. The rate of movement varies from a few inches per day to 150 ft per day; the former is more common. The centre flows quicker than the edges (hence the curved bands of detritus) and the middle flows quicker than the beginning or terminus.

Because the upper layers are brittle, variations in flow or changes in the underlying rock causes the ice to fracture into crevasses. If there is a large declivity, this may result in an ice-fall.

Piedmont glaciers

These spread out laterally at the foot of mountain ranges and are not common. An example is the Bering Glacier of Alaska, 1,500 sq. miles.

Since the last Ice Age, glaciers have had periods of advance and retreat. There is evidence to suggest this is fairly consistent on a world-wide basis, but the Alps will serve as an example. During the Middle Ages, the glaciers were not so extensive as they now are; it was possible, for example, to walk from Zermatt to Sion over what is now the icy Col d'Hérens. Their first advance is not recorded but they made substantial advances 1830-45 and 1875-92. They are now generally in retreat: of 93 Swiss glaciers observed in 1962-3, ten were advancing, six stationary and the rest retreating. The largest advance was the Cambrena Glacier, 93 ft, and the largest retreat was the Ferpècle Glacier, 600 ft. Several were retreating at the rate of about 200 ft per annum.

(See also BERGSCHRUND, CREVASSE, GLACIER TRAVEL, HANGING GLACIER, ICE FALL, MORAINE, SERAC, SNOW-BRIDGE.)

GLACIER CREAM

Heavily pigmented cream which is applied to all exposed parts of the body, particularly the nose, neck and ears, before venturing above the snow-line. It reduces the effect of solar radiation (ultra-violet rays) and must be worn even in a mist. Ordinary sun oil is not satisfactory. The lips also suffer heavily from solar radiation on snow-fields and glaciers, and special lip salves (e.g. Labiosan) are excellent for protection. If this is not available, glacier cream must be applied thickly.

Glacier cream wears off through perspiration and should be reapplied at periods throughout the day. Most climbers dislike "creaming up" – it is a messy business.

GLACIER TABLE

A feature of some dry glaciers. A rock, lying on the ice, has protected the underlying ice from the sun's rays. As the surrounding ice melts the rock is left perched on an ice pedestal, looking somewhat like a mushroom.

GLACIER TRAVEL

The chief requirements for glacier travel are common sense and a general knowledge of glacier formation. The dangers are real; they should neither be exaggerated nor ignored.

Before embarking on a glacier, even on a dull day, exposed parts of the flesh should be rubbed well with glacier cream which cuts out ultra-violet rays. Sensitive parts – neck, forearm, tip of nose and ears –

13 Mountain Rescue. An exercise in stretcher lowering on Tryfan in Snowdonia. (*right*) 14 A Climbing Wall. These are now fitted in many sports halls and allow ready practice in techniques.

A F Mummery

George Abraham

Peter Harding

Allan Austin

Don Whillans

Dougal Haston

15–20 Some Famous British Climbers

should be especially well creamed and the cream should be renewed at intervals during the day. Failure to do this will result in severe glacier burn. Tinted glasses or goggles should also be worn to prevent snow-blindness. An ice axe should be carried at all times.

A glacier which has no powder snow on it is known as a dry glacier. Crevasses on such glaciers are obvious and can be avoided or jumped. If they are not steep, such glaciers do not require a rope (e.g. Mer de Glace).

When crevasses are snow-covered, a rope is essential for safety (see CREVASSE RESCUE). Fifteen feet of rope between each pair is enough: the second can carry spare coils in his hand to give the leader more freedom and have the rest of the rope permanently coiled round his shoulders and securely tied off. The leader advances along his chosen route and the second follows, keeping the rope off the snow. Both men should be alert and ready to plunge their axes into the snow for a belay (*qv*). Where the leader suspects hidden crevasses (*qv*) he probes with the axe while his second belays him. He is also belayed while crossing snow bridges (*qv*). It is worth noting that crevasse covers are more likely to collapse after several hours of sunshine (hence the early start) and also that a ready beaten track in the snow made by previous parties is no guarantee of safety.

Ice falls present the danger of unstable seracs (*qv*). They should be avoided if this is feasible, or crossed as quickly as possible (e.g. in the Nantillons Glacier, Chamonix). Moraines (*qv*) are usually laborious but safe, though there is sometimes danger of falling stones (Arolla Glacier for example). On some glaciers surface streams can provide awkward obstacles (for instance, Gorner Glacier).

GLACIS
An obsolescent word indicating a gently sloping area of rock which can be walked up without the need for handholds.

GLENCOE
A valley in Argyll, Scotland; scene of the famous Massacre, 1692. In mountaineering terms, it may be said to begin at the Kingshouse Hotel on the edge of Rannoch Moor and run westwards to Glencoe village on Loch Leven, about 14 miles. High mountains and crags hem in the valley on both sides. One of the most popular climbing areas in Scotland.

On the N side of the valley the mountains form a simple ridge, the western end of which is the celebrated Aonach Eagach. The S side is more complex with a number of short, steep side valleys running up into the hills, chief of which are Bidean nam Bian (3,766 ft), Stob Coire nan Lochan (3,657 ft), Stob Coire Sgreamhach (3,497 ft) and Stob Dearg of Buachaille Etive Mor (3,345 ft) (*qv*). Below this latter, the long valley of Glen Etive joins Glencoe. Both Glen Etive and Glencoe have motor roads.

The only village is Glencoe, on the shores of Loch Leven. In the valley the accommodation includes the Clachaig and Kinghouse Hotels, Lagangarbh, Black Rock, and other climbers' huts, a private bunk house and a youth hostel. The principal camp site is near Clachaig.

The winter traverse of Aonach Eagach is a classic, but otherwise the principal climbing, summer and winter, lies on the complex crags of the south flank: Buachaille Etive Mor, Coire Gabhail, Beinn Fhada, Stob Coire Sgreamhach, Lost Valley Buttresses, Gear Aonach, Stob Coire nan Lochan, Aonach Dubh, Coire nam Beith, Bideam nam Bian, Stob Coire nam Beith. The first route made was Collie's Climb, Buachaille Etive Mor (Collie, Collier, Solly 1894).

Guidebooks: *Climbers' Guide to Glencoe and Ardgour* (2 vols), by L. S. Lovat and *Winter Climbs: Ben Nevis and Glencoe*, by I. S. Clough.

GLISSADING (Fr.: Ramasse)
If snow is of a sufficient hardness it is possible to slide down it using the boot soles in the manner of skis. A crouch position is adopted and an ice axe is trailed spike down in the snow to act as brake and rudder. The technique is difficult and many climbers end by sliding down on their rears, but experts can even do ski turns. It is a very quick way down long snow slopes, but also a prime cause of accidents. It is essential that the bottom of the slope should be visible, that the area is crevasse-free, and that the climber knows braking techniques should he get out of control. A rope glissade is very dangerous and is not recommended.

GLOVER, George Tertius (1870-1953)
Pioneer rock-climber who did much exploration in the far north of Scotland with Ling (*qv*) and others. Made the first ascent of Engineers' Chimney, Gable, Lake Dis-

trict (1899) and Glover's Chimney, Ben Nevis, 1902. Glover was a railway engineer.

GLOVES
Essential for winter climbing in Britain, as well as for Alpine and high-altitude climbing. There are three types: fingerless wool mitts (useful for rock-climbing in cold weather); mitts made of oiled wool (the general cold-weather glove of the mountaineer); and overmitts of nylon (which are wind and snowproof). In severe conditions all these may be worn in combination.

Despite the intense heat often encountered on Alpine glaciers, gloves should be worn as a protection, especially on a dry glacier where a slip can cause badly lacerated hands if gloves are not worn.

Braking gloves are specially designed leather gloves worn by a climber operating a belay (sometimes called belay gloves). In the event of another climber falling, braking gloves prevent the hands from being rope-burned.

GLYDERS
One of the most popular mountain groups in Snowdonia, separating the Ogwen and Llanberis valleys. The principal summits are Elidir Fawr (3,030 ft), Y Garn (3,104 ft), Glyder Fawr (3,279 ft), Glyder Fach (3,262 ft) and Tryfan (3,010 ft). The northern aspects of the chain (for such it is) forms magnificent cwms with fine crags and llyns (lakes) such as Llyn Idwal and Llyn Bochlwyd. The Llanberis flanks are less scenic but have many fine crags near the valley floor.

On the Ogwen side, the chief climbing interest lies in the crags of Cwm Idwal, Tryfan, Glyder Fach and Gallt yr Ogof, though there are many other cliffs as well. On the Llanberis side, there are the well-known Three Cliffs (qv). Both the Ogwen and Llanberis valleys contain numerous climbing huts. (See also LLANBERIS PASS, IDWAL, TRYFAN, OGWEN and THREE CLIFFS.)

Guidebooks: Llanberis North, by D. T. Roscoe, Tryfan and Glyder Fach, by A. J. J. Moulam, and Cwm Idwal, by A. J. J. Moulam.

GOBBI, Toni (1914-70)
One of the leading Italian post-war guides and an advocate of advanced winter climbing. First winter ascents of Hirondelles Ridge (1948), S Ridge of the Noire (1949), and Route Major (1953). He made a number of other first ascents in the Dolomites and Mont Blanc areas, the most notable being that with Bonatti (qv) of the Grand Pilier d'Angle (1957). He was a member of the Italian expeditions to Patagonia (1957-8) and Gasherbrum IV (1958). He visited the Caucasus in 1966 and Greenland in 1967 and 1969.

Though a trained lawyer, Gobbi preferred to live at Courmayeur where his equipment shop became a well-known meeting place for climbers. An expert skier, he was killed by an unfortunate skiing accident in the Dolomites.

GODWIN-AUSTEN, Lt.-Col. Henry Haversham (1834–1923)
Military surveyor who did outstanding work in the Himalaya between 1857 and 1877, when he retired. In 1861 he explored the Baltoro Glacier and sighted K2, second highest mountain in the world. For a short time K2 was known unofficially as Mt Godwin-Austen.

GOS, Charles (1885-1949)
A Swiss climber, son of the well-known painter, Albert Gos, and a writer of distinction. In his young days Gos was a keen non-guided man and he made the first unguided ascents of the Petit Dru and the Zmutt Ridge of Matterhorn. Illness brought his climbing career to an early end but he often wrote about mountains. His history of the Matterhorn, Cervin (2 vols, 1948), is his major mountain work but his most popular was Tragédies Alpestres (1940).

GOSSET, Philip Charles (1838-1911)
A Swiss surveyor who made the first ascent of the Kleine Doldenhorn (1862). It was during Gosset's winter attempt on the Haut de Cry (1864) that his companion and the guide J. J. Bennen (qv) lost their lives in an avalanche.

GOWER PENINSULAR
An area immediately west of Swansea, Wales, noted for its scenic beauty and fine sea cliffs. The cliffs are limestone and offer climbs of all grades, some in excess of 100 ft, but most much lower. The area is of post-war development.

Guidebook: Gower Peninsula, by J. O. Talbot.

GRADINGS OF DIFFICULTY
The purpose of grading climbs according to their difficulty is to indicate whether a

route is too hard or too easy for a given party. Like guidebooks (with which the growth of grading systems is closely linked), they were at first subject to disapproval. These early objections were quite valid – that so much depends upon the temperament and physical make-up of the climber, the weather, the wear and tear on the rocks and other variables, that a correct grading would be impossible. This has proved correct and the story of gradings is one of a continual search for improvement, but so far all but the simplest systems have been rejected by climbers as too complex.

The remarkable thing is that the simple systems, though far from perfect, work reasonably well. Almost every country now uses a grading system.

Britain

The original grades invented by O. G. Jones (*qv*) were: Easy, Moderate, Difficult and Exceptionally Severe. (In increasing difficulty.) Over the years these have become modified to: (Easy, Moderate), Difficult, Very Difficult, Severe, Very Severe, Extremely Severe.

The first two grades indicate exposed scrambling rather than technical climbing (for example on Innaccessible Pinnacle, Skye) and are not recognized by some modern authorities. The other grades can be further sub-divided by the prefixes Mild and Hard, for example, Hard Severe, Mild Severe. These indicate the climb's standing within its grade. The grade of Very Severe (V. S.) covers a wider range of difficulty than any other grade owing to the advance of standards over the years, and Hard Very Severe is now almost a grade unto itself. This leads to tortuous phrases like "an easy Hard Very Severe" – but a climber would know exactly what was meant. The grade of Extremely Severe (Extreme or X. S.) is reserved for the very hardest climbs.

Numerical systems have never found much favour in Britain, but are used on some outcrops, such as Helsby. The usual scale is 1–6 in increasing severity and may be subdivided into a, b, and c. So, 5a is less difficult than 5c.

Occasionally the two systems are married, with an overall adjectival grading for the route and a numerical grading for individual pitches. This system is growing in favour. It has the advantage of showing whether a climb is of sustained grading throughout.

Climbs involving artificial techniques are graded A1 to A4 according to difficulty. If drilling and bolting is needed the letter "e" is sometimes added, so "Very Severe, A4e" would indicate a climb involving hard free and artificial climbing, with some bolting.

The grading of snow and ice routes can be much more difficult than rock-climbs because conditions vary from year to year, but the Scottish system of I to V (increasing in difficulty) is now accepted throughout Britain.

It must be stressed that the grading of any route must be fairly imprecise. It may depend upon the climber making the first ascent, the compiler of the guidebook or, for well established climbs, a general consensus of opinion. The differences between regions (for example the Peak District and Lakeland) are perhaps less marked than they once were. Changes also occur in the nature of the rock through wear and tear, and climbs can be graded up or down accordingly over the years.

The graded lists which were once a feature of guidebooks, and in which all the climbs of a crag were listed according to difficulty from the hardest down to the easiest, have largely disappeared owing to the increasing number of climbs and the difficulty of the task. They were never very accurate. Instead, a quality grading (as opposed to difficulty) is now a feature of many guidebooks. Sometimes known as "star grading" it gives stars or asterisks to exceptionally enjoyable routes – three stars (maximum) being reserved for the great classics.

The Alps

With slight variations, Alpine countries adopt the French system, involving an overall descriptive grade and a numerical grade for any rock-climbing involved. The latter goes from 1–6, with + or – indicating Hard or Mild. The overall grades are: F (*facile* – easy), P.D. (*peu difficile* – a little difficult), A.D. (*assez difficile* – rather difficult), D (*difficile* – difficult), T.D. (*très difficile* – very difficult), E.D. (*extrêmement difficile* – extremely difficult).

These can be further sub-classified with the suffixes: *inf.* (*inférieur*) or *sup.* (*supérieur*), for below or above the grade respectively. This system is also used in English language guidebooks to Alpine areas. The grades should not be equated with those in use for English rocks.

U.S.A.
The system developed in Yosemite and adopted elsewhere compares with the French, though not exactly. There is an overall grade of I to VI, based upon time needed – Grades I–III take up an increasing number of hours, IV and V are for climbs lasting a day or just over, Grade VI is for multi-day climbs. Technical difficulty is based on the numbers 1–5: Grades 1–4 are for walking and scrambling, Grade 5 for serious rock-climbing. Grade 5 is further divided into 5.1, 5.2 and so on up to 5.11. Theoretically there is no upper limit. Grade 5.7 is about equal to average V. S. in Britain. There are grades for artificial climbing ranging from A1 to A5.

Other systems
In Australia, an open-ended numerical system is used for rock-climbs. At the moment it ranges from 1 to 21, in increasing order of difficulty. The Fang, at Tremadoc, H.V.S., is said to equal Grade 17.

In South Africa the grades are in ascending order of A to E.

In Russia routes are divided into three classes: (a) high-altitude class (above 6,000 m); (b) face ascents class (routes over 75°); and (c) traverse class (across two or more peaks). The difficulty is graded from 1 to 5 in ascending order with sub-divisions A and B.

GRAHAM BROTHERS
Peter Graham (1878-1961) and Alex Graham (b. 1881) were two brothers from Westland who became the leading New Zealand guides during the years 1894 to 1928, and made a number of first ascents in the New Zealand Alps. They were not related to the Graham who made the first ascent of Mt Cook (*qv*). (See autobiography: *Peter Graham – Mountain Guide*, published posthumously in 1964.)

GRAHAM, William Woodman (c. 1859–?)
An experienced mountaineer who made the first ascent of the NE summit (the highest point, 4,013 m) of the Aig. du Géant in 1882 with the guides A. Payot and A. Cupelin.

In 1883 Graham visited the Himalaya with the expressed intention of climbing "more for sport and adventures than for the advancement of scientific knowledge". Since von Déchy's visit of 1879 had been

failed because of illness, Graham thus became the first climber to specifically visit the Himalaya for purely climbing purposes. He took with him J. Imboden as guide, and when the latter became ill, replaced him with E. Boss and U. Kauffmann.

He first visited Sikkim, crossed two high passes and climbed a peak of about 20,000 ft. He next tried to force the Rishi Ganga in Kumaun (not accomplished for another 50 years) and to climb Dunagiri. He reached 22,700 ft on Dunagiri before retreating because of bad weather. He then ascended what he thought was Changabang (22,520 ft) but was probably some other peak. Returning to Sikkim he climbed Jobonu, explored Pandim and claimed the first ascent of the giant Kabru (24,002 ft).

This last has remained one of the great mysteries of Himalayan climbing. Himalayan authorities have argued for and against Graham's claim – all are agreed he climbed *some* big mountain, but was it Kabru? Cooke made the first undisputed ascent in 1935.

Little is known of Graham's later life. He is said to have lost his money and emigrated to the U. S. A., where he became a cowboy.

GRAIAN ALPS
A large area of the Alps stretching from the Cottians in the south to the Mont Blanc group in the north. The Graians form three principal ranges, roughly parallel, running N–S. These are the Central Graians, the West Graians (Tarentaise), and the East Graians (Mountains of Cogne).

The Central Graians are relatively unfrequented and the mountains easy. The highest is Pte. de Charbonnel (3,750 m). Rochemelon (3,538 m) was the first known ascent in the Alps (1358). The West Graians (known also as Tarentaise or Vanoise) are noted for their beauty. The highest peak is Grande Casse (3,852 m) and though most peaks are easy, the Aig. de Vanoise (2,790 m) offers good rock-climbing. Pralognan and Val d'Isere are the best centres.

The Eastern Graians are probably the most popular of these mountains, more so since the Mt Blanc Tunnel has made them fairly accessible to Chamonix. The centre is Cogne, near Aosta, and the highest peak is Gran Paradiso (4,061 m) one of the easiest of the big Alpine peaks. Other well-known mountains are Herbetet (3,778 m)

101   GRAY, D. D.

and Grivola (3,969m). Harder climbs are on the ridge which includes the Roccia Viva and Tour du Grand St Pierre. There are several huts and bivouac huts.

Guidebooks: *Graians West*, by R. Collomb, and *Graians East*, by R. Collomb.

GRAND CAPUCIN (3,838m)
An impressive pinnacle on the southern slopes of Mont Blanc du Tacul. Though first climbed by a minor route in 1924, it was the ascent of its stupendous East Face by Bonatti and Ghigo in 1951 that attracted attention. It is almost 1,500ft of artificial climbing. Very popular.

GRANDES JORASSES (4,208m)
One of the most important mountains in the Alps. Part of the Mont Blanc group, and on the frontier above Val Ferret. The mountain is a long crest with six summits: Pt Young (3,996m) Pt Marguerite (4,065m), Pt Croz (4,110m), Pt Hélène (4,045m), Pt Whymper (4,184m) and Pt Walker (4,208m). The first ascent of Pt Whymper was made by E. Whymper with M. Croz, C. Almer, F. Biner in 1865 and of Pt Walker by H. Walker with M. Anderegg, J. Jaun, J. Grange, 1868. Both ascents were by the fairly easy SW Face – the only really easy routes on the mountain.

There are four important ridges: the W and E Ridges, and the Tronchey and Pra Sec Ridges running S from the Pt Walker. These were climbed:

1911 W Ridge – G. W. Young, H. O. Jones with J. Knubel.
1923 Pra Sec Ridge – F. Ravelli, G. Rivetti, E. Croux.
1927 E Ridge (Hirondelles Ridge) – A. Rey, A. Chenoz with G. Gaja, S. Matteoda, F. Ravelli, G. Rivetti.
1936 Tronchey Arête – T. Gilberti, E. Croux.

It is worth noting that in 1911 Young's party descended the Hirondelles Ridge and in 1928 the American Rand Heron's party climbed the Tronchey Arête by an indirect variant.

There are four faces: the SW Face (the ordinary route), the S Face (between the Tronchey and Pra Sec ridges), the E Face (between the Tronchey and Hirondelles ridges) and the spectacular N Face, overlooking the Leschaux Glacier. The E Face of Pt Walker was climbed by G. Gervasutti and G. Gagliardone in 1942 and is one of the hardest climbs on the mountain. The S Face of Pt Walker was climbed in 1972 by A. Gogna and G. Machetto. It is one of the

largest faces in the Alps, but subject to stonefall.

A number of other hard climbs have been done on the south flanks of the mountain, but climbing attention has been mainly focussed on the great N Face. This extends along the whole mountain and consists of a series of spurs and couloirs. The first ascent was by the Croz Spur (R. Peters, M. Meier, 1935) but the great prize was the Walker Spur (R. Cassin, L. Esposito, U. Tizzoni, 1938) one of the most famous climbs in the Alps and the subject of numerous attempts in the thirties. It was these attempts that provoked Charlet's comment, "*C'est pas de l'alpinisme, ça, c'est la guerre*". (First winter ascent: W. Bonatti, C. Zappelli, 1964; first solo ascent: A. Gogna, 1968.)

There are now nine different routes on the N Face. Most notable of the rest are: The Shroud, 1968 – R. Desmaison, R. Flematty, winter; Central Couloir, 1972 – Y. Kanda, Y. Kato, H. Miyazaki, T. Nakano, K. Saito, winter; E Flank of Walker Spur, 1973 – R. Desmaison, G. Bertone, M. Glaret, winter.

Guidebook: *Selected Climbs in the Range of Mont Blanc Vol II*, by R. Collomb and P. Crew.

GRANITE
An igneous rock of crystalline quality. Granite varies from place to place but is always sound to climb upon and a great favourite with climbers. There are good granite rocks in Chamonix and Cornwall.

GRAY, Dennis Dillon (b. 1935)
A gritstone climber who played a large part in re-founding the Rock and Ice Club (*qv*). Gray seconded H. Drasdo on the first ascent of North Crag Eliminate, Castle Rock in 1952. He made the first ascents of Grond, Dinas Cromlech (1958), The Scene and Apolyon Ledge, Coire Ardair (1966), Gargoyle Wall, Nevis (1963), winter ascents of last three and various outcrop climbs including Frisco Bay, Stoney Middleton (1953), and Wombat and Macabre (1964) at Malham. He has made a number of first British ascents in the Alps and climbed in many different parts of the world.

In 1961 Gray attempted Indrasan in Kulu but failed on the W Ridge, though he succeeded in climbing the adjacent two highest Manikaran Spires. He was joint leader of the unsuccessful 1964 Gaurisankar Expedition, but two years later led the successful first ascent of the N Ridge of Alpamayo in Peru. He was leader of the 1968 Mukar Beh Expedition.

Dennis Gray was the first National Officer to be appointed by the B. M. C., and later, the first General Secretary. He is author of an outstanding autobiography, *Rope Boy* (1970).

GREASY ROCK
A term indicating rock which is slippery when wet. Mountain limestone seems to be prone to greasiness. Other rocks are often made greasy by mud from climbers' boots and by lichen.

GREAT GABLE (2,949 ft)
An immensely popular fell of the Lake District rising at the junction of Ennerdale, Borrowdale and Wasdale, and usually approached from the last two valleys. The war memorial tablet of the F.R.C.C. adorns the summit. There are two important groups of crags on the fell: Napes Ridges overlooking Wasdale and Gable Crag, overlooking Ennerdale.

The Napes are an unusual set of spiky ridges and buttresses which attracted the pioneers, together with the adjacent outcrop of Kern Knotts. Napes Needle (*qv*) was climbed by Haskett Smith (*qv*) in 1886 and is the symbol of the birth of rockclimbing as a sport. In fact, Haskett Smith also climbed the ridge above it (Needle Ridge) two years earlier. Other earlier ascents of note are:

1892 Eagle's Nest Ridge Direct – Solly, Slingsby, Baker, Brigg
 Arrowhead Ridge – Slingsby, Waller, Brant, Baker, Brigg
1893 Kern Knotts Chimney – Jones, Fowler, Robinson
1897 Kern Knotts Crack – Jones, Bowen
1921 Innominate Crack – Bower, Beetham, Wilton

Gable Crag has never been popular, though the Central Gully gives a fine winter climb.

Guidebook: *Great Gable, Wasdale and Eskdale*, by P. L. Fearnehough.

GREAT ORME'S HEAD
Well-known coastal cliff at Llandudno, North Wales. Limestone, with huge overhangs giving artificial climbs. The nearby Little Orme's Head is similar.

GREEN, William Spotswood (1847-1919)
An Irish clergyman who made some of the earliest explorations of the New Zealand Alps and the Canadian Rockies. In 1882 he made the first ascent of Mount Cook, though he turned back a few feet from the actual summit in order to avoid benightment. In 1888 he visited the Selkirks, making the first ascent of Glacier Crest, Terminal Peak and Mount Bonney. He wrote accounts of his expeditions in *The High Alps of New Zealand* (1883) and *Among the Selkirk Glaciers etc.* (1890). His survey resulted in the first map of the Selkirk Range. There is a Mount Green in both New Zealand and the Selkirks, and Green's Saddle in New Zealand; all commemorate the pioneer.

In his later years he was Government Inspector of Irish Fisheries.

GREENLAND, CLIMBING IN
This vast island consists essentially of a great central ice cap rising to 10,000 ft, surrounded by ranges of mountains. The highest are the Watkins Mountains, on the east coast, south of Cap Brewster, and the highest summit is Gunnbjorn Fjeld (12, 139 ft, L. R. Wager, 1935). The Watkins Mountains were discovered by Gino Watkins in 1931, but since the thirties they were unvisited until 1969 when both M. Slesser and A. Allen attempted to reach and climb Ejnar Mikkelsen Fjeld (10,700 ft), the highest unclimbed peak of the Arctic. Both failed because of bad weather, and the peak was climbed in 1970 by a remarkable small expedition: A. Ross, G. Williams, N. Robinson and P. Lewis.

The Staunings Alps in Scoresby Land (east coast) are lower than 10,000 ft (Dansketinde, 9,170 ft, J. Haller, W. Diehl, 1954). The peaks are shapely and there have been numerous expeditions in recent years – it is probably the best-known area of Greenland.

Further south on the east coast lie the Alpefjord mountains and other groups, including Mt Forel (11,024 ft, 1938) and in the extreme south are the peaks of Cape Farewell. On the west coast are the Sukkertoppen, Umanak Fjord area and the Melville Bay area, which have all attracted at least one expedition. There are many more mountain groups worth exploring.

Guidebook: *The Staunings Alps*, by D. J. Bennet.

GREGORY, Alfred (b. 1913)
Photographer and lecturer. Gregory took part in Shipton's Cho Oyu Expedition of 1952 and the following year was a member

of the final assault team on the summit of Everest. At a height of 27,900 ft, Gregory, Lowe and Ang Nyima dumped loads for the final camp, leaving Hillary and Tenzing to stay the night and climb to the summit next day (first ascent).

Gregory led a number of other expeditions: Rowaling, Nepal (1955), when 19 first ascents were done, an attempt on Disteghil Sar (1957) and a return to the Everest region in 1958. He visited the Cord. Blanca (1962) and Ruwenzori (1960). Wrote: *The Picture Book of Everest* (1953).

GRID REFERENCE
The Ordnance Survey use a system of imaginary squares covering Britain as a reference for pin-pointing any place with great accuracy. The basic squares are of 100 km side and extend north and east from a point of origin which lies approximately SW of Cornwall. There are ten such squares northwards and seven eastwards. The co-ordinates for the square including London, for example, would be 51, meaning the square whose bottom left corner was 500 km E of the point of origin and 100 km N of the point of origin. The eastings are always given first.

On the map scales commonly used by climbers (one-inch and two and-a-half inch to the mile) the maps are subdivided into squares of 1 km and these are similarly numbered from bottom left. Thus, on the Lakeland map, Friar's Crag falls in square 26,22. It is possible to estimate by eye further subdivisions into tenths, and Friar's Crag thus becomes 263,222, giving the position to the nearest 100 m. More detailed estimation is only accurate on very large-scale maps. For Friar's Crag, the figure is written 263222, and is known as the normal grid reference. However, since these figures will repeat themselves every 100 km, it may be necessary to give the 100 km square number – in this case, 35. The full grid reference thus becomes 35/263222. No other place in Britain can possibly have this reference except Friar's Crag.

Grid lines are only approximately N–S and E–W, the difference being the grid variation. (See MAGNETIC VARIATION.)

GRIGNA (Italy)
Limestone mountains near Lecco (Como) offering good climbs on sharp pinnacles. Many routes are hard and the area is well known as a training ground for famous Italian climbers such as Cassin and Mauri.

(No English guidebook.)

GRILL, Johann (1835-1917)
Known as 'Der Koderbacher'. Grill came from Berchtesgaden and all his early climbs were done on the peaks of Tyrol where he made the following notable first ascents amongst others:
1868 Traverse of Watzmann's three peaks
1873 Pflerscher Tribulaun
1881 East Face of Watzmann

He made a winter ascent of the W Face of the Weisshorn and expressed a wish to attempt the Eigerwand (1882!).

GRINDELWALD
A popular tourist and climbing resort in the Bernese Alps, overlooked by the Wetterhorn and Eiger (qv). It was from here that Wills (qv) made his ascent of the Wetterhorn in 1854, an event often regarded as the beginnings of Alpine sport. The village has always been famous for guides. (See also KLEINE SCHEIDEGG.)

GRITSTONE
The geographical term, millstone grit, is never used by climbers. Gritstone comes in many varieties, all modified sandstones, but with a common abrasiveness which aids friction climbing. Incut holds are not common, which, combined with the usual steepness of the rock, leads to superior technique. Gritstone climbing has a long history, beginning even before J. W. Puttrell, 'the father of gritstone', who started climbing at Wharncliffe in 1885, and continuing with such notables as Herford, Kelly, Kirkus, Longland, Harding, Brown and Whillans, all of whom began on gritstone. The transference of gritstone techniques to mountain crags by these and others has led to the continual rise in climbing standards.

Gritstone is found in the Pennines (qv) as natural outcrops (edges and tors) and quarries. The most popular is Stanage Edge (qv), near Sheffield. Gritstone climbs seldom exceed 100 ft and are usually shorter.

Guidebooks: *Rock Climbs in the Peak: Sheffield Stanage, Chew Valley Area, Sheffield Froggatt, Chatsworth Gritstone, Bleaklow Area, Kinder Area, Staffordshire Gritstone Area.* Also *Yorkshire Gritstone,* by M. Bebbington *Lancashire,* by L. Ainsworth.

GROEGER, Gustavus
An Austrian climber who made a number

of first ascents in the Eastern Alps including the first guideless ascent of Piz Bernina (1879). He emigrated to U. S. A. in 1881 and recorded an ascent of the highest point of the Break Neck Mountains (1883). Returned to Europe 1900.

GROHMANN, Paul (1838–1908)
One of the founders of the Austrian Alpine Club (1862). He made a number of the early first ascents in the Dolomites, including Sassolungo and the Cima Grande (both 1869).

GROOVE (G.: Verschneidung; Fr.: Dièdre; Am.: Dihedral)
A V-shaped fissure in the rock, not deeply incised, but rather flat and varying, from place to place, from a few inches to a few feet in width. The term is used loosely. Rounded grooves are sometimes called 'flutings' and are common on gritstone, for example, Robin Hood's Stride.

Grooves also occur on ice climbs. In couloirs deep grooves can be caused by avalanche debris – they form natural chutes for falling stones and are best avoided.

GROUGHS
Erosion channels in the peat surface of a moor. Large groughs can be 15 ft deep and very wide. Groughs sometimes form complex patterns which make walking difficult. The best-known examples are on Bleaklow and Kinder in the Peak District (qv).

GROUPE DE HAUTE MONTAGNE (G. H. M.)
An elitist group of climbers founded in 1919 in France. The standards of entry are very high, but the group is not restricted to French nationals. It issues an annual bulletin of new Alpine climbs and is associated with the C. A. F. in La Montagne. It is an influential and highly respected body in the climbing world. The British A. C. G. (qv) is similar, but of more recent foundation.

GROVE, Florence Crauford (1838–1902)
President of the A. C. (1884-86) and one of the best climbers of the period. His first ascents include: Dent d'Hérens, Parrotspitze (1863), Jungfrau from Rottal, Zinal Rothorn (1864), Aig. de Bionnassay (1865) and Elbruz (Caucasus 1874). In 1867 Grove made the first ascent of the Italian ridge of the Matterhorn by an amateur, which was also the first ascent of the mountain by anybody since the great affair of Whymper and Carrel in 1865. He climbed the mountain again the following year, making the fifth ascent from Zermatt, and was thus the first man to have climbed the Matterhorn by both the routes then known, though Tyndall (qv) had traversed it from Breuil to Zermatt a few weeks earlier.

Grove was with Moore, Gardiner and Walker in the Caucasus in 1874 and wrote an account of their travels in The Frosty Caucasus (1875).

GRUBER (or GRUEBER), G.
An Austrian climber with wide experience of the Alps, who made the second ascent of Mont Blanc via Mont Blanc de Courmayeur (1880) and the third ascent of the Brenva Face (1881). The Rochers Gruber of the Fréney Glacier are named after him. Gruber died in 1899.

GUGLIERMINA BROTHERS
Giuseppe F. (1872–1960) and Giovanni Battista (1873–1962) were two Italian brothers from the Val Sesia who made notable new routes on the Monte Rosa and Mont Blanc massifs including the first crossing of the Col Emile Rey (1899), Brouillard Ridge (1901, G. B. with J. Brocherel), Aig. Verte from the Nant Blanc Glacier (1904) and Punta Gugliermina (1914). An account of all their climbs, Summits, was compiled by Lampugnani and illustrated by photographs taken by G. F. who usually carried a heavy plate camera. It is suggested that this is why many of their expeditions involved bivouacs. They usually climbed without guides and G. B. led the rope. G. B. made his last first ascent at the age of 80 – on the Punta Giordani.

GUIDE
A professional mountaineer who earns all or part of his living by acting as a paid leader on climbs. It is not a guide's job to instruct, though in fact many do act as instuctors on courses. Most Alpine guides are also ski instructors and derive a considerable part of their income from this. Many mountain huts (qv) are looked after by guides or ex-guides.

A guide may be hired for a period of time at a rate agreed between him and the client, though there are minimum charges laid down. The guide provides the rope, but the client must pay his expenses for travel and food. (Guides are not usually charged for overnight accommodation in huts.) The guide's licence extends to all Alpine areas. In a good season, hiring a guide by the week or month is the cheapest method.

A guide may also be hired for a specific climb. Each route is graded by the local association and a fixed charge applies; it is often based on the time taken rather than the difficulty. For difficult climbs a guide will satisfy himself that the client is up to the required standard of competence. Charges are fairly high and because of this some local guides' associations run collective courses in which the guide(s) take a group of clients on a previously advertised route.

The training and examination of guides varies from place to place but the Austrian system might serve as an example. Previously organized by the Austrian Alpine Club, training is now in the hands of the Guides' Association (Verband der Österr. Berg -u Schi-führer). It is financed by the Government and private industry. A candidate must enter for the Aufnahmeprufung (a two-day entrance exam), in which he demonstrates an ability to climb to Grade V+ on rock, climb steep ice and be a good skier. About one-third of entrants pass. The successful entrants then proceed to a Felskurs (rock-climbing) lasting 15 days, the last three of which are examinations. The subjects include techniques and rescue, as well as various topics related to climbing, such as tour planning. Again, about one-third pass. Successful candidates then proceed to the Eiskurs, where another 15 days are spent on ice-climbing, crevasse rescue, etc. If he passes this the candidate proceeds to the Schifuhrerlehrgang (15 days) where subjects covering snow types, avalanches, etc. are learnt. If a candidate is successful on all these courses, he becomes a qualified guide. Refresher courses every year help to keep him abreast of new techniques and to ensure that the same methods are taught throughout Austria.

A British mountain guide obtains his carnet from the B. M. C. (*qv*). There are two parts, a summer and a winter carnet. It is possible to hold Part One only, but Part Two (winter) can only be taken by those who already hold Part One. The tests for each part last five days, and are both practical and written, covering a wide range of mountain subjects. A candidate must be able to lead medium V. S. on rock, and A2 artificial. For the winter carnet he must be able to lead Grade IV, ice. He must hold a First Aid Certificate and be at least 22 years old. A detailed account of his experience is required and he must have two sponsors. A carnet is valid for five years, and British guides are retired at 60.

It can be seen from the above that a modern guide is a highly competent mountaineer and on the Continent it is fashionable for the best amateurs to take a guide's examination. Guides frequently take part in expeditions. Guides are responsible for the well-being of their clients and in Switzerland are accountable in law.

The pioneer guides were local peasants who adapted themselves to the high Alps and saw in the new sport of mountaineering a way to earn a good living. Many of them were poor at their work but the best men were true mountaineers in their own right and very skilful; they led most of the early climbs in the Alps. They were lauded by their clients (employers, was the current term) and their services were avidly sought. For many years it was considered dangerous folly to climb without the services of at least one guide.

Chamonix was the first place to form an official Guides' Association (owing to Mont Blanc) but the restrictive practices it invoked led to many disputes with climbers in the nineteenth century.

Guides figure prominently in all the early climbing literature and in much of the later literature too (for example, Young). Some guides have written their own autobiographies (for instance, Klucker). Many are entered in this encyclopaedia but see also *Pioneers of the Alps,* by Cunningham and Abney (1887) and *The Early Alpine Guides,* by Clark (1949).

GUIDEBOOKS
Specialized handbooks designed to help climbers achieve their objective. The books point the way, explain the difficulties, usually give a grade (*qv*) to a climb, give the time needed (for higher mountains), and facilities such as huts, chairlifts, etc. Some guidebooks give brief notes on climbing history, local geology, flora and fauna. Most give the names of those climbers who made the first ascents. Present-day guidebooks are usually in pocket format and may have a protective plastic cover.

Guidebooks are often published by clubs, either directly or through some agency. The various Alpine clubs publish books on their own areas: in Britain the Fell and Rock Club, Climbers' Club, Scottish Mountaineering Club, Federation of

Mountaineering Clubs of Ireland and the Alpine Club, each publish several volumes and various small clubs produce more local guides. In the U. S. the American Alpine Club, the Appalachian Club and the Sierra Club publish guidebooks. A few books are published privately and there are, in Britain, two commercial guidebook firms, Cicerone Press and West Col Publications.

The principal difficulties with guidebooks are keeping them reasonably up to date and verifying their accuracy. In the Alps and other high mountains, this is especially difficult. Assessment of difficulties are subjective and frequently disputed.

Early Alpinists used Murray (*qv*) as their guide until it was superseded by Ball's Alpine Guides (*qv*), 1863-8. The first technical descriptions came with the Conway and Coolidge Guides (1881-1910). The first British climbers' guide was *Climbing in the British Isles* (2 vols), by W. P. Haskett Smith (1894-5).

Some guidebooks have had a profound effect on the development of the sport. In Britain notable examples are:

1897 *Rock Climbing in the English Lake District*, by O. G. Jones (the first guide to give a grading system)

1908 *The Island of Skye* – various authors (published by the Scottish M. C.; the first club guide)

1909 *The Climbs on Lliwedd*, by J. M. A. Thomson and A. W. Andrews (published by the Climbers' Club)

1913 *Some Gritstone Climbs*, by J. Laycock (first guidebook to gritstone climbing)

1922 *Doe Crag and Climbs Around Coniston*, by G. S. Bower (the first Fell and Rock guidebook; start of the 'Red' series)

1950 *Cornwall*, by A. W. Andrews and E. C. Pyatt (first guide to sea cliff climbing)

1955 *Llanberis Pass*, by P. R. J. Harding (contained the supplement recording the new climbs of the Rock and Ice Club and others)

1957 *Further Developments in the Peak District*, by E. Byne and W. B. White (first record of the 'gritstone explosion')

1961 *Rock Climbs on the Mountain Limestone of Derbyshire*, by G. T. W. West (first record of the 'limestone invasion'; the 'Blue Guide')

Guides of more local significance not included.

GUIDELESS CLIMBING

A term used well into the present century to denote climbs done in the Alps without professional guides. It was often used censoriously, as guideless climbing was thought to be foolhardy. Guides were always taken on the early expeditions to the Himalaya, Andes and Caucasus. Though guides are still employed by many climbers, guideless climbing is the norm today and the phrase has lost all meaning.

GULLY (Fr.: Couloir)

The rift between two buttresses caused by erosion. May be very wide or narrow (see CHIMNEY) and may contain a stream. They may be so easy that they contain a path, but many are genuine rock-climbs. A gully filled with small stones is known as a "scree gully" and often forms a quick way down from a crag. In the Lake District a gully is called a "gill" or "ghyll".

Unique features of some gully climbs are chockstones, where the gully is blocked by boulders, and waterfall pitches.

Most gullies are more difficult under ice and snow conditions when even simple summer scrambles can become serious climbs; perversely, *some* gullies become easier if there is a heavy snow layer (for example, Gardyloo Gully, Ben Nevis). Gullies are natural avalanche chutes and winter gullies should not be tackled until the snow has consolidated. Many gullies provide classic winter climbs, especially in Scotland. (See GULLY EPOCH; COULOIR.)

GULLY EPOCH

A term used to describe the pioneering days of British rock-climbing when the major routes followed the most natural lines, that is, gullies. It ended about the turn of the century: Great Gully, Craig yr Ysfa, 1900; Savage Gully, Pillar Rock, 1901.

GUSSFELDT, Paul (1840-1920)

German scientist and Privy Councillor to the Kaiser Wilhelm II, whom he accompanied on numerous journeys, Gussfeldt was also one of the outstanding mountaineers of the nineteenth century. Gussfeldt had very much the same sort of determination as Whymper (*qv*) and, like Whymper, he employed the best guides – in his case, Burgener, Rey and Klucker.

Among many climbs, two outstanding ones are the first crossing of the Col du

Lion from S to N with Burgener (1881) and the first winter ascent of the Grandes Jorasses with Rey (1891).

It was in the Bernina, however, that Gussfeldt first made his name, putting up two fine routes: the Scerscen Eisnase in 1877 and the first complete traverse of the Biancograt of Piz Bernina in 1878.

Later, Mont Blanc became his favourite mountain and he made the fourth ascent of the Brenva face (1892). In the following year came the traverse of Aig. Blanche de Peuterey (the second ascent) followed by the first complete ascent of the Peuterey Ridge to Mont Blanc de Courmayeur and Mont Blanc, with a return to Courmayeur. The climb lasted 88 hours and the guides were Rey and Klucker. Gussfeldt was 53 years old.

As an explorer, Gussfeldt was less successful. He spent 1873-5 on the West Afri-can coast trying to organize an expedition into the interior for the German Africa Company, but misfortune attended his efforts and the whole project ended in a shambles.

In 1876 he spent a month in the Arabian desert with Schweinfurth, but his next major venture was to the Chilean Andes in 1882-3, where he made the first ascent of Maipo (17,717 ft) but failed in two attempts on Aconcagua.

Gussfeldt wrote a number of books, the best known of which are: *In den Hochalpen* (1885) and *Der Mont Blanc* (1894).

GYALTSEN NORBU (d. 1961)
The first Sherpa to climb two of the world's 8,000 m peaks: Makalu (8481 m) in 1955 and Manaslu (8125 m) in 1956. He also climbed Api (7132 m) in 1960. Killed by an avalanche on Ganchen Ledrub (7245 m).

HADOW, Douglas (1846–65)

The young friend of Charles Hudson whom the latter insisted should join the Matterhorn party of 1865 (*qv*). It was Hadow's first season and he had made only two minor ascents together with a rapid ascent of Mont Blanc with Hudson. During the descent of the Matterhorn Hadow slipped and fell against Croz (*qv*) thus precipitating the famous accident.

HALL, Carl Christian (1848-1908)

A Danish treasury official who, after one season in the Alps (1878) devoted himself to the exploration of Norwegian mountains. Hall was comparable with the much better-known Cecil Slingsby (*qv*). From 1880 to 1900 he made numerous first ascents, particularly in the Romsdal and Jotenheimen regions, amongst which might be mentioned the first tourist ascent of the Romsdalhorn (1881), his 7th attempt, and the first ascent of Store Trolltind (1882).

HALL, William Edward (1835-95)

A wealthy barrister, traveller and adventurer who made the first ascents of Lyskamm (1861), Dent d'Hérens and Parrotspitze (1863).

HAMEL–DR HAMEL'S PARTY

A famous mountaineering accident, and the first on Mont Blanc. In August 1820 a party organized by Dr. Hamel, a Russian, set out to climb Mont Blanc. There were 14 men: Hamel, Selligue (Swiss), Joseph Durnford and Gilbert Henderson (Oxford students), and ten guides or porters led by Balmat and Couttet. After waiting a day for bad weather to clear at the Grands Mulets rocks, Seligue and two porters returned to Chamonix while the others attempted the summit. The snow was soft, and some 400ft up the Ancien Passage, above the Grande Crevasse, it avalanched carrying the party with it. Incredibly, eight survived, but Balmat, Tiarraz and Carrier were buried in the crevasse. Their remains reappeared below the Bossons Glacier forty-one years later.

HAMILTON, Arthur Bold (1848-1902)

A barrister whose brief Alpine career was spent exclusively at Arolla where he made the first travellers' ascent of the Tsa (1870) and first ascents of Dent Perroc and Dents des Bouquetins (1871).

HAMMOCK

Special lightweight hammocks are used for bivouacs (*qv*) where there are no suitable ledges, on some Yosemite climbs, for instance. The hammocks are slung from pitons or bolts.

HAND TRAVERSE

A sideways movement across rock where the weight comes mostly on to the hands owing to an absence of footholds. A hand traverse should be carefully assessed and executed quickly. Strenuous, but fairly common.

HANGING GLACIER

A subsiduary glacier set at a higher level than the main glacier or valley. It may be independent and hang over the valley with great ice-cliffs or it may join the main glacier by means of a steep ice-fall.

HARDING, Peter Reginald James (b. 1924)

One of the greatest rock-climbers of the post-war years in Britain. In partnership with Moulam (*qv*) and others he raised the standards of rock-climbing to new heights and was the natural forerunner of Brown (*qv*) and others. His lead of Suicide Wall, Cratcliffe, in 1946 is regarded by some authorities as the beginning of modern high-standard climbing, though this can be no more than a symbol. Like Brown and others who came slightly later, Harding began on gritstone and found full expression in the Llanberis Pass. On Cloggy he only did the West Girdle (1949, G. Dyke). His important new climbs include:

1945 Lean Man's Eliminate, Black Rocks – A. J. J. Moulam
1946 Girdle Traverse, Black Rocks – A. J. J. Moulam
Suicide Wall, Cratcliffe – Miss V. Lee
Valkyrie, Roches – B. Black
1947 Spectre, Grochan – E. H. Phillips

Ivy Sepulchre, Cromlech
Pheonix, Shining Clough
Goliath's Groove, Stanage
1948 Trilon, Wastad – N. L. Horsefield
Girdle, Wastad – P. R. Hodgkinson
Kaisergebirge Wall, Grochan – A.
Disley, A. J. J. Moulam ·
1949 Unicorn, Wastad – P. R. Hodgkinson, N. G. Hughes
Lion, Wastad – Moulam
Halan, Wastad – G. Dyke
Brant Direct, Grochan
Green Caterpiller, Cyrn Las – G. Dyke
Green Necklace, Cyrn Las – Dyke
West Girdle, Clogwyn du'r Arddu – Dyke
Demon Rib, Black Rocks – A. J. J. Moulam

Almost all of these climbs are now regarded as modern classics. In 1951 he brought out for the Climbers' Club *Llanberis Pass*, a guidebook which had a profound effect on a whole generation. In it two new categories were introduced for the new hard climbs: Extremely Severe and Exceptionally Severe. Universally known for a time as X.S., they have since been modified.

Harding has been credited with the invention of the modern hand-jam technique and the use of thin slings for runners – now replaced by tape, and essential to modern protection.

With Moulam he produced the guidebook to the *Black Rocks and Cratcliffe* (1949), the first time that the Climbers' Club had sponsored a gritstone guidebook. In private life, Harding is an engineer.

HARDING, Warren
A leading American rock-climber from Yosemite (*qv*). In 1958 he made the first ascent of the Nose of El Capitan – an outstanding achievement, though his siege tactics (*qv*) did not meet with universal approval. Harding has always adapted his tactics to meet the situation as he sees it. Other routes include:
1964 S Face Mt Watkins
1970 S Face, Half Dome
Wall of Early Morning Light (Dawn Wall)

HARD MAN
Used in climbing to mean someone who climbs at a high standard. Other forms: "a hard climber", or simply, "hard" ("he's hard" means he climbs hard climbs). The phrase returned to vogue in the 1960s but was in use in the nineteenth century when the meaning was slightly different, indicating someone who was a "good goer" in the Alps.

HARDY, Rev. John Frederick,
An Original Member of the A.C. who took part in several of the early Alpine ascents, particularly with Kennedy (*qv*). Amongst his first ascents were: Finsteraarhorn (1857, first English ascent), Piz Bernina (1861, first English ascent) and Lyskamm (1861). With Hudson and others he made the first traverse of the High Level Route (*qv*) from Zermatt to the Gt St Bernard (1861).

Hardy also climbed Mt Etna and visited Norway. He was an early exponent of guideless climbing.

HARNESS (Fr.: Baudrier)
A method of attaching a climber to the rope so that in the event of a fall the shock and strain will be minimized. The first type was the chest harness, originally made from spare rope, and used in the Alps for many years. This was later adapted into permanent chest harnesses of webbing, but in Britain these gave way to thigh harnesses of which the best-known example is the Whillans Harness (see illustrations). In the Alps the baudrier developed into a combination of chest and thigh harness, similar to a parachute harness.

HARPER, Arthur Paul (1865-1955)
Co-founder, with G. E. Mannering, of the New Zealand Alpine Club (1891) and one of the earliest explorers of the glaciers of Westland. Wrote: *Pioneer Work in the Alps of New Zealand* (1896) and *Memories of Mountains and Men* (1946).

HARRER, Heinrich
An Austrian climber who was a member of the team which made the first ascent of the Eigerwand, 1935. In 1939 he reconnoitred the Diamirai Face of Nanga Parbat, and was interned in India at the outbreak of war. He escaped to Tibet where he became friend and confidant of the Dalai Lama. In 1962 Harrer made the first ascent of the Carstensz Pyramide, New Guinea. He has also visited S. America.

His books are: *Seven Years in Tibet* (1953), *The White Spider* (1959), and *I Come from the Stone Age* (1964).

HARRISON'S ROCKS
A sandstone outcrop popular with London climbers for whom it is fairly accessible.

Short climbs of all standards. The rocks are near Groombridge in Sussex and the area contains numerous similar outcrops, many of them private. Bowles Rocks, near Eridge, are part of an outdoor pursuits centre.

Guidebook: *South-East England*, by E. C. Pyatt.

HART, Henry Chichester (1847-1908)
Irish explorer who was on the Nares Arctic Expedition (1875-6) and the Hull Expedition to Sinai and Palestine (1883-4). He made a number of ascents during the latter, including the Pyramids. Hart was the author of the Irish section of Haskett Smith's (*qv*) *Climbing in the British Isles* (1895).

HARTLEY BROTHERS
James Walker (1852-1932) and Francis Chisholm (1854-98) Hartley were two Liverpool brothers who took part in a number of difficult climbs in the Alps, particularly with Davidson (*qv*). J. W. Hartley was with C. T. Dent on the first ascent of the Dru (1878).

HASKETT SMITH,   Walter   Parry (1859–1946)
Barrister and philologist, regarded as the founder of British rock-climbing.

He first visited the Lake District in 1881, when he spent two months at Wasdale Head with fellow university students from Oxford. Here he met F. H. Bowring (*qv*) who led the students on fell-walking excursions, which probably included some simple scrambles. In the following year Haskett-Smith returned, accompanied by his brother, and began to climb rocks for their own sake: Deep Ghyll, Scafell; West and Central Jordan, Pillar Rock; and Great Gully, Pavey Ark, were climbed, and a brave attempt made on what later became the North Climb, Pillar Rock – an attempt which nearly ended in tragedy, when a loose block came away.

It was Haskett Smith's conception of rock-climbing for its own sake and pursuit of that aim which marks him out as the founder of British climbing, rather than the climbs themselves. There had been earlier climbs, in the Lakes and elsewhere, but usually as a means of achieving a *summit*. Broad Stand on Scafell was climbed early in the nineteenth century and the Old West on Pillar in 1826. Other early routes are North Climb and Mickledore Chimney, both on Scafell (1869) and the Slab and

Notch, Pillar Rock (1863). Mention might also be made of Richard Pendlebury's (*qv*) climbs during the 1870s: Pendlebury Traverse on Pillar Rock, Jack's Rake on Pavey Ark, and the gullies of Clogwyn y Person.

It was in 1886 that Haskett Smith made his most famous climb: the first ascent of the striking Napes Needle on Great Gable. He climbed it solo, with "no ropes or other illegitimate means", to quote his own famous phrase. It was not repeated for three years, but then the fame of the pinnacle spread and became very popular, which it still is. Haskett Smith describes the climb in a classic article written many years after the event (F. R. C. C. Journal 1914).

Haskett Smith climbed with another pioneer, J. W. Robinson (*qv*) and with the A. C. members who took to rock-climbing in the later 1880s, such as Slingsby, the Hopkinsons, and Hastings (*qv*), making ascents in the Lake District, Wales and Scotland. He visited the Alps and Norway on several occasions and walked in the Pyrenees with Packe (*qv*).

In 1894 he published *Climbing in the British Isles – England*, the first volume of a three-part work dealing with climbing in Britain, and the first climbing guide to British crags. The second volume, dealing with Wales and Ireland, followed in 1895, though he was helped considerably in this by O. G. Jones, Bowring and Hart (*qv*); Ellis Carr (*qv*) drew the diagrams. The Scottish volume never appeared.

HASLER, Gustav Adolf (1877-1952)
Wealthy Swiss industrialist and notable Alpinist at the turn of the century. Made many climbs especially in the Oberland and including the first ascent of the Scheidegg Wetterhorn (1901) and the Hasler Rib of the Aletschorn (1902). His outstanding achievement was the first ascent of the NE Face of the Finsteraarhorn with F. Amatter in 1904: the first great north face to be climbed and still graded T. D. *sup*.

HASTINGS, Geoffrey (1860-1941)
A Yorkshire climber, friend of Slingsby (*qv*) and Mummery (*qv*) and one of the leading mountaineers of his time. He began climbing with Slingsby in 1885 when they made an unsuccessful attempt on Deep Ghyll, Scafell, a climb they accomplished in the following year (second ascent). In 1887, with one of the Hopkinsons (*qv*), they climbed Needle Ridge on

Gable – probably the first ascent, though this is not certain. In 1889 Hastings made the second ascent of Napes Needle, three years after Haskett Smith's climb (*qv*). His importance to Lakeland climbing can be seen from the fact that he took part in the following important first ascents, ("L" indicates he led): 1888, Slingsby's Chimney, Scafell and Great Gully, Dow Crag (L), 1890, Shamrock Gully, Pillar Rock (L); 1891, North Climb, Pillar Rock; 1892, Moss Ghyll, Scafell and Great Gully, Screes (L).

He first visited the Alps in 1887 when he made a guideless ascent of the Dru, but it was in 1892-4, with Mummery, that he came to the fore, taking part in the first traverse of Grépon, the first ascent of Requin, first ascent of W Face of the Plan, a new route of Grand Combin (Mummery missed this), first guideless ascent of the Brenva Face of Mont Blanc, second ascent of the Moine Ridge of the Verte, and first traverse of the Col des Courtes.

In 1895, with Mummery, Collie and Bruce (*qv*) he made the first exploration of Nanga Parbat in the Himalaya, during which Mummery was killed.

In addition to this Hastings was in the large A. C. party which visited Skye in 1890 (first ascent of Bhastier Gorge) and, with Collie, he made the second descent of Alum Pot in Yorkshire (1893). He visited Norway in 1889, 1897, 1898, 1899 and 1901 with Slingsby, Collie and others, making a number of first ascents. He made a notable early exploration of the Lyngen district during his 1897 visit.

HASTON, Dougal (b. 1940)
A Scottish climber who sprang to prominence with his ascent of the Eiger Direct in the winter of 1966 (see *Eiger Direct*, by D. Haston and P. Gillman). The following year he made a winter ascent of the Matterhorn Nordwand and was a member of the British Cerro Torre expedition (*qv*). In 1969 he made the first winter ascent of the N Face of Argentiere, and then in 1970 he took part in the successful S Face of Annapurna expedition. Haston, with Whillans, reached the summit.

He again partnered Whillans in the International Expedition to the SW Face of Everest, 1971, and they reached the highest point yet reached on the face. Though he returned with Bonington's post-monsoon expedition of 1972, the party was defeated by high winds and extreme cold.

In 1967, Haston became Director of the International Mountaineering School in Leysin, Switzerland, founded by John Harlin who was killed during the Eiger Direct assault. Haston's autobiography, *In High Places*, appeared in 1972.

HAUTE SAVOIE ALPS
The large area between the Lake of Geneva and the Chamonix valley. The principal summits are those of the Dents du Midi, above Champery (highest top: 3,257m). Above the Chamonix valley, the Aigs. Rouges are popular viewpoints (highest top: 2,965m), easily reached by cablecar to Le Brévent (2,526m). There are also considerable rock-climbs on the Aig. Rouges. A little further north Le Buet (3,099m) is also a popular viewpoint.

The area also provides limestone climbing of quality. Best known are the crags of Mont Salève (about 400ft high), immediately south of Geneva. At Sallanches there is the Croix de Fer which gives two miles of cliff some 700-800ft in height and there are numerous crags in the region of Annecy. Plenty of scope for exploration.

Guidebook: *Dents du Midi*, by R. Collomb.

HAWKER, Rev. William Henry (1827-74)
Attempted the Ebnefluhjoch with Whymper in 1865, but he usually climbed with his wife. They made early explorations of the mountains of Corsica and the Maritime Alps.

HAWKINS, Francis Vaughan (1833-1908)
A London barrister who had a brief but interesting climbing career. He took part in the second ascent of Monte Rosa (1855 – his first Alpine season) and the following year attempted, unsuccessfully, to make new routes on Mont Blanc. In 1859 he reconnoitred the Matterhorn and joined Tyndall (*qv*) the following year in an attempt on the summit from Breuil. (The third attempt on the mountain; they reached 13,000ft, the highest point at that date.) Hawkins was an Original Member of the A. C. but resigned in 1861.

HEARDMAN, Fred (1896-1973)
One of the great bogtrotters of the Pennines, contemporary with Thomas (*qv*). In 1925 he set a record for the Scottish 4,000s (*qv*) with H. Gilliat (11 hr. 8 min.) and in 1926 with J. F. Burton and H. Gerrard he created the classic Colne-Rowsley Walk (73 miles). At Heardman's suggestion the Tan Hill Walk was done in 1953 (120 miles,

Desmond, 1953, 54 hr. 10 min.).

HECKMAIR, Anderl (b. 1906)

One of the leading German climbers of the pre-war era, a member of the so called 'Munich School'. He began climbing in the Wilder Kaiser in the 1920s, and like many of his companions found plenty of time for climbing because he was out of work. He made the first direct ascent of the Charmoz North Face, and made several attempts on the Walker Spur, but is best known for the first ascent of the Eigerwand (1938) which he led. As a guide in the post-war years, Heckmair has climbed in many parts of the world.

HEDIN, Sven Anders (1865-1952)

A Swedish explorer who did a great deal of work in Central Asia. Mapped large areas of the Pamirs and Tibet, but his only attempt at a major ascent was in 1894 when he tried to climb Muztagh Ata and failed at 20,160 ft. He wrote many books about his adventures and was honoured by many scientific societies, but his pro-Nazi sympathies in later years damaged his reputation.

HEIGHT CONVERSION

The heights of mountains are expressed either in metres or feet.

Using the table below the same method can be used to convert feet to metres.

Conversion Table

Metres	Feet or Metres	Feet
0·305	1	3·281
0.610	2	6·562
0·914	3	9·842
1·219	4	13·123
1·524	5	16·404
1·829	6	19·685
2·134	7	22·966
2·438	8	26·247
2·743	9	29·528

Example: convert 5,894 m to feet

5,000 m	= 5 × 1,000	=	16404 ft
800 m	= 8 × 100	=	2624·7 ft
90 m	= 9 × 10	=	295·28 ft
4 m	=		13·123 ft
5,894 m			19337·103 ft = 19,337 ft

To make an approximate calculation of metres to feet, multiply by three and add 10 per cent. The result will be high. For instance, in the above example: 3 × 5,894 = 17682 + 1768 = 19,450 ft.

HELSBY CRAG

Overlooks Helsby in Cheshire. A fine sandstone outcrop with climbs of all standards. The crag has a long history, being the training ground for climbers like Kirkus (qv), Hargreaves, Banner and Carsten. There are also short gymnastic problems on the nearby Frodsham Hill.

Guidebook: *Helsby Crag*, by J. O'Neil.

HEMMING, Gary

An outstanding American rock-climber who began his career in the early fifties at Tahquitz Rock, San Diego. Hemming climbed in Yosemite, High Sierra, Tetons and Britain, but his greatest achievements were in the Chamonix area. In 1962, with Kendall, he made the first American ascent of the Walker Spur, Grandes Jorasses and with Robbins (qv), a direct start to the W Face of the Dru. In 1963 he climbed the S Face of the Fou with Frost, Harlin and Fulton. These two routes marked the introduction of Yosemite techniques to the Alps – both are extreme rock climbs. In 1966 he made solo ascents of the Couturier Couloir (Verte) and the N Face of Triolet, and was one of the leaders in a dramatic rescue of two trapped climbers on the Dru West Face.

A moody, temperamental person, Hemming died tragically by committing suicide in 1969.

HERFORD, Siegfried Wedgwood (1891-1916)
A fine rock-climber, who applied his grit-stone training to the bigger crags in Lake-land, especially Scafell. He began climbing in the Peak District about 1910 and quickly became the companion of gritstone experts like Laycock, Jeffcoat and A. R. Thomson. Laycock's guidebook to the outcrops, *Some Gritstone Climbs* (1913), was dedicated to Herford.

In 1912 Herford visited Scafell Crag. He made the second ascent of Botterill's Slab and Jones's Direct, completed Hopkinsons' Gully, made the first girdle traverse, and finally made a direct ascent to Hopkinsons' Cairn – a problem which had baffled experts for years.

In 1914 came the first ascent of the Central Buttress of Scafell, including the famous Flake Crack. The party was Herford, Sansom (who led the upper part of the climb), Gibson and Holland. It remained for many years the most difficult rock-climb in Britain and is still treated with respect.

Herford also climbed in Wales, Scotland, the Alps and the Dolomites. He was killed at Ypres in 1916.

HERZOG, Otto (1888-1964)
A German climber who is claimed to be the man who first used karabiners (*qv*). Amongst a number of very fine first ascents, that of the North Face of Dreizin-kenspitze, done in 1921 with G. Haber, was outstanding – probably the first Gr 6+ climb in the Alps.

HEY, Wilson Harold (1882-1956)
Distinguished Manchester surgeon and President of the Mountain Rescue Committee from 1939-56. Hey insisted on the need for morphia in the rescue kits and was prosecuted for this, being fined a nominal £10 and costs. The case showed that there was a need for morphia and the authorities eventually gave in to common sense. Hey was a considerable rock-climber and Alpinist.

HIGH-ALTITUDE CLIMBING
The term is relative, but is usually reserved for climbing in those ranges which exceed 20,000 ft, that is, Himalaya, Andes, Alaska, Pamirs, Tian Shan, Hindu Kush. Much of what follows, however, may well apply to lesser ranges which are nevertheless remote.

The special problems associated with the climbing of big mountains are: transport, logistics, diet, high-altitude equipment, physiology and weather. There may also be problems of human nature brought on by the temperaments of the climbers, the ability of the leader and morale in general. Ultimately, there are the tactics for the actual assault on the peak.

Political restrictions apart, transport to almost any area of the world is now quick and easy, though possibly expensive. Even the Everest Base Camp is within the range of tourists these days; though much preliminary work will need to be done over customs clearance, and so on. In the closer approach, animals or human porters will be needed and these are usually hired at the local villages en route. In the Himalaya, Sherpas are used for high-altitude porterage; they take up where the village porters leave off. On a big expedition the Sherpas will include a foreman or Sirdar, a cook, high-altitude Sherpas and ordinary Sherpas. The H. A. Sherpas may take part in the final assault (for example, Tenzing on Everest). In the Moslem areas of the Himalaya, Sherpas are not permitted (Karakorum, for instance) and Hunzas are often used instead (see SHERPAS). There does not seem to be the equivalent of the Sherpa outside the Himalaya, though local men have from time to time assisted expeditions and gone high.

With a large expedition, radio communication now plays a vital part. There is usually a strong radio link from Base to civilization and from Base to Advanced Base. Walkie-talkies are used from the Camps to communicate with Advance Base.

The logistic problems increase with the size of the expedition and the remoteness of the peak. Expeditions vary from solo efforts (one climber supported by porters) to vast national and international armies. The problem is pyramidical – the more climbers you need to support at the apex, the more porters you need at the base. In large expeditions there will be specialists for important functions such as supplies, communications, Base Camp management, medicine etc. The leader of such an expedition might be an overall manager and take no part in the climbing. On smaller expeditions, the various tasks are undertaken by the climbers. Every attempt is made to pack the requirements into loads of manageable proportions for the porters (up to 70 lb) and according to how they will be needed en route.

The diet for the climbers must not only be balanced but tempting because there is a general reluctance to face food. Cooking – even the boiling of water – can take a long time and a conscious effort.

High-altitude equipment includes double boots and overboots, down suits, Whillan's boxes (*qv*) and possibly oxygen. Oxygen increases work rate and also allows proper sleep in the thin atmosphere. Acclimatization helps with this major physiological problem and with proper acclimatization a man may climb up to about 27,000 ft without oxygen and stay there for a length of time, but deterioration will set in and probably nobody could do it more than once; recovery takes weeks. However, individuals vary and there have been some considerable feats of endurance in this sphere. (see: oxygen equipment). Failure to acclimatize properly can result in pulmonary or cerebral edema (*qv*).

The climb itself is done from a Base Camp and there may be an Advanced Base Camp if the approach to the climb is difficult. As the climb advances further camps are established until one is sufficiently near the top for a summit assault to be made (say, 2,000 ft). The whole business may take several weeks, with climbers and porters moving up and down, ferrying loads, making the route, and returning to Base for rest periods. This may be helped by leaving fixed ropes on the route (*qv*). The whole art is to get the right two men into the top camp at the right moment for a summit assault. Under favourable conditions the ascent may be repeated by other members of the party and it is not unknown for all members of an expedition to reach the summit. On the return, as much gear as possible is collected and taken down, but quite often considerable amounts are left. (see also HIMALAYA.)

HIGH LEVEL ROUTE (Fr.: Haute Route)

A route from Chamonix to Zermatt originated in 1861 by members of the Alpine Club and utilizing the high mountain passes. The original route was: Chamonix – Col d'Argentière – Val Ferret – Orsières – Bourg St. Pierre – Col de Sonadon – Col d'Oren – Praraye – Col de Valpelline – Zermatt.

In 1862 the Col des Planards was discovered and Orsières bypassed, and the route gradually tended further north after the Col de Sonadon as mountain huts were developed. It is usual now to include Arolla in the itinerary.

The route makes an excellent ski tour through some of the grandest scenery in the Alps and this is its principal function today.

Guidebook: *High Level Route*, by E. Roberts.

HIGH TOR, MATLOCK

An impressive limestone crag above the R. Derwent in Derbyshire offering modern, high-grade climbs. The crags extend down the banks of the river as far as Cromford, the principal ones being (besides High Tor) Wild Cat Crags and Willersley Crags.

High Tor Gully (Puttrell, Smithard, Bennett, 1903) led to the dissolution of the famous Kyndwr Club (*qv*). The first ascent of the crag's main face was by P. Biven and T. Peck in 1957 (Original Route).

Guidebook: *The Southern Limestone Area*, by P. Nunn.

HILLARY, Sir Edmund Percival (b. 1919)

A New Zealand climber, who, in 1953 was the first man to reach the summit of Everest (with Tenzing, *qv*). During an expedition to Garwhal in 1951 Hillary met and joined the Everest Reconnaissance and in the following year he joined Shipton again in the attempt on Cho Oyu. He made further expeditions to the Himalaya in 1954, 1961, 1963 and 1964, when he became involved in providing schoolhouses for the Nepalese children.

In 1956-8 he made a crossing of Antarctica, reaching the South Pole in December, 1957.

Hillary has written several books: *High Adventure* (1955), *The Crossing of Antarctica* (1958, with Fuchs), *No Latitude for Error* (1961) *High in the Thin Cold Air* (1963) and *Schoolhouse in the Clouds* (1965).

HILL-WALKING (FELL-WALKING)

The basic mountain craft, hill-walking can cover anything from a simple stroll over the Downs to a winter crossing of the Cairngorms. It involves an ability to walk over rough, hilly country with an economy of effort that does not leave one exhausted at the end. Hill-walkers need good walking boots (not shoes and not climbing boots), protective clothes for bad weather, map and compass. A thorough grasp of the art of navigation is vital.

In winter hill-walking can become part of the greater mountaineering scene, akin to walking in the Alps. Good winter gear and an ice axe are essential, crampons and rope often useful, and it is important to know how to use these things. On long treks, such as over the Cairngorms, the Carneddau or the Bleaklow-Kinder massifs, it is useful to have an emergency sleeping bag in case of accident or exposure.

The majority of hill-walkers are simply after an enjoyable and not too strenuous day on the hills, but there are some long testing courses for those who wish to extend themselves. Amongst these might be mentioned: the Welsh 3,000s; the Scottish 4,000s; the Lakeland 24-hour record; the Lyke Wake Walk; the Four Inns Walk; the Derwent Watershed; and the Yorkshire Three Peaks Walk. There are several others. All these have been done in record times by fell-runners – a specialized and strenuous form of the activity.

Long distance walks spread over several days (over trails or ways) are fairly common in both America and Britain. They usually have some theme: Offa's Dyke, for example. The best-known British walk of this kind is the Pennine Way which stretches from Edale in Derbyshire to Kirk Yetholm in Scotland, 250 miles.

If we disregard the crossing of glaciers or permanent snow as being outside the scope of hill-walking (and this is arguable), there is still a considerable amount of hillwalking done in the Alps, and especially in the Eastern Alps, where hut to hut tours in the limestone regions are commonplace. Walking up to huts in the Western Alps, lunching and then walking down again, is a popular pastime.

HIMALAYA

The greatest range of mountains in the world, lying between India in the south and Tibet in the north. The name comes from the Sanskrit words *hima* (snow) and *alaya* (abode).

The Himalaya is some 1,500 miles long, stretching from the Indus in the west to the Brahmaputra in the east and is about 100 miles in width. For most of its length it can be divided into three parts: the Siwalik range, rising from the Ganges plain, forested and never more than 3,000 ft high; the complex and wide middle range known as the Lesser Himalaya whose average height is 15,000 ft, limestone, and wooded on the lower slopes, with hill stations like Simla and Darjeeling; and finally the Great Himalaya, composed mostly of granites and gneisses, and seldom less than 18,000 ft in height. The highest summit is Everest (29,028 ft). There are 13 others over 26,000 ft and, in all, at least 31 peaks exceeding 25,000 ft. (There are considerable problems in determining the exact height of any great mountain and figures are revised from time to time.)

For most of its distance, the Great Himalaya is bounded on the north by the bleak Tibetan plateau, but at the western end of the range there are important transHimalayan ranges parallel with the main one, the best known and most important being the Karakorum (*qv*).

In 1907 Burrard divided the Himalaya into sections from west to east (revised by Mason, 1955). These are 1. Punjab Himalaya, 2. Trans-Himalaya, 3. Kunmaun Himalaya, 4. Nepal Himalaya, 5. Sikkim Himalaya and 6. Assam Himalaya. (see individual headings).

All of these sections are of interest to the climber, though of the 50 peaks exceeding 25,000 ft (including the trans-Himalaya) only nine are outside the Nepal or Karakorum sections. Four of these are in Sikkim, two each in Kunmaun and Punjab and one in Assam. The largest glaciers in the world, outside sub-polar regions, are found in the Karakorum.

Each group of mountains is known as a *himal*. Within each *himal* there is one or more principal peak and a number of subsiduary peaks, for example the Dhaulagiri Himal has four summits over 25,000 ft and at least five more only a little less high. As the main summits are climbed, so greater attention is paid to the others, and peaks previously unnamed are being regarded as mountains in their own right; thus the sum total of Himalayan mountains is constantly changing, making any list an approximation. Some mountains have alternative names: Baltoro Kangri *or* Golden Throne, Gasherbrum I *or* Hidden Peak. The Chinese invariably use their own names: Everest is Chomo Lungma, Gosainthan is Shisha Pangma. The difficulty over heights has already been mentioned but for a technical description see K. Mason, *Abode of Snow*.

Politically the Himalaya embraces the states of India, Pakistan, Tibet (China), Kashmir (in dispute), Bhutan, Nepal and Sikkim. Religious and political differences have made much of the area sensitive and access to some parts is difficult, even impossible, because of this. Physical access to some areas has been much improved in recent years by better roads and internal air services, but many areas are still so remote as to be virtually unknown to climbers. Financial handicaps are more recent: it is common now for the various governments to demand a fee for an attempt on a particular peak – and popular peaks, like Everest, have to be "booked" years in advance. The planning of an assault on a great Himalayan peak requires considerable organization and financial resources.

The weather can be a deciding factor in Himalayan climbing. The range is affected by the monsoon, more so in the east than the west. In Nepal it arrives at the end of May or beginning of June and lasts until

while in the former June to September are the best months, in the latter late June to early August are considered more favourable. In Kumaun, the monsoon arrives a little later than Nepal and seems to end earlier – there is a chance of success immediately after the rains in August (Nanda Devi climbed 29 August, 1936).

In the post-monsoon period the weather is colder and the winds on the high mountains are fierce – 100 mph is common. Kabru in Sikkim was climbed on 18 November 1935, but post-monsoon attempts in Nepal or the eastern ranges have met with scant success. The weather is

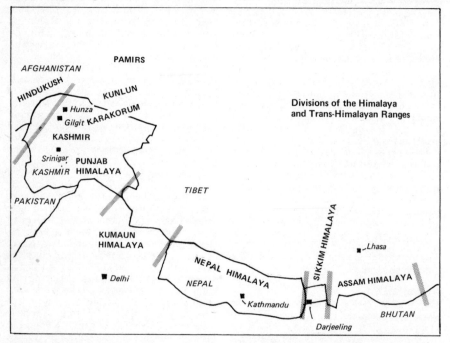

Divisions of the Himalaya and Trans-Himalayan Ranges

September. Precipitation is heavy, though there might be the occasional fine day, and climbing is virtually impossible. Access to the hills is made more difficult by swollen rivers.

The pre-monsoon period, between March and June, is usually chosen for climbing because the weather is warmer. There may well be local storms, and for three weeks or so before the monsoon arrives the weather might be unsettled (the *Chhoti barsat*). Climbers have mistaken this for the arrival of the monsoon proper. Further west, in Punjab and Karakorum, the effect of the monsoon is much less, so

often very dry during this period, however, and it is excellent for exploration of the valleys and for photography.

In the history of Himalayan climbing there has always been a strong element of exploration and the two have often gone hand in hand as principal aims of expeditions. The early surveyors, for example, ascended peaks which in other regions would have counted as major ascents but which were minor by local standards. Outstanding, perhaps, is the local surveyor who climbed Shilla (23,050 ft) in 1860 to plant survey poles, though this has recently been disputed.

The first climber to make a special visit to the Himalaya was M. Déchy in 1879, but illness prevented him from doing any climbing. Then came W. W. Graham with the guide J. Imboden and later, the guides E. Boss and U. Kauffmann in 1883. Graham claimed ascents of Changabang and Kabru, but these are disputed. Before the First World War the highest summit reached was Trisul, 23,360 ft (Longstaff, 1907), and the highest point attained was 24,600 ft on Chogolisa, (25,110 ft) (Duke of the Abruzzi, 1909). Other notable events were:

1892 Conway's Karakorum Expedition
1895 Mummery's attempt on Nanga Parbat
1899 Freshfield's circuit of Kangchenjunga
1902 Eckenstein's attempt on K2
1905 Guillarmod's attempt on Kangchenjunga
1907 Rubenson's attempt on Kabru
1910 Ascents of Pauhunri (23,180 ft) and Chomiomo (22,430 ft) by Kellas
1913 Meade's attempt on Kamet
1914 Ascent of Kun (23,250 ft) by Calciati

Between the Wars the Himalaya were notable for the successes of small parties on important peaks:

1931 Kamet (25,447 ft) – Smythe, (highest to date)
1933 Trisul (23,360 ft), second ascent – Oliver (first repeat of a big peak)
1935 Kabru (24,002 ft) – Cooke
1936 Nanda Devi (25,645 ft) – Tilman and Odell (highest pre-1950)
    Siniolchu (22,600 ft) – Bauer
    Nanda Kot (22,510 ft) – Takebushi
1937 Chomolhari (23,997 ft) – Chapman (smallest party: two, plus three Sherpas)
1939 Dunagiri (23,184 ft) – Roch
    Nanda Devi East (24,391 ft) – Karpinski
    Tent Peak (24,157 ft) – Schmaderer

The inter-war years also saw the great national and international expeditions to the highest peaks. None met with success and deaths were numerous. The highest point reached was 28,126 ft on Everest by Norton (1924) and Harris, Wager and Smythe (1933). The expeditions were: Everest (British) 1921, 1922, 1924, 1933, 1935, 1936, 1938 Kangchenjunga (German) 1929, 1930 (International), 1931, Nanga Parbat (German) 1932, 1934, 1937, 1938, 1939 K2 (American) 1938, 1939.

Post-war expeditions are too numerous to list in detail. The first peak of over

8.000 m Peaks

Name	Ht (m)	Ht (ft)	Section	First ascent
Everest	8848	29,028	Nepal	1953, British
K2	8611	28,253	Karakorum	1954, Italian
Kangchenjunga	8597	28,207	Sikkim	1955, British
Lhotse	8501	27,890	Nepal	1956, Swiss
Makalu	8481	27,824	Nepal	1955, French
Dhaulagiri I	8172	26,811	Nepal	1960, Swiss
Manaslu	8156	26,760	Nepal	1956, Japanese
Cho Oyu	8153	26,750	Nepal	1954, Austrian
Nanga Parbat	8125	26,658	Punjab	1953, Austro-German
Annapurna I	8078	26,504	Nepal	1950, French
Gasherbrum I*	8068	26,470	Karakorum	1958, American
Broad Peak I	8047	26,400	Karakorum	1957, Austrian
Gasherbrum II	8035	26,350	Karakorum	1956, Austrian
Gosainthan†	8013	26,291	Nepal	1964, Chinese

*Also called Hidden Peak
† Also called Shisha Pangma

Note. Kangchehjunga II (27,803 ft) has recently been regarded as a separate peak, in the climbing sense. Formerly ignored.

(See individual headings for details, also entries for EVEREST, K2, KANGCHENJUNGA and NANGA PARBAT. See also individual climbers, SHERPAS, HIGH-ALTITUDE CLIMBING.)

8,000 m (26,248 ft plus) to be climbed was Annapurna I (Herzog, 1950) and Everest itself was climbed in 1953 by John Hunt's expedition. By 1960 all the known 8,000 m peaks had been climbed, except the disputed Gosainthan. (See list.) By 1961, 63 7000 m peaks had been climbed (Dhyrenfurth). The greatest single factor in this was the opening of Nepal to exploration in 1949; it had previously been closed to foreigners.

Several peaks have had second and further ascents, for example Trisul, Everest, Nanda Devi, Nanga Parbat, etc. and Himalayan climbing is now entering into a new phase, comparable with the Alps in 1865, where new routes are being tried on "old" mountains. Notable are:

1951 Unsuccessful French attempt to traverse from Nanda Devi to Nanda Devi East. Duplat and Vignes killed.

1963 Successful American traverse of Everest by W and S ridges.

1970 Successful German traverse of Nanga Parbat S to NW.

South Face of Annapurna, first ascent by Bonington's expedition.

1969 to date. Various attempts on the SW Face of Everest.

HIMALAYAN CLUB

Formed in 1928 by the amalgamation of the original Himalayan Club and the Mountain Club of India, both of which were founded in 1927. The club is based in India and its aim is to encourage Himalayan climbing and exploration. It publishes *The Himalayan Journal* (1929), an authorative source of Himalayan information.

HINCHLIFF, Thomas Woodbine (1825-82)

A leading spirit in the formation of the A. C. of which he was President from 1875-7. Hinchliff's book *Summer Months in the Alps* (1857) was one of those that began the Golden Age of Alpine climbing, though his own achievements were fairly modest: first ascent of Wildstrubel Mittelgipfel, probably first ascent of the Oldenhorn (1857), and first ascent of Alphubel (1860) are the most notable. In 1862 he injured his hand in a gun accident which prevented him from further climbing. The discoverer of Melchior Anderegg (*qv*) in 1855.

HINDU KUSH

A 500-mile range of mountains west of the Indus and lying almost entirely within Afghanistan. Much of the range is unin-

teresting but there is an area of about 1,000 sq. m centred around the highest summit, Tirich Mir (25,263 ft) frequently visited by expeditions. The accessibility of the area, freedom from the monsoon and medium height of most of the peaks makes it an excellent area for small parties.

Principal summits

Tirich Mir (25,263 ft) – P. Kvernberg, A. Naess, H. Berg, A. Streather, 1950

Tirich Mir East (25,263 ft) – R. Höibakk, A. Opdal, 1964

Noshaq (24,581 ft) – Japanese and Polish parties, 1960

Istor o Nal (24,272 ft) – J. Murphy, T. Mutch, 1955

Pk (24,190 ft), NE of Istor o Nal – ascent not known.

Saraghrar (24,112 ft) – F. Maraini, 1959

Many other peaks 20,000-24,000 ft.

HOARE, Henry Seymour (1848-1930)

Made a number of new routes in the Alps in the company of Davidson, Hartley, etc. Made the first ascent of the Gross Engelhorn (1876) and of Mont Maudit (1878). In 1875 he made the first crossing of the Nantillons Col, which was not repeated for 29 years.

HOAR FROST

In conditions of extreme cold, frost crystals grow out from rocks, especially on exposed ridges. They can achieve remarkable sizes and look marvellous, but they do little to affect the climbing.

HODGKINSON, Rev. George Christopher (1816-80)

Was with Hudson (*qv*) on the first ascents of the Bosses Ridge of Mont Blanc and the Moine Ridge of the Aig. Verte. Also made the first ascent of the Col de Triolet (1863).

HOGGAR MOUNTAINS

Sometimes called Ahaggar Mountains. A wide area of volcanic pinnacles in the Sahara Desert, southern Algeria. Several expeditions have visited the area and many of the pinnacles climbed. The highest is Tahat (9,870 ft).

HOLDER, Henry William (1851–?)

Made three important visits to the Caucasus, 1888, 1890 and 1896, during which he made a number of first ascents including Adai Khokh (1890).

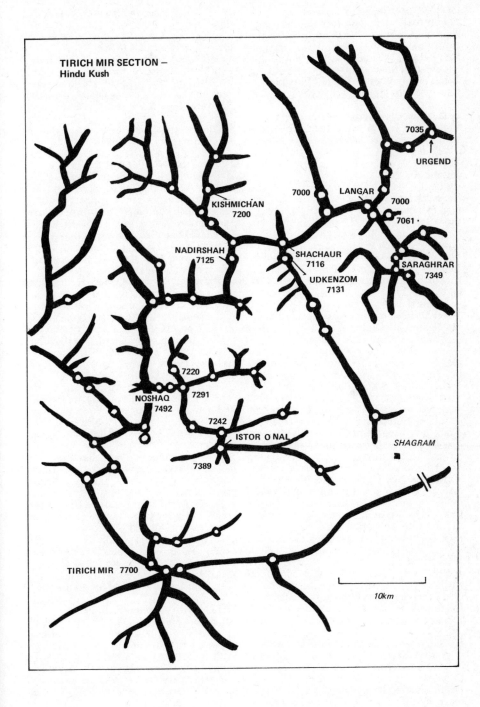

TIRICH MIR SECTION –
Hindu Kush

7035

URGEND

KISHMICHAN
7200

7000   LANGAR

7000

7061

NADIRSHAH
7125

SHACHAUR
7116

SARAGHRAR
7349

UDKENZOM
7131

7220

7291

NOSHAQ
7492

7242

ISTOR O NAL

7389

SHAGRAM

10km

TIRICH MIR 7700

HOLDS (It: appiglio; Fr: prise)

The cracks and rugosities on which a climber places his hands and feet in the course of a climb. They vary in size and shape and in their relative position to one another and these factors contribute to the difficulty or otherwise of a climb. Other factors are the type of rock, its friction and soundness.

The use of footholds usually offers little choice: one either places the foot on the hold – possibly just a toe – or, in the case of a suitable crack, jams it into the hold. There are occasional side pressure holds suitable for feet.

Handholds vary considerably. The easiest to use are those incut ones that the fingers can curl round and afford a pull; these are often called "jugs" if they are large. Pressure holds are holds where there is no grip as such and one relies on the friction of the rock. They may be sideways. There is also the "pinch grip", where the rock can be squeezed between fingers. A jammed hold (jamming) is when the hand is jammed into a crack for a pull. An undercut hold is one that is upside down, but it can be useful. All these holds may vary considerably in size and shape.

Loose holds occur on some climbs but may have to be used – a hold which might not bear a pull might bear using as a pressure hold. Some holds are friable and need gentle handling – thin flakes, for example, or sandstone flutings. All holds should be tested before use. Nevertheless, holds have been known to come away for no obvious reason, even on climbs which have been done many times.

On ice, handholds may have to be cut with the ice axe. This is usually done ladder fashion, each hand alternately. The same holds are used for the feet. Where handholds are not required, the footholds used in snow and ice work are known as steps. (See SNOW-CLIMBING and ICE-CLIMBING.)

HOLSTER

A stiff, conical tube attached to a harness for holding a piton hammer or hammer-axe. In modern ice-climbing it is common for the climber to wear two holsters, one for each ice axe.

HOLZMANN, Sir Maurice (1835-1909)

A German scientist who came to London in 1895 to research in chemistry but became instead an official of the royal household. He was a very active climber and made a number of first ascents in the East-ern Alps. He was an Original Member of the Climbers' Club.

HONG KONG, CLIMBS IN

The hills of Hong Kong have been compared with those of the Lake District: a walker's paradise. There are also good climbing areas: Lamtong Island, Kowloon Peak and Lion Rock with routes up to H. V. S.

Guidebook: *Rock Climbing Guide to Hong Kong*, by J. F. Bunnell.

HOPKINSON BROTHERS

A distinguished Manchester family related by marriage to the Tribes, Slingsbys, etc., and with them playing an important part in early British climbing. The brothers were: John (1849-98), Alfred (1851-1939), Sir Charles (1854-1920), Edward (1859-1921), Albert (1863-1949). Sir Charles was an M.P. and lawyer, Albert a surgeon, the others engineers – all brilliant.

The Hopkinsons kept few records and much of their climbing is unknown, but they were certainly among the originators of the sport. In 1882 they descended the E Face of Tryfan, four years before Haskett Smith climbed Napes Needle. In 1892 they ascended NE Ridge, Ben Nevis and descended Tower Ridge, two years before Collie (*qv*) paid his visit.

Hopkinson's Cairn was erected on the face of Scafell Pinnacle by Edward in 1887, and acted as a magnet to early climbers, who tried to reach it from below (see SCAFELL). It was not climbed until 1912 (Herford).

Either together or singly they took part in several of the famous early ascents, for example, Slingsby's Chimney, Scafell (1888, Edward). Their best-known routes are on Dow Crag: Great Gully Direct (1889) Intermediate Gully (1895) and Hopkinson's Crack (1895).

In the Alps they made a few minor routes, but in 1898 John Hopkinson and three of his children were killed climbing the Petite Dent de Veisivi, Arolla. The other brothers never climbed again.

HORNBEIN, Thomas F. (b. 1931)

An American doctor who began climbing at the age of 14 when he ascended Signal Mt in Colorado. He was on the Masherbrum expedition of 1960 but not in the summit party. Invited to join the American Everest Expedition for 1963, he was put in charge of oxygen and improved the system. With W. Unsoeld he climbed the West

Ridge of Everest (first ascent) and descended the South Ridge (first traverse),
bivouacking on the latter at 28,000 ft.
before reaching Camp 6 next day. One of
the most outstanding mountaineering
achievements ever accomplished. Wrote:
Everest – the West Ridge (1966).

HORNBY AND PHILPOTT

The Rev. James John Hornby (1826-1909)
and the Rev. Thomas Henry Philpott
(1839-1917) formed a famous partnership
which lasted from 1861-6. They crossed a
number of difficult passes and made the
first traverse of Aletschhorn (1864), the
first ascent of Lauterbrunnen Breithorn
(1865) (this was technically the second –
they arrived about ten minutes after von
Fellenberg!), and the NW Face (Ridge) of
the Silberhorn (1865). They might well
have done the first ascent of the Brenva
Route in 1863 had the idea not been vetoed
by their guide, Almer (*qv*).

Philpott was a student of Hornby's at
Durham University. Both men were strong
and good athletes, and Hornby was a
noted oarsman. The partnership ended in
1866 and Hornby retired from climbing
two years later on becoming Headmaster
of Eton. Philpott returned after a lapse of
26 years and did a couple of seasons, which
included some difficult routes.

HORT, Rev. Fenton John Anthony (1828-92)

Distinguished scholar and Professor of
Divinity at Cambridge. Hort made two
strenuous tours of the Alps in 1854 and
1856 but ill health later confined him to
topographical and botanical work. He
took an active part in the founding of the
A.C.

HOUSTON, Charles S. (b. 1913)

American medical professor noted for his
contributions to research on high-altitude
effects and diseases. Houston began climbing in the Alps in 1925 and had three seasons there. In 1936 he was leader, with
Tilman, of the successful team that made
the first ascent of Nanda Devi. Two years
later he led an American expedition to K2;
they reached c.26,000 ft. With Tilman
again in 1950 he led a small party into
Nepal and they were the first to see the
south side of Everest and the Western
Cwm. Houston was also leader of the
American K2 expedition of 1953 which encountered disaster at 25,000 ft and in which
Gilkey died.

Since 1967 Houston has been director of
high-altitude physiology programmes at
the laboratory (17,500 ft) on Mt Logan,
opened every year.

Besides numerous medical
contributions to books he is co-author of
Five Miles High (1939) and *K2, The Savage
Mountain* (1954).

HOWARD, Tony (b. 1940)

Played a leading part in the development of
the Dovestone area and the limestone dales
of Derbyshire in the early 1960s, but is best
known for his climbs in Romsdal, Norway
where he made the first ascent of the formidable Troll Wall (1965), said to be the
highest rock face in Europe. Besides
contributing to several Peakland guides he
wrote *Selected Climbs in Romsdal* (1965)
and later expanded this to *Walks and
Climbs in Romsdal* (1970). He is a well-
known equipment manufacturer (Troll).

HOWARD-BURY, Charles Kenneth (1883-1963)

An army officer with some experience of
exploration in Central Asia (Tien Shan,
1913) and subsequently chosen to lead the
first Everest Expedition (*qv*) in 1921 for
which he received the Founder's Medal, R.
G.S.

HUDSON, Rev. Charles (1828-65)

One of the greatest of the early Alpine
pioneers, killed in the Matterhorn tragedy
of 1865.

Hudson was one of the hardest men of
his day. At the age of 17 he averaged 27
miles a day on a walking tour of the Lake
District, and, according to Whymper,
could average 50 miles a day in his prime.
In 1853 he bivouacked in a sleeping bag at
7,000 ft in February when the temperature
was 13 degrees below zero, Fahrenheit. In
the same year he made a solo winter attempt to reach the Aig. du Goûter to
reconnoitre a new route up Mont Blanc.
He was an early exponent of guideless
climbing, making ascents of the K1, Matterhorn and Breithorn in 1855, and in the
same year, the first guideless ascent of
Mont Blanc (the first ascent from St. Ger-
vais). With Kennedy (*qv*), who accompanied him, he wrote a book about the
expedition: *Where there's a Will, there's a
Way* (1856).

Not all Hudson's climbs are recorded,
but among the most famous are the first
ascent of Monte Rosa (1855), first ascent
of Mont Blanc by the Bosses Ridge (1859),

and the first ascent of the Moine Ridge of the Aig. Verte (1865). (The ascent of the Bosses Ridge, claimed by Marie Couttet in 1840 and shown in some guidebooks, is now generally discounted.)

In 1865 Hudson, Hadow (a young novice) and their guide, Croz, were to attempt the Matterhorn from Zermatt when they were joined at the last moment by Whymper, Lord Francis Douglas and the Taugwalders, father and son. The combined party reached the summit at 1.40 p.m. on 14 July, but during the descent Hadow slipped, the rope broke and Hudson, Hadow, Croz and Douglas fell to their deaths. (See Whymper.)

Amongst his contemporaries, Hudson was held to be the finest mountaineer of all and there is much to support this idea. However, he twice took complete novices on difficult new climbs (see BIRKBECK) and on both occasions the result was a serious accident.

Hudson had been a Chaplain during the Crimean War (1854-5). At the time of his death he was Vicar of Skillington, Lincolnshire.

HUDSON, John Alfred (1838-74)
Took part in the first ascent of Lyskamm and the first traverse of the High Level Route from Zermatt to the Gd St Bernard (1861). Was later a companion of Girdlestone (qv) on the latter's guideless climbs.

HULTON, George Eustace (1842-1909)
A Manchester businessman who made the first ascent of the Arbengrat on the Gabelhorn and of the popular Cresta Rey on Monte Rosa (both 1874). With the Pilkingtons he later became interested in guideless climbing and made with them the first guideless ascents of Piz Kesch, Piz Roseg and Monte della Disgrazia (all 1882).

Hulton was also a pioneer of British climbing and the instigator of regular A.C. meets in Wales and the Lake District, usually in winter. He took part in the first ascent of Cust's Gully (qv) and the first ascent of Deep Ghyll, Scafell (1882). In 1883 he was with Pilkington and Walker in Skye when they made the first ascent of Bidein Druim nan Ramh and the second (or possibly third) ascent of the Inaccessible Pinnacle.

His brother, F. C. Hulton, also did a season in the Alps in 1873, when the two brothers made the 50th ascent of the Matterhorn.

HUNT, John Henry Cecil (b. 1910)
An army officer who led the successful Everest Expedition of 1953, for which he was knighted. Hunt had been on James Waller's spirited attack on Saltoro Kangri in the Karakorum in 1935, but was considered by the medical board not fit enough for the Everest Expedition of 1936. In 1937, with Cooke and Mrs Hunt, he explored the approaches to Kangchenjunga from the Zemu side and succeeded in reaching the SW Summit of Nepal Peak (23,440ft).

Hunt played a leading part in the foundation and organization of the Duke of Edinburgh's Award scheme and later in various social enquiries for the government. President of the A. C., 1956-8. Created Baron Hunt of Llanvair Waterdine. Wrote: *The Ascent of Everest, Our Everest Adventure*, and, with C. Brasher, *Red Snows*.

HUTS (G.: Hutte, Haus; Fr.: Refuge, cabane; It.: Rifugio, Capanna)
A mountain hut is a purpose-built refuge situated at some strategically high place in the mountains so that one or more peaks are readily accessible from it. It may vary from a simple bivouac shelter to something resembling a small hotel in size and facilities.

Huts were built to enable climbers to do away with the bivouacs endured by the pioneers. They mostly belong to the various Alpine Clubs, but there are a few belonging to university clubs and, in Tyrol, even to private families. All huts are open to anyone wishing to use them, though they are cheaper for club members and there are reciprocal rights between the various Continental clubs.

Huts are cared for by a guardian (G.: *Huttenwarte*), who is often a guide or ex-guide. In the larger huts he will have several assistants, often his family. It is unusual for a hut to remain open the whole year, but with the growth of skiing, many now open for the winter months as well as summer. When a hut is closed, some outbuilding or separate room is often left open for emergency use. Bivouac huts and some remote huts have no guardian.

There is no standard pattern to the facilities of the huts, even within one area, and the following can only be taken as generalizations:

French Alps: *dortoir*; meals provided; self-catering allowed.

Swiss Alps: *dortoir*; meals provision

(except simple soups) not general but increasing; no self-catering – the guardian cooks food brought by the party.

Austrian Alps (including Germany and Italy): *dortoir*, but also small rooms with bunks; meals provided, including a cheap *bergsteiger essen*.

Dortoir accommodation consists of communal bunks (G.: *Matratzenlager*). It is usual to sleep fully clothed, ready for a quick start in the morning (often 3a.m. – 4a.m.), though blankets are provided. In unguardianed huts there are often just the bare necessities, and climbers may have to provide their own fuel for cooking.

Supplies for huts were previously brought up by porters or on mules, but the téléférique or helicopter is more usual today.

The highest mountain hut in the Alps is the Capanna Margherita on the Signalkuppe of Monte Rosa (4556 m). It holds 25 climbers and is guardianed. The largest hut is probably the Berliner in the Zillertal range, Tyrol. It would be difficult to estab-lish which hut was the oldest but many were established in the 1860s and 1870s.

British mountain huts are usually valley bases, owned by various climbing clubs and available only to club members or those with reciprocal rights from another club. They have no resident guardian. At Glen Brittle, Skye, there is a hut built to commemorate climbers killed in the last war and this is open to members of all clubs affiliated to the British Mountaineering Council.

The Mountain Bothies Association repairs and maintains old shepherds' huts which serve as high-level bivvy huts for climbers.

HUT SHOES

It is forbidden to wear climbing boots inside Alpine huts. Boots are left in the porch and the climber wears hut shoes. These may be soft chamois leather slippers he has brought up from the valley or wooden soled clogs provided by the huts. Not all huts provide clogs.

ICE AXE (G.: Pickel; Fr.: Piolet; It.: Piccoza)

An essential piece of equipment wherever ice and snow-climbing is involved. The axe consists of a head, a shaft and a ferruled spike. The head is of hardened steel with one end fashioned into an adze or blade and the other into a pick. The shaft is straight-grained hickory or ash, though this is now being rapidly ousted by metal shafts or synthetic materials, which are stronger and do not deteriorate. The spike and ferrule are of hardened steel. The axe may or may not be equipped with a wrist strap.

Axe shafts vary in length from 60–90 cm – the longer ones are often known as walkers' axes, though in fact they are suitable for all but the very steep ice-climbs (see below). The trend over the years has been for ever shorter ice axes.

More recently, even shorter axes have been developed to cope with the very steep ice encountered in modern ice-climbs and the new techniques of climbing. These often have a hammer head replacing the adze (a hammer axe) and specially curved picks to allow maximum front pointing techniques.

There are four functions of an axe to be considered and these have changed in emphasis over the years:

1. As a WALKING STICK. The so called "third leg". Modern short axes often make this impossible and the use has virtually died out. It is still used in the special case of traversing, but otherwise the axe is best carried in a position of braking (below).

2. FOR STEP-CUTTING. Once the main function and still useful for this, though modern crampon techniques have reduced the importance of steps. (See STEPS.)

3. As a BELAY (qv). Again, still useful for this, but ice screws and snow anchors are better.

4. As a BRAKE. The axe can be used as a brake to arrest a slip on snow or snow-ice. The axe is held across the body and if a slip occurs the victim presses the spike gradually into the snow, thus braking. For most climbers this is now the most important function of an axe. The technique needs practice on safe slopes.

Ice axes have been in use from early pioneering days and seem to have originated from peasant's implements. Many climbers designed their own. The axe was contemporary with the alpenstock (qv) but had virtually supplanted the latter by the 1870s.

Early axes were ponderous affairs, very long and heavy, designed for chopping steps by the hundred. There have been continuous changes and many variations, including axes which unscrewed into sections, so that they could be carried easily when packed.

Ice axes can be dangerous weapons. The spike and head need covering when not in use – this is compulsory on many Continental transport systems. (See ICE-CLIMBING.)

ICE-CLIMBING

An important part of mountaineering techniques, ice-climbing is currently undergoing revolutionary changes (1973) brought about by new equipment.

The original art in climbing ice was that of step-cutting (qv), which depended on an ice axe and good nailed boots. Steps were cut using the pick of the axe either straight up the slope, or, where the ice was very steep, in zig-zag fashion with a large bucket step, or turning step, at each bend. The nailed boots gave admirable grip on hard ice though they tended to ball up in snow. Some very difficult climbs were completed in this way, including several of the early nordwands (qv). Protection was not possible until ice pegs came into use, about the 1920s.

The greatest single advance in ice equipment was the crampon (qv), which allowed progress on fairly steep ice which would have otherwise needed steps. Crampons were introduced quite early, but were regarded with suspicion and even hostility by many climbers. They were adopted in the Eastern Alps, however, and by the English climber Eckenstein (qv) who improved their design. With the introduction of the rubber-soled boot in post-war years (pre-war on the Continent) their use became virtually imperative. Many climbers, particularly in Scotland, still preferred nails, and mixed soles of rubbers and nails were used for a time.

As steeper ice-climbs were attempted, particularly in Scotland, the disadvantage of the long axe became obvious and the Scots used slater's picks to cut the hand and footholds necessary. (See *Mountaineering in Scotland*, by W. H. Murray.) By the 1950s, the general advantages of shorter axes were becoming acknowledged in the Alps, and the so-called dagger technique was evolved. In this, a short axe was used in one hand and an ice dagger (often a sharpened piton) in the other. The technique depended upon the front points of the crampons, the "lobster claws", and consisted of simply stabbing one's way up the face, using axe, dagger, and front points alternately. The method was tiring, though quick, and it was usual to cut resting steps at intervals. Belays and runners were provided by ice screws which came in during the fifties.

Though the early climbers had disdained the use of any attachment to their ice axes, the loss of an axe during a climb is so potentially serious that wrist straps were introduced. It is safe to say that the majority of ice-climbing is still done using a combination of the methods outlined above – that is general cramponing with occasional steps and moderately long axes.

Quite recently it has been shown in Scotland and elsewhere that steep ice can be climbed much more quickly by combining front pointing techniques with specially curved or angled ice-axe blades. The "Terrordactyl" and the "Chouinard" are the most common of these, the former having an angled pick at 55° to the shaft, and the latter a deeply curved pick. With the Terrordactyl, the ice is stabbed and a pull given to the axe which then sticks firmly in place; a blow from a Chouinard has the same effect. It is then possible to pull up on the axe, stabbing with front points, then place the second axe higher, and so on. Two axes are needed, but they are very short – little longer than a hammer. Vertical ice can be climbed in this way and a number of standard hard climbs such as Zero and Point Five Gullies on Ben Nevis have been done in remarkably short times using the new methods. The axes are usually attached to the harness by cords.

On moderately steep ice it is often possible for two climbers to move together, possibly using runners but not stances. This is quick, but demands a good understanding between the two climbers. Where the ice steepens, one climber cuts a stance and belays to an ice screw (or possibly more than one) while the other climbs. The leader runs out the full length of rope then he in turn cuts a stance and belays, to bring up the second, and so on.

Belaying on ice is a sensitive business. The best belay is a rock peg, if there is any rock conveniently placed, otherwise a strong ice peg, such as the tubular kind, is needed. If no screws or pegs are carried, a direct belay round the pick of the axe is the only security. Where pegs are used, a normal rock-climbing belay procedure is followed.

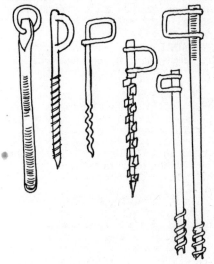

Ice-climbs vary from season to season. In Britain the best ice-climbs are found in Scotland in winter, particularly on Ben Nevis and in the Cairngorms and Glen Coe – all popular areas. They are graded in difficulty from the easiest (I) to the hardest (V). South of the border conditions are even less certain, but the Great End gullies in the Lakes, Kinder Downfall and Back Tor in the Pennines, and occasional routes in Wales can give good climbs.

See *Modern Snow & Ice Techniques*, by W. March.

ICE-FALL

When a glacier flows over a steep declivity, the ice fractures into enormous crevasses and pinnacles (seracs, *qv.*). Such an area is an ice-fall. They sometimes have to be crossed; this is often difficult and always potentially dangerous because the glacier is moving slowly downhill and this causes the seracs to fall. Well-known examples include the Géant ice-fall on the Mer de Glace and the huge two-mile long ice-fall descending from the Western Cwm of Everest.

ICELAND, CLIMBING IN
The island is well known for its volcanic scenery: geysers, hot springs, volcanos. The interior of the country is very bleak, though there are spectacular waterfalls, and travel is difficult. The largest of the ice sheets is the Vatna Jokull, which rises to almost 7,000 ft and there are numerous peaks, mostly 4–5,000 ft, but much of the rock is poor and there is not a great deal of interest for the climber.

ICE SCREWS
Ice screws have largely superseded ice pitons (qv) for belays and runners in steep ice-climbing.

The two principal types are the corkscrew and the tubular: the first is self explanatory, the second is hollow and threaded on the outside, in the manner of a soil sampler. Each has a closed ring at the top to hold a karabiner (qv). They are screwed into the ice and are easier to place and remove than a piton and less damaging to the ice.

Under a hot sun, ice screws (like ice pitons) should not be left in place for too long because heat is conducted down the metal and melts the surrounding ice. The screw then works loose. Belays should be repositioned from time to time if necessary. (See diagram on p. 125)

IDWAL
One of the most popular climbing areas of Snowdonia, it comprises a series of cliffs surrounding Llyn Idwal, a hanging valley above Ogwen. The principal cliffs are: Idwal Slabs, Slabs East Wall, Holly Tree Wall, Gribin Facet (Clogwyn y Tarw), Upper Cliff of Glyder Fawr and the Devil's Kitchen Cliffs (Clogwyn y Geifr). There are a number of minor cliffs, too, and Y Garn usually offers easy snow-climbs in winter.

The Slabs offer mostly easy climbing of some length but without variety: frequently used by novices under instruction. Their East Wall is steep and fierce. The Devil's Kitchen is a deep and striking

gully, famous in pioneering days and a trap for the unwary.

The first climb was the Central Gully of Glyder Fawr by J.M.A. Thomson (qv) in 1894. Other notable first ascents include:

1895 Grey Rib, Glyder Fawr – J.M.A. Thomson
     Devil's Kitchen (Twll Du) (winter ascent) – Thomson, Hughes
1897 Slabs Ordinary – Rose, Moss
1898 Devil's Kitchen – Reade, McCulloch
1899 Hanging Garden Gully – O. G. Jones, Abraham brothers
1905 Monolith Crack, Gribin – Abraham brothers
1912 Zig Zag, Gribin – Herford, Laycock, Milligan, Hodgkinson
1915 Hope, Slabs – Mrs Daniell, Richards, Roxburgh, Henderson
1918 Original, Holly Tree Wall – Richards, Holland, Miss Pilley
1919 Tennis Shoe, Slabs – Odell (solo)
1929 Heather Wall – Hicks, Hargreaves, Stewardson
1945 Suicide Wall – Preston, Morsley, Haines

Guidebook: *Cwm Idwal*, by A. J. J. Moulam.

ILKLEY
On the edge of the famous moor there are some gritstone outcrops. The three main climbing areas are Cow and Calf Rocks, the Quarry, and Rocky Valley. Fairly short and all standards. Popular.

Guidebook: *Yorkshire Gritstone*, by M. Bebbington

IMSENG, Ferdinand (1845-81)
A guide from the Saas valley, though he lived from the age of 20 in Macugnaga. Imseng sprang to fame suddenly when he persuaded the Pendlebury's (qv) to attempt the East Face of Monte Rosa in 1872, with great success. A few weeks later he accompanied Passingham and Dent on the first ascent of the Zinal Rothorn from Zermatt, and in 1879 was Penhall's guide in the latter's race with Mummery for the Zmutt ridge of the Matterhorn. Their route, via the West Face, has seldom been repeated.

Whilst repeating the Monte Rosa climb with Signor Marinelli in 1881, Imseng and his party were overwhelmed by an avalanche. Marinelli and his two guides were killed; a porter escaped. The climb is now known as the Marinelli Couloir.

INNERKOFLER, Michael (1848–1888)
A member of the pioneer Dolomite guiding family who made a number of first ascents in that region including Zwolferkogel (1875), Elferkogel (1878), Grohmannspitze (1880) and Cima Piccola de Lavardedo (1881). He died in an accident on Monte Cristallo.

INNERKOFLER, Sepp (1865-1915)
One of the most famous pioneer guides of the Dolomites with numerous first ascents to his credit. Killed making an attack on an Italian observation post on the summit of the Paternkofel.

INTERIOR RANGES, BRITISH COLUMBIA
Comprise four major ranges: Selkirks, Purcells, Monashee and Cariboo. The Selkirks, which contain the highest peaks, form the western side of the great Rocky Mountain Trench. On their western sides the ranges tail away towards the larger coast ranges (*qv*). The highest peak is Mt Sir Sanford (11,590 ft – Palmer, Holway, Aemmer, Feuz, 1912). The northern Selkirks are difficult of access.

The most accessible parts of the Selkirks are those around Glacier, opened to climbers when the C.P.R. pushed a railroad through the Rogers Pass in 1885. W. S. Green (*qv*) made a number of ascents in 1888 and the impressive Mt Sir Donald (10,818 ft) was climbed by E. Huber, C. Sulzer, H. Cooper. Sir Donald remains the most popular peak in the area.

More recently, interest has been centred on the Purcell range where the splendid Bugaboo spires give some of the best rockclimbing in North America (*qv*).

Guidebook: *Climbers' Guide to the Interior Ranges of British Columbia*, by W. Putnam.

IRAN (PERSIA), CLIMBING IN
The borders and coasts of Iran are guarded at almost every point by mountains, many of which are virtually unknown to climbers. Best known, and highest, is the great snow cone of Demavend (18,603 ft), first climbed (as far as is known) by Sir W. Taylor Thompson in 1836. Demavend is the summit of the Elburz Mountains of which other interesting peaks are Alam Kuh (15,880 ft) and Takht-i-Sulieman (15,154 ft). The range has been well explored by British, German and French parties.

Other mountains explored include Kuh-

i-Savalan (Kuhha-ye Sabalan) in Azerbaijan, whose height of 15,788 ft seems in dispute. The same applies to the little-known mountains of the Zagros Range, where Zard Kuh is given the height of 14,920 ft and Kuh i Dena, 14,030 ft (The latter has also been given 16,995 ft; a considerable difference!) There are several peaks here of 12–13,000 ft. In the east, near Baluchistan, lies the old volcano of Kuh-i-Taftan, 13,268 ft. (See *The Mountains of Elburz*, by B. Pierre, *A. J.* 61.)

IRELAND, CLIMBS IN
The principal Irish mountain groups are: Mournes (Slieve Donard, 2,796 ft), Sperrin Mountains (Sawel, 2,240 ft), Wicklow Mountains (Lugnaquillia, 3,039 ft), Blackstairs Mountains (Mt Leinster, 2,610 ft), Silvermine Mountains (Keeper Hill, 2,278 ft), Derryveagh Mountains (Errigal, 2,466 ft), Blue Stack Mountains (Blue Stack, 2,219 ft), Cuilcagh Mountains (Cuilcagh, 2,188 ft), Macgillicuddy's Reeks (Carrauntual, 3,414 ft, the highest mountain in Ireland), Brandon Peak (3,127 ft), Slieve Mish Mountains (Baurtregaum, 2,796 ft), Slieve Miskish Mountains (Maulin, 2,044 ft), Caha Mountains (Hungry Hill, 2,251 ft), Shehy Mountains (Knockboy, 2,321 ft), Galtee Mountains (Galtymore, 3,048 ft), Knockmealdown Mountains (Knockmealdown, 2,609 ft), Comeragh Mountains (Fauscoum, 2,597 ft), Murrisk Mountains (Mweelrea, 2,688 ft), North Mayo Hills (Nephin 2,646 ft) Twelve Bens (Benbaun, 2,395 ft). (This list runs approximately north to south and east to west.)

There are also considerable areas of sea cliffs, especially in the West, some rising to over 1,000 ft and virtually unexplored.

Though Haskett-Smith wrote about Irish climbing at the end of the nineteenth century, the sport there did not make much advance until after the last war when due to the efforts of climbers like J. P. O'F. Lynam, W. R. Perrott, P. Kenny, F. Winder, F. Maguire, P. Gribbon and A. Kopczynski, numerous climbs of all standards were put up. The principal climbing areas are Luggala, Glendalough, Ben Corr – but there are many developments taking place in other parts. The Irish Mountaineering Club is at present producing modern guides to Glendalough, the Mournes and Donegal.

IRVINE, Andrew Comyn (1902-24)
A member of the Oxford Spitzbergen

Expedition of 1923, on the strength of which he was chosen to go to Everest on the 1924 expedition, though his mountaineering qualifications were negligible. Inexplicably, Mallory chose Irvine instead of the experienced Odell as his partner for the summit assault. Both disappeared above Camp VI (8 June 1924).

IRVING, Robert Lock Graham (1877-1969)

A Winchester schoolmaster and writer whose pioneering work with pupils in the Alps caused a stir at the turn of the century. His most famous pupil was Mallory (*qv*).

Irving's books were popular with a wide public. They are: *La Cime du Mont Blanc* (1933), *Romance of Mountaineering* (1935), *The Mountain Way* (1938), *The Alps* (1939), *Ten Great Mountains* (1940) and *A History of British Mountaineering* (1955).

ISLE OF MAN, CLIMBS IN

The highest point of this popular holiday island is Snaefell (2,034 ft), but most of the climbing is on the coastal cliffs in the south where there has been considerable development of late. The sea-stack called the Sugarloaf, 160 ft, was climbed by A. W. Kelly in 1933.

Guidebook: *Rock Climbs in the Isle of Man*, by G. Gartrell.

JACKSON, Mrs. Edward Patten (1843 – 1906)

One of the most outstanding Victorian lady climbers, with about 140 major climbs to her credit. She climbed mainly with her husband until his early death, aged 39, in 1881. She made a new route on the Weissmies (1876) and what seems to be second traverse of the Matterhorn by a woman (1877). In 1884, with Dr K. Schultz, she made a descent of the Ferpècle Arête of the Dent Blanche, five years before its first ascent. In 1888 she made the first winter ascents of Gross Lauteraarhorn, Pfaffenstöckli, Gross Viescherhorn and first winter traverse of Jungfrau, all in the space of 12 days. Mrs Jackson's career deserves further research by Alpine historians.

JACKSON, James (1845-1926)

A very strong climber noted for carrying out expeditions in a single day, for example, Breuil to Zermatt over Matterhorn (1872), Monch from Wengern Alp, Eiger (first traverse, 1872), etc. In 1876 he made the first ascent of the Michabelgrat of the Täschhorn.

JACKSON, Rev. James (1796-1878)

Eccentric vicar of Rivington, Lancashire, who repaired his own church weathercock and was thereafter known as Steeple Jackson. He celebrated this event in one of his many doggerel verses:

Who has not heard of Steeple Jack
That lion hearted Saxon?
Though I'm not he, he was my sire
For I am Steeple Jackson!

Resigned in 1856 and lived in Cumberland where he made some long walks suitable for a man half his age: 46 miles in 14½ hours, followed two days later by 56 miles in 18 hours and a day later, 60 miles in under 20 hours. He was then 69.

On 31 May 1875 (aged 79) he climbed Pillar Rock, alone. He called himself Patriarch of the Pillarites. Three years later he tried to repeat the ascent but fell and was killed.

JACOMB, Frederick William (c1828-93)

Made the first ascent of Castor and Monte Viso (1861) as well as several cols and minor peaks. Played a large part in establishing the High Level Route (qv).

JAMES, Ronald (b. 1933)

Leading British guide and educationalist: head of the Outdoor Pursuits at the I. M. Marsh College of Education, the only degree course of the kind in Britain.

James was the founder of the Ogwen Cottage Mountain School (1959), the most successful private venture of its type, until it was taken over by an education authority in 1964. He remained as Warden until 1969. During this period he led 350 mountain rescues.

Ron James is perhaps best known for the new Welsh climbs he has originated. These total 80, amongst which might be mentioned: Touch and Go (1957), Mean Feet (1957), Grey Arête (1959), Devil's Nordwand (1959), Connie's Crack (1961), Lavaredo (1961), Meshach (1962) Epitaph (1962), Plum (1964) and Ampitheatre Girdle (1966).

He has made many British first ascents in the Alps, often with his wife, Barbara James, who has one of the best climbing records, Alpine and British, of any woman climber today.

His books are: Rock Climbing in Wales (1970) and Rockface – The Technique of Rock Climbing (1974).

JAMMING (Fr.: Coincement; it.: Incastro)

An important method of crack climbing where progress is made by wedging one's feet and hands in the crack and relying upon the friction. There are all types of jams: foot-jam, toe-jam, finger-jam, etc. One of the most important is the hand-jam, in which the hand is places sideways into the crack and then the thumb is brought across the palm, locking the hand into place. Improvements made in jamming techniques has been one of the factors responsible for the advancement of modern rock-climbing.

JAN MAYEN ISLAND

A small island nearly mid-way between

Iceland and Spitsbergen. The Beerenberg (7,680 ft) is an extinct volcano, climbed in 1921.

JAPAN, CLIMBING IN

The highest mountain in Japan is Fujiyama (12,390 ft), the well-known volcano shrine standing isolated and splendid about 50 miles west of Yokohama. It was reputedly first climbed by a monk, Enno Ozuno, in the seventh century. Ski mountaineering has taken place on the peak since 1913.

Most of Japan is mountainous, but the chief climbing interest lies in the Japanese Alps where Kitadake (10,470 ft) is the highest point, and the second highest mountain in Japan. The Japanese Alps are divided into three ranges: North, Central and South with 26 peaks of 3,000 m or more, steep-sided, sharp-ridged and composed of granite. In summer they are bare rock, above the tree line, but in winter they are often deeply snow-covered and temperatures can drop to −20° C. Both summer and winter climbing is popular. The Northern Alps are the most frequented with splendid peaks like Tsurugidake (9,835 ft), Yarigadake (10,433 ft) and Hodakadake (10,466 ft). There are no permanent glaciers. There are Japanese guidebooks to all the regions. Some winter climbing is also done in the Kurile and Sakhalin Islands.

There are Shinto shrines on the summit of many Japanese mountains and the importance of mountains in their religious beliefs has accustomed the Japanese to the special ambience of mountains, and made modern climbing readily acceptable to them. The Rev. Walter Weston (qv) was the father of Japanese mountaineering, helping to found the Japanese Alpine Club in 1905. It was Weston who first called the Japanese mountains 'alps'. At first the sport was taken up only by students from the privileged classes. With the aid of Swiss guides, Yuko Maki made the first ascent of the Eiger Mittellegigrat in 1921 and Mt Alberta in the Rockies in 1925.

Since those early days, Japanese climbing has developed along familiar lines: increasingly difficult ascents at home, new and hard climbs in the European Alps, and expeditions to the Himalaya and elsewhere. In expeditions, they outnumber every other country − possibly all other countries added together. For instance, in 1965, Japan mounted 53 overseas expeditions. Their successes, and failures, have

been in proportion. Outstanding was their first ascent of Manaslu (8156 m) in 1956. They were the first to attempt the South West Face of Everest (1969) and in 1970 they made the 15th and 16th successful ascent by the S Ridge.

JAYAL, Narendra Dhar (1926-58)

First Director of the Himalayan Mountaineering Institute at Darjeeling, Jayal was an Indian Army officer with considerable Himalayan experience including the second ascents of Abi Gamin (1952) and Kamet (1955). Died of pulmonary oedema attempting the second ascent of Cho Oyu.

JONES, Owen Glynne (1867-99)

One of the pioneers of British rock-climbing and a close friend of the Abraham brothers (qv). He began climbing at Cader Idris in 1888 but first visited the Lake District, where he was to make his mark, in 1890, when he climbed on Pillar. He knew none of the climbing fraternity and made many ascents solo, or with chance acquaintances. In 1893 he soloed Moss Ghyll under winter conditions, fell and cracked his ribs, but completed the ascent, and repeated the climb three days later. Apart from Cader Idris, where he had made the first ascent of the Cyfrwy Arête (solo), his next first ascent seems to have been the minor East Pisgah Chimney on Pillar (solo).

In 1893 he met J. W. Robinson, with whom he climbed Sergeant Crag Gully and Kern Knotts Chimney − both first ascents. He met the Abrahams in 1895 and climbed frequently with them thereafter; he posing for their photographs and they helping him with his guidebook compilation. (See list of climbs below.)

In 1896 he published *Rock Climbing in the English Lake District* − a guide to the climbs. In it he laid out the first system of classification of difficulty (see GRADINGS). These were: Easy, Moderate, Difficult, and Exceptionally Severe.

Jones was not an easy companion and rather abrupt in manner. His climbing was far from elegant − rough and spasmodic, was how George Abraham described it, but he was immensely strong. He thought little of his British climbs, hoping to make a name for himself as an Alpinist. This he never achieved, though he did many of the standard climbs and made a good winter ascent of the Schreckhorn in 1897. He was killed on the Dent Blanche in 1899 while attempting the Ferpècle Arête (sometimes known since then as the Jones Arête). His guide, Furrer, fell and pulled off Jones and a second guide, Vuignier. The rope broke between Vuignier and the last, man, Hill, who was left to make an incredible solo escape. Jones was buried at Evolene. In private life he was a science teacher.

List of first ascents

LAKE DISTRICT		*Companions*
1892	East Pisgah Chimney	–
1893	Sergeant Crag Gully	J. W. Robinson
	Kern Knotts Chimney	W. H. Fowler, J. W. Robinson
1896	Jones's Direct from Deep Ghyll	Abraham brothers
1897	Central Chimney, Dow	G. Ellis
	C Gully, Screes	H. C. Bowen
	Kern Knotts West Chimney	C. W. Patchell
	Kern Knotts Crack	H. C. Bowen
1898	Jones's Route, Dow	W. J. Williamson
	Jones's Direct from Lords Rake	G. T. Walker
	Jones and Collier's Climb, Scafell	–
	Pisgah Buttress, Scafell	Abraham brothers
	B Chimney, Overbeck	G. Abraham
1899	E Chimney, Overbeck	G. Abraham, A. E. Field, J. W. F. Forbes
	Walker's Gully, Pillar	G. Abraham, A. E. Field

NORTH WALES		
1888	Cyfrwy Arete, Cader Idris	—
1895	Craig Cau Gullies, Cader Idris	Haskett Smith
1899	North Buttress, Tryfan	Abraham brothers
	Terrace Wall Variant Tryfan	Abraham brothers
	Milestone Buttress Ordinary	Abraham brothers
	Devil's Staircase, Geifr	G. Abraham
	Hanging Garden Gully, Geifr	Abraham brothers

DERBYSHIRE
1897 Boulder Climb, Robin Hood's Stride
       Probably others. Companions probably the Abrahams and Puttrell.)
    This list is noteworthy in that many of these climbs are still among the most popular in Britain.

JORDAN, William Leighton (1837-1922)
A widely travelled climber noted for his great strength. He made the first ascent of the Italian Ridge of the Matterhorn by the Maquignaz's variation (1867) and later donated the fixed ladder known as the Echelle Jordan.

JOURNALS
Many clubs issue a journal or newsheet. The important ones are listed on p. 132.

JULIAN ALPS, THE
A group of limestone mountains on the Jugoslav – Italian borders. The chief summit is Triglav (2,863m), whose North Face has a number of good climbs, though the ordinary ascent is easy. Other good peaks are Jalovec (2,643m), Skrlatica (2,738m) and Canin (2,587m). There are many others. Bohinjska Bistrica is a well-known tourist village central to the area, but other good centres are Kranjska Gora, Mojstrana and Jesenice. Numerous huts for climbers. (No English guidebook.)

JUMAR CLAMPS
A device for prusiking (*qv*) up fixed ropes (*qv*). The most comfortable and effective device for this technique, jumars consist of a clamp fitted with a handle. A jumar can be moved upwards, but will hold a downwards pull unless the locking mechanism is opened. They are less secure when used

horizontally, as on a traverse.

Besides their use on fixed ropes, they have obvious uses in crevasse or cliff res-cue. The word is frequently used as a verb, "to jumar", and one speaks of "jumaring".

JOURNALS
(A = annual; Q = quarterly; B = bi-monthly; M = monthly)

British
Alpine Climbing	A	Alpine Climbing Group
Alpine Journal	A	Alpine Club
Climber & Rambler	M	commercial publication
Climbers' Club Journal	A	Climbers' Club
Fell & Rock Journal	A	Fell & Rock Climbing Club
Mountain	M	commercial publication
Mountain Life	B	commercial publication
Rocksport	M	commercial publication
Rucksack Club Journal	A	Rucksack Club
Scottish M.C. Journal	A	Scottish Mountaineering Club

American
American A.C. Journal	A	American Alpine Club
Ascent	A	Sierra Mountaineering Club
Canadian A.C. Journal	A	Canadian Alpine Club
Summit	M	commercial publication

Others
Les Alpes (*Die Alpes*)	M,Q	Swiss Alpine Club
Alpinismus	M	German commercial publication
Les Annales	A	Groupe de Haute Montagne (French)
Der Bergsteiger	M	Austrian Alpine Club
Himalayan Club Journal	A	Himalayan Club (India)
La Montagne	Q	French Alpine Club
Revista Mensile	M	Italian Alpine Club

K2 (28,253ft)

The second highest mountain in the world. It lies in the Central Karakorum (*qv*). The name Mt Godwin-Austen has never been officially recognized, and is now obsolete; the name Chogori has been suggested by Dyhrenfurth, but the peak is still best known by its original survey number.

K2 rises in splendid apparent isolation at the head of the long Baltoro Glacier, where the latter divides into the Savoie and Godwin-Austen Glaciers. There are six ridges, but only that to the west and that to the north-east join the main line of muztagh and even on these the next big peaks are far enough away to give the mountain its tremendous solitary appeal. Nevertheless, within a fifteen-mile radius there are other stupendous groups, such as Masherbrum, Chogolisa, Gasherbrum and Broad Peak. (See KARAKORUM.)

The head of the Baltoro Glacier was first explored by Conway (*qv*) in 1899. In 1902, Eckenstein (*qv*), who had been with Conway, led the first attempt on the peak: Guillarmod and Wesseley reached a height of about 21,400ft on the NE Ridge. Then followed:

1909 Duke of the Abruzzi's Expedition. Reconnoitred all the southern ridges; reached 22,000ft on the Abruzzi Ridge, 21,870ft on the NW Ridge.

1938 Houston's Expedition. Houston and Petzoldt reached *c*.26,100ft on the Abruzzi Ridge.

1939 Wiessner's Expedition. An ill-fated attempt by an American party which ended in the death of D. Wolfe and three Sherpas on the Abruzzi Ridge.

1953 Houston's Second Expedition. Bad weather foiled attempts and in a desperate retreat down the Abruzzi Ridge with the sick Gilkey, five climbers fell simultaneously and were held by P. Schoening – an almost unparallelled feat. Gilkey died.

1954 Desio Expedition. L. Lacedelli and A. Compagnoni reached the summit on 31 August.

KAIN, Conrad (1883-1934)

An Austrian guide who played a large part in opening up the mountains of Canada. Kain began guiding at the age of 19 and rapidly developed into a skilful and daring climber. He was chosen for expeditions to Spitsbergen in 1901, Egypt in 1902 and the Altai in 1912.

In 1909 Kain visited Canada at the invitation of the Canadian A. C. and it became his home. He crossed the Purcells with Longstaff and Wheeler in 1910, and this was to remain his favourite range. In 1913 he made the first ascent of Mt Robson (12,972ft) the highest peak in the Rockies, with A. H. MacCarthy and W. W. Foster. In 1916 he made the first ascent of the Howser and Bugaboo Spires; the latter was his most difficult climb. (See BUGABOOS.) Several peaks are named in his honour: Kain, near Robson, Conrad Spire and Glacier in the Purcells, Nasswald Peak after his Austrian home village and Birthday Peak after his birthday.

Kain visited New Zealand several times, acting as a guide at the Hermitage and elsewhere. In 1916 he traversed Mt Cook with Mrs Thompson, a remarkable feat for the time. This brought some criticism and there is no doubt that Kain was regarded by some climbers as too rash.

Kain had a great eye for nature, and told the most amazing tall stories. His autobiography (edited by J. M. Thorington from Kain's notes) appeared shortly after his death: *Where the Clouds Can Go.*

KAISERGEBIRGE (WILDER KAISER)

A small and compact group of limestone peaks immediately east of Kufstein, Tyrol. The highest peak is Elmauer Halt (2,344m), but despite the general lack of height and small area, the Kaiser are among the most important of the North Tyrolese Alps. The peaks are sharp and there are enormous limestone walls, all of attraction to the climber, including:

Fleischbank East Face – H. Dulfer, W. Schaarschmidt, 1912

Predigstuhl North Ridge – H. Matejak, 1908

Totenkirchl West Face – H. Dulfer and W. von Redwitz, 1913

There are several huts and the area is very accessible and very popular.

Guidebook: *Kaisergebirge*, by J. O. Talbot.

KAMMKARTE

From the German, *Kamm* (ridge), *Karte* (map). A map on which only ridges are shown, as black lines, with summits indicated by a dot or triangle. Inadequately surveyed country may be indicated thus and the technique is also used for simple maps in books. There are several in this book.

KANDERSTEG

Popular tourist and climbing centre at the western end of the Bernese Alps (Balmhorn, Altels, Wildstrubel, Blumlisalp, etc.). It is connected to Leukerbad by the Gemmi Pass (cable car).

KANGCHENJUNGA (28,707 ft)

Third highest mountain in the world, being a mere 46 ft less than K2. It lies in the Sikkim Himalaya; the central point for two huge ranges which run N–S and E–W. There are thus four faces: NW, approached by the Kangchenjunga Glacier; NE, by the Zemu Glacier; SE, by the Talung Glacier; and SW, by the Yalung Glacier. The supporting ridges contain some fine peaks:

North – Nepal Peak (23,443 ft), Tent Peak (24,162 ft), Pyramid (23,295 ft)

South – Talung (24,111 ft), Kabru (24,076 ft)

East – Simvu (22,360 ft), Siniolchu (22,600 ft)

West – Kangbachen (25,782 ft), Jannu (25,292 ft)

On the South and North ridges especially, the list could be extended.

The Kangchenjunga region was easy of access and well known to the pioneers. In 1899, Freshfield made a classic circumnavigation of the mountain (see *Round Kangchenjunga*, by D. Freshfield), and in 1905, Guillarmod made an attempt on the mountain which ended in disaster (see CROWLEY). Pache and three porters were killed. In 1929, P. Bauer led a German reconnaissance of the Zemu approach and Allwein and Kraus reached 24,250 ft; the expedition was an epic of endurance. In 1930, Dyhrenfurth took a large international party to the NW Face, but after the death of a Sherpa, the attempt was abandoned, though ascents were made of other nearby peaks. In 1931, Bauer returned with a second German party to the Zemu Glacier. Schaller and a porter

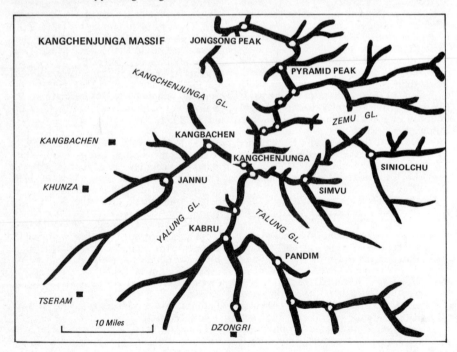

KANGCHENJUNGA MASSIF
JONGSONG PEAK
KANGCHENJUNGA GL.
PYRAMID PEAK
ZEMU GL.
KANGBACHEN
KANGBACHEN
KANGCHENJUNGA
SINIOLCHU
KHUNZA
JANNU
SIMVU
YALUNG GL.
KABRU
TALUNG GL.
PANDIM
TSERAM
10 Miles
DZONGRI

were killed, but a height of 25,263 ft was attained before retreat became inevitable. This was another feat of endurance. (See *Himalayan Campaign*, by P. Bauer.)

In 1954 J. Kempe led a reconnaissance of the SW Face and in the following year an expedition led by R. C. Evans was successful in climbing the mountain; J. Brown and G. C. Band reached the summit on 25th May, followed next day by H. R. A. Streather and N. Hardie.

KARABINER (G.) (Fr.: Mousequeton; E.: Snap-Link; It.: Moschettone)

The German word is now used exclusively, often shortened to "krab". A karabiner is an oval or D-shaped metal link, one side of which opens by means of a spring clip. It is used for belays, runners, abseiling, roping-up etc. (all *qv*) and is the universal attachment mechanism of climbing. On some karabiners the spring clip (gate) can be locked by a screwed collar (screwgate krab).

Karabiners are made in steel (or steel alloys) or in aluminium alloys. The breaking load should be at least equal to that of the rope and all the leading makes are well above this limit. The screwgate type is recommended for main belays, for tying on and for abseiling, as there are circumstances in which the gate can inadvertently open if not locked. For runners, the non-screwgate is usually preferred because of the speed of handling, and the same goes for artificial climbing (*qv*). Alloy krabs are only half the weight (or less) of steel ones.

Karabiners need to be examined from time to time: the springs can become faulty and the jaws of the gate do not always lock properly – an incompletely closed karabiner is obviously much weaker than a fully closed one. A little light machine oil should be applied to the spring from time to time.

Karabiners are said to have developed from a pear-shaped clip used by Munich firemen in the early years of this century. They were adapted for climbing by Otto Herzog (*qv*).

KARAKORUM

A vast complex of high mountains in the trans-Himalaya, lying behind and almost parallel with, the Punjab Himalaya (*qv*) at the western end of the great range. It is about 250 miles long, from the Batura Gla-

cier in the west to Saser Kangri in the east. The Lower Shyok and the Indus separate it from the Punjab Himalaya and the Shaksgam from the Aghil Mountains. Within this area it is extremely complicated topographically, but can conveniently be divided into the Greater and Lesser Karakorum. The Greater Karakorum includes the main crest zone of the system and includes K2, the second highest peak in the world (28,252 ft); the Lesser Karakorum lies between the Greater Karakorum and the Indus: it is shorter, but contains many important peaks such as Rakaposhi and Masherbrum.

The Karakorum has 19 peaks over 25,000 ft – only Nepal, with 22, has more. It also contains the world's greatest glaciers outside the sub-polar regions: Hispar-Biafo, 76 miles; Siachen, 45 miles; Baltoro, 36 miles; Batura, 36 miles.

The Greater Karakorum is divided into groups known as *muztagh* (Muz tagh = ice mountain), named after the glaciers draining their slopes.

Much of the area is uninhabited, but the Hunzas live in the Hunza valley to the west, the Baltis in the centre, round Askole, and the Ladakhis in the east. All have been used as porters, especially since Partition, when Sherpas were forbidden to enter the region. The Hunzas are regarded as the most reliable.

The area has always attracted explorers: Younghusband, Conway, Cockerill, the Workmans, Longstaff and Visser amongst others. There are still parts, particularly in the east, virtually unknown. Conway's Karakorum Expedition of 1892 was the first large-scale expedition to visit the Himalaya. They explored the Hispar, Biafo and Baltoro Glaciers and made some minor ascents. Captain H. H. Godwin-Austen of the Indian Survey had explored here in 1861 and in 1888 it was proposed that K2 should be named Mt Godwin-Austen, but it was not officially accepted.

8,000 m peaks

K2 (8611 m, 28,253 ft), 1954 – Desio Expedition

Gasherbrum I (8068 m, 26,470 ft), 1958 – P. K. Schoening, A. Kauffman

Broad Peak (8047 m, 26,400 ft), 1957 – M. Schmuck, F. Wintersteller, H. Buhl, K. Diemberger

Gasherbrum II (8035 m, 26,350 ft), 1956 – F. Moravec, S. Larch, H. Willenpart

(Gasherbrum I is also known as Hidden Peak)

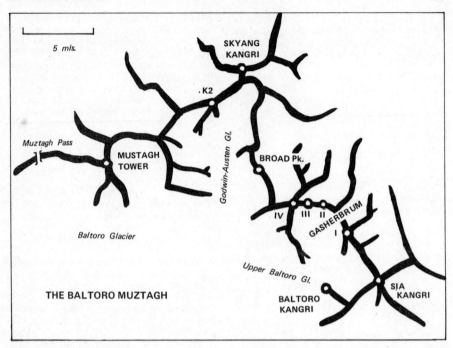

SKYANG KANGRI

·K2

Muztagh Pass

MUSTAGH TOWER

Godwin-Austen Gl.

BROAD Pk.

IV   III II GASHERBRUM I

Baltoro Glacier

Upper Baltoro Gl.

THE BALTORO MUZTAGH

BALTORO KANGRI

SIA KANGRI

5 mls.

Other important Peaks
Gasherbrum III (26,090 ft), unclimbed
Broad Peak II (26,017 ft) —
Gasherbrum IV (26,000 ft), 1958
Disteghil Sar I (25,868 ft), 1960
Masherbrum East (25,660 ft), 1960
Rakaposhi (25,550 ft), 1958
Hunza Kunji I (25,540 ft), 1959
Kanjut Sar (25,460 ft), 1958
Saltoro Kangri I (25,400 ft), 1962
Trivor (25,329 ft), 1960
Disteghil Sar II (25,250 ft), —
Saser Kangri (25,170 ft), 1970
Chogolisa I (25,110 ft), 1958
Muztagh Tower (23,863 ft), 1956
(Many more peaks below 25,000 ft)
Note. Gasherbrum III is at present the highest unclimbed mountain in the world (1973)
(See also K2, CONWAY, BUHL, J. BROWN, etc.)

KARWENDELGEBIRGE
An important group of limestone peaks between the Inn valley and Mittenwald, on the Austro-German border. As they rise immediately above Innsbruck (the Nordkette range) they give that town its celebrated background, and Hafelekar (2,334 m) can be reached by cable car.

There are four main ranges running east to west with deep valleys between, and crossing from north to south can be difficult. Scharnitz is perhaps the best general centre and there are several huts, of which the Falken Hutte with its views of Laliderer, is best known.

The peaks are typical of the North Tyrol ranges, with ridges and steep walls, but the climbs are generally longer than those of, say, the Kaiser or Wetterstein. The highest point is the Birkkar Spitze (2,756 m) but others of interest include: Kaltwasserkarspitze (2,733 m), Lamsenspitze (2,508 m), Grosser Bettelwurf (2,725 m) and Lalidererspitze (2,594 m). The area is famous for its steep walls, best known being the Lalidererwand (M and G. Mayer with A. Dibona and L. Rizzi, 1911.).

Guidebook: *Karwendal*, by M. Anderson.

KAUFMANN, Christen (1872-1939)
Grindelwald guide who was with Whymper in the Rockies in 1901. He returned to Canada every summer until 1908, making numerous first ascents. In the winter he climbed in the Oberland. Kaufmann was the guide who led Winston Churchill up the Wetterhorn in 1894.

KENNEDY, Edward Shirley (1817-98)
A remarkable Victorian mountaineer who, though wealthy, was an expert on the underworld of his day. He was one of a small group, which included Hudson (*qv*), which undertook guideless climbs and was with Hudson on the first guideless ascent of Mont Blanc (1855). Co-author, with Hudson, of *Where there's a Will, there's a Way*. He took part in the first ascent of the Disgrazia (1862) and the first English ascents of the Finsteraarhorn (1857) and Piz Bernina (1861). He may have made the first ascent of the Aig. de l'M in 1854, though this is not certain, and he claimed a guideless ascent of the Täschhorn in a list he made out in 1876, but nothing is known of this.

Kennedy was deeply involved in the founding of the A. C. of which he was President (1860–62). He edited *Peaks, Passes and Glaciers* (2nd series, 1862).

He died relatively poor, having lost his money in a financial crash in 1860.

KENNEDY, Thomas Stuart (1841-94)
One of the hardest climbers of his day, comparable with Hudson (*qv*), with whom he made the first ascent of the Moine Ridge on the Aig. Verte in 1865. (They climbed Mont Blanc *the next day*!)

His most notable first ascents were: Dent Blanche (1862), Aig. de Leschaux (1872) and the North Summit of Aig. de Blaitière (1873).

His record shows he was in many ways ahead of his time, especially in rock-climbing. He made the first ever attempts on peaks such as Lyskamm, Verte and Dru and an incredible winter attempt on the Matterhorn in 1862.

In 1883 he visited the Himalaya but a fever prevented him from making any ascents or attempts.

Kennedy was an all-round athlete and one of the best horsemen and polo-players of his day. His daring was legendary: he once rode the Nile cataracts on a log for fun. Despite this, he was a quiet man; his chief relaxations were mathematics and mechanics.

KILIMANJARO (KIBO, 19,340ft)
An extinct volcano on the Tanzania –Kenya border, and the highest mountain in Africa. The three principal peaks are Kibo (19,340ft), Mawenzi (16,890ft) and Shira (13,140ft). The first ascent of Kibo was made by H. Meyer and L. Purtscheller in 1889. Mawenzi was first climbed by E.

Oehler and F. Klute in 1912. Shira has no climbing interest.

The ordinary route up Kibo is simple and there are huts *en route*, but there are more serious climbs on the Heim and Kersten Glaciers of the S and SE Faces. Mawenzi provides good rock-climbing of a high standard; the N Face and W Face are 2,000 ft high and the E Face is 4,000 ft high:

1958 North Face – Tremonti and Bianchi
1964 East Face – Edwards and Thomson
1972 North Spur – Knowles and Kempson
1972 East Face Variant – Jugoslav team

Guidebook: *Mount Kenya and Kilimanjaro* – Mountain Club of Kenya.

KILNSEY CRAG
Above Kilnsey in Wharfedale, Yorkshire. A limestone crag famous for its overhangs. The Main Overhang, about 35 ft, is the largest in England (Original Route, R. Moseley, 1957). The climbs here are long and hard.

Guidebook: *Yorkshire Limestone*, by F. Wilkinson.

KINDER SCOUT (2,088ft)
A high peat plateau in the Peak District, between the Snake Pass on the north and Edale on the south. Groughs (*qv*) make the going hard, and the walks across the moor are famous, notably the Marsden-Edale (*qv*) and the Pennine Way, which begins at Edale. The moor often holds snow in winter and Edale is a ski centre. There are winter climbs on Kinder Downfall and the nearby Back Tor and Mam Tor. Numerous gritstone crags rim the perimeter of the moor but, except for the Downfall area, none are of much significance.

Guidebook: *Kinder Area* (Rock Climbs in the Peak Vol. 7) – Climbers' Club.

KING, Sir Henry Seymour (1852-1933)
Made a number of first ascents in the Alps, the best known of which are those of the Kingspitze in the Engelhorner (1887) and the Aig. Blanche de Peuterey (1885); the latter a considerable *tour de force* for the time.

King was a banker, M.P., and first Mayor of Kensington. He was knighted in 1892.

KIRKUS, Colin (1910–40)
A brilliant rock-climber from Liverpool whose most creative period was cut short by a tragedy on Ben Nevis (1934) in which he was seriously injured and his partner,

Linnell, killed. He made the first climb on Scafell's East Buttress (Mickledore Grooves, 1930), and played a significant part in the opening up of Clogwyn du'r Arddu, for which he is said to have coined the name "Cloggy". His best-known first ascents are: Lot's Groove, Glyder Fach; Central Route, Tryfan; Great Slab, Chimney Route, Pedestal Crack, Birthday Crack, Curving Crack – all on Clogwyn d'ur Arddu; Kirkus's Route, Cwm Silyn; Direct Route, Dinas Mot; Pinnacle Wall, Craig yr Ysfa.

Kirkus expected to be chosen for the 1933 Everest expedition but was disappointed. Instead he went on Marco Pallis's Gangotri Expedition.

He recovered from the Ben Nevis accident sufficiently to compile the Glyder Fach guidebook (1937). He also compiled a book for novices, *Let's Go Climbing*.

Kirkus was killed when his plane was shot down over Germany during the War.

KITSON, John Hawthorne (1843-99)
Made the first traverss of the Weisshorn (1871) and of the Eiger (1872). He also made the first ascent of the Rifelhorn from the Gorner Glacier (1871).

KLEINE SCHEIDEGG
A hotel complex on the col which separates Grindelwald (*qv*) and Lauterbrunnen. A mountain railway joins these villages via Kleine Scheidegg and Wengen. The Jungfraujoch Railway starts at Kleine Scheidegg. The col offers superb views of Jungfrau, Monch and Eiger.

KLETTERSCHUHE (G) (It.: Scarpetti)
Literally, climbing-shoe. Kletterschuhe were developed in the Eastern Alps, particularly the Dolomites, where they consisted of a canvas upper with felt or cord soles, which gave a good grip on the limestone of the region. Modern Kletterschuhe have vibram type soles, thinner than normal, and are essentially a light climbing boot. In Britain, they have been largely replaced by P. A.s (*qv*).

KLUCKER, Christian (1853-1928)
One of the greatest of all Alpine guides, Klucker came from Sils in the Engadine, where he was schoolmaster and later inspector of schools. Small, thickset and powerful, he was an excellent rock-climber and equally good on ice, as his climbs show. As a guide, his list of *difficult* new climbs has perhaps never been equalled,

even by Josef Knubel (*qv*).

He made 44 new ascents of peaks and 88 new climbs. His experience ranged from the Dolomites to Dauphiné and he once went to Canada with Whymper (1901). In his own district of Engadine he made the first ascent of many of the popular pinnacles and ridges, for example, Punta Rasica, Ago di Sciora. He was with Rey (*qv*) and Gussfeldt (*qv*) on the famous 88-hour traverse of the Peuterey Ridge in 1893.

Klucker's best season was that of 1890 when with Norman – Neruda (*qv*) he made the following difficult new climbs: NE Face, Lyskamm; NE Face, Piz Roseg; NE Face, Piz Bernina; NW Face, Piz Scerscen; Wellenkuppe-Obergabelhorn traverse.

He climbed until the year of his death. Even in 1927, aged 74, he made a new double traverse of the East Arête of Torrione del Ferro. He wrote *Adventures of an Alpine Guide*, published posthumously in 1932.

KNOTS
See facing page

KNOWLES, Guy John Fenton (1879-1959)
Friend of Eckenstein (*qv*) and a member of the ill-starred expedition to Kangchenjunga in 1902, where he was threatened at pistol point by Crowley (*qv*). Engineer and supervisor of the Copyright Agency for the Copyright Libraries.

KNUBEL, Josef (1881-1961)
Born in St Niklaus, Valais, Knubel came of a guiding family and was himself one of the most important guides of the present century. Small, modest and given to heavy smoking, he was an extremely strong goer and fine climber. His adventures with G. W. Young (*qv*) are chronicled in the latter's books.

His first climb was the Matterhorn in 1896, when he was aged 15, where he acted as a porter for his father. The same year he climbed the Dom and Monte Rosa. In 1903 he led the American climber, Oliver Perry-Smith, over a number of Zermatt peaks, including the Teufelsgrat of Täschhorn. He gained his guide's certificate the following year.

Among his many first ascents, the following are particularly outstanding. With Young and others: SE Ridge of Requin (and descent), 1906; SW Face of

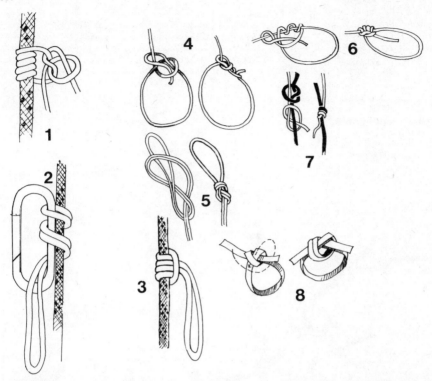

The diagrams show knots in common use by climbers: 1. Penberthy – crevasse rescue; 2. Bachmann – crevasse rescue; 3. Prusik – crevasse rescue; 4. bowline – tying on; 5. figure of eight – tying on; 6. Tarbuck – tying on; 7. fishermans – tying rope ends together eg. slings; 8. tape – tying two ends of tape together.

Täschhorn, 1906; Younggrat, Breithorn, 1906; E Face of Zinal Rothorn, 1907; W Ridge of Grandes Jorasses, 1911; Mer de Glace Face of Grépon (via Knubel Crack), 1911; W Ridge of Gspaltenhorn (Rote Zähne), 1914. With Kurz (*qv*): First winter ascents of Wellenkuppe, Obergabelhorn, Schallihorn and Täschhorn, all 1920. With Zurcher and others: W Face of Piz Bernina, 1930; Lauper Route, Eiger 1932.

His great staying power is demonstrated by the following:
Charmoz-Grépon-Blaitière (Central and North) in a day: Meije Traverse in 6 hr 20 min.: double traverse of Weisshorn in two days.

With Thomas (*qv*) and Zurcher, he climbed all the 4,000 m peaks of the Alps.

KUFFNER, Moriz von (1854-1939)
Wealthy Viennese brewer and intellectual who became Burgener's (*qv*) employer, after Mummery. Von Kuffner climbed most of the 4,000 m peaks of the Alps and made several first ascents, including the first ascent of Lagginhorn from Laggintal (1885), first descent of the Mittellegi Ridge (1885), first ascent of the Frontier Ridge, Mont Blanc (1887), first ascent of the N Ridge of the E Peak, Piz Palu (1899).

In 1938 Von Kuffner lost all his possessions to the Nazis on the invasion of Austria. He fled to Zurich, where he died.

KUGY, Julius (1858-1944)
An Austrian climber noted for his explorations of the Julian Alps, although he also climbed extensively in the Western Alps. Wrote several books, the best known being *Alpine Pilgrimage*.

KUNMAON HIMALAYA
Lies between the Sutlej in the west and the borders of Nepal in the east. There are three main ranges: the Great Himalayan crest zone which contains Nanda Devi

(25,645 ft), the Lesser Himalaya to its south with peaks of less than 23,000 ft and joining the Great Himalaya at Chaukhamba, and the Zaskar Range to the north, forming the boundary with Tibet and containing important peaks like Kamet (25,443 ft).

Kamet (25,443 ft), 1931
Nanda Devi East (24,391 ft), 1939
Abi Gamin (24,130 ft), 1950
Mana (23,862 ft), 1937
Mukut Parbat (23,820 ft), 1951
Chaukamba (23,412 ft), 1952
Trisul (23,360 ft), 1907

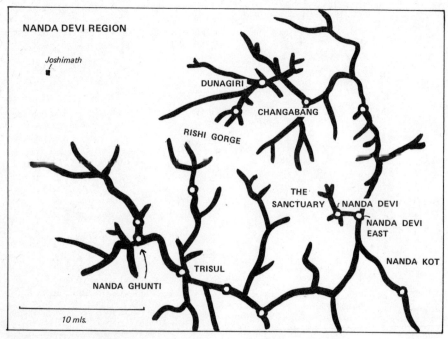

NANDA DEVI REGION

Joshimath

DUNAGIRI

CHANGABANG

RISHI GORGE

THE SANCTUARY / NANDA DEVI

NANDA DEVI EAST

NANDA KOT

TRISUL

NANDA GHUNTI

10 mls.

Only the two peaks mentioned exceed 25,000 ft, but the area has always been popular with climbers. It was one of the earliest to be explored – Graham 1883, Longstaff, 1907, Meade, 1910-13. Trisul (7120 m) was the first 7,000 m peak to be climbed (Longstaff, 1907) and Kamet (7755 m) was the highest peak ever climbed (Smythe, 1931) until Nanda Devi (Tilman, Odell, 1936), displaced it.

Nanda Devi (25,645 ft) is surrounded by a ring of high mountains with only one means of access – the Rishi Ganga river which cuts an enormous gorge. The struggle to force a way through the Rishi Ganga into the "Sanctuary" is one of the classic mountaineering feats: eight attempts were made until Shipton and Tilman succeeded in 1934.

Kunmaon is an ideal area for small parties.

Important Peaks
Nanda Devi (25,645 ft), 1936

Satopanth (23,213 ft), 1947
Dunagiri (23,183 ft), 1939

KURZ, Marcel Louis (1887-1967)
Noted Swiss topographer and guidebook writer. Though employed initially by the Swiss Federal Institute of Topography, he later worked freelance, and his work on the Mount Olympus area of Greece brought universal recognition (1921). He worked several times with his father on the *Carte de la Chaîne du Mont Blanc* (1910, 1924, 1929).

Kurz was an accomplished winter mountaineer of the old school (first ascent of Grand Combin on ski, 1907). In 1926 he visited New Zealand with H. E. L. Porter where they made the first traverse of Mt Tasman and in 1930 he was on the Dyhrenfurth Kangchenjunga Expedition and took part in the first ascent of Jonsong Peak (7459 m). (See SMYTHE.) He visited the Himalaya again in 1932 and 1934.

Kurz's guidebooks are models of accuracy and detail. Besides ski guides he wrote guides to Bernina and the Urner Alps and revised his father's guide to the Mont Blanc region. His most famous work, however, was the *Guide des Alpes Valaisannes* (4 vols., 1920-37).

In 1934 he wrote *Le Problème Himalayen*, a topic which absorbed the later years of his life and resulted in *Chronique Himalayenne* (1959). Other books are *Le Monte Olympe* (1923) and *Alpinisme Hivernale* (1925). From 1947 to 1953 he was Editor of *The Mountain World*.

KYNDWR CLUB
The first club based on a gritstone tradition; it was founded in 1900 by J. W. Puttrell, E. A. Baker and other Peak District enthusiasts. Its activities included walking and caving as well as climbing. The club explored many of the Peak District rocks, and notes of climbs were included (by Baker) in the Climbers' Club Journal. Baker later published *Moors, Crags and Cave of the High Peak* (1903), the first detailed account of gritstone climbs in book form.

The club dissolved because of a quarrel over the High Tor Gully, Matlock (*qv*). Baker and his friends attempted this twice without success and denigrated it as a route. Puttrell, Smithard and Bennett climbed it in 1903 and Smithard praised it as a climb. The argument continued for some time and the club broke up. Puttrell and his friends formed the Derbyshire Pennine Club (1907), but Baker had by then moved to the south of England.

LADDOW ROCKS

One of the earliest gritstone outcrops to be developed, Laddow consists of a series of fine buttresses above Crowden Great Brook in the north of the Peak District. The best approach is from Longdendale. There are climbs of all standards.

Guidebook: *Bleaklow Area* (Rock Climbs in the Peak Vol. 6) – Climbers' Club.

LAKE DISTRICT

A mountainous area of north-west England famous for its scenic beauty and literary associations. It contains the highest mountain in England, Scafell Pike (3,206 ft).

The area can be roughly divided into three unwieldy regions: in the north, the Skiddaw group (Skiddaw 3,054 ft); in the east, the eastern fells, whose highest point is Helvellyn (3,113 ft); and the central or western fells culminating in Scafell Pike. It is the last of these groups which demonstrates a radial pattern, like the spokes of a wheel, whose hub is the *col* of Esk Hause.

Long and beautiful glaciated valleys (dales) separate the ridges and contain the lakes: Windermere, Esthwaite Water, Coniston Water, Wastwater, Ennerdale Water, Buttermere, Crummock Water, Loweswater, Derwentwater, Thirlmere, Elterwater, Ullswater and Haweswater. Of these, Windermere is largest and Wastwater deepest. There are numerous smaller lakes, called "tarns".

The mountains are known locally as "fells"; hence, fell-walking – a term now used beyond the locality. There are 225 fells of 2,000 ft or more (F. Simpson, 1937), but this includes individual tops of the same fell; otherwise the number is 112 (Monkhouse and Williams, 1972). Only four exceed 3,000 ft (cf. Snowdonia): Scafell Pike (3,206 ft), Scafell (3,162 ft), Helvellyn (3,113 ft) and Skiddaw (3,054 ft).

The Lake District 3,000s Walk joins these in a single outing, and is not nearly so popular as the Welsh counterpart. The Lake District Record (*qv*) is a marathon fell-walk, rarely attempted; it is perhaps the toughest trial of its kind in the world.

The principal centres of tourism are Windermere, Ambleside and Keswick but the smaller places such as Coniston and Wasdale Head are perhaps more important to the mountaineer.

Because of the high central massif it is seldom easy to reach one valley from another by motor road and this has helped preserve the unique nature of the area. The fell-walking is superb and immensely popular; in fact there are problems of human erosion on some paths, such as Mill Gill and Sty Head. The area is a National Park (centre: Brockholes, near Windermere) and the principal landowner is the National Trust.

Because of the difficult road communications, rock-climbing tends to be centrist but there are good crags throughout the area, though those of the eastern fells are not so well developed as those further west. Popular crags include: Dow Crag (Coniston), Scafell Crag and East Buttress (Scafell), Napes Ridges (Great Gable), Pillar Rock (Pillar), Shepherd's Crag (Borrowdale), Gimmer Crag (Langdale) and Castle Rock (Thirlmere). There are many others. The climbs are of all standards. The best winter climbs (snow and ice) are on Great End (Scafell group).

There are numerous huts for climbers in the area, mostly belonging to the Fell and Rock Climbing Club (F. R. C. C.). The club is one of the most important in Britain.

Traditionally, the Lake District is the birthplace of rock-climbing as a sport (see HASKETT SMITH).

Guidebooks: *A Pictorial Guide to the Lakeland Fells* (7 vols), by A. Wainwright; *Climbing Guides to the English Lake District* (8 vols) – F. R. C. C. *Climbs in Cumbria* (3 vols) – Cicerone Press.

LAKE DISTRICT FELL RECORD

"The aim of these walks is to ascend the greatest possible number of peaks over 2,000 ft and to return to the starting point within twenty four hours." (Wakefield.) One of the most arduous tests of endurance in the mountains. There is no set course.

Long Lakeland walks had been recorded by Elliott (*qv*), the Pilkingtons (*qv*) and others in the nineteenth century, but

Wakefield's attempt of 1905 gave modern form to the Record. He did 59 miles, ascended a total of 23,500 ft and took 22 hr. 7 min. Thomas (*qv*) improved on this and in 1932 Bob Graham lifted it to 68 miles and 26,000 ft (42 summits). Graham's record stood for 28 years, and anyone who can match or improve it is entitled to belong to the Bob Graham 24-hour Club.

Graham's record was beaten by Alan Heaton in 1960, who did 42 peaks but in slightly shorter time. In 1961 his brother, Ken Heaton, raised it to 51 peaks in 22 hr. 13 min. and in 1963 Eric Beard (*qv*) did 56 peaks in 23 hr. 35 min. The present record (1973) is held by Joss Naylor who in 1971 did 61 peaks in 23 hr. 37 min.

LAMB, Robertson (1865-1927)
A well-known Liverpool rock-climber and Alpinist, Lamb's name is perpetuated in the famous Wayfarer's hut, Langdale, usually known as "R. L. H.".

LAMMER AND LORRIA
Eugen Guido Lammer and August Lorria were two Austrian mountaineers who made a number of very daring ascents during the last two decades of the nineteenth century. Both were advocates of extreme guideless climbing, believing that objective danger, such as stonefall, was all part of the game. Lammer in particular was an advocate of this; he was a follower of Neitzche, and in his old age, an ardent Nazi (see *Jungborn*, by E. G. Lammer). He was a strong advocate of naturalism in climbing, deploring anything that came between the climber and the mountain, and advocated the removal of any man-made structure above the timber line, including climbing huts.

Though constant partners, the two men often did solo climbs as well, and of the highest calibre for the time (for example, Lammer on the N Ridge of Hinterer Brochkogel – first ascent, 1898). They also climbed at night and in bad weather.

In 1887 they attempted Penhall's route on the Matterhorn (*qv*) and were carried away by an avalanche which they miraculously survived without serious injury. Lammer crawled from the Stokje to Stafel Alp to obtain aid for Lorria.

With Purtscheller and the Zsigmondys (*qv*) they represented an approach to climbing totally alien to the traditional, and were (and still are) heavily criticized for their extremism, and for the "do or die" attitude it engendered in some Continental

climbers during the thirties. With modern equipment (of which Lammer would have disapproved) the argument is now largely academic.

Lorria, with E. A. Martel, was joint author of an unusual guidebook, *Le Massif de la Bernina* (1894) – well illustrated.

LANCASHIRE, CLIMBS IN
South of the Lake District there are climbs in various quarries, including limestone near Lancaster and sandstone at Cronton, near Liverpool. Most important are the gritstone quarries of the Bolton Moors and neighbourhood, especially Hoghton, Wilton and Anglezarke which have climbs of 100 ft, mostly hard. Cadshaw Rocks is a natural outcrop giving many easier gritstone climbs.

Guidebook: *Lancashire*, by L. Ainsworth.

LANGDALE
Strictly, Great Langdale, to distinguish it from the adjacent Little Langdale. The valley stretches westwards from Ambleside and culminates in a fine valley head of rocky peaks, including the Langdale Pikes, Crinkle Crags and Bowfell. The principal passes out of the valley head are Stake Pass (to Langstrath), Rosset Gill (to Sty Head), The Band (to Eskdale) and Blea Tarn (to Little Langdale). Only the last is motorable.

Langdale is a very popular climbing centre. The chief villages are Elterwater and Chapel Stile, but most climbers prefer to stay nearer the valley head where there are the two famous hotels, the "Old" and "New Dungeon Ghyll", as well as a camp site and numerous climbing huts.

The principal crags are: Gimmer, White Ghyll, Bowfell, Raven, Pavey Ark and Raven Crag Walthwaite. They offer a wide variety of climbs, particularly in the middle and upper grades. For beginners there is Middle Fell Buttress, Scout Crag and Tarn Crag.

The first real climb in the area was Haskett-Smith's ascent of Great Gully on Pavey Ark in 1882. (See individual crags.)

Guidebook: *Great Langdale*, by J. A. Austin.

LANTERN
Because many Alpine climbs begin before dawn it is necessary for climbers to carry a light. Originally this was a folding candle lantern, still in use after the Second World

War. A torch with long life batteries is now used; this can sometimes be clipped on the helmet (head torch).

LAPSE RATE
The lapse rate is the drop in temperature with altitude. Dependent upon humidity it is approximately 4°F per thousand feet of rise. (See also WIND CHILL FACTOR.)

LARDEN, Walter (1855-1919)
A well-known climber at the turn of the century, though with few first ascents to his credit; the first complete ascent of the W Ridge of Schreckhorn with Coolidge (qv) is probably his most notable.

Larden did much to popularize Arolla as a climbing centre. He collected together all known routes in the area and made them available in the Mont Collon Hotel (1883). He then brought the information up to date and published it as *Walks and Climbs around Arolla* (1908). His other books are *Recollections of an Old Mountaineer* (1910), *Argentine Plain and Andine Glaciers* (1911) and *Inscriptions from Swiss Chalets* (1913).

LASSOING
Where the rope is thrown over a projection to help the leader. Rope Wall on Tryfan, Wales, is a route on which it is used, or the top block of the Aig. de République at Chamonix. Not very common.

LAUENER BROTHERS
Among the best-known of the early Oberland guides were Ulrich, Christian, Jakob and Johann Lauener of Lauterbrunnen. Ulrich (1821-1900) was the most famous: he took part in the ascent of the Wetterhorn in 1854 by Wills (qv) and the first ascent of Monte Rosa (1855). Christian (1826-91) was for many years Tuckett's guide (qv) and made the first ascent of Cimon della Pala (1870). The other brothers never achieved the same degree of fame. Johann was killed by an avalanche on Jungfrau in 1853.

LAUPER, Hans (1895–1936)
A Zurich dentist and classical scholar who made a series of difficult north face climbs in the Oberland between 1915 and 1932, including the Stockhorn, Kamm, Mönch and Jungfrau. His most famous climb is the Lauper Route on the Eiger (1932), accompanied by Alfred Zurcher and the guides Joseph Knubel and Alexander Graven.

LAYBACK (Am.: Lie-back)
A crack-climbing technique, used for corner cracks or cracks where one edge protrudes more than the other. Feet are placed flat against the protruding edge and hands grip the nearer edge, thus setting up opposing forces. Hands and feet are moved alternately upwards. A difficult and strenuous technique. Alternative methods, e.g. jamming (qv), are used whenever possible.

The term is said to have been invented by Rice Evans, an American who climbed at Stanage in the twenties. On the Continent it is known as "à la Dulfer', after the climber of that name.

LEADER
The first man on a climbing rope. His part in the climb is said to be "leading" and anyone who has completed a climb as leader is said to have "led the climb". Because leading is much more difficult than following, the leader is usually the most experienced member of the rope. In a rope of two, where both may be of equal ability, it is usual for each climber to lead alternate pitches. This is called "leading through".

Because the leader goes up first he is not protected by a rope from above as his companions are. He must make his own protection (qv) and the consequences of a fall could be serious on an unprotected pitch. A leader obviously needs considerable experience and judgement: the fate of the party rests in his hands, especially on a long climb.

In descent, the leader comes down last, so that he can protect the party from above. On fairly easy ground the leader may decide to descend first if there are route-finding problems which he judges his companions cannot solve.

On high-altitude expeditions the leader is the man responsible for the expedition as a whole, particularly its strategy. He may or may not take an actual part in the climbing.

LEAF, Walter (1852-1927)
A London banker who made a number of minor new routes and first ascents in the Alps between 1871 and 1893. His brother Herbert Leaf was with him for the first two seasons.

LECHTALER ALPS
A long range of limestone mountains between the Lechtal and Inn. There is no one centre and to reach one side of the range

Peter-Taugwalderſohn
Nov. 1843-1923.

Edward Whymper
1840-1911.

Peter Taugwalder
Vater, 1820-1888.

rd f. Douglas
1847-1865

Rev. Chs. Hudson
1828-1865

D. Hadow
1846-1865.

Michel A. Croz
1830-1865.

Die ersten Besteiger des
Matterhorns 14 Juli 1865
in der Reihenfolge des abstieges, nach zeitgemässen aufnahmen.
Oben die drei damals Ueberlebenden. (Zusammengestellt v. P. Montandon)

21 THE MATTERHORN. Members of the party who made the first ascent, 14th July 1865.
Only Whymper and the two Taugwalders survived the accident on the way down.

22 Ice Technique. Fashioning steps in descent. (*right*) 23 Modern Ice Technique. Bill March on Hells Lum Crag in the Cairngorms. He relies on the front points of his crampons and the picks of his short ice axes. The picture also shows the type of gear worn by the modern climber.

from the other involves a lengthy car journey. The highest peak is the Parseierspitze (3,040m). Other peaks of interest are: Wetterspitze (2,898m), Freispitze (2,887m), Platteinspitze (2,639m) and Heiterwand (2,638m). (No English guidebook.)

LEDGE (G.: Band; Fr.: Vire; It.: Cengia)
A flat or slightly sloping area on a rock face or mountain side. Ledges often provide resting places, stances and belays (qv). On the easier rock-climbs, belays are almost always on large ledges. Ledges can be almost any size – some go right across a face. Quite a number of ledges have been given names, for example The Oval, Scafell.

LEHNE, Jorg (1936-69)
A leading German post-war climber who, with Brandler, Hasse and Low made a famous Direct Route on the Cima Grande; a major advance in artificial climbing. He was responsible for a number of winter first ascents in the Eastern Alps but his most famous venture was as leader of the team that made the first ascent of the Eigerwand Direct (Harlin Route) in 1968. Killed by stonefall at Chamonix.

LEICESTERSHIRE, CLIMBS IN
Hangingstones at Woodhouse Eaves is a natural granite outcrop with short climbs and there are a number of quarries which have been developed.
   Guidebook: *Rock Climbs in Leicestershire*, by K. S. Vickers.

LEPONTINE ALPS
A vast area of mountains between the Simplon and Splügen passes, south of the Furka-Oberalp line and north of the Italian lakes. It is bisected, N–S, by the popular St Gotthard Pass. The eastern part is sometimes known as the Adula Alps. It is an area of low peaks suited to mountain walking and is very beautiful, though little frequented. The chief peaks are Monte Leone (3,553m), Blinnenhorn (3,370m), Basodino (3,273m) – all in the W – and Rheinwaldhorn (3,402m) in the Adula. A good deal of rock-climbing exploration could be done, especially in Val Maggia.
   Guidebook: *Mittel Switzerland*, by M. Anderson.

LETTER BOX
A narrow slot or hole in a ridge is sometimes called a letter box. There is a well-known one on Grey Knotts Face, Borrowdale. Rather archaic.

LINE
The thinnest rope made for climbing, No. 1 circ. ⅝ inch (see ROPE). Used for making étriers and prusik loops. Line slings have been replaced by tape (qv).

LOMBARD ALPS
The southern limits of the Alps between Como and Trento, south of the Bernina – Ortles massifs and north of the Milan – Verona motorway. It includes the lakes of Como, d'Iseo, d'Idro and Garda and is easily accessible from the towns of northern Italy. The area lies entirely within the Italian borders.
   The name is one of convenience invented by Ball (qv) and taken up by Coolidge (cf. NE Switzerland) to describe several disparate groups. The highest peaks are those of the Presanella – Adamello groups: Adamello (3,554m), Cima Presanella (3,556m), Caré Alto (3,462m). This is a snowy region with wild glens, but the climbing is mostly easy. There are several huts and the best centre is Pinzolo.
   Immediately to the east of these rise the Brenta Dolomites (qv), a complete contrast in form.
   West of the Aprica Pass lie the Bergamesque Alps whose highest peak is Pizzo di Coca (3,052m). It is an area for mountain walking, though in the extreme west, above Lecco, lies the Grigna (qv). Except for the Brenta, there are no English guidebooks.

LONGEURS (Fr.)
The dull and uninteresting sections of a hill-walk, or the easy sections of a rock-climb. A climb with too many longeurs is said to be scrappy.

LIGHTNING
Can be a hazard in the mountains, especially on exposed ridges and pinnacles, but it can also cause stonefall on faces and in gullies, etc. In Alpine regions particularly, thunder storms form quickly. Since lightning tends to strike the highest points, it is prudent to keep as low as possible, off the crest of a ridge and away from summits. Ice axes emit a strange humming noise when electrical discharge is near ("singing"). They should not be carried pointing upwards, strapped to a rucksack, but the old idea that they should be abandoned is not always desirable or necessary.

LIGURIAN ALPS

The western extremity of the Alps immediately beyond the Col de Tende, though not accepted as such by Coolidge (see ALPS). Collomb points out correctly (1971) that these hills must belong to the Alps or Appenines and fit more logically into the former. Coolidge left them out because they do not have the characteristics of the Alps: they are largely wooded and though there are a few rock faces, they are of little interest to the climber. The highest summit is Mt Marguareis (2,659 m).

LIMESTONE

A sedimentary rock formed from the compacted remains of tiny marine organisms. The main types of the rock are: chalk, oolitic limestone, carboniferous or mountain limestone, and dolomite or magnesium limestone. Marble is limestone which has undergone a metamorphic change. The rock is noted for containing fossils, minerals and caves.

Limestone is extremely common rock, occurring in many parts of the world. In the Alps it forms much of the Oberland and the Eastern Alps, and in Britain much of the Pennines (all *qv*).

Mountain limestone is the commonest form of the rock. Despite its popularity in the Alps for many years it was much distrusted in Britain as a suitable rock for climbing until after the last war, (though there had been spasmodic climbs made ever since the sport started). This was because of the nature of the rock – heavily fractured and not always sound. Major ascents began in the 1950s, often heavily protected by pegs, but the present tendency is for hard climbs and only a few pegs, if any. All the major artificial routes of Britain (*qv*) are on limestone: a supreme example being the Kilnsey Overhang in Yorkshire. Other favourite limestone cliffs include Stoney Middleton, High Tor and cliffs along the Wye, all in Derbyshire; Malham Cove and Gordale Scar in Yorkshire; Avon Gorge and Cheddar Gorge in Somerset; and Swanage in Dorset.

LING, William Norman (1873-1953)

Companion of Raeburn (*qv*) and Glover (*qv*) and one of the outstanding mountaineers at the turn of the century with first ascents in the Lakes, Scotland, Norway, the Alps and Caucasus. Ling Chimney (1899) on Gable, Lake District, is named after him.

LIVEING, Robert (1834-1919)

A short but notable Alpine career. In 1859 he made the first ascent of the Rimpfischhorn, second ascent of the Dom and second (first English) ascent of Weissmies. In the following year he made the first known ascent of the Oberaarhorn and first ascent of Blümlisalphorn.

LLANBERIS PASS

A long, sombre valley stretching NW from Pen y Pass, Snowdonia, to Nant Peris and one of the most popular climbing areas in Britain. It is known simply as "The Pass". The nearest centre is Llanberis, but there are climbing huts in the Pass, and a good motor road along its length makes it easily accessible from all parts of the district.

The crags are numerous and their arrangement intricate. On the north side of the road the chief crags are: Craig Ddu, Clogwyn y Grochan, Carreg Wastad, Dinas Cromlech. On the south side they are: Clogwyn y Ddysgl, Cyrn Las, Clogwyn y Person, Crib Goch, Dinas Mot and Dinas Bach. There are others.

Pen y Pass (*qv*) was an early centre of Welsh climbing and notable ascents included:

1897 The Black Cleft, Dinas Mot – J. M. A. Thomson
1898 The Parson's Nose – Kitson, Corbett, Evans, Bedford
1904 Great Gully, Cyrn Las – Thomson, Smith
1906 Schoolmasters' Gully, Cyrn Las – Mitchell, Barker, Drew, Atchison
1908 Reade's Route, Crib Goch – Reade, Bartrum

All these were on the south side of the Pass. The north side began to be developed in the thirties, chiefly owing to J. M. Edwards (*qv*), though there were fine leads elsewhere, most notably Main Wall, Cyrn Las (Roberts, Cooke, 1935), The Direct Route and West Rib, Dinas Mot by Kirkus (1930, 1931) and Diagonal Route, Dinas Mot (Birtwistle and Parkinson, 1938).

After the War the Pass, along with Clogwyn du'r Arddu, played the most significant part in the rise of rock-climbing standards. Those involved included Harding, Moulam, Brown, Whillans and others and the era can be symbolized by the first ascent of Cenotaph Corner, Dinas Cromlech (Brown, Belshaw, 1952). (See also THREE CLIFFS and the various persons and crags named.)

Guidebooks: *Llanberis North,* by D. T. Roscoe; *Llanberis South,* by P. Crew; *Cwm*

Glas, by P. Crew and I. Roper.

LLIWEDD (Y Lliwedd) (2,947 ft)

A mountain in the Snowdon massif with a spectacular N Face overlooking Llyn Llydaw. There are actually two summits – West (2,947 ft) and East (2,940 ft). The crag (also Lliwedd) is one of the largest in Wales and offers numerous climbs in the middle grades. Usually approached from Pen y Pass (*qv*).

Though not popular today, Lliwedd holds a special place in the history of Welsh climbing. The first ascent of the West Buttress (Stocker, Wall, 1883) marked the start of Welsh climbing and the Girdle Traverse (Thomson and Reynolds, 1907) of the mountain was the first in the world. Almost all the classic lines are of early date when the cliff was dominated by J. M. A. Thomson (*qv*). It was regarded as the crag for the expert and consequently many famous names appear among the first ascents. Of the later climbs, only Central Gully Direct (Dodd, Edwards, 1938), is of note.

Guidebook: *Lliwedd,* by H. Drasdo.

LLOYD, Robert Wylie (1868-1958)

A self-made, wealthy businessman from Lancashire, who spent 30 seasons with Josef Pollinger and made a number of good Alpine routes. A supporter of clubs and expeditions, the R. W. Lloyd Hut (Ynys Ettws), Llanberis, is named after him. Lloyd amassed a number of collections in art, stamps, coins, and so on, some of which were internationally renowned.

LOCHMATTER FAMILY

A famous family of guides from St Niklaus, Switzerland, related to the Pollingers and close friends of the Knubels, who were also well-known guiding families.

They first came to notice as three brothers, all guides: Franz (b. 1825) Joseph-Marie (b. 1833) and Alexander (b. 1837). Joseph-Marie, led J. M. Elliott up the Hörnli Ridge of the Matterhorn in 1868 – the first time it had been climbed after the tragedy of 1865. In 1873 he made the first ascent of Le Rateau; in 1879, the first ascent of the W Ridge of Chardonnet; and in 1881 probably the first traverse of the Zinal Rothorn from Zermatt to Zinal. He climbed with many of the best climbers of the day. He was killed in 1882 on the Dent Blanche, together with his eldest son, Alexander. The other brothers had less distinguished careers.

Joseph-Marie Lochmatter had six sons, all good climbers, but especially outstanding were Franz and Joseph who were guides to V. J. E. Ryan (*qv*). The E Ridge of the Aig. du Plan (Ryan-Lochmatter Route), 1906, the NW Ridge of the Aig. de Blaitière, 1906, and the S Face of the Taschhorn (1906) are perhaps the best known of their ascents. (See KNUBEL, YOUNG, RYAN.)

LONGLAND, Sir John Laurence (b. 1905)

One of the best English rock-climbers between the wars. In 1928 he led Birch Tree Wall at the Black Rocks of Cromford, and his famous Longland's Climb on the West Buttress of Clogwyn du'r Arddu. In 1933 Longland was on Everest where, with Wyn Harris, Wager and eight Sherpas, established Camp VI at 27,400 ft – the highest camp ever at that time. Longland returned leaving Wager and Wynn Harris and during the descent was caught by a storm through which he shepherded the porters to safety. A great feat.

As Director of Education for Derbyshire, Jack Longland was responsible for the establishment of White Hall Outdoors Pursuits Centre in 1951, the first of the many local authority centres in Britain.

Longland has served on various Government enquiries and is well known as a broadcaster. He was knighted in 1970.

LONGMAN, William (1813-77)

An Original Member of the A.C. and President 1872-4. Longman was the publisher of many early Alpine classics, including Ball's Alpine Guides (*qv*), *Peaks, Passes and Glaciers* and the *Alpine Journal* (until 1930). His climbing career was undistinguished.

LONGSTAFF, Tom George (1875-1964)

One of the greatest of the early Himalayan climbers and explorers. As a man of private means he was able to indulge his passion for exploration and besides the Alps he visited the Caucasus, the Rockies, the Selkirks, the Arctic (five times) and the Himalaya (six times). He qualified as a doctor but never practised.

In 1903 his Caucasus journey resulted in first ascents of Tiktingen, Latsga, Lakra, Bashiltau and the formidable West peak of Shkhara. In 1905 he made his first visit to Nanda Devi's "Ring" and reached the rim of the Sanctuary. He made remarkable but unsuccessful attempts on Nanda Devi East, Nanda Kot and, during a quick visit to Tibet, Gurla Mandhata. In 1907 he returned, failed to force the Rishi Ganga into the Sanctuary, but climbed Trisul (23,360 ft). It remained for 21 years the highest peak ever attained.

In 1909 he visited the Karakorum, crossed the Saltoro Pass and discovered the great Siachen Glacier. In 1922 he went as technical adviser on the second Everest expedition. Awarded Gill Memorial (1908) and Founder's Medal (1928) of the R. G. S. President A. C. 1947-9.

His autobiography, *This My Voyage*, was published in 1949.

LUNDY

An island in the Bristol Channel, 2½ hours by boat from Ilfracombe or Bideford. The cliffs offer considerable climbs of high quality in all grades on good granite. One of the largest slabs in the country, The Devil's Slide, 400 ft, lies in the NW of the island. Permission from the Agent is necessary for a visit.

Guidebooks: *Rock Climbing in Devonshire*, by R. D. Moulton; and *Lundy Rock Climbs*, by R. D. Moulton.

LUNN, Sir Arnold (1888–1974)

One of the great ski mountaineers and the man who, more than most, helped to shape the sport of skiing in its early days. He made many of the first ski and ski-aided ascents in the Alps, including the Dom, the Eiger and the Weisshorn. A world authority on skiing.

Sir Arnold was an honorary member of several famous clubs including the Alpine Club, Dr. h. c. of Zurich University and Citoyen d'honneur of Chamonix. Founder of the Oxford M. C. and Alpine Ski Club.

His books on mountaineering are: *The Alps* (1913), *The Alpine Ski Guides* (*Bernese Oberland*, 1920 – the first ski mountaineering guide), *Alpine Skiing at all Heights and Seasons* (1921), *The Mountains of Youth* (1925), *A History of Skiing* (1927), *Mountain Jubilee* (1943), *Zermatt & the Valais* (1955), *Mountains of Memory* (1956), *A Century of Mountaineering* (1957), *The Bernese Oberland* (1963), *Matterhorn Centenary* (1965). He was Editor of the *Climbers' Club Journal* 1912-13, and the journals of the Alpine Ski Club from 1908 to 1974.

MACCARTHY, Albert H. (1876–1956)

Born in the U. S. A. but went to live in British Columbia in 1910 where he and his wife began climbing. Formed partnerships with W. W. Foster and the guide, Conrad Kain (*qv*), with whom he made new ascents in the Purcells and elsewhere. Notable first ascents were: Mt Robson from the N (1913), NW Ridge of Mt Sir Donald (1913), Mt Louis (1916), Bugaboo Spire (1916) and first traverse of Mt Assiniboine (MacCarthy, Wakefield, Hall, 1920). He was the leader of the expedition to Mt Logan (1924-5), Yukon; the second highest peak in North America. Reached the summit on 23 June 1925.

"Mack" visited the Alps in 1926, doing 101 peaks in 45 days. He returned to the U. S. A. in 1930, as an hotelier in Annapolis.

MACDONALD, Claude Augustus (1859-1949)

A sheep farmer from Wagga Wagga who made a number of first ascents in the Alps and New Zealand. His most remarkable exploit was the first ascent of the NW Face of Ebnefluh in 1895, still regarded as a hard climb.

MACDONALD, Reginald John Somerled (c. 1840-76)

The companion of many of the pioneers. Made first English ascent of Pelvoux with Whymper in 1861, second ascent of Mönch (first English, and now the normal route), first ascent of Dent d'Hérens, first ascent of Parrotspitze (1863) first ascent of Jungfrau from the Rottal (1864) and first ascent of Aig. de Bionassay.

MacDonald died at the early age of 35 and has perhaps not been given the credit he deserves for his early ascents.

MACINNES, Hamish

One of the most active Scottish mountaineers of the post-war years. His interests have touched on every aspect of the sport and have had a lasting influence.

At home he has climbed many new routes, especialy in Glencoe, and often with members of his winter climbing courses. He no longer publishes new climbs, but among his earlier routes the first winter ascent of Raven's Gully, Buachaille Etive Mor (1953, Bonington) and Zero Gully, Ben Nevis (1957, A. G. Nicol, T. W. Patey) are outstanding. Zero Gully, especially, can be regarded as one of the big breakthroughs in British climbing.

In the Alps he made an attempt, with Bonington, on the Eigerwand in 1957, and took part, with Bonington, Whillans and others in the first British ascent of the Bonatti Pillar of the Dru (1958) when he was seriously injured by stonefall.

MacInnes has climbed in New Zealand, Caucasus and the Himalaya. He was with Cunningham (*qv*) in the celebrated Creag Dhu Everest Expedition, which consisted of two men (1953) and in the Yeti hunting expedition of 1957 in Lahul. He was also part of the Everest SW Face teams in the two expeditions of 1973. Outstanding among his other climbs is the traverse of Shkhelda, Caucasus, with G. Richie (1961). This was the first major Caucasus traverse by a British party.

Living in Glencoe, he has organized winter climbing courses there for many years and been leader of the rescue team in the valley. He was one of the first to advocate the use of dogs in rescue work. He also turned his attention to equipment, developing a new, improved rescue stretcher, and designing the first ice axe to break away from the old pattern – an all metal axe. Later he developed the inclined pick which has had an influence in modern ice techniques.

MacInnes is a considerable photographer. He has written: *Scottish Climbing*, 2 vols (1971); *International Mountain Rescue Handbook* (1972); *Call Out* (1973) and *Climb to the Lost World* (1974).

MACKENZIE, John (1856-1933)

Best known of the Skye guides during the pioneering days on the island. Made a number of first ascents including Sgurr a'Ghreadaidh, Sgurr Thearlaich and Sgurr Mhic Coinnich (Mackenzie's Peak). Was the constant companion of Collie (*qv*) with whom he made the first crossing of the Thearlaich–Dubh Gap and the first ascent of the Cioch. (See also CUILLIN OF SKYE.)

MACKINDER, Sir Halford John (1861-1947)
Distinguished geographer and politician. Mackinder founded geography as a university subject in the 1880s (Oxford). With C. Ollier and J. Brocherel, he made the first ascent of Batian, Mt Kenya (*qv*) in 1899. Knighted, 1920.

MACNAMARA, Arthur (1861-90)
Classical scholar and barrister, who, with Slingsby, Barnes and Topham, had a memorable Arolla season in 1887 when he did first ascents of the E Ridge of Mont Blanc de Cheilon, and the S Peak of the Aig. Rouges, descending by the celebrated Crête de Coq. He also made the first ascent of the Satarma Pinnacle.
Macnamara was killed descending the Düssistock in 1890.

MACPHEE, George Graham (1898-1963)
A Scottish doctor who was the first to climb on the Castle Rock of Triermain, Lake District (Yew Tree Climb, 1928) and to investigate Green Gable as a climbing ground. He was with Kirkus on the first ascent of Great Slab, Clogwyn du'r Arddu (1930). Macphee also made a number of climbs on Ben Nevis and elsewhere in Scotland, and compiled the Ben Nevis guidebooks of 1936 and 1954.

MAESTRI, Cesare (b. 1929)
Italian climber and guide from Trento, notable for his hard Dolomite routes and for his solo exploits. Maestri made the first two ascents of the Cerro Torre in Patagonia (*qv*) and both ascents aroused controversy.

MAGNETIC VARIATION
The difference between true north and magnetic north, expressed in degrees, e.g. 6° W means that magnetic north is 6° west of true north, and of course, it is to the magnetic north that the compass needle points. The magnetic variation differs from place to place and changes slowly year by year (at the moment in Britain it is decreasing from the W by about $\frac{1}{12}$° per annum). The relevant information is given at the bottom of all good maps.
When navigating in the hills, the magnetic variation must be taken into account. In Britain, where the O.S. maps have the grid system (*qv*) it is easier to use a false variation calculated by subtracting the grid variation from the real magnetic variation, and then assuming the grid lines are true north. The Silva type compass makes all these calculations very simple. (See also COMPASS.)

MAITRE, Jean (d. 1927)
A French mining engineer who made a number of notable ascents in the Dauphiné. The Pic Maitre of the Grande Ruine (1887) is named after him.

MALCZEWSKI, Antoni (1793-1826)
A Polish count and noted poet who climbed the lower (N) summit of the Midi with J. M. Balmat and five Chamonix guides in 1818 – the first Chamonix aiguille to be climbed. He ascended Mont Blanc a few days later: "a pleasurable journey after the sad and terrible Aiguille du Midi."

MALHAM
Village and tourist area in the Yorkshire Dales famous for its limestone scenery. The principal climbs are at Malham Cove and Gordale Scar: long, mostly hard, free and artificial. Popular. Several other limestone cliffs are used for climbing hereabouts notably Attermire Scar.
Guidebook: *Yorkshire Limestone*, by F. Wilkinson.

MALKIN, Arthur Thomas (1803-88)
With his wife was among the earliest of English travellers to the Alps, immediately before the Golden Age. They were the second English group to visit Saas and Mrs Malkin was the first Englishwoman to visit the Théodule. They also possibly made the first ascent of the Eggishorn. (All this in 1840.) Continued to climb for many years after.

MALLORY, George Herbert Leigh (1886-1924)
An almost legendary figure in British climbing, whose name is forever associated with Everest. Mallory's actual total of new climbs in Britain and the Alps was small, and none are of great importance. Nevertheless he was regarded as the Golden Boy of the climbing world for some years – Young (*qv*) called him Sir Galahad, and his striking features, character and intellectual brilliance, as well as his undoubted ability, made him the centre of the popular Pen y Pass gatherings.
Mallory came from Cheshire, but it was Irving (*qv*), who was his schoolmaster at Winchester, who first took him to the Alps in 1904. He did not climb in Britain until 1906, when he was at Cambridge, and led a party of undergraduates up Lliwedd. He

met Young at this time and became a member of his circle.

Mallory was a teacher at Charterhouse until the 1921 Everest Expedition (except for war service). He married in 1914 and had a son and his two daughters, Clare and Berridge, both became well-known climbers.

Everest became his ruling passion. He was a member of the first three expeditions (*qv*) and was in the parties which were the first to see the North Face and reach the North Col. He was also the first to see the Western Cwm, from whence the success of 1953 was gained; he considered it impracticable.

On 8 June 1924, Mallory, with the inexperienced Irvine (*qv*) as partner, set out from Camp VI to climb the last 2,000 ft to the summit. They were seen by Odell (*qv*) through a break in the cloud, at the first step of the NE Ridge. What happened after that remains a mystery: they did not return and no trace was found of them. In 1933 an ice axe, belonging to one of them, probably Irvine, was found at about 27,600 ft and it is presumed that an accident occurred at this spot and the two climbers fell to their deaths. It is unlikely that they reached the summit.

Mallory is famous for two quotations: "Have we conquered an enemy? None but ourselves"; and, in reply to a question as to why he wanted to climb Mount Everest, "Because it is there."

MALTA, CLIMBS IN
The sea-cliffs of this Mediterranean island offer various rocks-climbs, initially developed by the commandos.
Guidebook: *Malta Climbers' Guide*, by J. D. Graham.

MANK
Colloquialism for bad weather – mist, cloud, snow. "The mank is right down" means that the peaks are obscured by cloud. Probably from the French, *manqué*.

MANNERING, George Edward (1862-1947)
One of the founders of the New Zealand Alpine Club. Inspired by W. S. Green (*qv*), he attempted Mt Cook five times between 1886 and 1890, reaching a point 140 ft from the summit before being forced back. Wrote *With Axe and Rope in the New Zealand Alps* (1891) and *Eighty Years in New Zealand* (1943).

MANTELSHELF (Am.: Chinning; Fr.: Retablissement)
A move in rock-climbing to overcome a very high step. The palms are placed on the hold (often a ledge) and a press-up made until one foot can be raised to the same hold. A very delicate movement is then made to stand upright. If there are holds on the facing wall, it is easier, but often it is a question of balance alone. Common on many climbs. One-handed mantelshelves are not unknown, particularly on gritstone.

MAPS (G.: Karte; Fr.: Carte)
Used with the compass (*qv*), an indispensable aid to mountain navigation. Apart from the question of accuracy, maps for use in the mountains should be of convenient scale, suitably contoured and contain as much detail as is consistent with clarity. It is essential, too, that the magnetic variation is shown, with date, and the annual increase or decrease. Colour layering and hatchuring make relief clearer.

In Britain, the Ordnance Survey (O.S.) maps of the scale one inch to one mile are commonly used, though some rock-climbers may prefer the $2\frac{1}{2}$ inch to one mile series. The larger the scale, the less area any single sheet will cover and convenience must be balanced against detail requirements. There are commercial maps available but these have no advantages over the O.S. maps. The single exception in Britain is the S.M.C. map to the Cuillins of Skye, which shows these complicated peaks in great detail. In 1974 the O.S. 1" series was being replaced by metric maps of 1:50,000.

Alpine maps are in the scales: 1:100,000, 1:50,000, 1:25,000 (France 1:20,000). The first of these is useful for giving a general picture of an area but the practical maps are in the larger scales. The usual series are, for France: Carte de France (I.G.N.), for Switzerland: Carte Nationale (G.: (C.N.) landeskarte (L.K.), for Austria and the German Alps: Alpenvereinskarte (O.A.V.) and Freytag-Berndt (F.B.), for Italy: Touring Club Italiano (T.C.I.). Note that many maps of one country overlap considerably into neighbouring states – particularly in the case of Italy. Note also that Austro-German maps usually give the old Austrian Empire names for Italian peaks (e.g. Tre Cima becomes Drei Zinnen and, more confusing, Mt Cevedale becomes Konigspitze).

Maps to the popular Alpine areas can usually be relied upon, especially the newer

1:25,000, but this is not always the case with less popular areas where the maps are based on older surveys. All maps become out of date when new roads, cable cars, buildings, dams are added (hydro-electric works provide considerable alterations) and, too, many glaciers are shrinking. Heights, on all maps, tend to vary with new surveys.

A Kammkarte is a map where the ranges are drawn as black lines and the peaks as triangles or dots with height added. They are usually to scale, but are not really good enough for navigation. In remote areas, however, they may be the only available information. It should be noted that the secondary purpose of many mountaineering expeditions to remote areas is to draw adequate maps of the region.

MAQUIGNAZ, Jean-Joseph (1829-90)

The best-known member of a family of guides from Breuil. His career closely parallels that of J. A. Carrel (*qv*), his great rival. Maquignaz was with Carrel on the abortive attempt on the Italian Ridge of Matterhorn in 1865. In 1867, with his brother Jean-Pierre, he succeeded in climbing the ridge direct (Carrel had made a detour near the top). Other members of the party were left at a col below the final peak, named Col Félicité in honour of Félicité Carrel who was with them. In 1868, the two brothers led Tyndall (*qv*) on the first traverse of the mountain, and five days later reversed the traverse with another party. He made the first winter traverse with V. Sella (*qv*) in 1882.

Maquignaz's best work was done with members of the Sella family, for whom he became almost a family retainer (and consequently prosperous). With four of the Sellas he made the first ascent of the Aig. du Géant (1882) – though not to the true top, as it turned out, and with considerable aid from fixed ropes.

Maquignaz disappeared while climbing Mont Blanc in 1890.

MARITIME ALPS

The main Alpine chain between the Col de Tende and the Col de Larche, considered by Coolidge to be the beginning of the Alps at the western end, though the Ligurian Alps are now included. The nearness of the Mediterranean (the mountains are scarcely 40 km from Nice) and relative lack of height make permanent snow and ice scarce, though there is a little. Generally rock peaks which offer ridge and face climbs. The area has been compared with Skye. The highest summit is Punta dell'Argentera (3,297 m) and the best centre is St Martin.

Guidebook: *Maritime Alps*, by R. Collomb.

MASON, Alfred Edward Woodley (1865-1948)

Novelist and mountaineer, and one of the few men to write successful mountaineering novels. After Oxford Mason went on the stage for a time but began writing about 1895, describing in articles some adventures in the Tyrol. His first novel was *A Romance of Wasdale*. He had started climbing in 1891 (Wetterhorn) and in the Lake District about the same time. He continued to climb until 1910, doing many of the usual Alpine and British climbs of the period. He was Liberal M. P. for Coventry, 1906-10.

Mason's best-known novel today is probably *The Four Feathers* (1902) but his main climbing novel is *Running Water* (1907), inspired by Mummery's guideless ascent of the Old Brenva on Mont Blanc. It is said that the character of Mr Kenyon is Leslie Stephen (*qv*) and the villain, Skinner, is an amalgam of Dent, Davidson and Mummery (all *qv*).

MATHEWS BROTHERS

The three Mathews brothers, William (1828-1901), Charles Edward (1834-1905) and George Spencer (1836-1904) were central figures throughout the pioneering days of Alpine climbing. Their experience was vast and they took part in a number of the great first ascents, including Grand Casse, Castor and Monte Viso (William), and Moore's famous ascent of the Brenva Face of Mont Blanc (George Spencer). There was also a cousin, Benjamin St John Attwood-Mathews, who made a number of ascents with William, including the first English ascent of Finsteraarhorn. It was at his father's house that, in 1857, it was finally decided that the Alpine Club (*qv*) should be formed. William Mathews (together with Kennedy (*qv*) was principally responsible for the Club.

C. E. Mathews played a prominent part in the start of Welsh climbing by organizing winter meets at Pen y Gwryd Hotel (including one attended by Melchior Anderegg (*qv*) in 1888). He formed the Society of Welsh Rabbits (1870) (*qv*) and the Climbers' Club of which he was first President (1898-1901).

William was President of the A.C. (1869-71) and C. E. Mathews was President (1878-80).

C. E. Mathews was a solicitor with a strong interest in local politics; a friend of Joseph Chamberlain. The other brothers were in the family business of land agents. The family had great influence in Birmingham and Worcestershire.

MATTERHORN (4477·5 m) (Fr.: Cervin; It.: Cervino)

Famous in shape and history; along with Everest, the best-known mountain in the world. It stands in a peculiarly isolated position between Breuil (Italy) and Zermatt (Switzerland). In its honour, Breuil has been recently renamed Cervinia; the Swiss have more sense.

The mountain has four distinct ridges and four faces, and the top is a concave crest, about 80 m long, the W end of which forms the true summit and the E end the Italian Summit (4476·4 m). (*Note*. It is *not* the highest mountain in the Alps (Mont Blanc) nor even in Switzerland (Dom).).

The easiest way up is by the NE Ridge (Hörnli). Long and confusing, sometimes subjected to stonefall from careless parties above, it is mostly rock at an easy angle, with snow to finish. There are fixed ropes at the most difficult part. The Solvay Hut (*qv*) (emergency only) is at 4,000 m on the ridge.

The S-W Ridge (Italian Ridge) is a rock-climb of some difficulty made easier by fixed ropes and ladders. The N-W Ridge (Zmutt) is a lovely snow crest which ends in some teeth; the climb then goes to the right of this over slabs to the top. The S-E Ridge (Furggen) is the hardest to climb, rising in three big towers to the summit; the final tower is usually avoided on the left.

The North Face is one of the great Grade VI Alpine routes: loose rock, stonefall. The technicalities of this Face are not extreme but its seriousness cannot be questioned. The other faces are of minor interest.

A summary of important ascents is given below:

1865 (14 July) First ascent, Hörnli Ridge – Whymper, Hudson, Hadow, Douglas, Croz, Taugwalders, father and son (see WHYMPER, *et al.*)
1865 (17 July) Italian Ridge – Carrel and Bich (see CARREL)
1867 (13 Sept) Italian Ridge, present route – Maquignaz brothers (*qv*)
1868 (27 July) First traverse, Breuil-

Zermatt – Tyndall and Maquignaz brothers (*qv*)
1868 (3 August) First traverse, Zermatt-Breuil – Hoiler, Thoily and Maquignaz brothers.
1871 First ascent by a woman – Gardiner, F. Walker and Lucy Walker, with five guides.
1874 First double traverse, Breuil to Breuil – J. Birkbeck Jun., Petrus and Bic
1876 First guideless ascent – Cawood, Colgrove and Cust (*qv*)
1879 Zmutt Ridge – Mummery, Burgener, Gentinetta, Petrus
1879 West Face – Penhall, Imseng, Zurbriggen (see PENHALL)
1911 Furggen Ridge – Piacenza, Carrel and Gaspard.
1931 North Face – F and T, Schmid
1931 South Face – Benedetti, Carrel and Bich
1932 East Face – Benedetti, Mazzotti, and four guides
1959 First solo ascent, North Face – Marchart
1962 Direct Ascent, West Face – Ottin and Daguin
1962 First winter ascent, North Face
1965 First ascent of North Face by a woman – Yvette Vaucher and party Direct Route, North Face – W. Bonatti (*qv*)
1966 All four ridges climbed in a day – two Zermatt guides.

The Matterhorn has been subjected to various records and stunts. The fastest recorded ascent (Hörnli) is 1 hr, 3 min.

MAUD, John Oakley (1846-1902)

Was with Cordier and Middlemore on the first ascent of the Verte from the Argentière Glacier in 1876, and in the same season made the first ascents of Les Courtes and Les Droites. He later made new routes on the Bietschorn and Lauteraarhorn and twice tried the Mittellegi Ridge (1879, 1881) but without success. In 1878 he was with Dent (*qv*) for three attempts on the Dru.

MCNAUGHT-DAVIS, Ian (b. 1929)

A leading British post-war climber with various new routes to his credit, including Cioch Grooves, Skye (1951), The Kame, Foula (1972) and Stochastic Groove, Gogarth (1966). He seconded Brown on several other Gogarth climbs.

McNaught-Davis made a number of British first ascents in the Alps and in 1956 was a member of the Muztagh Tower Expedition (first ascent). In 1960 he made the first ascent of Hjornespitze and Bersearkerspitze in Greenland and in 1962 climbed the Peak of Communism in the Pamirs. He visited the Ruwenzori in 1955.

He is well known to the public for his part in several recent television climbing programmes.

MEADE, Charles Francis (b. 1881)

British Alpinist noted for his first descent of the NE Ridge of Jungfrau, 1902 and for his Himalayan campaigns of 1910, 1912 and 1913 when he attempted to climb Kamet. In 1913 he reached the *col* between Kamet and Abi Gamin (Meade's Col, 23, 420ft) and camped there; until the Everest expeditions this was the highest mountain camp known. The lightweight tent used is named after him. Meade wrote: *Approach to the Hills* (1940) and *High Mountains* (1954).

MER DE GLACE

Perhaps the most famous glacier of the Alps and the longest in the Mont Blanc group (14 km). Its principal feeding ground is the Géant Glacier, which, with the Vallée Blanche, extends from the Aig. du Géant to the Aig. du Midi. The Géant glacier descends the spectacular Géant Ice-fall to the Tacul Glacier which almost immediately effects a junction with the glaciers of Leschaux and Talèfre to form the Mer de Glace. There are numerous subsidiary feeder glaciers on either bank. The stream issues from the ice above Les Tines and is largely canalized to its junction with the Arve.

The Mer de Glace is usually dry (see GLACIERS) and though heavily crevassed, is fairly gently inclined and seldom presents difficulties. The chief mode of access is from Montenvers (*qv*).

MERKL, Willy (1900-34)

A leading climber from the great Munich school of the late 1920s. Merkl made many daring ascents in the Eastern Alps, including the Dolomites, and some first-rate iceclimbs in the Western Alps before visiting the Caucasus in 1929, where the third ascent of the S Peak of Ushba was made, and also the first ascent of the N Ridge of Koshtantau.

In 1932 he adopted Welzenbach's plans (*qv*) for an attempt on Nanga Parbat and led an expedition which succeeded in finding a practicable way to the top, though

had not the resources to carry it out. In 1934 he returned to the attack but the party was overtaken by storm and in a fearful retreat, four Germans and six porters died. Merkl himself died between Camps 7 and 6. His leadership of both expeditions has been strongly criticized.

MERZBACHER, Gottfried (1846-1926)

Bavarian climber who played a part in the opening of the Dolomites. In 1891 he was with Purtscheller in the Caucasus, then visited the Tien Shan. He later visited the great Bogdo Ola group, though by then his interests had turned to exploring rather than climbing.

MESSNER, Reinhold (b. 1944)

A mountaineer from the Tyrol, well known for his solo ascents of hard climbs, for example, Phillip/Flamm, 1969. An outspoken champion of free climbing. In 1970 Messner, with his brother Gunther, took part in the Nanga Parbat Expedition and both reached the summit by the Rupal Flank (first ascent). Gunther was taken ill and his brother decided they should descend by the little-known Diamiri Face. Without even a rope they managed to descend successfully, but Gunther was killed near the foot of the face, presumably by an avalanche.

MEURER, Julius D. (1838-1924)

Founder and first President of the Austrian Alpine Club (1878), but later disagreed with the vogue for guideless climbing and resigned. He was the author of many climbing guidebooks to the Eastern Alps. He made the first ascent of Pala di San Martino (1878).

MEXICO, CLIMBING IN

The highest peaks in Mexico are the three volcanoes, Citlaltepetl (Pico de Orizaba) (18,700ft), Popocatapetl (17,888ft) and Ixtaccihuatl (17,000ft). The famous Popocatapetl was reputedly climbed by the Conquistadores in 1519. The peaks are of little use to mountaineers. Good rock-climbing is reported near Mexico City and Durango.

MIDDLEMORE, Thomas (1842-1923)

In the early 1870s Middlemore was companion of a number of hard climbers, including Gardiner, T. S. Kennedy and Eccles. In his last season he joined Cordier and Maund on the first ascents of the Verte from Argentière Glacier, Les Courtes and

Les Droites. With Cordier he also made the first ascent of Pizzo Bianco and Piz Roseg from the Tschierva Glacier, (all in 1876). His passage of the Col des Grandes Jorasses with Kennedy in 1874 (the first) created a fierce controversy as to the moral justification of persuading guides to undertake climbs involving objective dangers.

His brother, S. G. C. Middlemore, also did a few Alpine seasons, but of a less ambitious character.

MIEMINGER KETTE
A small group of limestone mountains between the Fern Pass and Telfs in the Tyrol. Highest point is the Griesspitze (2,739 m). Ehrwald is the best centre (No English guidebook.)

MILESTONE BUTTRESS
A buttress below the N Ridge of Tryfan (Snowdonia); it is quite close to the road which is here marked by the tenth milestone from Bangor, and hence the name. It was first climbed by O. G. Jones and the Abraham brothers (qv) during Easter 1899 since when it has become possibly the most popular beginners' climb in Britain. There are several routes on the cliff, now, mostly easy. The rock is very worn.
Guidebook: *Tryfan and Glyder Fach*, by A. J. J. Moulam

MILLERS DALE
A Derbyshire dale with a wide selection of limestone climbs. In its middle reaches the dale is known as Water-cum-Jolley, and there is a branch dale, Ravensdale, which also offers fine climbing. Raven's Tor in Miller's Dale is noted for its artificial climbs.
Guidebook: *The Northern Limestone Area*, by P. Nunn.

MIXED CLIMBING
A term used in the Alps to indicate a route which involves both rock climbing and snow or ice-climbing.

MOELWYNS
A group of mountains in the south of Snowdonia whose principal summits are Moelwyn Mawr (2,527 ft), Moelwyn Bach (2,334 ft) and Cnicht (2,265 ft, the "Matterhorn of Wales". Immediately E of these are the vast slate quarries of the Blaenau-Ffestiniog region. There are dozens of crags and *llyns* (lakes). Many crags offer climbs, mostly short, the best being those near Llyn Stwlan (The Moelwynion). On

the W edge of the area is Carreg Hyll-Drem and on the E is Carreg Alltrem, both popular cliffs with hard climbs.
Guidebook: *Snowdon East*, by A. J. J. Moulam.

MONOLITH
A tall block of rock resting against a crag. The crack or chimney between the monolith and the face often provides a climb, for example, Monolith Crack, Shepherd's Crag, Borrowdale. Perhaps the most famous is the Monolith Crack on the Gribin, Wales, climbed by the Abraham brothers (qv) in 1905.

MONTAGUE, Edward Charles (1867-1928)
Author and journalist, sometime acting editor of the *Manchester Guardian*. A keen climber, he is best known for his story *In Hanging Garden Gully*.

MONT AIGUILLE (12,086 m)
A fantastic limestone peak some 36 miles south of Grenoble in the Vercors. It consists of a fine grassy plateau surrounded on all sides by steep limestone walls varying between 500 ft and 1,000 ft in height. Its impressive appearance guaranteed its notoriety from medieval days and it is mentioned by English writers as early as 1211, when it was known as Mons Inascensibilis!

In the summer of 1492, Charles VIII of France, on his way to Italy, was so impressed by the peak that he ordered Antoine de Ville, Lord of Domjulien and Beaupre, to attempt its ascent. The noble lord was successful, several men reaching the top by means of ladders and "subtle engines". They stayed three days, erecting a hut (surely the first bivouac hut?) and three crosses. Chamois were found on the summit.

Today the mountain offers numerous very hard climbs. There are no easy ways up. (See *Josias Simler* by W. A. B. Coolidge.)

MONTANDON, Paul (1858-1948)
A Swiss banker who was one of the early exponents of guideless climbing. He made the first guideless ascents of numerous peaks including the Eiger (1878), Schreckhorn (1883), Gspaltenhorn (1885) and the first guideless traverse of the Bietschorn (1888). One of the earliest skiers in Switzerland. He remained active all his life, and ascended Cevedale at the age of 75.

MONT BLANC (14,807 m)

The highest summit in Western Europe and one of the most important mountains for climbers, not only for its height, but for the variety of climbing it offers. It stands immediately south of Chamonix (qv) on the Italian frontier, though the summit is entirely in France. It forms a distinctive high ridge with the Dôme du Goûter, north-west, and Mont Maudit, north-east, and the latter extends to Mont Blanc du Tacul. From Mont Blanc itself a short ridge runs south to Mt Blanc de Courmayeur. All these peaks are over 4,000 m. The northern face (towards Chamonix) presents great glaciers and snow-fields, well seen from the Brévent on the opposite side of the Chamonix valley, but the south (Italian) side is a complex series of glacier cwms separated by high and often difficult ridges.

The easiest ways to the summit are on the Chamonix side, that via the Goûter Route being the commonest, though the Grands Mulets is also easy. The only really easy route from Italy is via the Dôme Glacier. All three of these routes reach the Col du Dôme and then traverse the Bosses Ridge to Mont Blanc summit. All are fairly lengthy snow/ice climbs.

The three long high ridges of Brouillard, Innominata and Peuterey are seldom climbed throughout since their southern ends connect with peaks which are climbs in their own rights. The Peuterey integrale is one of the hardest ridge climbs in the Alps. Between the Brouillard and Innominata Ridges are the important Brouillard Pillars and between the Innominata and Peuterey are the important Frêney Pillars. Beyond the Peuterey is the wide high face of the Brenva terminating in the Brenva Ridge. Strictly speaking, this is the limit of the Italian side of Mont Blanc proper.

The Brenva Face is of particular importance since it contains a number of ridges offering great climbs. These are quite different from the long ridges previously mentioned, being steeper and definitely a part of the face. They face east and are, from the south (Peuterey): Eckpfeiler Buttress (Grand Pilier d'Angle), Pear Route (Via della Pera), Route Major, Sentinelle Rouge, and the Brenva Ridge (Old Brenva).

Beyond the Brenva, above the upper bay of the Brenva Glacier, the SE Face of Mt Maudit is an important climbing area and this is limited by the long ridge known as the Frontier Ridge, since the frontier here turns E and follows the ridge to the Tour Ronde. Note. The correct name of this ridge is the Arête de la Brenva; not to be confused with the Brenva Ridge. Beyond this again is the glacier bay of the Cirque Maudit, on the far side of which is the Diable Ridge of Mont Blanc du Tacul and the various spectacular pinnacles, of which the best known is the Grand Capucin.

All these climbs, from the Brouillard to the Capucin, are long, remote and fairly difficult. Some are extremely difficult and the area is one of the most important for climbing in the Alps.

In 1760, de Saussure (qv) offered a prize for the first ascent of Mont Blanc. Attempts were made in 1775, 1783, 1784 and 1786, the last two reaching the start of the Bosses Ridge. The summit was finally attained by J. Balmat and M. Paccard on 8 August 1786. The first English ascent was by Col. M. Beaufoy in 1787 and the first woman to reach the top was Marie Paradis in 1808. The first American ascent was by W. Howard and J. Van Rensselaer, 1820. (See The First Ascent of Mont Blanc, by Brown and de Beer.) Other important first ascents include:

1827 Corridor Route – C. Fellows, W. Hawes with nine guides.
1840 (c) Grands Mulets Route – M. Couttet
1861 Goûter Ridge – L. Stephen, F. Tuckett, with M. Anderegg, J. J. Bennen, P. Perren
1865 Brenva Ridge – G. S. Mathews, A. W. Moore, F and H. Walker with J and M. Anderegg
1887 Frontier Ridge – M. von Kuffner with A. Burgener, J. Furrer and a porter
1901 Brouillard Ridge – G. B. Gugliermina with J. Brocherel
1919 Innominata Ridge – S. L. Courtauld, E. G. Oliver, with A. Aufdenblatten, A and H. Rey
1927 Peuterey Ridge – L. Obersteiner, K. Schreiner
1927 Sentinelle Rouge – T. G. Brown, F. S. Smythe
1928 Aigs. du Diable Ridge – Miss M. O'Brien, R. Underhill with A. Charlet, G. Cachet
1928 Route Major – T. G. Brown, F. S. Smythe
1933 Pear Route – T. G. Brown with A. Graven, A. Aufdenblatten
1951 Gervasutti Pillar – P. Fornelli, G. Mauro

1957 Eckpfeiler Buttress – W. Bonatti, T. Gobbi
1961 Central Pillar of Frêney – C. Bonington, D. Whillans, I. Clough, J. Deugosz
Guidebook: *Selected Climbs in the Mont Blanc Range* Vol I, by R. Collomb and P. Crew

MONT BLANC GROUP

The principal range between the Col de la Seigne and the Grand Col Ferret in the Western Alps. The mountains run SW–NE and are limited on the northern side by the vale of Chamonix and on the southern by the Val Veni and Val Ferret. In practical terms they are limited to the west by the Val Montjoie (Col du Bonhomme) and in the east by the Swiss Val Ferret. In area they do not compare with many other Alpine groups, but their importance to Alpinism is unquestionable.

alp above the Mer de Glace and an important starting point for expeditions. On the Italian side, Courmayeur is the best centre. The two villages are connected by the Mont Blanc Tunnel (road only) and by a téléphérique system. There are several other villages important for certain ascents, as well as téléphériques, etc. There are numerous huts.

The presence of the highest mountain in the Alps, and the intensive development of climbing in this area, means that every important peak, and almost every climb, is redolent of history. Only a broad picture can be given here:

The earliest attempts were on Mt Blanc itself and culminated in the first ascent by Dr M. G. Paccard and J. Balmat, 8 August 1786. Tourist ascents followed. The ascent of other peaks followed the general pattern of Alpine pioneering in which the highest peaks were the general goal. Typical is the

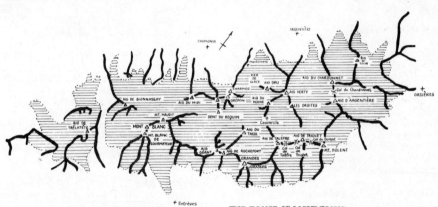

THE RANGE OF MONT BLANC.

The mountains are divided between France, Italy and Switzerland, the borders meeting at the summit of Mont Dolent (3,820m) near the Col Ferret. Most of the area is in France. There are 25 tops of over 4,000m of which the highest is Mont Blanc, 4,807m: the highest summit in Western Europe. The area is heavily glaciated and the rock (granite,) runs to superb pinnacles (*aiguilles* = needles) giving fine climbing of all standards. The snow and ice-climbing is equally good and varied and the region is immensely popular.

Chamonix (*qv*) is by far the most important centre, and connects by rack railway with Montenvers, a hotel complex on an

first ascent of the Aig. Verte (E. Whymper with C. Almer, F. Biner, 1865).

Towards the end of the nineteenth century the aiguilles assumed importance as rock-climbing skills increased: Aig. du Grépon (A. F. Mummery with A. Burgener and B. Venetz, 1881), Aig. du Grand Dru (C. T. Dent, J. Walker with A. Burgener, K. Maurer, 1878). First ascents of the numerous aiguilles continued well into this century.

The first ascent of the Brenva Ridge (G. S. Mathews, A. W. Moore, F and H. Walker, with J and M. Anderegg, 1865) was outstanding for its time. The other great ridges were then climbed at intervals well into the present century, for example, the Hirondelles Ridge of Grandes Jorasses (G. Gaia, S. Matteoda, F. Ravelli, G. A. Rivetti with A. Rey, A. Chenoz, 1927).

The decade prior to the Second World War saw attempts on various N Faces and include the first ascent of the N Face of the Dru (P. Allain, R. Leininger, 1935) and the Walker Spur of Grandes Jorasses (R. Cassin, G. Esposito, U. Tizzoni, 1938).

Between the wars, too, came the development of the Brenva Face, beginning with Sentinelle Rouge (T. G. Brown, F. S. Smythe, 1927).

Of the numerous hard post-war climbs, one might pick out the Bonatti Pillar of the Dru (W. Bonatti, 1955) and Central Pillar of Frêney (C. Bonington, I. Clough, D Whillans, J. Dlugosz, 1961) as particularly interesting. (See also MER DE GLACE, CHAMONIX AIGUILLES, MONT BLANC, AIG. DU DRU, GR. JORASSES.)

Guide books: *Selected Climbs in the Mont Blanc Range*, (2 vols), by R. Collomb and P Crew.

MONTENVERS

A favourite and historically famous starting point for climbs in the Mont Blanc range. It is a shoulder of alp above Chamonix, on the left bank of the Mer de Glace (*qv*) near the glacier terminus. There is a hotel, cafe, bunkhouse, mountain zoo, and (on the glacier) ice grottoes. Plenty of camping space, and the site is easily joined with the extensive Plan de l'Aiguille by a good track. Extremely popular with tourists. It is connected with Chamonix by a rack railway.

MONTE ROSA (4634m)

A complex mountain mass between Switzerland and Italy. The Swiss side faces Zermatt, the Italian side Macugnaga. It has the third highest summit in the Alps (Dufourspitze, 4634m) which is also the highest summit in Switzerland. The other summits are:

4609m Nordend
4596m Grenzgipfel
4563m Zumsteinspitze
4556m Signalkuppe (Punta Gnifetti)
4436m Parrotspitze
4341m Ludwigshohe
4321m Corno Nero
4215m Pyramide Vincent
4046m Punta Giordani

As the cols between the ridges do not fall below 4,000m, the mountain as a whole is the largest 4,000m massif in the Alps.

The mountain is very popular, especially from Zermatt. The ordinary route is long but not very difficult, though rather more so than Mont Blanc. There are rock-climbs, notably the Cresta Rey and Cresta di Santa Caterina, and some famous ice-climbs on the immense East Face, notably the Marinelli Couloir, but generally the mountain offers long mixed traverses from peak to peak. The highest hut in the Alps, Capanna Margherita, is on the summit of the Signalkuppe.

The first ascent (Dufourspitze) was by J. G. and C. Smyth, E. J. Stephenson with U. Lauener, J and M. Zumtaugwald in 1855. It quickly became one of the most popular climbs in the Alps and certainly the most popular from Zermatt until displaced by the Matterhorn in that respect.

Other notable first ascents include:

1861 Nordend – Buxton bros, J. Cowell, M. Payot
1872 Marinelli Couloir – Pendlebury bros, C. Taylor, F. Imseng, G. Spechtenhauser, G. Oberto
1874 Cresta Rey – E. Hulton, P. Rubi, J. Moser
1876 Via Brioschi – L. Brioschi, F and A. Imseng
1887 Cresta Signal – H. W. Topham, A. Supersaxo, a porter
1906 Cresta di Santa Caterina – V. J. E. Ryan, F and J. Lochmatter
1931 NE Face, Signalkuppe – J. Lagarde, L. Davies

Guidebook: *Selected Climbs in the Pennine Alps* Vol I., by R. Collomb.

MONTSERRAT

A mountain some 4,000 ft high situated about 35 miles from Barcelona, Spain, and famous for its monastery. The name means the serrated or sawn mountain and it consists of numerous pinnacles of conglomerate, some in excess of 500ft, giving climbs in the upper grades. The best-known pinnacle is the Cavall Bernat (Costa-Boix and Balaguer, 1935).

MOORE, Adolphus Warburton (1841-87)

One of the greatest Victorian mountaineers. Moore's career embraced practically all the then known difficult climbs in Alps: frequently as the second or third ascents. His own first ascents began in 1862 with the Sesia Joch, Jungfraujoch and Gross Fiescherhorn, but his finest seasons were 1864 and 1865. In 1864, mainly with Whymper (*qv*) and H. Walker (*qv*) he made six major first ascents of peaks or *cols* and several second, third or fourth ascents. In 1865 he raised this to nine first ascents, including Piz Roseg, Ober Gabelhorn and the Brenva Face of Mont Blanc.

The Brenva climb took place the day following Whymper's ascent of the Matterhorn and, just as Whymper's climb symbolized the end of the Golden Age, Moore's Brenva endeavour symbolized the birth of a new age of difficult climbing. It is significant, too, that the adverse public reaction to climbing following the Matterhorn tragedy, which threatened the Alpine Club with extinction, was countered by Moore's Secretaryship (1872-4).

In 1866, 1867 and 1869, Moore did some winter climbing in the Alps, including the second ascent of the Brèche de la Meije. In 1868 he visited the Caucasus with Freshfield and Tucker, making first ascents of Kasbek and the E summit of Elbruz. He paid a second visit in 1874 with Gardiner, Grove and Walker.

In private life Moore was a senior official in the India Office and one-time private secretary to Lord Randolph Churchill. Twice offered the Presidency of the A. C., he declined on the grounds of his official duties.

In 1867 Moore privately published his diary of his great 1864 season: *The Alps in 1864*. An enlarged public edition was published in 1902.

MORAINE (It.: Morena)

The detritus of glacier found at the snout (terminal) and edge (medial). Moraines are formed of boulders, mud and even old ice, crushed together by the grinding action of the glacier's movements. In the Alps, where the glaciers are retreating, the moraines may be extensive. The older ones are usually well compacted and have well trodden paths. New moraine is loose and unpleasant.

MORSE, Sir George Henry (1857-1931)

Brother-in-law of the Pasteurs (*qv*); climbed frequently with them and with Wicks and Gibson (*qv*). He made new routes on the Aig. de Talèfre (1892) and Aig. d'Argentière (1893). He took part in the first guideless ascent of Grépon (1892) and the first traverse of it from S to N (1893).

Morse was President of the A.C.(1926-7) and an Original Member of the Climbers' club. He climbed frequently in Britain. He was knighted for political services in 1923.

MORSHEAD, Frederick (1836-1914)

A very active Alpine pioneer who made many early ascents (though no first ascents of great note), especially with Moore (*qv*) and C. E. Mathews (*qv*). With the latter, he was a founder of the Climbers' Club.

MOSELEY, William Oxnard, Jun. (1848-79)

Born in Boston, U.S.A. and a doctor in Massachusetts, Moseley was a keen climber with many ascents in the Alps and Sierra Nevada to his credit. He was killed while descending the Hörnli Ridge of the Matterhorn; a celebrated accident, but one which seems to have been his own fault. His boots were badly nailed and he insisted, against the wishes of his guides and companion (Craven, *qv*), in unroping too soon. He slipped on the slab which now bears his name, and fell 2,000ft to his death.

MOULAM, Anthony John James (b. 1927)

A leading post-war British rock-climber, and partner to P. R. J. Harding (*qv*) on many climbs in Llanberis and the Black Rocks, Derbyshire. Moulam's own routes include Mur y Niwl, Ysfa (1952), Ogof Direct, Silyn (1952), Shadrach (1951) and Scratch (1953) both at Tremadoc. (Many others too.) He began climbing at the Black Rocks in 1940 and has climbed in many parts of Britain and the Alps. He has appeared on various T. V. climbing programmes.

Tony Moulam was President of the Climbers' Club, 1970-2, and of the B. M. C., 1971-3. He held the latter Presidency during a period of change and upheaval, initiated many reforms, but finally resigned over policy disagreements.

He has compiled a number of post-war guidebooks: *A Guide to Black Rocks and Cratcliffe Tor* (with Harding, 1949. Revised as part of Chatsworth area guide, 1970), *The Carneddau* (1951, 1966), *Tryfan and Glyder Fach* (1956, 1964), *Cwm Idwal* (1958, 1964) and *Snowdon East* (1970).

MOUNTAIN

An elevated mass of land, circumscribed in area and surrounded by valleys or plains. The highest point is known as the summit and there may be other eminences known as subsidiary summits or tops (e.g. Monte Rosa). These may have separate names or may be given a compass name, e.g. Wildspitze, N Summit, S Summit. Or they may simply be given a spot height e.g., Pt

2365 m. Where several such summits exist, the highest is known as the Principal summit.

The sides of the mountain are known as the flanks and are given a compass name or, more rarely, are named after the valley they overlook (e.g. Rupal flank, Nanga Parbat). If the flank is very steep it is called a face or wall. Where the faces meet they form a ridge – often the easiest way up the mountain. Ridges are given compass names or are named after places nearby, people who made the first ascent or attempt, some feature of the ridge, or even some nickname, such as Viereselgrat, Dent Blanche (Four Asses Ridge).

Some mountains are plateaux, that is, the top is almost equal in area to the bottom and is fairly level, e.g. Kinder Scout, Derbyshire. Not all plateaux are mountains, however. Particularly sharp-pointed mountains are often given special names: Spire, Tower, Aiguille, etc. Mountains formed by special geological processes are also given identifying names – mesa, nunatuk, and so on.

Though some mountains exist alone (e.g. Ararat), many are linked by ridges to other mountains. The result is also called a ridge (e.g. Mischabelgrat in Switzerland). A compact group of mountains is known as a massif and a bigger group as a range or chain (obsolete). These last three words are used somewhat indiscrimately: one hears, for example, of the Range of Mont Blanc, the Chain of Mont Blanc or the Mont Blanc massif. An imaginary line linking the principal summits of a range is known as the crest line, or, because it determines the flow of rivers, the watershed.

The qualities of a mountain which appeal to climbers are the height, the shape of the mountain, and the intrinsic difficulties of an ascent.

In Britain, any peak over 2,000 ft in height is usually regarded as a mountain.

MOUNTAIN CAMPING

Good quality equipment designed for ordinary lightweight camping is perfectly adequate for most mountain camping in summer. A dry site should be chosen, preferably sheltered from prevailing winds and free from hazards such as flooding, stonefall and avalanches. Pegging is often difficult owing to the stony nature of the ground, and stones can be used instead to hold the tent down. In exposed sites, a windbreak of stones might be desirable.

However, for high-altitude camping, winter camping and other extreme conditions, specially designed mountain tents are best. These are tough, light, and easy to erect. They usually have a sleeve entrance which can be drawn into the tent and tied off for further comfort, and they all have a built-in ground sheet (common in many ordinary tents now) and a wide valance on which rocks or snow can be placed to help hold the tent down against blizzards. On stony slopes it may be necessary to build a platform for the tent, or to dig out a platform from a snow slope. On level ground a windbreak is useful (see above), although snow can be used instead. It may also be possible to dig a hole for the tent, further protecting it from strong winds. On recent high-altitude expeditions, the box tent (Whillans Box, *qv*) has been used in preference to ordinary tents because of its greater comfort and strength.

In cold conditions, good down sleeping bags and duvet equipment is necessary and only boots and outer windproofs are removed for sleeping. Even these must be kept somewhere warm, if possible, to prevent them freezing. Cooking and eating are performed while lying in the bags.

MOUNTAINEERING (Am.: Mountain climbing; G.: Bergsteigen; F.: Alpinisme; It.: Alpinismo)

The sport of climbing mountains, or, the exploration of high mountains for scientific purposes or simply conquest. The term, like the activity, is capable of wide interpretation, but basic to it is the acknowledgement of some degree of difficulty, only overcome by skill on the part of the mountaineer.

Mountaineering involves four major activites: walking, rock-climbing, snow or ice-climbing, and navigation. To these may be added: mountain camping, ski mountaineering, mountain rescue, high-altitude planning. Knowledge of weather, food values, physiological changes and other allied subjects may also be of value in certain circumstances. Physical and mental fitness is required, but probably experience counts for more, for the sport can be continued into old age, and frequently is.

The philosophy of the sport varies according to where it is taking place, and though certain countries (e.g. U.S.S.R.) lay down dogmatic rules for climbers, in general all the conditions of an ascent must come from within the climber himself, guided by the prevailing opinion. To take an extreme example: any climber found

24 A Hard Dolomite Rock Climb. The North Face of Cima Grande. (*right*) 25 A Classic Alpine Snow Ridge. The Biancograt of Piz Bernina.

26 JOE BROWN. One of the greatest climbers Britain has ever produced is seen here climbing Tensor, at Tremadoc, North Wales.

using pitons to help him up the easy Ordinary Route of Milestone Buttress in Wales would be ridiculed, but nobody would complain if he used pegs and bolts on some of the fierce walls of Yosemite, California. Similarly, under present conditions, siege tactics would be ludicrous on the Hörnli Ridge of the Matterhorn, but not on the South Face of Annapurna. There is a thin dividing line between what is acceptable and what is not, and here mountain ethics (*qv*) play their part. Generally speaking, the best ascent to date is taken as the standard, so that if a climb *can* be done with four pegs, it is unethical to use more. If someone reduces the number of pegs required to say, two, then that becomes the new standard. In Alpine climbing or winter mountaineering, where snow and ice are involved, these unwritten rules can be blurred by weather and other factors. It must be stressed that all of this is left to the individual conscience.

The aims of mountaineering pass through three phases: to reach the summit; to create a more difficult route; to reduce the aid needed on a difficult route. Each takes precedence in turn over the next. If we examine three areas:

Britain
Reaching the summit counts for little. There are only a handful of summits in Britain that cannot be reached by simple walks. The route, and the way in which it is climbed, are both of great importance (see above).

Alps
The summit is still of importance, since many are difficult to reach by any route. The routes, too, are of great importance but the techniques used are more open to debate, though extreme misuse would cause criticism.

Himalaya
The summit is still the prime objective by any route and any technique within reason. A new route on a mountain already climbed is a major event, and the techniques employed are left to the first ascenders. (This will certainly change in the near future.)

Men have been climbing mountains for utilitarian reasons or curiosity since time immemorial. The first sporting ascent is frequently taken as that of Sir Alfred Wills (*qv*) and his party on the ascent of the Wetterhorn in 1854 – but this is highly debatable.

MOUNTAINEERING ASSOCIATION (M. A.)
In 1945, the then emergent British Mountaineering Council (*qv*) was asked to undertake the training of would-be climbers as part of its function. The B.M.C. felt it could not undertake this task and as a result of this decision a group of climbers, led by J. E. B. Wright, a former professional guide, founded the Mountaineering Association in 1946. It was a non-profit-making trust and it quickly established itself as the premier training organization in Britain, with about 1,200 students per year taking its courses. The instructors included many top names in British climbing (e.g. Clough, MacInnes, Scott).

Jerry Wright was Director of Training, and the Association published several books by him and others as well as a popular quarterly. When Wright retired, the organization faltered and came to an end in 1968.

MOUNTAINEERING ROUTE
A phrase used in Britain to indicate a climb of considerable length, where the difficulty is secondary to the fine positions. It is also used by some climbers disparagingly when the lack of difficulty disappoints them.

MOUNTAIN HEIGHTS
A casual glance at mountain literature or mountain maps will quickly show that there are often discrepances in the heights attributed to mountains. This is particularly the case of mountains in remote areas. There are good technical reasons for this; survey heights vary from survey to survey. Among the causes are: refraction, earth curvature, vertical deflection caused by unequal gravity, the depth of snow on the summit during observations, and the exact meaning of "mean sea level", since sea-level is not spheroid. Heights are usually the average of several calculated observations with all possible corrections applied.

Where the peaks have been inadequately surveyed, or not surveyed at all, the heights may be those attributed to the peaks by climbers who have used an aneroid (altimeter) or possibly hypsometer. Variations in temperature and air pressure make these readings highly inaccurate. In some cases the heights given are merely estimates based on climbers' judgements.

National pride has been known to affect published data. This is especially the case when a height approaches a "magic figure" for example, 6,000 m. If a height is estimated at, say, 5,985 m, the addition of another 20 m seems of little account and makes the peak all the more impressive.

Another source of error is attributable to converting metres to feet and vice versa, and rounding down or up to the nearest unit. For difficulties over Himalayan heights see *Abode of Snow*, by K. Mason. (See also HEIGHT CONVERSION.)

MOUNTAIN LEADERSHIP CERTIFICATE (M.L.C.)

A certificate designed to ensure that the holder has a basic proficiency which would enable him or her to lead a party on simple hill expeditions in safety. It is gained after a course which includes instruction and a minimum of 12 months experience, and gains widest acceptance by teachers, youth leaders and others concerned principally with taking parties on hill-walking expeditions.

The Mountain Instructor's Certificate (M.I.C.) is a more advanced qualification designed principally for instructors working at outdoor pursuits centres, and there is an advanced certificate for the more proficient. All these are administered by the Mountain Leadership Training Board.

Other qualifications include a Scottish Winter Certificate and the Guide's Certificate.

The proliferation in recent years of "paper qualifications" in mountaineering has come in for heated argument.

MOUNTAIN RESCUE

The organization of mountain rescue in Britain is done by the Mountain Rescue Committee (*qv*). Teams of volunteers are established in all the mountain areas. There is an experienced leader for each team and the members undergo rigorous training in rescue techniques. Additional volunteers may be co-opted on the spot to assist with arduous procedures such as long carries or sweep and search patterns. The police are often co-opted too and, if necessary, the R.A.F. Mountain Rescue. Each team is fully equipped with the necessary gear, including land rovers and radios. Helicopters are available when required. In addition, the M.R.C. maintain mountain rescue boxes at various strategic places in the hills for immediate use in the event of

an accident. There is no charge made for mountain rescue in Britain.

Rescue in the Alps is usually the province of the local guides who call upon such services as they require, including helicopters. The victim has to pay for these services, or in the event of death, his relatives, and the charges can be high. In some parts of the Alps, there are special avalanche rescue teams, mainly concerned with skiing accidents.

In both Britain and the Alps dogs have been trained to take part in search operations: a trained dog is reckoned to be worth 20 searchers.

The procedure for calling out the mountain rescue team in Britain is that a messenger goes from the scene of the accident to the mountain rescue post, or telephones the police, using a 999 call, whichever is quicker. In the case of overdue parties, a contact should be made after a reasonable time, say three hours, and the team leader will then decide whether a search should be started. (See ACCIDENTS.)

More information is contained in the *International Mountain Rescue Handbook* by H. MacInnes and the annual *Mountain and Cave Rescue* by the M.R.C.

MOUNTAIN RESCUE COMMITTEE

The coordinating committee for mountain rescue in England and Wales, representing the interests of all those who are concerned with rescue work (climbing clubs, caving clubs, police, R.A.F.). There are separate committees for Scotland and Ireland. It is a voluntary body and charitable trust.

The scope of the M.R.C.'s work is wide. It includes the equipping of rescue posts, assisting in the raising and training of teams, research into improved rescue techniques and facilities, and general fundraising to promote these activities. Basic equipment is supplied by the N.H.S. through the M.R.C.

The M.R.C. had its origins in the The Joint Stretcher Committee of The Rucksack Club and F.R.C.C. formed in 1933 to produce a stretcher suitable for use in the hills (Report 1935, see THOMAS). The Committee was widened to include other clubs in 1936 and later. It became the M.R.C. in 1946. (See *Mountain & Cave Rescue*, the annual M.R.C. handbook. This gives current lists of teams and posts throughout Britain.)

MOUNTAIN RESCUE STRETCHERS

Specially designed stretchers are necessary

for the safe evacuation of injured persons from a mountain. The main types are: Mariner, Thomas, MacInnes and (in emergency) the Pigott rope stretcher. The Thomas and MacInnes are the ones used by British rescue teams.

The Thomas stretcher is issued to M.R. teams in England and Wales. It has long extending handles, yoke straps to distribute weight, and wooden runners to allow it to be slid down suitable slopes. There are two models, the standard and the split two-piece (each half can be carried separately in the latter).

The MacInnes stretcher is used by Scottish teams and the R.A.F. It can be folded, and since it weighs only 33 lb can be carried by one man. The patient is secured by a clever system of straps, and there is a wheel attachment which allows the stretcher to be trundled over easy ground.

The Pigott rope stretcher is only used in emergency. It is difficult to carry and uncomfortable for the patient and it should not be used where there is possible spinal injury. It is made from a normal climbing rope.

MOUNTAIN SICKNESS
The effect of altitude on certain people, who begin to feel lethargic and queasy. Ac-companied by a severe headache. Usually only happens above about 10,000 ft and is probably caused by insufficient acclimatization. Not as common as many people think. The only cure is to go down.

MOUNT EVEREST (29,028 ft)
The highest mountain in the world (29,028 ft), lying in the Kosi Section of the Nepal Himalaya (qv). Three ridges run down from the summit: the S Ridge to the S Col, the W Ridge to the Lho La and the NE Ridge which connects with various ridges in Tibet. A branch of this ridge turns NW towards the N Col and Changtse. Between these ridges lie the N Face, the SW Face and the E Face. Below the N Face lies the long Rongbuk Glacier, below the E Face the Kangshung Glacier and below the SW Face the Khumbu Glacier, noted for the famous Khumbu ice-fall which guards access to the mountain. The whole of the north and east sides of the mountain lie in Tibet, the whole of the south and west sides in Nepal. All the earliest expeditions approached from the north by the Rongbuk Glacier and all the later ones, with the exception of the Chinese, from the south by the Khumbu Glacier. The eastern side and the Kangshung Glacier seem virtually unknown.

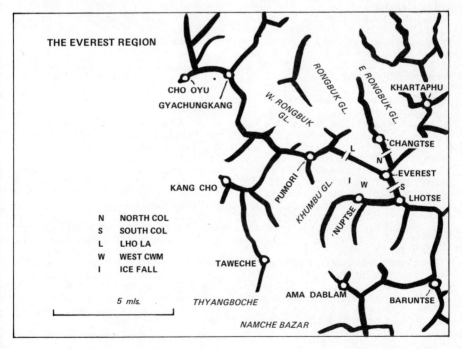

Though both Tibet and Nepal were forbidden to explorers and surveyors, a number of the highest peaks were visible from a distance and these were measured by theodolite in the years following 1846. Upon computation of the results in 1852, Peak XV was found to measure 29,002 ft, thus dispacing Kangchenjunga and Dhaulagiri as the highest-known mountains. Later surveys have changed the height to 29,028 ft. Exhaustive enquiries to find a local name for it failed. The most popular suggestion was the Tibetan name, *Chomo Lungma* (used today by the Chinese), but this name refers to the whole district and not the mountain itself. After 13 years, the mountain was named Mount Everest in honour of Sir George Everest, a former Surveyor General of India.

The general problems of climbing Everest are those of any high and remote peak in the monsoon zone. There are two climbing periods – before and after the monsoon – but on Everest, post-monsoon parties have met with little success owing to the high winds and extreme cold. The great height of the mountain has led all the parties to use oxygen (but see the Chinese, below) and it does not seem possible to climb the mountain without it.

The northern route
Immediately prior to the First World War, a number of Everest expeditions were mooted, but none came to fruition. In 1921 political difficulties were overcome and Lt.-Col. Howard Bury led a reconnaissance party through Tibet to the north side of Everest. The route they found was used by all subsequent expeditions.

The route goes steeply up from the Rongbuk Glacier to the N Col, then follows the NE Ridge, or the N Face, to the top. Above the N Col is a band of limestone, 1,000 ft thick, stretching across the face, and above that two other bands, steeper, which cut into the ridge and form two distinct steps. The steps can be avoided by a dangerous traverse across the face to a gully which cuts through the bands and gives access to the final 700 ft pyramid. The key is, therefore, either the rock steps or the gully. Both have been tried.

The expeditions of 1921, 1922 and 1924 were dominated by Mallory (*qv*), who lost his life, with Irvine, during the 1924 expedition. In all, 12 people, including seven Sherpas died on the three expeditions. In 1924 Norton reached 28,126 ft on the N Face – a height record equalled by Harris,

Wager and Smythe in 1933, but not surpassed until 1952. Bad weather spoilt most of the other pre-war attempts.

Since the War there have been two attempts on the N face by Westerners – Denman, a Canadian, in 1947, and a small party of Americans in 1962. Neither had permission to enter Tibet and both expeditions were complete failures. At least they survived, which is more than Maurice Wilson did in his hair-brained solo attempt of 1934.

In 1952, reports reached the West of a Russian expedition to the N Face which failed disastrously. This has never been confirmed. In 1960, the Chinese claimed the first ascent of the N Face, completed at night and without oxygen. Details of the climb are confusing and the ascent is doubtful. The Chinese failed in a second attempt in 1966, but claim to have climbed the peak again in 1969 (surveyors, climbing solo). The fact is that there have as yet been no ascents from the north not subject to serious doubts.

The southern route
In 1949 Nepal became open to climbers and in the following year Tilman and Houston reconnoitred the Khumbu Glacier. In 1951, Shipton made a full-scale reconnaissance and climbed the Khumbu ice-fall. With the key thus solved a strong Swiss team reached the S Col and Raymond Lambert and Sherpa Tenzing reached a height of about 28,200 ft on the S Ridge, in 1952. The following year, John Hunt's party was successful – Hillary and Tenzing reached the summit at 11.30 a.m., 29 May.

The southern route begins from a base on the Khumbu Glacier, climbs the notoriously dangerous Khumbu ice-fall to the Western Cwm, a huge snow basin cradled between Everest, Lhotse and Nuptse. It then crosses the steep flanks of Lhotse to the S Col. The S Ridge is then followed to the S Summit (28,700 ft) and finally the summit.

The ascent has been made several times since 1953 (see list) but the only new route was the traverse of the mountain by the Americans, Unsoeld and Hornbein, in 1963, by the W and S Ridges – one of the greatest mountaineering feats of all time.

In 1969, the Japanese made the first attack on the SW Face. The face is about 7,000 ft high and soars above the Western Cwm. The first 5,000 ft are ice-slopes of about 45°, then there is a rock band cut into

by gullies – in particular the gully continuation of the ice-slope, and a chimney over
to its right (Whillan's Chimney). Both have
been attempted, but nobody has yet penetrated the rock band (1973). The SW
Face, and the unknown E Face are the only
remaining problems on Everest.

Leaders of Everest expeditions to 1953
1921 Lt.-Col. Howard Bury
1922 General Bruce
1924 General Bruce (retired ill), Major E.
      F. Norton.
1933 H. Ruttledge
1935 E. Shipton
1936 H. Ruttledge
1938 H. W. Tilman
1950 H. W. Tilman and C. Houston
1951 E. Shipton
1952 Dr E. Wyss-Dunant
1953 Col. J. Hunt

List of known expeditions
1921 British – N Face/NE Ridge
1922 British – N Face/NE Ridge
1924 British – N Face/NE Ridge
1933 British – N Face/NE Ridge
1933 First flight over Everest (Houston)
1934 Wilson's solo attempt (unofficial) –
      N Face/NE Ridge
1935 British – N Face/NE Ridge
1936 British – N Face/NE Ridge
1938 British – N Face/NE Ridge
1947 Denman's solo attempt (unofficial) –
      N Face/NE Ridge
1950 Anglo-American – Khumbu glacier
1951 British – Western Cwm
1952 Swiss (2 expeditions) – S Ridge
1952 Russian (unconfirmed) – N Face
1953 British first ascent – S Ridge
1956 Swiss, second and third ascents – S
      Ridge
1960 Chinese, fourth ascent (uncon-
      firmed) – N Face
1960 Indian – S Ridge
1962 Indian – S Ridge
1962 American (unofficial) – N Face
1963 American, fifth, sixth, seventh
      ascents, first traverse – W Ridge & S
      Ridge
1965 Indian, eigth, ninth, tenth, eleventh
      ascents – S Ridge
1966 Chinese – N Face
1969 Chinese, twelfth, thirteenth, four-
      teenth ascents (unconfirmed) – N
      Face
1969 Japanese – SW Face
1970 Japanese, fifteenth, sixteenth ascents
      – S Ridge & SW Face
1971 International – SW Face & W Ridge
1971 Argentine – S Ridge
1972 International – SW Face
1972 British – SW Face
1973 Italian, seventeenth, eighteenth
      ascents – S Ridge
1973 Japanese, nineteenth ascent (first
      post-monsoon) – S Ridge & SW
      Face

Note 1. The Chinese claims are included in
the above list. Some authorities regard
these as suspect, especially those of 1969.

MOUNT EVEREST FOUNDATION
Formed after the 1953 first ascent of the
mountain to administer the funds accumulated from book and film rights. The Foundation is jointly controlled by the Alpine
Club and the Royal Geographical Society.
Grants from the Foundation are made to
expeditions. It is necessary for the expedition to show that it has a worthwhile objective (though not necessarily a large one)
and that the Leader and other members are
competent to undertake the expedition.

MOUNT KENYA (17,058 ft)
An impressive volcanic peak rising from
the highlands N of Nairobi. The Central
core is a volcanic plug forming the twin
peaks of Batian (17,058 ft) and Nelion
(17,022 ft), separated by a high *col* called
the Gate of Mists. Other peaks of the core
are Lenana (16,355 ft) Pt Pigott (16,265 ft),
Pt John (16,020 ft) and Midget Peak
(15,420 ft), and others of less importance.
The former rim of the volcano has also left
some high peaks nearby, though not such
good rock, nor as impressive: Tereri
(15,467 ft), Sendeyo (15,433 ft). The name,
Kenya, derives from the native name
Kiima kya nyaa (the mountain of the
ostrich), the country is named after the
mountain.
   The mountain was discovered by the
missionary Krapf in 1849 and was
explored by Teleki and Von Hohnel in
1887 and Gregory in 1893. Sir H. Mackinder, with the guides C. Ollier and J. Brocherel, made the first ascent of Batian in
1899. Other notable climbs include:
1929 Nelion first ascent. Batian, second
      ascent – E. Shipton, P. Wynn Harris
1930 Traverse of Nelion and Batian – E.
      Shipton, W. Tilman
1938 First woman's ascent, Batian – Miss
      U. Cameron
      First Kenya native ascent, Nelion –
      Mtu Muthara
1944 North Face – A. Firmin's party

1946 S Face and SW ridge – A. Firmin, J. W. Howard
1955 W Face – R. A. Caukwell, G. W. Rose
1959 First Kenya native ascent, Batian – Kisoi Munyao
1963 NE Pillar, Nelion – G. B. Cliff, D. Rutowitz
E Face, Nelion – H. Klier, S. Aeberli, Cliff
1964 Traverse Pt Pigott–Pt John – R. Baillie, T. P. Philips
1973 Diamond Couloir – Y. Laulan, P. Snyder

Many other routes have been established, both on the major peaks and the lesser pinnacles. Of the latter, Midget Peak is reputed most difficult. Mention should be made of the attempt to climb the mountain by escaped prisoners of war (see *No Picnic on Mt Kenya*, by F. Benuzzi).

Considerable rock-climbing is done on Lukenya, S of Nairobi, and other rocks.

Guidebook: *Mt Kenya and Kilimanjaro*, by Mitchell (Mountain Club of Kenya).

MOUNT MCKINLEY (20,320 ft)

The highest mountain in North America, situated in the Alaska Range of south-central Alaska. The Indian name for the peak was *Denali* (The Great One). The modern name was given in 1896 in honour of President W. McKinley of the United States.

The upper two-thirds of the mountain are covered permanently in snow and ice – a great complex of snow-fields and glaciers. The north side is the more easily accessible, especially since the Denali highway was built. The McKinley area is a National Park.

The first attempt to climb the mountain was by J. Wickersham in 1903, followed by that of F. A. Cook and E. Barrille in 1906. Cook's claim to have reached the top is now discounted. In 1910 came the famous "Sourdough Expedition" organized by Lloyd and comprising tough local miners and trappers (sourdoughs). Using home-made axes and crampons they attacked the Karstens Ridge, chopping a 4,000 ft stairway of ice steps. At last, two of the men, P. Anderson and W. Taylor, carrying a 14 ft fir flagpole, made a summit "dash" of 8,500 ft and reached the North Summit (19,470 ft). The flagpole was clearly seen by H. P. Karstens, H. Stuck, W. Harper and R. Tatum on the occasion of the first ascent of the South Summit (20,320 ft) in 1913.

A series of photographs published by Bradford Washburn in the *American Alpine Journal* in 1947 led to renewed activity, and the peak has been visited frequently since then. Because of the great size of the mountain, the glaciation and terrible weather, all climbing on McKinley is expeditionary in character.

Important ascents include:
1951 West Buttress – Washburn's party
1954 South Buttress and Traverse – Argus, Thayer, Viereck, Wood
West ridge of North Peak – Wilson, Beckey
1961 South Face – Cassin, Canali, Alippi, Zucchi, Perego, Airoldi

1963 Wickersham Wall – Gmöser, Prinz, Schwartz
1967 West Buttress – Davidson, Genet, Johnston
1967 South Face Direct – Eberl, Laba, Seidman, Thompson

See *A Tourists' Guide to Mount McKinley*, by B. Washburn.

MOUNT OLYMPUS (2,917 m)

The fabled home of the Greek gods, and indeed, one of the subsiduary peaks is called the Throne of Zeus (2,909 m). The highest summit, Mitka (the Point), was first reached by D. Baud-Bovy, F. Boissonnas, K. Kakalos in 1913. The ascent is not difficult, but the rock of the area seems rotten. The Greek Alpine Club was inaugurated on the summit of Olympus in 1927.

MUMM, Arnold Louis (1859-1927)

A London publisher who liked to combine climbing with travel. He was with Freshfield (*qv*) in the Ruwenzori in 1905, and on Longstaff's Himalayan Expedition (*qv*) in 1907, though he did not reach the summit of Trisul with Longstaff. Mumm took with him some small oxygen cylinders prepared by Siebe Gorman & Co. – the first use of oxygen for high-altitude climbing.

In 1909 Mumm visited the Canadian Rockies for the first time and returned on several later occasions. He made the first ascent of Mumm Peak and Mt Resolution (1910), Mt Hoodoo and Mt Bess (1911) and several minor peaks. He became a member of the American A.C.

He wrote a book about his trip with Longstaff: *Five Months in the Himalaya* (1909), but he is particularly noted for his compilation of *The Alpine Club Register* (3 vols 1923-8), which gives details of the lives and expeditions of all members of the A.C. elected between 1857 and 1890.

Mumm was a man of immense intellectual capacity (Triple First, Oxford) but shyness and a total lack of ambition prevented him from reaching eminence. He died at sea in 1927.

MUMMERY, Albert Frederick (1855-95)

The foremost climber of the second half of the last century, with justifiable claims to be regarded as the founder of modern Alpinism. His number of first ascents was relatively small, but all were important, as were the climbs he attempted but failed to achieve, such as the Furggengrat of Matterhorn and the North Face of the Plan. In climbing circles he was a legend in his own lifetime with a number of staunch disciples, and not a few enemies, such as Whymper and Davidson (qv). Conway called him "the greatest climber of his, or any other, generation", but Winthrop Young thought his achievements overrated. The truth lies in between, but it cannot be denied that his influence on the development of Alpinism was profound.

Mummery was born in Dover, Kent, in 1855, the son of a successful tannery owner. He was a weak, rather sickly child, and this left him with a permanent deformity and myopic vision. He was never able to carry great loads. His social background, too, was exploited to keep him out of the A. C.; he was blackballed in 1880 and not elected for another eight years.

His career as a climber can be divided into two parts: first his partnership with the guide Alexander Burgener (qv), and second his conversion to guideless climbing (about 1890).

He began climbing in 1871 but it was in 1879 that he met Burgener and his outstanding career really began: his first ascents are:

1879 Fletchhorn (new route), Sonnighorn, Zmutt Arête of Matterhorn
1880 Traverse of Col du Lion, Grands Charmoz, Furggengrat and E Face of Matterhorn (The first time this had been done; they failed on the upper Furggengrat and traversed across the E Face to reach the ordinary Hörnli Ridge)
1881 Charpoua face of the Verte; Grépon
1887 Täschhorn by the Teufelsgrat – (Mrs Mummery also took part)
1888 Dych Tau (Caucasus) – guide, Zurfluh

His guideless climbing began next year:

1889 Schreckjoch, first crossing – with Petherick, his brother-in-law
1892 First traverse of Grépon – Hastings, Collie, Pasteur
1893 Dent du Requin, first ascent – Slingsby, Hastings, Collie
West face of the Plan, first ascent – Slingsby, Hastings, Collie
1894 Col des Courtes, first ascent – Collie, Hastings
Old Brenva Route, Mont Blanc, first guideless ascent – Collie, Hastings
1895 Died on an expedition to Nanga Parbat

This list includes only the outstanding climbs and takes no account of the enterprising but unsuccessful attempts on other routes, for instance, his attempt on the Hirondelles Ridge of Grandes Jorasses with the guide Emile Rey in 1892. His famous "easy day for a lady" was a traverse of Grépon in 1893, which he made with Slingsby and Miss Bristow (qv). The quote comes from the heading of Chapter 6 of his book, which is: *The Grépon. An inaccessible peak – The most difficult climb in the Alps – An easy day for a lady*. These he regarded as the three stages through which all mountains were doomed to pass; the phrase itself was invented by Leslie Stephen (qv).

Before he left for the Himalaya in 1895, his book *My Climbs in the Alps and Caucasus* was published. It quickly became one of the classics of climbing literature and the final chapter "The Pleasures and Penalties of Mountaineering", which contains Mummery's climbing philosophy, showed the way the sport had to develop. It had a profound influence, more especially on the Continent.

Mummery went to the Himalaya with Collie and Hastings, and they were joined by Bruce (qv) and two Gurkhas, Raghobir and Goman Singh. They chose Nanga Parbat as their goal because it was reasonably accessible and big, but the area was, of course, largely unknown. It seems likely that they underestimated the scale of the climbing, and particularly Mummery, judging from his letters home – though this may have been deliberate playing down to comfort his wife. After various reconnaissances, and an attempt on the Diamiri Face, the party decided to move to the Rakhiot valley on the other side of the mountain: Collie and Hastings to go round with the porters, Mummery and the two Gurkhas to try a new pass over the intervening ridges. They set off on 24 August 1895, but when Collie and Hastings arrived at Rakhiot, there was no sign of Mummery. Despite intense search, Mummery and the two Gurkhas were never seen again, and it is generally presumed that they were overwhelmed by an avalanche.

THE MUNICH SCHOOL
A name given to the Austro-German climbers of the late twenties and thirties who were putting up hard-face climbs in the Alps. Many, but by no means all, came from the Munich area. The term was coined by British traditionalists as one of disparagement (others were: "the dangle and whack school", "the do or die school"). In recent years the term has been revived as one of historical convenience and respect.

MUNRO
Denotes any summit or top of 3,000 ft or more in Scotland. It derives from Munro's Tables, first published by Hugh Munro in the S. M. C. Journal of September, 1891. This listed 538 tops, of which 283 were regarded as separate mountains (revised by Inglis in 1921 to 543 tops or 276 mountains). The definition of what constitutes a separate top, or even mountain, is somewhat vague. "Munro bagging" is quite popular: many people have bagged them all – but not Munro himself; he died with two tops unvisited.

The Tables are now published as a booklet: *Munro's Tables and other tables of Lesser Heights.*

MURITH, Laurent-Joseph (1742-1816)
A Canon of the Gt St Bernard Monastery and friend of de Saussure (*qv*) and Bourrit (*qv*). Explored the glaciers of Valsorey,

Orny and Otemma and in 1779 made the first ascent of Mont Velan (3,734 m).

MURRAY, John (1808-92)
Publisher, and originator of popular handbooks for travellers, giving detailed information regarding routes, inns, etc. The Alpine volumes were indispensable to the early climbers until superseded by Ball (*qv*). John Murray's firm also published Whymper's great books.

MURRAY, William Hutchison (b. 1913)
Scottish climber and author noted for his pre-war ice-climbs, and later for his Himalayan expeditions. While he was a prisoner of war, he wrote *Mountaineering in Scotland* (1947), one of the modern classics of climbing literature. His routes include (winter); Crowberry Ridge by Garrick's Shelf (1937), Deep Cut Chimney, Stob Coire nam Beith (1939), Twisting Gully, Stob Coire nan Lochan (1946) and (summer): Clachaig Gully (1938), Great Gully of Garbh Bheinn of Ardgour (1946). (Numerous others.)

In 1950, Bill Murray led the Scottish Expedition to Garhwal and Almora, and the following year he was Deputy Leader to Shipton on the Everest Reconnaisance. In 1953 he climbed in the Api range. He was awarded the Mungo Park Medal of the R.S.G.S. in 1953 and the O.B.E. in 1966.

His books are: *Mountaineering in Scotland* (1947), *Undiscovered Scotland* (1951), *The Scottish Himalayan Expedition* (1951), *The Story of Everest* (1953), *Highland Landscape* (1962), *The Hebrides* (1966), *Companion Guide to the West Highlands* (1968), *The Western Isles of Scotland* (1973), *The Scottish Highlands* (1974). He also compiled the climbers' guide to Glencoe (1947) and is the author of five novels.

NAILS

The early mountaineers nailed their boots with hobs of the common sort. These were later supplemented by special edging nails known as wing nails or clinkers and the hobs gave way to muggers, which were of soft iron like the hobs and allowed the rock to bite into them. Immediately prior to 1914 a new nail, the tricouni, was invented on the Continent: it had three flattened prongs and was of hard steel – the nail bit into the rock. On all these nails there were many variations

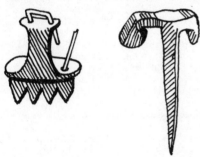

The ways boots should be nailed – pattern, type and number – were a constant source of discussion. Though nails did lead to a precise sort of climbing they had several disadvantages: they were heavy, they balled up in snow, and they wore away the holds, especially on soft rocks. They were gradually but irrevocably superseded by the vibram (*qv*) sole and had practically disappeared by the 1960s.

NAISMITH, William W. (1856-1935)

Scottish Alpinist and rock-climber who took part in many of the early Scottish first ascents, such as the Black Shoot of Stob Maol in 1892, King's Chimney and Sgurr Coire an Lochan (1896) and winter ascents of the Castle and South Castle Gully of Ben Nevis (1896). He also climbed in the Alps and Norway.

In January 1889 Naismith wrote a letter to the *Glasgow Herald* proposing the formation of a Scottish Alpine Club: the suggestion resulted in the formation of the Scottish Mountaineering Club a month later. Naismith is best remembered today for his famous "Rule" (*qv*).

NAISMITH'S RULE

A simple rule for determining in advance the time required for a mountain journey, and first formulated by W. W. Naismith. The rule is: allow one hour for every three miles on the map plus an additional hour for every 2,000 ft of climbing.

The rule does not take into account any halts, nor does it work for very short or very long journeys, but it is fairly satisfactory for an average day. Further refinements can be made (see *Mountain Leadership* by E. Langmuir), but these spoil the essential simplicity of the calculation.

NANGA PARBAT (26,658 ft)

An impressive mountain standing at the great bend of the Indus in the Punjab Himalaya. As the river is at 3,500 ft, Nanga Parbat presents a spectacular 23,000 ft face of rock and ice on this side. There are three flanks to the mountain: that to the south, the Rupal Flank, above the Rupal Nullah, long and very steep; the Rakhiot Face, above the Rakhiot Glacier; and the Diamiari Face above the Diamiari Glacier (see map). All three have been climbed.

NANGA PARBAT MASSIF

Because of its easy accessibility, Nanga Parbat was the first really big Himalayan peak to be attempted (Mummery, 1895). It has a disastrous history of fatalities.

Principal Expeditions

1895 Mummery Expedition – Mummery and two Gurkhas killed.

1932 W. Merkl (German) – Rakhiot Peak (23,210 ft) climbed (Aschenbrenner, Kunigk).

1934 W. Merkl (German) – Drexel died of edeoma. Merkl, Wieland, Welzenbach and six Sherpas killed.

1937 K. Wien (German) – Seven climbers (including Wien) and nine Sherpas buried by avalanche.

1938 P. Bauer (German) – Bad weather foiled attempts.

1939 P. Aufschnaiter (German) – Reconnoitred Diamirai Face.

1950 Thornley, Crace, Marsh – Thornley and Crace killed.

1953 K. M. Herrligkoffer (German) – Buhl reached summit, solo.

1962 K. M. Herrligkoffer (German) – Diamirai Face climbed.

1970 K. M. Herrligkoffer (German) – Rupal Face climbed and Diamirai descended by Messner brothers. G. Messner killed.

NANTGWYNANT
A valley in Snowdonia between the Pen y Gwryd (*qv*) and Beddgelert. On the north side of the road there are three popular valley crags. From E to W these are Clogwyn y Bustach, Clogwyn y Wenallt and Craig y Gelli. Lockwood's Chimney (Bustach) (A. Lockwood, 1909), is an easy old favourite but most of the other routes here are hard. Oxo (Wenallt) (Lees, Roberts, Trench 1953) was the first of the modern climbs.

Guidebook: *Snowdon South*, by T. Jones.

NAPES NEEDLE
A prominent pinnacle, about 60 ft high, standing at the foot of the Needle Ridge of the Great Napes, on the Wasdale side of Great Gable (Lake District). It is famous for its first ascent (27 or 30 June, 1886) by W. P. Haskett Smith (*qv*) solo: an event traditionally regarded as the birth of rockclimbing as a sport. Certainly its spectacular appearance in photographs did much to stimulate interest in the sport.

The original route was the Wasdale Crack. The climb was not repeated until 1889, when it was climbed three times:
17 March, G. Hastings
22 June, F. Wellford
12 August, J. W. Robinson

The first lady's ascent was by a Miss Koecher on 31 March 1890. Most ascents (over 600) by J. E. B. Wright (professional guide) who also made the fastest ascent (1930s).

Notable first ascents are:

1892 The Lingmell Crack – O. G. Jones, Mrs Commeline, J. N. Collie

1893 The Crowley Route – E. A. Crowley

1894 The Arête – W. H. Fowler

1912 The Obverse Route – S. W. Herford, W. B. Brunskill

1928 Direct from the Gap – H. G. Knight, H. M. Kelly, W. G. Standring

The most popular route today is The Arête (Mild Severe).

NEB
A jutting gritstone roof, e.g. High Neb, Stanage. It is a north country term meaning peak, as in peaked cap (neb cap).

NEPAL HIMALAYA
One of the largest and most important parts of the Himalaya, lying between the Kali River to the west and massif of Kangchenjunga to the east. Nepal is an independent native state whose capital is Kathmandu. Everest (29,028 ft), the highest mountain in the world, lies on the Nepal–Tibet border, and there are at least 22 other summits in excess of 25,000 ft. Because of its size, it is convenient to divide Nepal into three sections, based on the principal rivers:

Karnali Section (West Nepal)
There is a long northern crest line with Gurla Mandhata in the west to the Dhaulagiri Himal in the east. In the west the main watershed lies parallel with this and contains the Api and Saipal massifs while further east there is a long spur known as the Kanjiroba Himal.

Gandaki Section (Central Nepal)
From the Kali Gandhaki River to the Sun Kosi River. The mountains range from Annapurna in the west, though Manaslu and Himal Chuli to Gosainthan in the east.

Kosi Section (East Nepal)
From the Sun Kosi to the Arun River. The shortest of the three sections but contains peaks such as Gauri Sankar, Cho Oyu, Makalu and Everest.

Until 1949, Nepal was closed to foreigners and the only survey was that done on a small scale in 1925-7 by Indian surveyors,

who were allowed to survey the main val-
valleys. All our knowledge of the peaks
has been gathered since 1949, except in so
far as the largest had been fixed by long

8,000 m Peaks
Everest (8848 m, 29,028 ft) – 1953, British
Lhotse (8501 m, 27,890 ft) – 1956, Swiss
Makalu (8481 m, 27,824 ft) – 1955, French

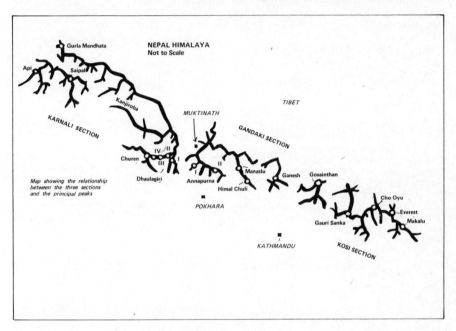

Map showing the relationship
between the three sections
and the principal peaks

distance survey from other parts of the
Himalaya. Much detail remains unknown.
All the highest peaks have been climbed,
but in this area especially, the term is relative – there are, for example, several summits of Nuptse awaiting ascent and
Dhaulagiri IV continues to offer resistance
(1973). Apart from these, and similar multiple summits, there are many peaks above
20,000 ft unclimbed, and unknown.

In 1949, a Swiss party entered Nepal to
explore Kangchenjunga and climbed
Pyramid Peak (see Sikkim). In the same
year Tilman began a series of explorations
in various parts of the country, including
the route to Everest (1950). In 1950 a
French team climbed Annapurna I, the
first 8,000 m peak to be climbed, and in
1953 the British climbed Everest. Of the
many expeditions since one might note
particularly the American traverse of Everest in 1963, the ascent of the South Face of
Annapurna by Bonington's team in 1970
and the various attempts on Everest's SW
Face. (See EVEREST, HIMALAYA).

The famous Sherpa porters are natives
of Nepal (*qv*).

Dhaulagiri (8172 m, 26,811 ft) – 1960,
Swiss
Cho Oyu (8153 m, 26,750 ft) – 1954, Aus-
trian
Manaslu* (8125 m, 26,658 ft) – 1956,
Japanese
Annapurna I (8078 m, 26,504 ft) – 1950,
French
Gosainthan** (8013 m, 26,291 ft) – 1964,
Chinese
*Also called Kutang I
** Also called Shisha Pangma

Other Important Peaks
Annapurna II (7937 m, 26,041 ft) – 1960,
British
Gyachung Kang (7922 m, 25,990 ft) – 1964,
Japanese
Himal Chuli (7864 m, 25,801 ft) – 1960,
Japanese
Nuptse (7879 m, 25,850 ft) – 1961, British
Peak 29 (7835 m, 25,705 ft) – 1970,
Japanese
Chomo Lonzo (7815 m, 25,640 ft) – 1954,
French
Dhaulagiri II (7751 m, 25,429 ft) – 1971,
Austrian

Gurla Mandhata (7728 m, 25,355 ft) – unclimbed

Dhaulagiri III (7715 m, 25,312 ft) – 1973, German

Dhaulagiri IV (7,661 m, 25,135 ft) – unclimbed

Makalu II* (7,640 m, 25,066 ft) – 1954, French

* Also called Kangchunto.

NÉVÉ (G.: Firn)
The snow-slopes on a mountain above the bergschrund. The névé feeds the glacier with fresh snow or ice.

NEW ENGLAND, CLIMBING IN
Climbing in the north-eastern United States is rapidly developing under the pressures from the nearby large urban populations. The most popular areas at present are the Shawangunks and the White Mountains of New Hampshire (both qv). The latter offer ice-climbing of a high order as well as rock-climbs.

Other areas are the outcrop-type climbs of Quincy Quarry, Boston; Crow Hill, Massachusetts; and Ragged Mt, Connecticut; and the larger cliffs of Breakneck Ridge on the Hudson River; Pokomoonshine, Chapel Pond, Giant's Washbowl, and Wallface in Vermont. Smuggler's Notch in the latter state has good ice-climbs. There is said to be great potential in Mt Kineo and Mt Katadhin in Maine, but climbing is discouraged in that state.

R. Underhill, Miss M. O'Brien and F. Weissner began climbing in the area in the 1920s and 1930s, but the expansion of the last two decades has been tremendous and there are routes of all standards. It is more than likely that new cliffs will be found and developed.

Guidebooks: *Adirondack Mountain Guide*, – Adirondack M.C.; *Maine Mountain Guide* – Appalachian M.C.; *White Mountain Guide* – Appalachian M.C.; *Shawangunk Guide*, by A. Gran; and *Cathedral and White Horse*, by J. Cote.

NEW GUINEA, CLIMBING IN
A high mountain chain of 1,100 miles extends along the centre of this large Pacific island, with several summits in excess of 13,000 ft and some of 15,000 ft. The first of the high peaks to be climbed was Mt Victoria (13,363 ft), in the Owen Stanley Range at the east end of the island, by Sir W. MacGregor's expedition of 1888. The expedition continued along the crest of the range and accounted for most of the high summits (10,000 – 12,500 ft). The highest peak in the island is Carstensz Pyramide (16,500 ft) climbed by Harrer (qv), Temple, Kippax, and Huizenga in 1962, after several previous expeditions had failed. Mt Idenburg (15,750 ft) was also climbed by Harrer and Temple, who traversed a number of the peaks in the area (Nassau Range), including Ngga Boloe (16,400 ft), first climbed by A. H. Colijn in 1936. There are tremendous unclimbed rock walls in the Carstensz area.

Nothing appears to be known about the other high mountains.

NEWMARCH, Francis Wells (1853-1918)
A civil servant who visited the Caucasus in the three years 1893-5 with Cockin, Solly etc, (qv). The expeditions were notable in that they were guideless. Newmarch was a very strong walker.

NEWTON, Henry Edward (1873-1961)
Vicar of Ross, New Zealand, and one of the pioneers of climbing in the island. With the Graham brothers (qv) and others he explored the Fox and La Perouse Glaciers, 1903-06. Made first ascents of La Perouse and David's Dome (1906), Douglas Peak, Glacier Peak, Torres, Lendenfeld, Haast, Bristol Top, and Conway (1907). Returned to England that year but visited New Zealand in 1935, making the first ascent of Mt Eros with Alex Graham.

NEW ZEALAND, CLIMBING IN
The principal mountains of New Zealand are the Southern Alps and their southward extensions into Fiordland. The highest peak is Mt Cook (12,349 ft) and about 17 other peaks exceed 10,000 ft, though re-surveying keeps altering the number, to the chagrin of the many climbers who claim to have done all the 10,000 ft summits. Heavy precipitation ensures a good snow cover and there are numerous glaciers. The Tasman Glacier is 19 miles long. Snow and ice-climbing is the principal attraction because the rock (schists and greywacke), is generally poor.

The Southern Alps extend from Harper Pass in the N to the Hasst Pass in the S. Notable peaks are:

Mt Cook 12,349 ft – 1894, G. Graham, T. Fyfe, J. Clark*

Mt Tasman, 11,475 ft – 1894, E. Fitzgerald, M. Zurbriggen

Mt Dampier, 11,287 ft

Mt Hicks, 10,443 ft

Malte Brun, 10,421 ft

Mt Sefton, 10,359 ft

Mt Elie de Beaumont, 10,200 ft
Mt Douglas, 10,107 ft
La Perouse, 10,101 ft
Mt Haidinger, 10,059 ft
The Minarets, 10,022 ft
* In 1882 W. S. Green (*qv*) made what was
virtually the first ascent, stopping a few
feet short of the summit to avoid benight-
ment.

The chief centre is the Hermitage, but
there are others and there are numerous
huts.

South of the Alps, the mountains continue and rise to the Barrier Range where
Mt Aspiring (9,975 ft) and Mt Earnshaw
(9,250 ft) dominate the scene. The former is
one of the most dramatic mountains on the
island.

South again, in the Fiordland, the
mountains continue in complicated
ranges, where mention might be made of
Mitre Peak (5,560 ft) and Mt Tutoko
(9,042 ft).

North of the Alps the mountains extend
right across the island in the provinces of
Nelson and Marlborough. The Kaikoura
Ranges rise to over 9,000 ft, the Spenser
Range to over 7,000 ft and there are several
other ranges somewhat less in height.

By contrast, the North Island of New
Zealand, though it has peaks between
5,000 and 9,000 ft (highest is Ruapehu,
9,175 ft), offers little of interest to the
climber.

The weather of the New Zealand Alps is
often bad, mid-January to the end of
March being most favourable. For the
main ranges of South Island, an approach
from the east is always preferable, often
easy, but that from the west can be difficult
because of dense forest. The snow-line descends to 6,500 ft in the Southern Alps, and
avalanches are common.

By 1894, practically the whole of the
New Zealand Alps had been explored by
Harper and others, though a lot of detail
was unknown. Green's attempt on Mt
Cook stimulated others and Fitzgerald and
Zurbriggen came out from England for the
express purpose of climbing the mountain
in 1894, but in the event were forestalled by
local enterprise. They climbed Tasman,
Sefton, Haidinger, Silberhorn and Sealy –
all first ascents. Local climbers such as
Mannering, Fyfe and Clark were also active, some as professional guides. The great
guides, Peter and Alec Graham, dominated the New Zealand scene for 25 years.

New Zealand climbers have followed the
trend of other areas in attacking the harder
ridges and faces of their mountains in
recent years, and in sending expeditions
overseas. Sir Edmund Hillary, who
reached the summit of Everest with Tenzing in 1953, is a New Zealander. The New
Zealand Alpine Club was founded in 1891.

NICHE (It.: Nicchia)
A small recess in a rock face, usually with a
flat floor where a climber can stand. May
offer a stance and belay (*qv*). Niches are
sometimes difficult to quit. In the Alps the
word is sometimes used for a large hollow
in a face, e.g. the Niche des Drus.

NICHOLS, Robert Cradock (1824-92)
One of the early explorers of the Graian
Alps, where he made a number of first
ascents (1863-6).

**NICOLSON, Alexander (Sheriff Nicol-
son) (1827–93)**
One of the early explorers of the Cuillin,
Skye. Descended Nicolson's Chimney,
Sgurr nan Gillean, in 1865, and made the
first ascent of Sgurr Alasdair, the highest
peak of Skye in 1873 (Alexander's Peak).
His writings did much to popularize Skye
among the members of the Alpine Club.
(See CUILLIN OF SKYE.)

NIEDERE TAUERN
Used here to indicate the mountains of
Steiermark, north of Klagenfurt and Graz,
and east of the Radstatter Tauern Pass.
The area is composed of numerous small
groups, and the highest peak is Hochgol-
ling (2,863 m) in the Schladminger Tauern.
There is much rock-climbing and scram-
bling, and interesting peaks include the
Hochtor (2,365 m), Kleine Buchstein
(1,994 m) and Pfaffenstein (1,871 m). (No
English guidebook.)

NORMAN-NERUDA, Ludwig (1864-98)
One of the leading climbers of his day, his
outlook was comparable with that the
Zsigmondys (*qv*) or Mummery (*qv*). He
climbed with a great guide, Klucker (*qv*),
or without guides (usually with his wife,
May, as companion) or solo (e.g. Dent
Blanche, Croda da Lago).

His greatest season was with Klucker in
1890, when they made first ascents of
Scerscen NW Face (and descended the
same way!), Lyskamm NE Face, Piz
Roseg NE Face, and the first traverse of
Wellenkuppe – Gabelhorn. They also

made an attempt on the N Face of the Dent Blanche and did several other climbs of lesser character. The face climbs were outstandingly difficult for the period and are still highly regarded.

In one sense this early promise (it was his third season) was never fulfilled because he became increasingly involved with the pure rock-climbing of the Dolomites, where he made a number of new climbs. He died of a suspected heart attack while climbing he Schmitt Kamin of the Cinque Dita in 1898.

Norman was his father's surname and Neruda his mother's (later Lady Hallé). He was born in Sweden but lived most of his life in London. An account of his climbs, written in note form by himself and edited by his wife, called *The Climbs of Norman-Neruda*, was published in 1899.

NORTH-EAST SWITZERLAND
A division of the Alps (*qv*) invented by Coolidge to account for a number of outlying peaks of some interest. These are (from W to E): Gr. Mythen (1.899m), the Glärnisch (2,914m), the Churfirsten (Kurfürsten) (2,306m) and the Säntis (2,502m). These are limestone Alps offering rock-climbs of all grades, and all are readily accessible. The Säntis is of startling appearance. (No English guidebook.)

NORTHERN HIGHLANDS
The mountains N of the Kyle of Lochalsh – Inverness railway, in the counties of Sutherland, Ross and Cromarty. The area is considerable and, because it is penetrated by few roads, one of the most inaccessible in Britain. There is no centre suitable as a base for the whole area but the best-known groups can be reached as follows: Liathach (3,456ft), Beinn Eighe (3,309ft), Slioch (3,217ft) from the Torridon, Kinlochewe and Loch Maree areas; An Teallach from the Dundonell Hotel; Stac Polly from Ullapool; Suilven (2,399ft), Canisp (2,779ft), Ben More Assynt (3,273ft) and Quinag (2,653ft) from the Inchnadamph area. The northern-most peaks of interest are Foinaven (2.980ft), Ben Klibreck (3,154ft) and Ben Hope (3,040ft). The last is the most northerly 'Munro' (*qv*).

The gneiss, quartzite and sandstone produce spectacular scenery including some enormous crags (e.g. Coire Mhic Fearchair buttresses of Ben Eighe). The best-known climbing is that of Carnmore, on the N side of Fionn Loch (Carnmore Crag, Torr na H'Iolaire, A'Mhaighdean).

There is constant discovery going on in the area, but the nature of the rock, allied to the remoteness of the place, is unlikely to make it very popular. There is a move to suppress guidebooks to the area to preserve a spirit of discovery – but some do exist.

Guidebooks: *The Northern Highlands*, by T. Strang; and *Climbers' Guide to the Northern Highland Area*, by I. G. Rowe.

NORTHERN TYROLESE ALPS
Between Bludenz in the west and Vienna in the east there are numerous groups of limestone mountains forming an unbroken chain. West of Salzburg they are contained in an area roughly north of the Inn and south of Munich, forming the boundary between Austria and Bavaria, and for this reason are sometimes known as the Bavarian Alps. East of Salzburg they are less easily defined but may be considered to be immediately south of the Salzburg-Vienna autobahn, and limited by the Enns valley.

This eastern half is beyond the Radstatter Tauern Pass, which Coolidge defined as the eastern limit of the Alps (*qv*) but such a limit is not defensible when it excludes mountains such as Dachstein, almost 3,000m high. Only Vienna will serve as the true eastern limit.

Within these limits there are dozens of mountain groups, highly complex in arrangement. They are mostly fairly small, well confined in area. All have the familiar look of limestone – sharp peaks, steep crags, and airy ridges – and though there is some permanent ice and snow on the higher groups, it is of little consequence to the climber. They are predominantly mountains for the rock-climber and hill-scrambler; it is a common misconception that only hard rock-climbs exist. Huts are numerous and the whole area is very popular with Austro-German climbers.

The highest peak is the Parseierspitze (3,040m) in the Lechtaler Alps, near Landeck. The famous Zugspitze (2,963m) in the Wetterstein is frequently claimed as the highest mountain in Germany, though in fact it is on the German-Austrian border: the highest peak completely in Germany is Watzmann (2,713m), near Berchtesgaden.

From west to east the *principal* groups are: Allgauer, Lechtaler, Wetterstein, Karwendal, Kaiser, Berchtesgadener, Dachstein (all *qv*).

NORTH FACE (G.: Nordwand)
Many of the most important and serious

faces in the Alps have a northern aspect. The climbing of these faces is generally associated with the activities of the so-called Munich School in the 1930s (Welzenbach, the Schmids, Harrer and others) and the German word *nordwand* (north wall) came into general use among climbers. Tied in, as it was, with the political climate of the times, the climbing of nordwands and the Munich School in general came in for a good deal of criticism, especially from the conservative elements of British climbing. It is now seen to be an important step forward in the development of the sport.

In fact, the climbing of Alpine faces as distinct from ridges, goes back a good way before the Munich School: one might instance the climbs of Norman-Neruda (NE Face of Lyskamm, 1890), Mummery's attempt on the N Face of the Plan (1892), or the Marinelli Couloir of Monte Rosa (1872). Nor are all the big faces to the north: Monte Rosa and Mont Blanc are cases in point. Even in the thirties, big-face climbing was not an exclusive German affair: the Italians and French were active participants as well.

Nevertheless, the German participation in big-wall climbing has always been large and the mental outlook necessary was cultivated in the nineteenth century by climbers such as Lammer, Lorria, Purtscheller and the Zsigmondys. It certainly reached a climax with Welzenbach and others in the thirties. Outstanding was the Schmids' first ascent of the Matterhorn Nordwand in 1931 and the ascent of the Eigerwand by Harrer, Vorg, Kasparek and Heckmair, 1938. The nordwands still represent the epitome of Alpine climbing and leading climbers are now tackling them in winter, or solo, or making more direct lines up the faces. (See: *Big Wall Climbing* – D. Scott)

NORTH YORKSHIRE MOORS
Including the Cleveland Hills, they range from the Tees, south to the Vale of Pickering, separated from the Pennines (*qv*) by the Vale of York. The Lyke Wake Walk crosses the moors from Osmotherley to Ravenscar. There are a number of short rock-climbs on sandstone outcrops, best known of which are The Wainstones and Raven's Scar, both at Hasty Bank. There are longer and harder climbs on limestone at Peak Scar and Whitestone Cliff. All the climbs are post-war.

Guidebook: *North York Moors Climbers'* guide, by A. Marr.

NORTON, Edward Felix (1884-1954)
Leader of the 1922 and 1924 Everest Expeditions. During the latter he reached 28,126 ft – the highest known point on this side of the mountain – subsequently reached by Smythe, Wager and Wyn Harris (1933). Wrote: *The Fight for Everest 1924* (1925). Norton was a grandson of Wills (*qv*) and related to the Pasteurs (*qv*).

NORWAY, CLIMBING IN
The Norwegian coastline is over 1,100 miles long (12,000 miles if the fjords and islands are counted!) and along much of it rise mountains whose magnificence in Western Europe is only rivalled by the Alps and Pyrenees. In sheer wildness, the Norwegian mountains have the advantage even over these. Though they lack the height of the other two ranges, this is compensated for by the fact that many of them start, literally, at sea level.

Though much of the area is glaciated (the Jodalsbrae is the largest ice-field in Europe), the Norwegian mountains are predominantly rock-climbs on granite, syenite and gabbro. Despite intensive exploration by recent Norwegian climbers, and others, there is so much rock that any number of new ascents can be made. The highest summit is Galdhopiggen (8,098 ft) with Glittertind (8,009 ft) a close second; these are both in the Jotenheimen and are easy ascents.

The most popular mountain area is the Jotenheimen (Home of Giants) and particularly the impressive Horungtinder centered on the hotel of Turtegrø. The best-known peak is Skagastolstind (7,888 ft), one of the many obelisk-type mountains common in Norway. Almost equalling the Jotenheimen in popularity, because of recent explorations, are the mountains around Romsdal, including the Romsdalhorn (5,102 ft) and the 4,500 ft Troll Wall.

In the far north, the Lyngen Peninsula, the Tys Fjord area, and the islands of the Lofoten have equally good mountains, as indeed have Sunnmöre and Nordmöre. All have been explored by climbers, but there is still a lot of virgin rock.

The outstanding figure in early Norwegian climbing was W.C. Slingsby (*qv*), who first visited Norway in 1872 and paid 15 subsequent visits, exploring most of the mountain groups. His ascent, solo, of Skagastolstind in 1876, was a considerable achievement. The Danish climber, Hall (*qv*), was another notable pioneer, particularly in the Jotenheimen and Romsdal areas. More recently, Norwegian climbers such as A. Naess, A. Randers Heen and R. Hoibakk have put up routes of high quality, though the most famous climb of post-war years is unquestionably the Rimmon Route on the Troll Wall, Romsdal. (J. Amatt, A. Howard, W. Tweedale, 1965). (See ROMSDAL. Also see *Norway, the Northern Playground*, by W. C. Slingsby.)

NOYCE, Cuthbert Wilfrid Frank (1917-62)

Schoolmaster and writer, one of the best-known British climbers of the immediate pre-war years and one of the hardest goers the mountains have seen. With Armand Charlet in 1937-8 he did the Mer de Glace face of Grépon in 3¼ hours and the Old Brenva of Mont Blanc in 3½ hours. In the course of a single day in 1942 he did 4,500 ft of hard solo rock-climbing in Cwm Idwal and on Tryfan. In 1959, with Sadler and Mortlock, he climbed the Welzenbach Route of Dent d'Héréns, Furggen Direct of Matterhorn, NE Face of Lyskamm and NE Face of Signalkuppe.

In the Himalaya he made the first ascents of Pauhunri, Machapuchare and Trivor. He was a member of the 1953 Everest Expedition and forced the passage to the South Col.

He helped Edwards (*qv*) in the compilation of the guidebooks to Tryfan (1937) and Lliwedd (1939), making some new routes, including Scars Climb, Soap Gut and the first unaided ascent of Munich Climb.

Noyce wrote a dozen books either by himself or in collaboration with others. Apart from his poems, these were mainly concerned with mountaineering. Best known is *South Col*, his personal account of the successful Everest venture. Noyce was killed with R. Smith during a visit to the Pamirs in 1962.

NUDO DE APOLOBAMBA

A group of peaks on the Peruvian – Bolivian border. Most of them are between 5,000 and 6,000 m and several are unclimbed. The highest is Chupi Orco (19,830 ft), a snow-dome, and the next highest seems to be Palomani Grande (18,928 ft). They were both climbed by a German expedition in 1958.

Nudo means 'knot' and the Apolobamba is only one of several such groups in this region. They seem to offer little to the climber, especially with the Cordillera Real being so near (*qv*).

NUNN, Paul James (b.1943)

One of the leading post-war British climbers, Nunn sprang to prominence at the age of 16, when he repeated a number of the hard gritstone climbs and began putting up fierce new routes of his own such as Anniversary Arête, Stanage and the Girdle of the Lower Tier at the Roches (both 1959). He has since made some 40 gritstone and 60 limestone new routes and was natural successor to Eric Byne in editing the new series of Peakland guidebooks (Vols 5-8).

In Wales, Nunn has put up some 50 routes of which might be mentioned Nexus, Llanberis (with Boysen, 1963). In the Lake District his routes include Plagiarism, Falcon Crag; Daedelus, Eagle Crag and Eyrie, Gillercombe. (He edited the guide to Borrowdale, 1967.)

In Scotland he made a traverse of the Etive Slabs, Thin Red Line (1966), and climbed the Old Man of Stoer (1966) and The Maiden (1970) with Patey and others. It was during the descent of the latter that Patey was fatally injured. He has made a number of hard routes on Foinavon and elsewhere, summer and winter, including the first winter ascent of Emerald Gully, Ben Dearg (1970).

As well as making a number of first British ascents in the Alps, Nunn was a member of the Caucasus Expedition of 1970 which made the first ascent of Pik Shirovski N Face, and in 1972 was in Baffin Island to make the first ascent of N Summit of Asgard by NE Pillar. He has professed a dislike of large expeditions.

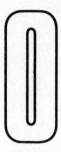

OBJECTIVE DANGERS
Dangers which cannot be overcome by climbing skill, e.g. stonefall. Routes subjected to objective dangers carry warnings in the guidebooks. Many modern Alpine climbs of the harder sort have objective dangers e.g. the Eigerwand.

OGWEN COTTAGE
A former guest house that was one of the great pioneering centres of Welsh climbing. The building is now a mountaineering school and stands by Llyn Ogwen. The adjacent Idwal Cottage Youth Hostel is also a well-known mountaineering base and figures in Elizabeth Coxhead's novel, *One Green Bottle*.

OLD MAN OF HOY
A sea-stack off the island of the same name in the Orkneys – 450 ft, sandstone. (First ascent: 1966, Baillie, Patey, Bonington.) St John's Head, nearby, one of the largest sea-cliffs in Britain (1,141 ft), was climbed by J. Street, E. Ward-Drummond, B. Campbell-Kelly, A. Evans, and L. Dickinson in 1969. The ascent took three days.

ON SIGHT
A climb is said to have been led "on sight" when the leader has made no previous inspections, such as climbing it on a top rope (*qv*). Reserved for hard climbs and new (previously unsolved) problems.

ORDINARY ROUTE
The usual way up a mountain or crag; that taken by the majority and usually the easiest, e.g. the Hörnli Ridge of the Matterhorn. Sometimes called the Tourist Route if the mountain is popular. On British crags the word is sometimes built into the name, e.g. Milestone Ordinary, Tryfan.

ORIGINAL ROUTE
The first route up a mountain or crag.

Sometimes so named, as in Original Route, Holly Tree Wall, Idwal.

ORMSBY, John (1829-95)
Made the first ascent of Grivola in 1859 (the subject of the first lecture paper to the new Alpine Club). Ormsby made interesting excursions into the Atlas Mountains and the Spanish mountains (Picos de Europa, etc.) when they were virtually unknown.

ORTLER ALPS
A fine group of mountains south of the Otztal Alps (*qv*) and separated from them by the Unter Vintschgau valley. The mountains, though now in Italy, were once Austrian and so carry dual German and Italian names. The highest summit is Ortles (Ortler) (3,899 m) but Gran Zebru (Konigspitze) (3,859 m) is more impressive. There are climbs of all grades and the region is particularly good for steep ice-climbs. Numerous huts. Trafoi is perhaps the best centre.
    Guidebook: *Ortler Alps*, by A. J. Thompson.

OTZTAL ALPS
A popular group of mountains on the Austro-Italian border south of the Inn at Imst. The highest peak is Wildspitze (3,772 m). Much of the area offers easy ascents but with large snow-fields and glaciers. There are many huts and hut-touring is popular. Harder climbs (mostly rock) are found in the Kaunergrat. The chief centres are Solden, Vent, Obergurgl and Mittelberg.
    Guidebook: *Otztal Alps*, by W. Unsworth.

OUTCROP (G.: Klettergarten; It.: palestia di roccia)
Crags which jut out from the flanks of a mountain ("valley crags") were said to be outcrops, for example Dinas Cromlech, but the term has now come to be exclusively applied to the lesser rocks which appear in many parts of the country, often away from the traditional mountain areas. The Derbyshire edges (*qv*) and the Devon tors are outcrops, as are the limestone cliffs of the Avon Gorge and elsewhere. There are over 400 such crags where climbs have been made in England alone. Quarries may be regarded as outcrops, sea-cliffs are more debatable. (See *The English Outcrops*, by W. Unsworth.)

OUTRAM, Sir James (1864-1925)

One of the pioneers of Canadian climbing, with Whymper, Collie and others. Climbed a number of peaks for the first time, outstanding being his first ascent of Mt Assiniboine (1901).

OUTSIDE ROUTE

Opposite to "through route" (*qv*). Where a chockstone blocks a chimney, it may be possible to go behind the chockstone (through) or over the front of it. The latter is the outside route – more exposed and often more difficult.

OVERHANG (Fr.: Surplomb; It.: Strapiombo)

(a) A rock face which is beyond the vertical is said to overhang;
(b) A sudden jutting out of the rock is called an overhang.

An overhanging wall may be quite short and climbed free; such pitches exist on many climbs. Alternately it may overhang for many feet and only be climbable by artificial techniques (*qv*).

Similarly, overhangs may be small and easily overcome but some are very big (e.g. Kilnsey Great Overhang, Yorkshire). The underneath of a large overhang is known as a roof. Overhangs are climbed by artificial techniques.

OXYGEN EQUIPMENT

Used to offset the effects of high altitude. Though the Chinese claim to have ascended Everest without oxygen, it is probable that Norton's height of 28,126 ft during the Everest attempt of 1924 is the highest reached by a climber not using oxygen.

The first use recorded is in 1907 by Mumm (*qv*), who took with him some small oxygen cartridges when he went to explore Nanda Devi, but his companions Bruce and Longstaff treated it as a joke. Equipment was developed for use on Everest in 1922, but the early sets were clumsy and their use limited by their weight. There was also strong ethical objections by some of the pioneers – the effects of high altitudes were not known – and only the postwar era has shown the necessity of oxygen from a health view-point.

There are two systems of oxygen apparatus, the closed and the open. In the closed system the oxygen is regenerated by chemicals, but this has never been found entirely satisfactory (though obviously cheaper and easier on porterage). Open systems are used today in which fresh oxygen is supplied in bottles carried by the climber. The rate can be regulated.

Sets are constantly being improved. One of the latest is the Blume system which is designed to give oxygen enrichment equivalent to a height of 17,000 ft, and is self-compensating to allow for different breathing rates. Bottles vary: the Luxfer (British) weighs 17 lb and holds 1,000 litres.

P.A.s

A special rock-climbing boot with canvas uppers and tight-fitting rubber soles stiffened by a shank, originally developed by Pierre Allain. P.A.s are extremely good on small holds, and are much lighter than normal climbing boots. Introduced in the fifties and at first used only by experts, they have rapidly become universal. There are now several types by various makers. Sometimes, inaccurately, known as klets (see KLETTERSCHUHE).

PACCARD, Michel-Gabriel (1757-1827)

A Chamonix doctor who, with Jacques Balmat (qv), made the first ascent of Mont Blanc. (Summit reached 6.30 p.m., 8 August 1786.)

Paccard made three attempts on the summit by the Goûter route: in 1775 with Thomas Blaikie, in 1783 with Bourrit (qv) and in 1784 with two guides. He also reconnoitred the Italian side of the mountain. After his successful climb he prepared a manuscript describing it but this was never published because of the scandalous attack made on him by Bourrit, who claimed that the real hero was Balmat. This began one of the greatest mountaineering controversies of all time. Bourrit's views persisted for many years and only diligent research by modern historians has established Paccard's prime role in the climb. It is believed that Paccard made later climbs and possibly ascended Mont Blanc again. His famous manuscript of the first ascent has never been discovered. (See: *The First Ascent of Mont Blanc*, by T. G. Brown and G. R. de Beer.)

PACKE, Charles (1826-96)

A devoted explorer of the Pyrenees and a contemporary of Russell (qv). He paid a brief visit to these mountains in 1853, but it was in 1859 that he began their systematic discovery. Published a guidebook to the area in 1862 (later extended and revised) and in 1893 made a donation to the C. A. F., which went towards the building of the Refuge Packe at the Col de Bugaret.

Packe also visited the Lake District many times. He was an enthusiastic bivouac man, and a keen botanist.

PACK FRAME

A lightweight metal frame with a shoulder harness like a rucksack. A bag can be fastened on to the frame. Useful for carrying very bulky loads.

PAMIRS

A large area of mountains north of the Hindu Kush in the Tadzhik Republic of the U.S.S.R. There are two main groups, both E-W orientated, and divided by a headwater of the River Oxus. Both groups contain peaks over 21,000 ft and in the northern group (the Trans Alay) is the Peak of Communism (24,590 ft), the highest mountain in the U.S.S.R. The Pamirs is a fairly bleak area, and holds some of the world's longest glaciers (see KARAKORUM), including the Fedchenko Glacier, 45 miles.

There are three 7,000 m peaks in the Pamirs:

Peak of Communism (7,495 m 24,590 ft) – V. Abalakov, solo, 1933

Peak Lenin (7,134 m 23,406 ft) – R. Rickmers party, 1928

Peak Evgenia Korzhenevskaya (7,105 m 23,310 ft) – A. Ugarov's party, 1953

The first two of these have been climbed several times by different routes, notably Peak Lenin, claimed to be the most climbed high mountain in the world. Outstanding are: first traverse by Kovalev's party, 1952, and the first ascent of the N Face by Arkin's party, 1960. Relatively little is known about Korzhenevskaya Peak. The Peak of Communism was formerly called Peak Stalin.

Mountaineering has developed rapidly since the thirties, and the Russians have put up some fine face routes and exceedingly long traverses (cf. Caucasus). Visiting parties from abroad are not unusual: Noyce (qv) and R. Smith were killed descending Peak Garmo in 1962.

Peaks over 21,000 ft include:

Peak Revolution, 22,924 ft
Peak Moscow, 22,260 ft
Peak October, 22,244 ft
Peak Karl Marx, 22,068 ft
Peak Fikker, 22,041 ft
Peak Dzerzhinsky, 22,025 ft
Peak Garmo, 21,637 ft

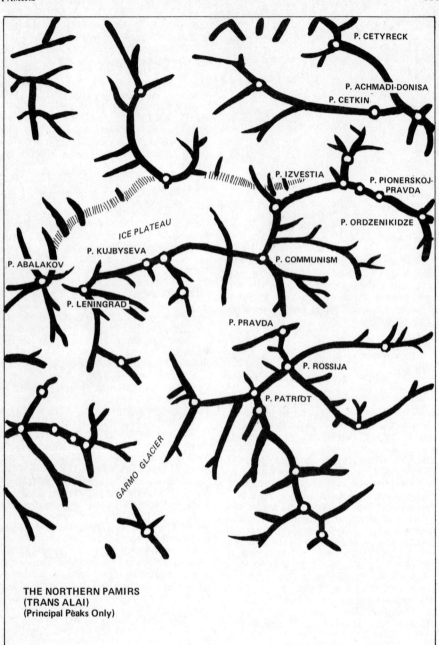

**THE NORTHERN PAMIRS
(TRANS ALAI)**
(Principal Peaks Only)

Peak Engels, 21,359 ft
Peak Leningrad, 21,349 ft
Peak Abalakov, 21,152 ft
Peak Pravda, 21,018 ft

PAPOOSE CARRIER
A rucksack type of frame to which is attached a seat for carrying a small child. Often used in British mountains. The child should be firmly secured in the seat.

PARKER BROTHERS
Charles Stuart Parker (1829-1910), Samuel Sandbach Parker (1837-1905) and Alfred Traill Parker (1837-1900) were three remarkable Liverpool brothers who were pioneers of guideless climbing. They climbed in Skye at a date prior to 1860 (Sgurr nan Gillean) and between 1857 and 1865 made a number of Alpine ascents and crossed several cols. They made the first guideless ascent of the Finsteraarhorn in 1865.

Their chief fame rests on the two guideless attempts they made on the Matterhorn in 1860 and 1861, at a time when even the best guides would not attempt it. They climbed from Zermatt (the first attempt from there) and reached about 11,000 ft in 1860 and somewhat higher the following year. Weather rather than difficulty forced them to retreat and they intended to try again in 1865 but arrived after the accident (See WHYMPER).

C. S. Parker was an M. P. and his brothers were in the family shipping business.

PARSON'S NOSE, THE (Clogwyn y Person)
The steep end of Crib y Person, a ridge in Cwm Glas, Snowdonia. First climbed by A. H. Stocker about 1884.

PASS
The way across a mountain ridge from one valley to another. Open to wide interpretation, but generally of three types:
(a) *motor pass* – accessible to vehicles, e.g. Llanberis Pass, Brenner Pass;
(b) *foot or mule pass* – accessible only to walkers and baggage animals, e.g. Sty Pass, Monte Moro Pass.

The top of these passes is known as the summit, and both types may be blocked during winter.
(c) *climbing pass* – the way over a high col (*qv*). In the Alps this may involve steep and serious ice-climbing (e.g. Moming Pass). The making of new passes was regarded

almost as highly as the first ascent of a mountain by the pioneers, but is seldom undertaken for its own sake today except in the exploration of new areas.

In pre-climbing days many passes in the Alps had been made for the purposes of trade: Coolidge estimates about 20 before 1600 and about 65 by 1800.

PASSINGHAM, George Augustus (1842-1914)
A climber noted as the outstanding "hard man" of his day, with some incredible journeys to his credit, for example the Dom from Zermatt and back in 17 hours. He took part in the first ascent of the Zinal Rothorn, 1872, and made a difficult climb on the W Face of the Weisshorn, 1879.

PASTEUR FAMILY
An English family of Swiss ancestry who have maintained a continuous record of mountaineering from 1846 to the present day. The founder was Henri Pasteur (1827-1909) who began with an ascent of the Buet in 1846 and climbed in the Alps regularly for the next 50 years. His two sons and three daughters were all climbers – the best known being Charles Henry Pasteur (1869-1955) who made the first ascent of L'Evêque (Verte), the first guideless ascent of Grépon, and the first traverse of Grépon, in 1892. Two of his sisters took part in the first of these climbs.

The family was related by marriage to Morse (*qv*) and Norton (*qv*). (For family details see *A. J.* vol. 60.)

PATAGONIA
The southernmost part of South America, from the Rio Negro to the Magellan Straits. In the west of this area, the Andes continue for about 1,000 miles. Unlike the ranges further north, the peaks here are broken into more individual groups. The top half of the range, from Rio Negro to Lago Buenos Aires, consists of forested country with several volcanoes, including El Tronador (11,253 ft) and, a little further south groups of glaciated peaks rising to about 8,000 ft. The area is little explored.

The chief mountaineering interest has centred on the southern half of the range, approximately from Lago Buenos Aires to Punta Arenas, and especially on the great Heilo Continental – an ice-cap extending from Lat. 46°S to 52°S and divided into two parts by the Canal Baker, an inlet which cuts into the range to the depth of 100 miles. The division gives rise to the North

L. BUENOS AIRES

H. NORD

L. SAN MARTIN

HIELO SUD

FITZROY

L. VICDURA

L. ARGENTINO

SANTA CRUZ

PUNTA ARENAS

TIERRA DEL FUEGO

Outline Map of
PATAGONIA

DARWIN

100 mls.

Patagonian Ice-cap (Heilo Patagonico
Norte) and South Patagonian Ice-cap
(Heilo Sur). The Chile-Argentine border
threads a circuitous route through this
country, most of the ice-caps being in
Chile, but the important Fitzroy Group
being in Argentina. The eastern (Argentine) side is open country but the western
side is wet and forested and the coast is
deeply indented with fjords. The ice-caps
reach sea level in various places. Throughout the range, the weather is notoriously
bad.

The Heilo Norte was crossed by
Shipton's party in 1963-4 and the highest
peak in Patagonia (Monte San Valentin,
13,204 ft), near the northern extremity of
the ice-cap, was climbed by O. Meiling's
party in 1958. The area is difficult of access
and there remains plenty of exploration
and climbing for future expeditions.

The Heilo Sur is much longer than its
northern counterpart. The crossing of the
ice-cap was attempted by F. Reichart in
1916 and 1933, but the first successful
crossing was by W. Tilman in 1956. He left
his boat, *Mischief*, in Calvo Fjord, and traversed to Lago Argentino and back. The
length of the ice-cap was traversed by
Shipton's party in 1960-61. There are
numerous peaks on the ice-cap but the
most famous groups are just to the east: the
Fitzroy Group, between Lagos San Martin
and Viedma, and the Paine Group, about
100 miles further south. These two groups,
though the peaks are not particularly high,
offer some of the most difficult climbing in
the world. Notable ascents include:

Fitzroy Group (also: FitzRoy, Chalten)
Cerro Fitzroy, 11,073 ft – C. Magnone,
L. Terray, 1952
Fitzroy Super Couloir – J. L. Fonrouge, C.
Comesana, 1964
Aig. Poincenot, 10,120 ft – D. Whillans, F.
Cochrane, 1962
Cerro Torre, 10,280 ft – C. Maestri, T.
Egger, 1959

Paine Group
Paine Grande, 10,600 ft – W. Bonatti, T.
Gobbi, 1958
Central Tower, 8,760 ft – C. Bonington, D.
Whillans, 1963
The Fortress, 9,400 ft – G. Hibberd, D.
Nicol, J. Gregory, 1968
The Shield, 8,800 ft – M. Dotti, M. Curnis,
1968
(See also CERRO TORRE.)

PATEY, Thomas Walton (1932-70)

One of the most outstanding British
mountaineers of the post-war era. Patey's
climbs revolutionized the game in Scotland, especially in the Cairngorms.

An Aberdonian, Patey tramped the
Scottish hills as a schoolboy and began
climbing in 1949. In 1950 he made the first
winter ascent of the Douglas-Gibson
Gully, Lochnagar, a breakthrough in the
winter standards at that time. There followed over 70 new routes in the Cairngorms alone, with others on the Ben and in
remoter parts of Scotland. Among his first
ascents the following are especially noteworthy:

1952 Tough-Brown Traverse, Lochnagar
     (winter)
1952 Parallel B Gully, Lochnagar
1953 Eagle Ridge, Lochnagar (winter)
1953 Sticil Face, Shelter Stone Crag
1954 Vertigo Wall, Creag an Dubh Loch
1955 Central Pillar, Creag Meaghaidh
     (winter)
1956 Parallel   Buttress,   Lochnagar
     (winter)
1957 Zero Gully, Ben Nevis (winter)
1957 Cresta Climb, Ben Nevis (winter)
1960 Cioch Nose, Applecross
1962 The Last Post, Greag Meaghaidh
     (winter)
1964 Diadem, Creag Meaghaidh (winter)
1965 Traverse of the Cuillin Main Ridge
     (winter)
1966 Old Man of Hoy

After qualifying as a doctor, Patey
joined the Royal Marines for a time and
then, in 1961, took up a practice at Ullapool. Lack of companions often forced
him into solo climbing, though he liked
this for its own sake too and he became a
leading exponent of the art. His solo routes
include The Nose Direct on Fuar Tholl
and Gnome Wall, Ben Eighe, but his finest
is the winter Girdle of Creag Meaghaidh
(1969). South of the border, he played a
part in the development of Chudleigh
Rocks in Devon.

He first visited the Alps in 1951 doing
traditional routes at Chamonix. He
returned in 1953 to make the first British
ascent of the Sans Nom Arête of the
Verte and, in 1955, the first British ascent
of the North Face of the Plan. He did not
return for eight years, then, with Brown,
Bonington and others made first ascents
of: W Face of Plan, NW Face of Aig.
Sans Nom (1963); SW Ridge of Leschaux,
N Face of Pt Migot (1964); W Face of
Cardinal (1965). SE Ridge of Aig. Rouge

de Rochefort (1968).

Patey was considered for the Everest Expedition of 1953 but was rejected on account of his youth. In 1956 he took part in the first ascent of the Muztagh Tower and in 1958 the first ascent of Rakaposhi. In 1959 and 1960 he made some first winter ascents in Norway.

Patey had made a number of climbs on Scottish sea-stacks and it was while abseiling from one of these, The Maiden, that he was accidentally killed.

Well known as a humorous writer of articles and songs for climbers, the best of this work was published posthumously: *One Man's Mountains*.

PAVEY ARK (2288 ft)

A very popular fell and crag rising above Stickle Tarn, Langdale. The crag is immense but broken into complicated buttresses and slabs. Across it runs Jack's Rake, a curious ledge by which it is possible to climb to the summit (first ascent: probably R. Pendlebury (*qv*) 1870-80). Great Gully was climbed by Haskett Smith in 1882 and was the first real climb in Langdale. After the pioneers climbed the easier routes the crag did not attract much attention until after the Second World War when routes like Cook's Tour (Cook and Elliott, 1943), Rake End Wall (Carsten and Phillips, 1945) and Astra (Austin and Metcalf, 1960) led to a revival.

Guidebook: *Great Langdale*, by J. A. Austin.

PAYOT, Alphonse (1852-1932)

Chamonix guide particularly noted for his association with James Eccles (*qv*). They made the first ascent of Mt Blanc from the Brouillard Glacier, and the first ascents of: Mt Blanc de Courmayeur, Aig. du Plan, Aig. du Rochefort, Aig du Tacul, Dôme de Rochefort, and Aig. Dorees. In 1882, with the guide A. Cupelin and W. W. Graham (*qv*), he made the first ascent of the Aig. du Géant.

PEAK DISTRICT

The Peak District embraces the southern limits of the Pennine Chain. The heart of the region is in Derbyshire, but the moors and crags spread themselves into the fringes of the adjacent counties. In effect the district forms a large triangle of open country between the heavily industrialized areas of South Lancashire, South Yorkshire and the Midlands. This alone is enough to ensure its popularity.

The northern part of the district comprises high moors covered in a thick layer of peat in which the weather has eroded a complex of deep channels called *groughs* (*qv*). The underlying rock is gritstone (*qv*), with outcrops in abundance. The principal summits are Kinder Scout (2,088 ft) (*qv*) and Bleaklow (2,060 ft) (*qv*).

The southern part is more complex. Gritstone moors are to be found east of the River Derwent and west of Buxton, though nothing as high and rugged as those further north. The main central core consists of gentle limestone hills intersected by deep valleys - the famous Derbyshire dales. Even here there are a few small gritstone caps: Stanton Moor and the Black Rocks of Cromford (*qv*), for example.

The difficult nature of the Kinder-Bleaklow massifs lends itself to arduous walking and these moors are well known for long, hard courses such as the Marsden-Edale Walk. By tradition, such walks are usually done in the winter months when the moors are particularly bleak and severe. They require good equipment, stamina and competent navigation. For less ambitious walks Edale is a good centre; it is a tiny hamlet which has also gained some popularity with skiers. By contrast, the limestone area further south, though very beautiful, affords only gentle walks.

Outcrops for climbing are to be found throughout the entire Peak District. The gritstone crags are famous: Stanage Edge (*qv*), the Roches (*qv*), Laddow (*qv*), Black Rocks (*qv*), Cratcliffe and many others have played a significant part in climbing history. The limestone crags are of more recent development: Stoney Middleton, High Tor, Chee Dale, Miller's Dale (*qv*), Ravensdale and Willersley are among the best known. In contrast with the relatively low gritstone rocks, the limestone crags provide climbs of two hundred feet or more, mostly of a serious nature. There are also some small outcrops of dolomite near Brassington - the only dolomite climbing in Britain.

Because the crags are widespread, there is no single centre which is suitable for climbing throughout the region. Roads are good, however, and the majority of crags are only a few minutes walk from a road.

Historically, the Peak District has been a womb of English climbing where new techniques have been developed, aided by the superb friction of the gritstone crags. Early pioneers included J. W. Puttrell (*qv*), E. A.

Baker and J. Oppenheimer, who took the knowledge gained on gritstone to the higher crags of Scotland and elsewhere. They were followed by S. W. Herford (*qv*) who made the first ascent of Scafell's Central Buttress in 1914, and H. M. Kelly, another climber who was to make his mark in the Lakes. The development of the Derwent edges after the last war by J. Brown (*qv*), D. Whillans (*qv*) and others played a significant part in the rise of British climbing standards.

The moors have been the training ground of many outstanding long-distance walkers, notably F. H. Heardman and E. Thomas (*qv*). (See PENNINE HILLS.)

PEEL
Traditional climbing jargon for a fall; noun or verb. "I peeled off" or "I had a peel".

PEG
A piton (*qv*). A peg route is one which relies entirely on pitons, i.e. artificial climbing. Using pitons is known as "pegging" and taking them out is called "de-pegging". This English word is gradually replacing the French one in Britain.

PEG HAMMER
A special hammer for placing and removing pitons (*qv*). The head is steel and there are various shapes; the shaft is hickory or metal. Hammers usually have a sling attached as a safety precaution against dropping them. A hammer-axe is a very short ice-axe in which the blade has been replaced by a hammer face. It is used in steep ice-climbing, and in Scotland replaces the pre-war slater's pick.

PENDLEBURY BROTHERS
The two Pendlebury brothers, Richard (1847-1902) and William Martin (1841-1921) were important Alpinists during the 1870s. They began in 1870 with a new traverse of the Wildspitze via the Mittelberg Joch: now one of the most popular climbs in the Alps. For most of the following two seasons they confined themselves to the Eastern Alps.

In July 1872, with Ferdinand Imseng (*qv*) they astonished the Alpine world by making the first ascent of Monte Rosa from Macugnaga by the route now called the Marinelli Couloir. The following year, after some new climbs in the Dauphiné, they made the first real attempt on the Dru, but failed, then the first ascent of

Schreckhorn from the Lauteraarsattel. Among other interesting expeditions were first ascents of: S Peak of Aig. de Blaitière (1876), Pic d'Olan (1875), Pic Sans Nom (1877). Their usual guide was Gaby Spechtenhauser of Otztal.

Richard can lay claim to being one of the founders of British rock-climbing (see HASKETT SMITH). With his brother and others he climbed the Pendlebury Traverse of Pillar Rock in 1872. He also climbed Jack's Rake on Pavey Ark and the Western and Eastern Gullie of Clogwyn y Person (1870s – exact date uncertain).

The brothers came from Liverpool, where William was in business. Richard was a Cambridge mathematician until he retired to Keswick a year before his death.

PENDULE (PENDULUM)
A horizontal abseil (*qv*) used to change a line of ascent or descent e.g. from one vertical crack to another.

PENHALL, William (1858-82)
A medical student noted for his strength and daring during his brief Alpine career. After some new routes with Conway (*qv*) in 1878 he turned his attention to the unclimbed Zmutt arête of the Matterhorn the following season. After one unsuccessful attempt he returned in an attempt to race Mummery (*qv*) to the top, and in so doing climbed the great West Face of the mountain, crossing the dangerous Penhall Couloir. The climb has seldom been repeated, and possibly never in its entirety. A few days later, he and Mummery climbed the Durrenhorn (first ascent), mistaking it for the Nadelhorn.

Penhall was killed on the Wetterhorn in 1882.

PENNINE ALPS, THE
The main range of the Alps from the Grand Col Ferret in the West to the Simplon Pass in the east. It is one of the largest Alpine groups and it has a greater number of 4,000 m peaks than any other – 42 tops exceed this height. Dufourspitze of Monte Rosa is the highest (4,634 m) and is the third highest mountain in the Alps. The Matterhorn (*qv*) is unquestionably the best-known peak.

The Swiss-Italian frontier follows the main range. Long valleys run down on the N and S flanks of this, those on the N (Swiss) side to the deep trench of the Rhône, those on the S (Italian) side to the Aosta valley or, in the E, the Lombardy

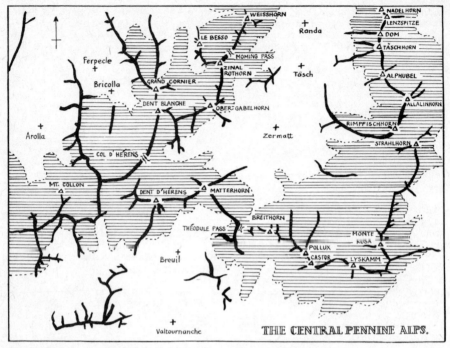

THE CENTRAL PENNINE ALPS.

plains. Between the valleys are ranges of high peaks, though on the S these are of little importance. On the N, these lateral valleys and ranges are of great importance to the climber. From W to E the valleys and ranges are:

Val d'Entremont (principal centre: Bourg St. Pierre), Combin group
Val de Bagne (Fionnay), Cheilon group
Val d'Hérens (Arolla), Dent Blanche group
Val d'Anniviers (Zinal), Les Diablons
Turtmanntal (Meiden), Weisshorn range
Mattertal (Zermatt), Mischabel group
Saastal (Saas Fee), Weissmies group
Simplon Pass

By far the most important centre is Zermatt (*qv*) followed by Saas Fee and Arolla. The others are of interest only for certain peaks. On the Italian side of the main range only Macugnaga in Valle Anzasca and Breuil in Valtournanche are of importance. There are numerous huts throughout the district.

The climbing here is more akin to that of the Oberland than it is to that of Chamonix. There are rock-climbs, but these do not seriously compare with those of the aiguilles nor is the rock as good. There are plenty of long, mixed climbs and of all standards. There are numerous glaciers, the longest being the Gorner Glacier (11 km, with the Grenz feeder).

With the exception of the Combin group, Lagginhorn and Weissmies, all the 4,000 m peaks are accessible from Zermatt, a fact which made it the pre-eminent mountaineering centre of pioneer days. All the important big peaks were climbed by the 1860s, leaving only the lower peaks and the more obscure ones such as Dürrenhorn (1879). Outstanding during this period was Whymper's struggle for the Matterhorn (*qv*). There followed the great ridge climbs, exampled by:

1879 Z'mutt Ridge, Matterhorn – A. F. Mummery with A. Burgener, J. Petrus, A. Gentinetta.
1882 Viereselgrat, Dent Blanche – J. S. Anderson, G. P. Baker with U. Almer, A. Pollinger
1887 Teufelsgrat, Taschhorn – Mr. & Mrs. Mummery with A. Burgener, F. Andermatten
1889 Ferpécle Arête, Dent Blanche – W. Gröbli with A. Pollinger
1895 Schaligrat, Weisshorn – E. Broome, with J. M. Biner, A. Imboden
1901 Rothorngrat, Zinal Rothorn – C. R. Gross with R. Taugwalder

1911 Furggengrat, Matterhorn – M. Piacenza with J. J. Carrel, J. Gaspard

However, some great face climbs were
also being done at this time, for example:

1872 Marinelli Couloir, Monte Rosa – R.
and W. M. Pendlebury, C. Taylor,
with F. Imseng, G. Spechtenhauser,
G. Oberto
1890 NE Face, Lyskamm – L. Norman-
Neruda with C. Klucker, J. Rein-
stadler
1906 SW Face, Täschhorn – V. J. E. Ryan
with F and J. Lochmatter, G. W.
Young with J. Knubel

The latter climb is still one of the most
difficult and dangerous in the Alps. In the
years following the Great War there were
still hard ridges and faces to climb:

1923 Gracey Route, Mont Collon – Miss
L. Gracey with M and M. Pralong
1925 Bouquetins Traverse – I. A.
Richards with J. Georges
N Face, Dent d'Hérens – W. Welzenbach, E. Allwein
1928 NNW Ridge, Dent Blanche – Mr.
and Mrs. Richards with J and A.
Georges
1931 N Face, Matterhorn – F and T.
Schmid
1938 N Face, Mt. Blanc de Cheilon – L.
Steinauer, W. Gorter

Outstanding post-war achievements
have been solo and winter ascents of these
and similar routes. The greatest new route
is Bonatti's North Face Direct on the Matterhorn, done by Bonatti solo, in winter
(1965).

Guidebook: *Selected Climbs in the Pennine Alps* (2 vols), by R. Collomb.

PENNINE HILLS, THE

An extensive range of hills stretching from
the upper Tyne valley in the north to Ash-
bourne in the south and varying in width
from about 12 miles to 50 miles. The chief
rocks are limestone and gritstone, though
there are some igneous intrusions (e.g.
High Cup Nick). The high moors of the
north and the Peak (*qv*) tend to give arduous, boggy walking (habitués are known as
"bogtrotters"), for example, Mickle Fell
area, Bleaklow, Kinder etc., but the limestone regions give easier going (Inglebo-
rough area, the Yorkshire and Derbyshire
dales). The highest summit is Cross Fell
(2,930 ft).

The Pennines may be divided into con-
venient distinct groups. These are (from N
–S): the Northern Moors, the Yorkshire
Dales, Forest of Bowland, Rossendale, the

High Peak and the Low Peak. There is
rock-climbing in all these areas, either on
natural limestone and gritstone outcrops
or in old quarries (see individual cliffs and
areas).

The Pennines are noted for long-
distance walks. The Pennine Way stretches
250 miles from Edale to Kirk Yetholm in
Scotland (it includes the Cheviots). Other
famous walks are: Tan Hill to Cat and
Fiddle, Three Peaks (Whernside, Inglebo-
rough, Penyghent), Marsden-Edale, Derwent Watershed and Derwent Edge Walk
(Woodhead – Robin Hood).

Guidebooks: *The Pennine Way*, by C.
Wright; *The Pennine Way*, by A. Wain-
wright; *Lancashire*, by L. Ainsworth; *York-
shire Gritstone*, by M. Bebbington;
Yorkshire Limestone, by F. Wilkinson; and
Rock Climbs in the Peak (9 vols)

PEN Y GWRYD

An inn in Wales standing at the head of the
Nantgwynant valley and famous as one of
the great pioneering centres of Welsh
climbing. The present landlord (1972),
Chris Briggs, is well known for his mountain rescue work.

PEN Y PASS (GORPHWYSFA HOTEL)

A former inn at the summit of Llanberis
Pass and the usual starting point for the
Pyg Track up Snowdon, or the Crib Goch
ridge. It achieved erstwhile fame as the
centre for G. W. Young's (*qv*) Welsh parties in the early days of this century. The
building is now a Youth Hostel.

PETERSEN, Theodor (1836-1918)

A German chemist who played an important role in the early days of the D.O.A.V.
Petersen made a number of first ascents in
the Otztal where the Petersenspitze was
named in his honour, though von Déchy
made the first ascent in 1874.

PFANN, Hans (1863-1958)

A Nuremburg climber who began climbing
in the Kaisergebirge in 1894 and became
one of the leading exponents in the Eastern
Alps. Climbed guideless and made the first
ascent of Pt Walker, Gd. Jorasses by the S
Face, first traverse of Les Droites, first
verse Matterhorn – Dent d'Hérens and the
first traverse of Ushba (Caucasus) (Pfann,
Leuchs, Distel, 1903). Made the first ascent
of Illampu (Andes) in 1928. Wrote two
books about his climbs: *Führerlose Gipfel-
fahrten*, and *Aus meinem Bergleben*.

PFANNL, Heinrich (1870–1929)
A High Court judge from Vienna with many first ascents in the Eastern Alps to his credit. With Maischberger and Zimmer in 1900 he made the first ascent of the Géant by the N Ridge and NW Face.

PHU DORJE (1924–69)
One of the outstanding Everest Sherpas. He visited the mountain six times: reached South Col on four of them and the summit with the Indian Expedition of 1965. He was killed on Everest when a snow bridge collapsed under him.

PIAZ, TITA (1879–1948)
One of the great Dolomite guides, comparable with Innerkofler (*qv*). A somewhat rough personality, he was known as The Devil of the Dolomites. His routes include:
1900 Punta Emma, NE Face (solo)
1907 Vajolet Torre Est, SE Face
1908 Totenkirchl (Kaisergebirge) W Face, Piaz Route
1911 Torre Delago, SW Ridge
Piaz was killed riding a cycle without brakes.

PICOS DE EUROPA
An important group of karst peaks on the northern edge of the Cantabrian mountains, near Santander. The highest summit is Torre de Cerredo (2,642 m). The unusual name is of unknown derivation, but ancient: Pena de Urrieles is sometimes used instead.

There are three main groups, Western, Eastern and Central: the Eastern is little visited by climbers; the highest point of the Western is Pena Santa de Castilla (2,586 m); but the Central area is the best known. Here is the Cerredo, the Torre de Llambrion (2,639 m) and the strange spire of the Naranjo de Bulnes (2.516 m). (First ascent: P. Pidal, G. Perez, 1904.) The best centre is Arenas de Cabrales.

The whole area consists of narrow gorges and serrated peaks, all closely packed into an area comparable with the Lake District. Travel is extremely difficult and the wildness, combined with the huge rock walls, is the chief attraction.

PIED D'ELEPHANT
A short, down, sleeping bag which covers the legs and hips. Used with a duvet jacket for bivouacking (*qv*).

PIGOTT, Alfred Sefton (b. 1895)
One of the leading British rock-climbers of the years following the First World War. Pigott followed the classical pattern of gritstone training and hard new routes in the greater mountain areas. Between 1920 and 1923 his best known gritstone routes were:
Laddow: Priscilla (shared with Morley Wood), Little Crowberry
Cratcliffe: Giant's Staircase, The Bower Route 1, The Girdle
Black Rocks: Sand Buttress, Lean Man's Climb, Curved Crack
Roches: Batchelor's Buttress, Crack and Corner, Black and Tan's Climb, Via Dolorosa.

With J. Wilding he made his eponymous route on the Comb Buttress of Ben Nevis, 1920; and in 1921 the S Face of Inaccessible Pinnacle, and the Direct Finish to the Crack of Doom, Skye. In 1922 he made the Direct Route, Central Buttress, Ben Eighe.

With Morley Wood, he made the West Route of Eagle Crag, Birkness Combe, 1925, and in 1927 his famous eponymous route on the East Buttress of Clogwyn du'r Arrdu (*qv*) – the first major breach in that cliff.

Fred Pigott was one of the founders of the Mountain Rescue Committee (*qv*) in 1933, and Hon. Sec. from its foundation until 1956. Chairman 1956-72; President 1972 to date. Awarded the O. B. E. in 1964.

PILKINGTON BROTHERS
Charles (1850-1918) and Lawrence (1855-1941) Pilkington were of the famous Lancashire glass-making family. Both were strong walkers and Lawrence is sometimes regarded as the founder of the Lake District Fell Record (1871). With Gardiner and Hulton they were pioneers of guideless Alpine climbing (1878 onwards) and made many first guideless ascents including the Meije and the Guggi route of the Jungfrau. Their influence on guideless climbing was considerable.

They were among the first to climb in Skye (1880), making first ascents of the Inaccessible Pinnacle and the Pinnacle Ridge of Sgurr nan Gillean. Later they made the first ascents of Sgurr MhicChoinnich, Clach Glas and Sgurr na h-Uamha. Sgurr Thearlaich is so named in honour of Charles (Charles' Peak). Mrs. C. Pilkington made the first woman's ascent of Inaccessible Pinnacle (1890).

Lawrence was injured in Piers Ghyll, Lake District, in 1884 and did little climbing thereafter, but Charles climbed regularly until 1911. He was President of the A.C., 1896-8.

PILLAR (G.: Pfeiler; Fr.: pilier; It.: pilastro)

A tall, narrow column of rock jutting out from the parent mountain to which it is usually attached by a narrow neck. A pillar has its own summit and the word implies that the rock is steep, e.g. Central Pillar of Frêney, Mont Blanc.

PILLAR ROCK

One of the most famous and spectacular crags in Britain with a wide variety of good climbs. The crag stands on the Ennerdale face of Pillar Fell in the Lake District, though it is usually approached from Wasdale Head by a fairly long walk. It is unusual (for Britain) in being an immense free-standing obelisk with two tops, High and Low Man, and two appendages known as Pisgah and the Shamrock. The summit (High Man) can only be reached by climbing, the easiest way being from the foot of East Jordan Gully by simple ledges – very exposed. There are climbs on all the faces and they are of all grades.

The first ascent of the Rock was made by J. Atkinson, a local man, in 1826, probably by the Old West Route, though this is not certain. It remained the only way to the top until 1863 when a large party, led by J. W. E. Conybeare found the present easy way described above. The Pendlebury brothers (*qv*) and others found the Pendlebury Traverse in 1872, but the first real climb was the West Jordan Climb by Haskett Smith (*qv*) in 1882. From then on it attracted almost all the leading pioneers. Notable early ascents are:

1890 Shamrock Gully – Hastings, Hopkinson, Robinson
1891 North Climb – Haskett Smith, Hastings, Slingsby
1899 Walker's Gully – Jones, G. Abraham, Field
1901 New West Climb – Abraham brothers, C. Barton, Wigner
     Savage Gully – Barton brothers, Meryon
1906 North West Climb – Botterill brothers, Oppenheimer, Taylor.

There was some loss of popularity in post-war years but the Rock has more recently been the scene of some new, hard climbs. (See JACKSON REV. J., and various pioneers such as HASTINGS, etc)

Guidebook: *Pillar Group*, by A. G. Cram.

PITCH (Fr.: Longeur de corde; It.: Lunghezza)

The distance between two belays (*qv*) that a climber has to travel. Thus, two belays may be 20 ft apart, but a climber may actually have to move 30 ft to get from one to the other: the pitch length is 30 ft. Pitches can vary from a few feet to over 100 ft. Guidebooks usually indicate the length of rock pitches.

PITON (Fr.) (E.: Peg; Am.: Pin; G.: Haken; It.: Chiodo)

Metal spikes which can be hammered into rock cracks. There is another type designed for use on ice.

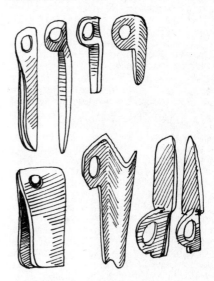

Pitons have four basic uses: 1. for protection as running belays; 2. for direct aid where the rock is holdless or overhanging; 3. as a belay point where no natural belay exists; 4. as an abseil point where there is no suitable natural feature.

Pitons were rarely used in Britain before the Second World War and are still used sparingly, on the understanding that to place a piton where one is superfluous lowers the grade of the climbing; it is, in fact, cheating. Even on artificial climbs (*qv*) the number of pitons is kept to the minimum. In general, the soundness of this philosophy has been proved in practice many times. Early piton climbs have often been subsequently led free, due to an improvement in climbing skills and the development of other methods of protection.

In the Alps and the United States there has always been a much freer interpretation of piton use, principally because the climbs there are longer, higher and subject to changes in weather. An Alpine route which is fully pegged is obviously a quicker proposition than the same route where pitons have to be inserted, but to bang in a piton is itself much quicker than searching about for ways to overcome difficulties.

In the Eastern Alps, and to a lesser extent in other places, some routes have permanent pitons cemented into the rock.

With the development of modern bivouac gear, long climbs are often much safer, weatherwise, than they were, and this is leading to a reappraisal of piton usage, especially in the U. S. A.

Pitons of various kinds have been in use throughout climbing history, but their wider use developed in the Eastern Alps during the early decades of this century. Made of mild steel, the essential parts were a blade or spike for inserting in the crack and a ring or hole into which a karabiner (*qv*) could be clipped. They were basically unchanged until the 1960s when chromolly-steel pitons of specially designed cross-sections were introduced from the United States. These were so superior in every way that they are now almost universally used. The major types are illustrated on p. 189.

A difficult climb on a big peak may require dozens of pitons, which represent a considerable weight for the climber to carry. There are Russian pitons of titanium, which is strong and very light, and this may well be the piton material of the future but at the moment titanium is far too expensive for commercial use.

Use
Pitons are normally carried in bunches clipped to karabiners and hanging on slings, bandolier fashion, though there are special piton-carrying clips and bags on the market. They are driven in with a piton hammer, usually carried in the hammer pocket of climbing breeches, or the holster of a harness (*qv*).

The choice of which piton to use is dictated by the cracks available and the pitons the climber is carrying. The aim is to choose the best combination of the two, bearing in mind the likely direction of strain. Properly placed, even a small piton such as a rurp can take considerable weight.

PLACIDUS à SPESCHA, Father (1752-1833)
"The monk of Disentis". Father Placidus was a Benedictine monk born at Truns near Disentis in the Grisons, Switzerland. He served in the Disentis Monastery and in local parishes and explored the local peaks making numerous first ascents: Stockgron (1788), Rheinwaldhorn (1789), Oberalpstock (1792), Piz Urlaun (1793), Piz Aul, Piz Scharboden (1801), Piz Terri (1802), Güferhorn (1806).

He devoted his entire life to the mountains (he attempted Tödi at the age of 72), an interest aroused in him by de Saussure's (*qv*) books. He met considerable opposition from his brother monks, who thought him mad or a French spy and upon the French invasion of the Grisons his valuable scientific collection was commandeered by the invaders while his manuscripts perished when the monastery was burned.

He was undoubtedly very much in advance of his time; he even suggested the formation of a club for tourists, "an alpine club". Coolidge ranks Father Placidus with de Saussure as one of the founders of Alpinism.

PLIMSOLLS
Before the introduction of P.A.s (*qv*), plimsolls were often used on hard British rock-climbs, especially gritstone climbs. The cheapest, thin-soled varieties gave the best results. Still useful.

POCKET
A small hollow in a rock face useful as a handhold. Common on gritstone and sandstone. Sometimes called pigeon holes, for instance, Pigeon Hole Wall, Helsby.

POLY BAG
A large polythene bag useful as a protective cover in case of benightment, exposure, and so on.

PONTESFORD ROCKS
A 200 ft crag on the side of Pontesford Hill, Shropshire, offering numerous climbs in the easier and middle grades.
Guidebook: *Pontesford Rocks*, by W. Unsworth.

PORGES, SIGMUND
An Austrian climber who made the first ascent of Mönch with Christian Almer (*qv*) in 1857, and the second ascent of the Eiger (1861).

PORTER
A person employed to carry a load either to

base camp or on a mountain. The Sherpas are the best-known modern examples (*qv*). In the pioneer days, porters were used in the Alps, usually to carry firewood etc. for the gîte (*qv*), though some took part in famous ascents. More recently, porters carried provisions to Alpine huts, but this practice seems to have disappeared with the advent of helicopters and téléphériques. They were usually trainee guides.

POWELL BROTHERS
W. W. R. Powell (b. 1849) L. S. Powell (b. 1855) and C. H. Powell (b. 1857) were three brothers who all made minor first ascents in the Alps in the closing years of the nineteenth century, though they do not seem to have climbed together much. The most important member of the trio was Charles Herbert Powell (Major-General, knighted 1917), who in 1889 joined Dent, Freshfield and Woolley in the Caucasus to search for Donkin and Fox (*qv*). Powell spoke Russian and was an experienced Asian traveller.

PRE-ALPS
The limestone hills which lap the main Alpine chain to north and south. They are invariably limestone and the Dolomites are the best known, though these are so important they are seldom regarded in this way. For climbers, the most important of the others are: the cliffs of Calanques on the French Mediterranean coast, Vercors and Grande Chartreuse near Grenoble, the Salève near Geneva, the Jura and Vosges on the Swiss-French border, and the Grigne near Lake Como in Italy. Numerous rock-climbs exist in all these areas. A selection of climbs at Vercors is given in the Dauphiné guidebook (*qv*), but there are no English language guides to the other areas beyond articles in journals.

PREUSS, Paul (1886-1913)
One of the best Austrian rock-climbers at the turn of the century. Preuss began climbing at the age of 11 with an ascent of the Grosser Bischofsmutze in the Dachstein – one of his favourite areas and where he made a number of first ascents. He climbed numerous new routes in the Gesause, Wilde Kaiser, Wetterstein, Silvretta and Dolomites, many of them solo. His most frequent companions were his sister or Paul Relly. Perhaps his finest ascents came in the last three years of his life: W Face of Totenkirchl (solo), NE Face of Crozzon di Brenta (with Relly), E Face and traverse of Campanile Basso (solo) – all 1911.

Though noted as a rock-climber, Preuss did a number of hard ice-climbs in the Ortler but did not climb in the Western Alps until 1912, when he met Eckenstein, who taught him additional ice techniques. He made the first ascent of the SE Ridge of the Aig. Blanche de Peuterey and was planning to attempt the Peuterey Ridge *integrale* in 1914 (not done until 1935). He made many winter climbs.

Preuss was killed attempting a solo first ascent of N Ridge of Mandlwand in the Gosaukamm. Preuss was a D.Phil of Munich University, a plant physiologist and a philosopher.

PROTECTION
A term used to indicate protection which a leader can arrange for himself as he climbs, i.e. runners (*qv*) of various kinds. A well-protected pitch is one where runners can be arranged to safeguard the leader on the hard moves. Artificial chocks (*qv*) have increased the protection on many climbs and have helped to push up standards.

PRUSIKS (PRUSIK LOOPS)
A system of self-help in crevasse rescue invented by Dr Prusik, a noted Austrian climber during the early part of this century. The climber, when crossing a snow-covered glacier, attaches a loop of thin cord to the main rope, about two feet from his waist, and tucks the other end into his pocket. The knot used for attachment is the Prusik knot which can be slid up the rope but will not slide down if there is pressure on the loop, that is, if a climber stands in it.

If the climber falls into a crevasse, his companion holds him (see CREVASSE RESCUE) while he takes the strain off his waist or chest by standing in his prusik loop. He then attaches two more prusik loops to the rope: a short one for under the armpits and another long one for his other foot. By moving each loop in turn up the rope he can raise himself out of the crevasse. This is seldom as simple as it sounds and the method can be very tiring; it is used only as a last resort.

Prusik knots can be awkward to tie and manipulate with gloved hands. A simpler variation using a karabiner was introduced by Bachmann in the 1950s. The "krab" provides a good handhold. A more recent variation is the Penberthy knot, also claimed to be easier to use than the Prusik knot.

There are at least four mechanical devices intended to make prusiking easier. The best known are jumars and hiebelers. They clamp the rope and replace the prusik knot. They are much less strenuous to operate and are used on expeditions and hard Alpine climbs for climbing fixed ropes (*qv*). They can, of course, be used for crevasse rescue as well.

In rock-climbing, prusik loops can be invaluable in relieving the strain on a climber who has parted company with the rock and is hanging free.

PUNJAB HIMALAYA

The westernmost section of the Himalaya between the Indus in the west and Sutlej in the east. Beyond it to the west lies the Hindu Kush and to the east the Kunmaon Himalaya, while behind it lies the trans-Himalaya of Ladakh and the Karakorum. At its heart is the beautiful Vale of Kashmir.

The area is noted for peaks in the region of 16,000–19,000 ft, many of which have been climbed, often by Service officers on leave or at the war-time Aircrew Mountain Centre at Sonamarg. Best known is Kolahoi (17,799 ft) (E. F. Neve, K. Mason, 1912). There is a well-known ski centre at Gulmarg.

There are only two great massifs: Nanga Parbat and Nun Kun. The former, seen from the great bend of the Indus or from Gulmarg, is one of the most impressive mountain scenes in the world. It was the first great Himalayan peak to be attempted (Mummery, 1895) and one with a notorious fatality rate.

Principal peaks
Nanga Parbat (26,658 ft) – H. Buhl (solo), 1953
Nun (23,410 ft) – P. Vittos, Md. C. Kogan, 1953
Kun (23,219 ft) – Count Calciati, 1913
(See also MUMMERY, BUHL, NANGA PARBAT, HIMALAYA.)

PURTSCHELLER, Ludwig (1849-1900)

A noted Austrian Alpinist whose list of ascents was said to be second only to that of Coolidge (*qv*). Purtscheller was a companion of the Zsigmondy brothers and made with them the first ascent of the Kl. Zinne and numerous other climbs in the Eastern Alps. In 1883 he visited the Western Alps and with the Zsigmondys and others made numerous guideless ascents, many of which were criticized as being reckless at that time. Like several Austrian climbers of the period, Purtscheller often climbed solo in the Tyrol, and this too was regarded as unconventional.

Purtscheller went with Hans Meyer to East Africa in 1889 and they made the first ascent of Kilimanjaro. In 1891 he visited the Caucasus. He died from influenza in 1900, his condition weakened by a serious accident he had sustained on the Dru six months earlier.

PUTTRELL, James William (1869–1939)

A Sheffield man who began climbing on Wharncliffe Crags in 1888 and is indisputably the founder of gritstone climbing. He climbed alone for two years, then was joined by W. J. Watson. In 1900, the growing band of enthusiasts became the Kyndwr Club (*qv*).

Puttrell did not visit other mountain areas until 1895 and had no contact with other pioneers. In this respect he was an independent founder of the sport of rock-climbing. Puttrell took part in the first ascents of Crowberry Ridge Direct, Glencoe (1900) and the Chimney of Ben Nuis, Arran (1901), a climb not repeated for 54 years.

PYE, Sir David Randall (1886-1960)

Distinguished scientist, friend of Mallory, Young *et al*, and the originator of three of Britain's best-known climbs: Faith and Charity (Idwal Slabs, Snowdonia, 1916) and The Crack of Doom (Corrie Lagan, Skye, 1918).

PYRENEES

A mountain range on the frontier between France and Spain. It is approximately 270 miles long and the highest summit is the Pic de Néthou (Aneto), 11,168 ft. The topography is very complicated and the rock varies from granite to limestone.

The Pyrenees are different from the Alps in several respects, apart from being generally lower. Glaciers are confined to the north slopes of the central range and the snow-line is about 9,000 ft. There are no large lakes, but many streams, and the waterfalls are the highest in Europe outside Norway. Passes are high and scarce. Most notable are the huge cirques heading many of the valleys, of which that at Gavarnie is famous.

Climbing interest is principally in the

27 THE MATTERHORN, PENNINE ALPS. The mountain is covered with an unusual powdering of snow after a storm. The Hornli ridge is towards the camera and the Zmutt ridge is on the right. Between the two lies the North Face. On the left is the Furggen ridge. The Italian ridge is on the side of the peak out of the camera.

28 THE GRANDES JORASSES, MONT BLANC GROUP. One of the great north faces of the Alps. The Walker Spur descends from the highest point of the picture. In the foreground is the Mer de Glace.

29 THE EIGER, BERNESE ALPS. Equalling the Matterhorn in popular fame because of the Eigerwand, the great bowl-shaped face well seen in the picture. On the left, the skyline forms the Mittelegi Ridge. (*right*) 30 YOSEMITE VALLEY, CALIFORNIA. The greatest rock-climbing centre of the United States with some of the world's hardest climbs. In the foreground is El Capitan with the East Buttress just beyond it. In the background is Clouds Rest and the distinctively named Half Dome.

central part of the range where there are peaks such as Nethou, Posets (11,073 ft), Mont Perdu (11,007 ft) and Vignemale (10,820 ft) among many others. There are several huts and the centres include Cauterets and Gavarnie in France and the Ordesa National Park in Spain. There are numerous climbs of all grades, including fine modern rock routes.

Guidebooks: *Pyrenees West* and *Pyrenees East* – A. Battagee

QUARRY-CLIMBING
Disused quarries frequently offer climbs which are steeper and longer than those of natural outcrops. Best known are the gritstone and limestone quarries of the Pennines, but limestone quarries are also used in other places (e.g. South Wales) and there are granite quarries in Leicestershire and slate quarries at Llanberis. In addition, many of the popular natural outcrops have been quarried to a greater or lesser degree: Stoney Middleton, Helsby and the Avon Gorge among others.

The upsurge in quarry-climbing came in the 1950s with the discovery of Dovestones, in the Pennines, as a superb climbing ground, but a few quarries have a much longer history, notably at Ilkley (1890s) and Brownstones, Bolton (1920s). Many quarries are near to industrial towns and offer good opportunities for a few hours' practice.

The longest quarry-climb (1972) is Midnight Buttress, Langcliffe, Yorkshire (405 ft, V. S.).

QUEEN ELIZABETH ISLANDS
The Arctic islands of Canada, north of Baffin Island (*qv*). Climbs have been reported on Ellesmere Island and Axel Helberg Island, up to 8,500 ft. The area is remote and difficult of access.

RADSTATTER TAUERN
The E end of the Alps by Coolidge's definition; a small group of peaks between Badgastein and the Radstatter Tauern Pass. The highest point is the Hochalmspitze (3,350 m) but the best-known peak is Ankogel (3,246 m). Hafnereck (3,061 m) is the most easterly snow peak in the Alps.

RAEBURN, Harold (1865-1926)
One of the greatest figures in Scottish mountaineering. He played a considerable part in developing Scottish crags after the English "invasion" by Collie, etc. (qv) in 1894. Raeburn's first notable exploit was the climbing of Church Door Buttress on Bidean in 1895, where he led the crux pitch, followed by the Direct Route up the Douglas Boulder on Ben Nevis, 1896.

His name is particularly associated with Ben Nevis, though he climbed in many parts of Scotland. He made 12 new routes on the Ben, including:
1898 The Castle
1901 Observatory Ridge (solo) – also first winter ascent, 1920
1902 Observatory Buttress (solo)
1908 Raeburn's Buttress

Raeburn was also a considerable Alpinist. With Ling (qv) and others he made several first British guideless ascents of difficult routes, including the Zmutt Ridge of the Matterhorn (1906). He often climbed solo, both at home and in the Alps, and made the first solo traverse of the Meije (1919).

In 1913 and 1914, Raeburn visited the Caucasus making nine new ascents and in 1920 made an attempt on Kangchenjunga and reached about 21,000 ft. He was chosen for the Everest Expedition of 1921 and though taken ill and evacuated, insisted on rejoining the expedition after his recovery, when he reached 22,000 ft. On his return home he had a complete breakdown from which he never recovered. He wrote *Mountaineering Art* (1920).

RAKE
Used in the Lake District to mean a long, slanting ledge or passage across a crag or mountain, for example, Jack's Rake, Pavey Ark; Lord's Rake, Scafell.

RAMSAY, Sir Andrew Crombie (1814-91)
Eminent nineteenth-century geologist instrumental in solving the geological structure of Snowdonia, and one of the leading protagonists in the great glacier controversy of his day. Took part in the first ascent of Lyskamm (1861).

RAVANEL, Joseph (1869-1931)
One of the great Chamonix guides noted for his climbs with E. Fontaine. Ravanel was one of the fastest movers ever seen in the Alps. One morning in 1904, he left the Couvercle, climbed the Verte and was back at Montenvers by 8.30 a.m.

Ravanel made many new routes among which were: Aig. du Blaitière, NW arête; Aig. du Fou; Aig. du Moine, N arête; Nom –Verte Traverse; Aigs. Mummery and Ravanel; Crocodile; Ciseaux; Peigne; and the Traverse en Z of the Drus. A typically strong day for Ravanel was his traverse from the Sans Nom over the Verte and down by the Moine (with Broadrick and Field (qv), 1902). He was one of the first guides to use skis. Ravanel was nicknamed "Le Rouge".

RAVEN CRAG, LANGDALE
An immensely popular line of rocks on the fellside above the Old Dungeon Ghyll Hotel, Langdale. It comprises Middle Fell Buttress (the first route; Laycock, Herford and Thomson, 1911), Raven Crag proper, and East Raven Crag. Middle Fell is easy and one of the most frequented climbs in the country, but other routes tend to be in the middle grades with a few harder. They are steep and clean.

Lower down the valley, near Chapel Stile, is Raven Crag Walthwaite, which also contains a number of good climbs.
Guidebook: *Great Langdale*, by J. A. Austin.

RAVEN CRAG, THIRLMERE
A crag near the northern end of Thirlmere, Lake District. It has a number of hard climbs and some in the middle grade, but it has never won universal popularity.
Guidebook: *Eastern Crags*, by H. Drasdo and J. Soper.

RÉBUFFAT, Gaston (b. 1921)

One of the greatest French guides of the post-war era. Born in Marseilles, he learned to climb on the Calanques and became a guide in 1942; accepted by the Chamonix guides' association in 1946. He made early ascents of some of the great north faces such as Eigerwand and Walker Spur and made a number of new climbs in the Mont Blanc area, the most popular being the Rébuffat Route on the Aig. du Midi (1956). He was a member of the Annapurna team in 1950.

Rébuffat has made a secondary career as writer and film-maker. His eleven books and four films (1973) are all about mountaineering; the best-known in England is *Starlight and Storm* (1956).

RECIPROCAL RIGHTS

The rights of a club member to use the facilities of another club with whom there is an exchange agreement, particularly for accommodation. When there are full reciprocal rights, a club member can use another club's hut(s) as if he were a member of that club, paying the same charges. Many clubs operate reciprocal rights but usually with some curtailment, e.g. previous notification of hut use, slightly higher charges.

The various alpine clubs have complete reciprocal rights with one another, though there are occasional disagreements.

REVERSE

To climb down. It may be applied to a single move or a whole climb. The old idea that a climber should not make a move which he cannot reverse is scarcely applicable today (see COMMITTING MOVE). When a climb is being reversed, the leader comes down last so as to protect the rest of the party. On very easy rocks and the majority of easier snow and ice-climbs it is better to come down facing outwards.

REY, Emile (1846-95)

A guide from Courmayeur, recognized as one of the finest of his day. Rey began guiding at the age of 30 but quickly rose to the top of his profession, being an excellent rock-climber. Perhaps his best-known route is the epic first ascent of the Peuterey Ridge with Gussfeldt (1893), which lasted 88 hours. He made the first ascent of the Aig. Blanche de Peuterey with Seymour King in 1885, and the first descent of the Scerscen Eisnase with Gussfeldt in 1887.

Rey was intelligent, well read, bi-lingual, and altogether different from most other guides of the times. Klucker perhaps came nearest to matching him and it is interesting they should share the Peuterey Ridge. Rey was immensely popular with his employers, despite the fact that he undoubtedly held a high opinion of himself. He regarded himself as "lucky". He died in a fall, unroped, from an easy part of the Aig. du Géant during a descent. There is little doubt that he suffered some sort of stroke or heart attack.

REY, Guido (1861-1935)

Wealthy Italian climber and romantic after whom the Cresta Rey on Monte Rosa was named, though he only made the third ascent. Rey made many fine guideless climbs in his youth but later climbed only with guides following the death of his brother in a guideless climbing accident. Obsessed with the then unclimbed Furggen Ridge of the Matterhorn he made several attempts on it but failed: an ascent was finally achieved with the aid of a rope ladder (1899). The first true ascent was made in 1911.

Rey is best remembered for his great work *The Matterhorn* (1904): the definitive volume on the mountain's early history. In 1914 he published *Peaks and Precipices*: his adventures in the Dolomites and the Chamonix Aiguilles.

RHUM (Rum)

One of the Inner Hebrides, reached by steamer from Mallaig or occasional boat from Glenbrittle, Skye. The island has some fine mountains, the highest being Askival (2,659 ft). There are numerous rock-climbs of all grades but the highest. The island is a Nature Reserve, but climbing is allowed. There is a bothy at Dibidil.

Guidebook: *The Island of Rhum*, by H. Brown.

RIB (G.: Rippe; Fr.: Nervure)

A small ridge on a mountain face or a crag. In rock-climbing it is used somewhat indescriminately and can mean almost any small protruberance.

RICHARDSON, Katherine (1854-1927)

One of the finest of the early woman climbers. She began in 1871 and her remarkable stamina first showed itself when she made the first traverse of Piz Palu in 1879. In 1885 she was the first woman to climb La Meije – a "record" later repeated on other peaks. In 1888 she made the first traverse from the Bionnassay to the Dôme de Goûter, long thought impossible, and in the following year made the first ascent of the West Face of the Tsa, and the first traverse, Petit–Grand Dru. Miss Richardson had two of the finest guides of the day: Emile Rey and J. B. Bich.

RICKMERS, Willi Rickmer (1873-1965)
German mountaineer, explorer and writer who made notable contributions to the knowledge of the Caucasus and Pamirs. Awarded the Patron's Gold Medal, R. G. S. in 1935. Rickmers, of British ancestry, climbed in Britain and the Alps, though he made no new routes. An accomplished skier, he was also noted for his sense of humour; once, posing as a Prof. Dustsucker, he claimed to have discovered Noah's Ark.

RIDGE (G.: Grat; Fr.: Arête; W.: Crib)
The crest where two opposing faces of a mountain meet and the feature thus formed. May be broad or narrow, rock or snow. Ridges may be horizontal, gradually sloping, or very steep, and may be interrupted by gendarmes (*qv*), gaps, or steps. On a lesser scale, a ridge can also be formed by two faces of a crag, e.g. Crowberry Ridge, Buachaille Etive Mor. In rock-climbing, the term is somewhat loose (see RIB, BUTTRESS).

THE RIVALS (YR EIFL) (1,850 ft)
Hills in the Lleyn Peninsula, North Wales with huge seaward-facing buttresses. Developed in the fifties, but the cliffs never became popular.

RIVER CROSSING
A number of mountaineers have lost their lives trying to cross swollen mountain torrents; but a procedure to make the crossing as safe as possible has now been devised. The leader ties on the middle of the rope and one man stands upstream holding one end of the rope and another man downstream with the other end. The leader wades across facing the current. If he should be swept off his feet the upstream control slackens the rope while the downstream control pulls the leader ashore. It is dangerous to pull against the current as the leader will be towed under. The second man to cross ties on to the two ends of the rope. The leader stands downstream and the third man upstream. The man crosses, the rope acting like an endless belt. Any

number can cross in this way. The last man crosses in the same way as the leader, but in reverse.

There are other methods, but the above is the surest. For a wide river ropes can be joined together. It is essential to choose the place where the current is weakest, even though the river might be wider at that point. (See *Mountain Leadership*, by E. Langmuir.)

ROBBINS, Royal
A leading American rock-climber noted particularly for his ascents in Yosemite, some of which are:
1957 NW Face of Half Dome
1961 Salethe Wall
1964 North America Wall

He has made altogether four major routes on Half Dome and three on El Capitan (*qv*). Of the six major El Capitan routes first established, Robbins made either the first or second ascent, except for Muir Wall, and in this case he made the first solo ascent (1968). It is regarded as one of the most difficult solo climbs ever made, and took ten days.

Robbins has climbed in Alaska and Britain, and in the Alps he made two very hard variants to the W Face of the Dru (Hemming and Robbins, 1962, Harlin and Robbins, 1965).

Robbins is the exponent of the single push theory of big wall climbing as opposed to siege tactics (*qv*).

He has written *Basic Rockcraft* (1971). (See YOSEMITE, EL CAPITAN, W. HARDING)

ROBERTS, James Owen Merion (b. 1916)
Former Gurkha officer, now Director of Mountain Travel, a Nepalese tours agency which employs many Sherpas for trekking duties. Since 1937 when he took part in the ill-fated Masherbrum Expedition, he has participated in over 13 major Himalayan expeditions, eight times as leader. His unrivalled experience in Himalayan travel and climbing makes him a valued member of any team going there and his services are much sought after. He acted as a transport officer for the successful 1953 Everest Expedition, and was a member of the American 1963 Everest team. In 1971 he was co-leader of the International Expedition to the SW Face and Bonington's deputy leader in the post-monsoon attempt of 1972.

ROBERTSON, Robert Augustus (1850-1948)

An Original Member of the Climbers' Club and the S. M. C. He was President of both 1907-09. Best known for his first ascent of the SW Ridge of L'Evêque (Arolla), now a popular climb (1894).

ROBINSON, John Wilson (1853-1907)

One of the pioneers of Lakeland climbing. Though he seldom led a climb, Robinson accompanied many parties on first ascents of Lakeland routes, notably Moss Ghyll, Scafell and the Great Gully of the Screes, both in 1892.

ROCHEMELON (3,538 m)

A mountain in the Graian Alps climbed in 1358 by Bonifacio Rotario, knight of Asti, and thought to be the first ascent of a high Alpine peak. (1 September 1358.) The Benedictine monks of Novalesa at the foot of the peak had tried an ascent as early as the eleventh century but had not succeeded. There is a small chapel on top, and the ascent is easy in Alpine terms.

ROCHES, THE

One of the finest of all gritstone crags, forming part of a distinct ridge with Hen Cloud and various lesser rocks, near Upper Hulme, Staffordshire. There are numerous routes of all grades, fairly long.

The crag was visited by the pioneers, and Laycock (qv) is reputed to be the first climber benighted on gritstone (Central Climb, Hen Cloud, 1909). The land was once a private zoo, and escaped wallabys still breed here!

Guidebook: *The Staffordshire Gritstone Area* (Rock Climbs in the Peak Vol. 9).

ROCK AND ICE CLUB

The most celebrated climbing club of the post-war era. It began as a small Manchester group of friends and was formed into a "club" on 26 September 1951. The original members were: N. Allen, D. Belshaw, J. Brown, D. Chapman, D. Cowan, J. Gill, P. Greenall, R. Greenall, R. Moseley, M. Sorrell, R. White, D. Whillans. Between them they were responsible for a major breakthrough in British climbing, especially with their routes in Derbyshire, Llanberis Pass and Clogwyn du'r Arddu. Most notable were J. Brown and D. Whillans (qv).

The Club foundered in 1958 but was reconstituted by N. Allen and D. Gray in February 1959.

ROCK-CLIMBING

One of the most important branches of mountaineering. It is the art of climbing steep rocks; of pitting skills, nerves and strength against the obvious dangers of gravity, weather, falling stones and fatigue. It is the acceptance of a challenge according to the climber's judgement of his own skill and endurance. This can vary enormously – a challenge to one man will be no challenge at all to another; some climbers find most satisfaction in taking the challenge to their own limit, whereas others are content to let the challenge be a minor part of the activity and climb well within themselves. In this, rock-climbing is closely allied to other branches of mountaineering (e.g. ice-climbing), but it is capable of finer development and to some it is a sport in its own right.

It is difficult to say where scrambling (qv) ends and real rock-climbing begins; the use of the rope is no criterion because many climbers solo difficult routes which less able climbers would climb roped. Broadly, a climb is one that comes within the system of gradings used for rock-climbs in the guidebooks (qv).

Rock-climbing may be treated under four headings: the skills of climbing, route-finding, protection and the psychological barrier. The first includes specific techniques (e.g. bridging) and balance, together with the special techniques associated with artificial climbing (qv). Route-finding can be difficult, especially on long Alpine rock-climbs, and is aided by guidebooks (qv) but much more by experience. Protection (qv) includes belays and runners. The psychological barrier has many components: doubt as to one's own ability, the worry of exposure, and a general fear of the unknown. Most climbs become easier (in this sense) with familiarity.

There are two common systems of rock-climbing. In the Alps and other high ranges, it is common for the climbers to move together on easy rock or for one to take a simple direct belay while the other climbs. This is for speed. On more difficult routes, the English system is used, whereby one man is belayed by an indirect belay, while the other climbs, and vice versa. Thus, only one man climbs at a time – if there are three or more in the party, this still applies. It is sometimes called the "pitch by pitch" system, since the distance between two belays is called a pitch. It is slower but much safer than the other

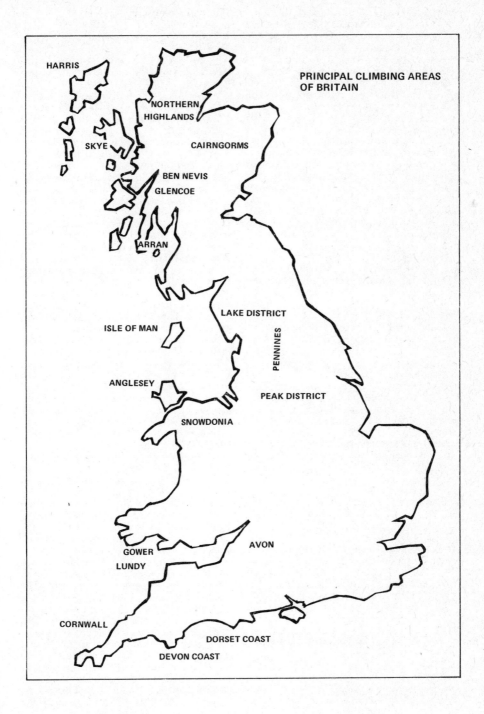

PRINCIPAL CLIMBING AREAS
OF BRITAIN

HARRIS

NORTHERN HIGHLANDS

SKYE

CAIRNGORMS

BEN NEVIS

GLENCOE

ARRAN

LAKE DISTRICT

ISLE OF MAN

PENNINES

ANGLESEY

PEAK DISTRICT

SNOWDONIA

GOWER

AVON

LUNDY

CORNWALL

DORSET COAST

DEVON COAST

method. Further safeguards are the waist belays of the stationary climber controlling the rope and the runners placed by the leader (see BELAYS, RUNNERS, PROTEC TION).

Solo climbing is often undertaken, sometimes with complicated rope protect-ion, sometimes with no protection. The extra danger involved is obvious.

Rock-climbing of various sorts has been done since time immemorial for practical reasons such as the collecting of birds' eggs for food (e.g. in the Hebrides). As a sport, in Britain, it was largely initiated by two men: Haskett Smith in the Lakes, and Put-trell in Derbyshire (qv). The ascent of Napes Needle in the Lake District is often taken as the start of rock-climbing (1886), but this is symbolical rather than historical fact.

ROGNON (Fr.) (G.: Fluh)
A rock island in a glacier, usually a safe resting place and frequently used as the site of a mountain hut.

ROMSDAL
The most popular rock-climbing area of Norway with some of the largest and steepest cliffs in Europe. The centre is Andalsnes reached by road from Bergen or Alesund or by rail from Oslo.

The Romsdalhorn (1,555 m) is a shapely peak first climbed by local peasants (C. Hoel, H. Bjermeland, 1827). Early ex-plorers included C. Hall (qv) and W. C. Slingsby (qv). There was intermittent pro-gress over the years, but after the last war this was stepped up by the Norwegian climbers, A. Randers Heen and R. Hoi-bakk, culminating in the East Pillar of Trollryggen in 1958.

The most spectacular climbs, however, are on the Troll Wall, 1,500 m high, and requiring artificial aid.

Troll Wall (Trollveggen) first ascents:
1965 The Norwegian Route – L. Petter-sen, J. Tiegland, O. D. Enersen, O. Eliassen, 11 days
1965 The English (Rimmon) Route – A. Howard, J. Amatt, B. Tweedale, five and a half days
1967 The French Direct Route – Deck, Boussard, Cordier, Brunet, Frehel, 21 days

There are still many new climbs to be made at Romsdal, particularly in the little-known outer ranges.

Guidebook: *Walks and Climbs in*

Romsdal, Norway, by A. Howard.

ROOF (G.: Dach, First; Fr.: Toit; It.: Tetto)
The underside of a large, sharply jutting overhang. Climbed by artificial techniques (qv).

ROPE (G.: Seil; Fr.: Corde; It.: Corda)
(a) The name given to a group of climbers tied together in climbing fashion, e.g. "Smith's rope reached the summit first";

(b) The actual rope used for climbing.

(a) The normal climbing rope is of two or three persons. In a rope of three, No 1 is known as the "leader", No 2 as "second" or "middleman", No 3 as "last man". The distances between them will depend on the climb but it is common on British rock now to have 120 ft or 150 ft be-tween each pair. On easier Alpine climbs, when the climbers can move together, 15 ft is sufficient, any extra rope being wound round the climbers' shoulders and tied off. Two ropes of two may combine to make a rope of four to cross a heavily crevassed glacier, because of the extra security this gives, but ropes of four or more are now usually only seen when novices are under instruction or on guided glacier tours.

(b) Modern climbing ropes are made of nylon (or perlon, which is virtually the same). There are two types (1) hawser laid (2) kernmantel. In the first type the fibres are twisted into three strands and the strands twisted into the rope. The kern-mantel rope consists of a bunch of strands running the length of the rope and covered by a woven outer sheath. Kernmantel has a higher breaking strain and is easier to handle since it does not kink as much as hawser rope. Hawser had the advantage in being more extensible under impact (an important point in a fall) but the new kern-mantels seem to be at least as good as the hawsers. Certainly kernmantel is now the chief type of rope used by climbers.

For a main climbing rope the recom-mended thicknesses are: Hawser $1\frac{3}{8}$ in. circ. (No 4): for kernmantel, 11 mm circ. The usual lengths are 120 ft or 150 ft. Some climbers prefer a double rope (sometimes called half rope) and use $1\frac{1}{4}$ in. hawser (No 3) or 9 mm kernmantel, usually bought in 300 ft lengths. As the name suggests, it is used doubled, and has advantages where the rope has to pass through many kara-biners, in that alternate ropes can be passed through alternate karabiners, reducing drag. It is also still used a great deal in artificial climbing (*qv*) and where sack-hauling (*qv*) is needed. The main disadvantage is that a double rope is rather more difficult to handle. For details of nylon ropes see table below.

Before nylon ropes were used, the common rope was "Alpine hemp", though cotton and silk were not unknown. All natural fibre ropes tend to rot fairly quickly (especially if badly stored) and soon lose strength. They also freeze in cold weather and become unmanageable. They are heavier than nylon and nowhere near as strong. As main ropes, hemp lingered on into the late fifties, especially on gritstone outcrops which were regarded as too abrasive for expensive nylon. Hemp rope is still used today as waistbands (*qv*) and as spare loops from which to abseil (see SLINGS).

Hawser rope (Viking)

No.	Circ.	Wt./100 ft	Breaking load	Uses
1	$\frac{5}{8}$ in.	$1\frac{1}{4}$ lb	1,000 lb	prusik loops
2	$\frac{7}{8}$ in.	$2\frac{1}{2}$ lb	2,000 lb	runners, abseil slings
3	$1\frac{1}{4}$ in.	$4\frac{1}{2}$ lb	3,500 lb	double rope, runners, abseil
4	$1\frac{3}{8}$ in.	$5\frac{1}{4}$ lb	4,200 lb	climbing rope, slings

Kernmantel rope (Edelrid)

Circ.	Wt./100 ft	Breaking load	Uses
4 mm	*	*	étriers
5 mm	*	*	prusik loops
7 mm	*	*	runners
9 mm	3 lb	3,200 lb	double rope, runners, abseil slings
11 mm	$5\frac{1}{2}$ lb	4,300 lb	climbing rope, slings

ROPE-LENGTH (Fr.: Longeur de corde)
A term used mainly in Alpine guidebooks to describe a distance in the course of the climb. It usually implies easy climbing which is not worth describing in detail, e.g. "traverse right for three rope-lengths to the foot of a crack". Often confusing.

ROTHSCHILD, Baron Albert de, (1844-1911)
Head of the famous banking firm and one of the world's richest men. From 1867-75 he had a very active Alpine career including most of the famous grand courses. He made a minor first ascent – Schwarzhorn, on Monte Rosa (1873).

ROUTE (G.: Weg; Fr.: Course, Voie; It.: Via)
(a) The directions followed in a mountain journey;
   (b) A climb. The two words are interchangeable, e.g. Murray's Route, Dow Crag.

ROUTE CARD
A card, prepared in advance, giving details of a proposed mountain journey. The information should include bearings for each leg of the journey, estimated time for each leg (see Naismith's Rule), bearings for easy ways off, if applicable, names or at least numbers of people taking part.

Route cards are generally used for extremely difficult journeys or, more common, by leaders taking large parties into the hills, school parties for example.

RUBBERS
Thin, cheap gym-shoes, once popular for difficult climbs but now superseded by P.A.s and similar footwear.

RUBENSON, Carl Wilhelm (1885–1960)
A Norwegian climber famous for his attempt on Kabru in the Himalaya in 1907. With a fellow countryman, Monrad Aas, he set out determined to make the highest climb then known, though neither were experienced mountaineers. They succeeded in reaching a point within 100ft of the summit when cold and darkness forced them down to their top camp. They descended by moonlight, Rübenson slipped

but was held by Aas and later they found the rope was almost parted.

Rübenson was befriended by Slingsby (*qv*) who induced him to make the first ascent of Stedtind (Rübenson, Schjelderup, Bryn, 1910) in Norway. He also made first ascents of Svolvaergjeita, Rørhoptind and Strandatind (Norway) as well as two minor summits in Kashmir. He later became a popular journalist.

RUCKSACK
A bag, fitted with shoulder straps, used for carrying gear and provisions. Usually made of canvas or nylon. A rucksack may or may not be fitted with a metal frame.

A framed rucksack, e.g. Bergen type, is usually a commodious bag with outside pockets, used for carrying a fairly large amount of gear. The bag is attached to a metal frame at the back and the shoulder straps are fixed to the frame. At the bottom of the frame is a waistband of canvas or leather. Thus the weight is carried on shoulders and hips. Such a rucksack is inconvenient when climbing because the frame gets in the way and the load is too low on the body.

A pack frame (back pack) is an adaptation of the framed rucksack in which the bag is detachable from the frame. When attached, it sits on a base plate. Pack frames are made so that the load is much higher and consequently more comfortable. Very large loads can be carried this way; useful on expeditions.

A frameless rucksack can be a small affair known as a "day sack" or the larger "Alpine sack". These are the sacks used in climbing. They should have external straps or cords for carrying an ice-axe and crampons and a strong metal ring for sackhauling (*qv*). The rucksack should be robust and waterproof and fastened with easily worked buckles. It should also "sit high" when loaded and carried. There are many varieties: outside pockets which are detachable, extendable sacks, and so on.

RUN-OUT
The length of rope between a leader and second man, as the leader climbs. A full run-out means the pitch (*qv*) has required all the rope available. It is usual for the second to warn the leader when he is approaching a full run-out by shouting "ten feet left". This gives the leader notice to seek a belay.

RUSKIN, John (1819-1900)
Writer, critic and social reformer; an aesthetic genius who had a profound effect on his times. Mountains, especially the Alps, were the ruling passion of his life and though he made very few real ascents (Buet, Salève, Rifelhorn and various travellers' passes), he knew and understood the mountain world better than most of his contemporaries. Through his writings, he made the world look at mountains in a new, more understanding way.

There is no doubt that Ruskin would have become a mountaineer in the true pioneering spirit of his times had it not been for his parents, and particularly his mother. They were especially possessive and protective, and both lived to a great age. Ruskin could never bring himself to break free from their influence (even his marriage was a failure.)

His sensibility over mountain scenery was offended by the activities of the new Alpine Club and in *Sesame and Lilies* (1865) appears his famous stricture:

"The Alps themselves, which your own poets used to love so reverently, you look upon as soaped poles in a bear garden, which you set yourselves to climb and slide down again with shrieks of delight. When you are past shrieking, having no human articulate voice to say you are glad with, you fill the quietude of their valleys with gunpowder blasts, and rush home, red with cutaneous eruption of conceit, and voluble with convulsive hiccough of self-satisfaction."

The reference to gunpowder comes from the then popular celebration of a successful ascent by firing cannon, especially in Chamonix after an ascent of Mont Blanc. Ruskin was in Chamonix (his favourite Alpine village) when Albert Smith returned from his celebrated ascent (*qv*) in 1851. Later he wrote, "true lovers of natural beauty ... would as soon think of climbing the pillars of the choir at Beauvais for a gymnastic exercise, as making a playground of Alpine snows." Despite this, he was elected a member of the Alpine Club in 1869.

He had some training in geology and entered into the glacier controversy with gusto, defending Forbes against Tyndall and Ramsay. His geological training probably helped with his sketching, for though he refused to recognize himself as an artist he was a superb draughtsman, especially of mountains. He claimed to have taken the first photograph of the Matterhorn (1849).

Ruskin's eminence as an art critic was unrivalled in his day, though it led him into some stormy waters. His books, in which art and life were blended (particularly the volumes of *Modern Painters*), are outstanding. Later in life he developed theories of socialism and reform much ahead of his time. He was extremely generous and gave away much of his personal fortune – about £200,000. He lived the last 29 years of his life at Brantwood, Coniston, and he is buried in the village churchyard there. His relatives refused the offer of a tomb in Westminster Abbey.

RUSSELL-KILLOUGH, Count Henri Patrick Marie (1834-1909)

Born of an Irish father and French mother, Count Henri Russell was, with Charles Packe (*qv*), the founder of Pyrenean climbing and exploration. His early life was adventurous, and he travelled in remote parts of the world, but from 1858 he settled down to a detailed exploration of his beloved Pyrenees. He made numerous first ascents, including Vignemale, a mountain he was to climb 33 times and on which he built a famous series of refuge-caves. He made only one visit to the Alps, 1867, when he ascended Mont Blanc and Breithorn.

Russell was a big man, very strong and with a pronounced sense of humour. He was one of the founders of the Club Alpin Française.

RUTTLEDGE, Hugh (1884-1961)

The leader of the 1933 and 1936 Everest Expeditions. He was an Indian civil servant with considerable experience of Himalayan travel but no real mountaineering background, and this led to difficulties and criticisms. He wrote *Everest, 1933* and *Everest, the Unfinished Adventure*.

RUWENZORI

A range of East African mountains fabled as Ptolemy's *Lunae Montes* or "Mountains of the Moon". They were discovered in 1888 by H. M. Stanley who gave them their present name, probably derived from the native words *Ru-enzururu* (snow hill). The highest summit, Margerhita (16,763 ft), was first climbed by the Duke of the Abruzzi, 1906. The area has been thoroughly explored and there are now mountain huts available. The weather is often bad.

Principal summits are:

Mount Stanley (Margerhita), 16,763 ft
(Alexandra), 16,703 ft

Mount Speke (also called Duwoni), 16,042 ft
Mount Baker, 15,889 ft
Mount Emin, 15,720 ft
Mount Gessi, 15,470 ft
Mount Luigi di Savoia, 15,178 ft
Guidebook: *Ruwenzori Range*, by D. Pasteur and H.A. Osmaston.

RYAN, Valentine John Eustace (1883-1947)

One of the most remarkable climbers of the turn of the century. With the Lochmatters, Franz and Josef, he made a series of climbs which were well ahead of their day for the Alps, and joined Young and Knubel (*qv*) in others. Their most famous combined ascent was that of the SW Face of the Täschhorn, in 1906, still regarded as one of the most difficult climbs in the Alps.

His climbing career began in 1898 with some small peaks in the St Gotthard area. He missed the following season but was out in the next three (1900-02), although he did nothing out of the ordinary. His army career took him to Malta in 1903 and he climbed on the cliffs there, but in May of that year an early visit to the Alps brought him into contact with the Lochmatter brothers for the first time. In the four seasons, 1903-06, they climbed in many parts of the Alps, including the Dolomites, doing all the hard climbs and making new ones. (For routes done with Young, *qv*.)

In 1904 he did 20 major climbs and made an attempt on the West Ridge of Grandes Jorasses. In 1905, he made 25 ascents including the second ascent of the Verte from Charpoua, second ascent of the W Face of the Plan, first ascent of the N Face of Charmoz and a number of difficult traverses. He first met Young this year, on the Furggen ridge of the Matterhorn.

In 1906 he made the three routes for which he is best known: the NW Ridge of Blaitière, the Ryan-Lochmatter Route on the Plan, and the Cresta di Santa Caterina on Monte Rosa.

Ryan resigned his commission in 1905 and planned to visit the Himalaya (he had been left an estate in Ireland), but instead he married (1906), and returned to the Alps as usual. Young later suggested that the Täschhorn climb might have put Ryan out, and certainly he did not revisit the Alps until 1909, when he did nothing of note. In 1914, however, he (with the Lochmatters) returned with his old ferocity: he made a new route up the Nantillons face of Grépon, various other new climbs and the

second ascent of Young's Mer de Glace
Face of Grépon, adding the finish which is
now the usual one.

But that was the end. He visited the Alps
a few times afterwards but did nothing – he
lost all interest in the sport, even becoming
"anti-climbing".

He left Ireland in 1921, during the
"Troubles" and settled in Jersey, which he
hated. He was always a difficult person,
disliked by many (he failed to gain membership of the A. C.). He never smiled, and
drove his guides remorselessly. Some notes
he compiled of his great climbs were lost by
Yeld (qv), to whom he had entrusted them
and he never bothered to rewrite them.
(See *Climbers' Club Journal*, 1949, for an
appreciation of Ryan by Young.)

SAAS FEE
Most important of the hamlets at the head of the Saastal in the Pennine Alps; the others are Saas Grund and Saas Almagell. Popular climbing and ski centre. The climbs are mainly centred on the Weissmies and Mischabel groups.

SACK-HAULING
On a difficult pitch a leader, and possibly others in the party, may have to do the climb without the encumbrance of a rucksack. Once the leader is up, the sack is tied to the rope by means of the hauling ring, and pulled up. It is essential that the leader have a double rope for this purpose, one strand for hauling, the other to connect him to the rest of the party.

SAFETY ROPE
A rope held from above to protect novices during abseiling (*qv*) practice. On a mountain climb which requires abseils, a separate abseil rope is carried and the climbing rope then acts as a safety rope for all the party except the leader, who comes down last. (See also TOP ROPE)

SALATHÉ, John
A Swiss born American who was one of the leading Yosemite climbers of the 1940's with routes to his credit such as the SW Face of Half Dome, Lost Arrow Chimney Route and the N Face of Sentinel Rock (as late as 1956). He was an experienced blacksmith who redesigned pitons, making them from harder steel.

SALBITSCHIJEN (2,981 m)
A granite peak in the Voralp Tal near Goschenan, Switzerland, famous for its rockclimbs, which are mostly hard. There are three main ridges: the South, East and West. The South and West are amongst the best of their type in the Alps.
1935 South Ridge (Gr. IV) – A and O. Amstad with Guido Masetto

1948 West Ridge (Gr. VI) – E. and B. Favre, L. Henchoz
The Salbit Hut and Salbit Bivouac Hut serve the area.
Guidebook: *Engelhorner and Salbitschijen*, by J. Talbot.

SALISBURY CRAGS
Popular basalt outcrop on Arthur's Seat, Edinburgh. There are climbs of all grades and the crag has a long history of climbing.

LE SAUSSOIS
A 200 ft limestone cliff above the R. Yonne in France. Hard climbs. Popular.

SAUSSURE, Horace - Bénédict de (1740-99)
A wealthy scientist of Geneva and one of the earliest mountain explorers. It was de Saussure who offered a prize for the first person to reach the summit of Mont Blanc on his first visit there in 1760. It was not claimed until the Paccard-Balmat ascent of 1786. In 1787 de Saussure himself reached the summit (third ascent). He also climbed the Pizzo Bianco near Macugnaga, and several other minor peaks, and was the first traveller to visit Zermatt (1789).

de Saussure enjoyed wide fame. He was elected F.R.S. in 1768. His book *Voyages dans les Alpes* (1779-96, 4 vols) contains the first detailed maps of Alpine areas. (See *The First Ascent of Mont Blanc* by T. G. Brown and G. R. de Beer.)

SCAFELL CRAG AND EAST BUTTRESS
Scafell Crag extends across the Wasdale Face of Scafell in the Lake District and is one of the largest and most important climbing crags in Britain.

The crag is bounded on the left by Mickledore, a deep gap between Scafell and Scafell Pike. Broad Stand is the route from Mickledore to the summit of Scafell: a popular but dangerous scramble. On the right of the main crag is the easy route of Lord's Rake, also leading to the top, and between Mickledore and the Rake is a tenuous ledge known as Rake's Progress from which most of the climbs start. Three enormous gullies divide the face: from left to right, Moss Ghyll, Steep Ghyll and Deep Ghyll. Beyond the Rake lies the Shamrock buttress and other rocks of less interest.

There are climbs of all grades, but they all have an air of seriousness. The East

Buttress is on the Eskdale side of Mickledore. It is steep and forbidding and all the climbs are hard. Other crags forming part of the Scafell group are: Pike's Crag, on the Wasdale side of Scafell Pike; Esk Buttress and Heron Crag, both on the Eskdale side of the range; Great End, the gullies of which offer good winter climbs.

Various ways up from Mickledore to Scafell were made in the middle of the last century. Deep Ghyll was descended in snow in 1882 by Mumm and King and similar scrambles were accomplished by Haskett Smith in the 1880s, but the first real climb was Slingsby's Chimney (Slingsby, Hastings, E. Hopkinson, Haskett Smith, 1888). Other notable ascents are:

1892 Moss Ghyll – Collie, Hastings, Robinson
1897 Keswick Brothers' Climb – Abraham brothers, Puttrell
1898 Jones's Direct from Lord's Rake – Jones, Walker
1903 Botterill's Slab – Botterill, Williamson, Grant
1912 Hopkinson's Cairn Direct – Herford, Sansom
Hopkinson's Gully – Herford, Sansom
Girdle Traverse – Herford, Sansom, Brunskill, Gibson
1914 Central Buttress – Herford, Sansom, Holland
1926 Moss Ghyll Grooves – Kelly, Miss Eden-Smith, Kilshaw
1931 Mickledore Grooves (East) – Kirkus, Waller, Pallis
1932 Great Eastern Route (East) – Linnell, Cross
1938 May Day Climb (East) – Birkett, Hudson, Wilson

Of these the Central Buttress (C.B.) was outstanding for its day and was long regarded as the hardest climb in Britain. It is now graded H.V.S. It contains the well-known Flake Crack. Among the spate of hard post-war climbs the following may be noted (leaders only):

1952 Hell's Groove (East) – Dolphin
1957 Phoenix (East) – Moseley
1959 Centaur (East) – L. Brown
1960 Ichabod (East) – Oliver
1966 Nazgul – L. Brown
1969 Lord of the Rings (East) – Adams /Read
1971 The White Wizard – Bonington

The most serious *rock-climbing* accident in Britain took place on Scafell Crag when, in 1903, R. W. Broadrick and three companions were killed attempting the slabs below Hopkinson's Cairn.
Guidebook: *Scafell Group*, by G. Oliver and L. J. Griffin.

SCHMID BROTHERS
Franz and Toni Schmid were two climbers of the so-called Munich School who made the first ascent of the Matterhorn Nordwand in 1931; a major event in climbing history. Toni Schmid was killed the following year on the Gross Wiesbachhorn.

SCHUCK, Otto
An Austrian climber in the second half of the last century who made a number of new routes in the Eastern Alps, particularly the first ascent of the East Face of Watzmann (1881).

SCHULTZ, Karl (1844-1929)
A German lawyer who was one of the outstanding climbers of the second half of the nineteenth century. A friend and companion of Purtscheller (*qv*) and the Zsigmondys (*qv*), and something of 'a stormy petrel' (*A.J.*). He attacked Gussfeldt (*qv*) in print and was himself attacked by Lammer (*qv*).

In the Western Alps he made the second ascent of the Biancograt (1883) and a week later the third ascent of the Marinelli Couloir on Monte Rosa, but his outstanding feat was the descent of the Ferpècle Arête of Dent Blanche with Mrs Jackson (*qv*), five years before the first ascent. A year later he made the first ascent of Crozzon di Brenta.

In 1885 he was with the Zsigmondys in an attempt on the S Face of Meije, during which Emil Zsigmondy was killed. From then on he climbed exclusively in the Eastern Alps, where he made a number of first ascents.

SCHUSTER, Claud (Lord Schuster) (1869-1956)
Mountaineer and skier. Though he made no notable first ascents, Schuster is remembered for three fine books: *Peaks and Pleasant Pastures* (1911), *Men, Women and Mountains* (1931) and *Postscript to Adventure* (1949). President of A.C. 1938-40. He succeeded in abolishing the traditional ballot for new members.

SCOOP
A rounded niche which may be vertical, or slanting across a rock face. Varies tremendously. A peapod is a scoop shaped like its

namesake – there is a famous one at Curbar, Derbyshire.

SCOTT, Douglas Keith (b. 1941)

A Nottingham mountaineer who has established himself as the leading exponent of artificial climbing in Britain. He has made both free and artificial routes in the Derwent Valley, Derbyshire, but is best known for climbs such as those at Strone Ulladale in the Hebrides: The Scoop (1969), Sidewinder, the Nose (both 1971). He also made the first ascent of the Big Overhang, Anglesey – the largest overhang in Britain (100 ft roof).

In the Dolomites he made the first British ascent of the Direct Route, Cima Ovest (135 ft roof), 1969, and in the Pyrenees the first British ascent of the Tozal del Mal, S Face. He has made a number of hard climbs in the Yosemite and in Romsdal, Norway.

Alongside his attacks on the big walls, Scott has built up a reputation as an expedition man. These are:

1965 Tibesti Mountains. First ascent Tarso Tieroko (10,500 ft)
1966 Cilo Dag. First ascent Cafer Kule pinnacle
1967 Hindu Kush. First ascent Koh-i-Sisgeikh West; first ascent. S Face of Bandaka (22,500 ft)
1971 and 1972. Two expeditions to Baffin Island making a number of hard first ascents
1972 A member of both the spring and autumn Everest expeditions.

Scott was Editor of *Alpine Climbing*, 1971-2, and is the author of *Climbs on Derwent Valley Limestone* (1965) and *Big Wall Climbing* (1974).

SCOTTISH 4,000s

Name given to a walk embracing all the 4,000 ft peaks in Scotland: four in the Cairngorms and three in the Ben Nevis group. First done by E. Thomas and friends from the Rucksack Club, and R. S. T. Chorley and friends from the Fell and Rock Club in 1924. Both groups used a car between the two mountain areas. The first traverse without car was by F. Williamson in 1954 (98 miles, 13,000 ft, 50 hours).

SCOTTISH HIGHLANDS

North of the Glasgow–Edinburgh axis, Scotland is predominately mountainous: 276 summits over 3,000 ft (Inglis, 1921). For climbers the most popular areas are: Glencoe, Ben Nevis, Cairngorms, Skye, Arran and Arrochar. Exploration of other regions has been sporadic, because of the difficulties of access, though many fine climbs have been done in the Northern Highlands, Harris and elsewhere. (See NORTHERN HIGHLANDS, CUILLIN OF SKYE, BEN NEVIS, GLENCOE, ARRAN, CAIRNGORMS, ETIVE SLABS, STRONE ULLADALE.)

Guidebooks: The District guides of the Scottish Mountaineering Trust by various authors. Currently: *The Islands of Scotland*; *The Southern Highlands*; *The Western Highlands*; *The Cairngorms*; *The Central Highlands*; *The Island of Skye*; *The Northern Highlands*. Also: *Munro's Tables and other tables of Lesser Heights* – S.M.T., and *Scottish Climbing* (2 vols), by H. MacInnes.

SCRAMBLING (Fr.: Varappe)

Used to indicate progress in places where occasional handholds are necessary, but not sufficient to make it a rock-climb in the proper sense. Such places are common: Crib Goch, Snowdon; North Ridge, Tryfan; Striding Edge, Helvellyn; many parts of the Cuillin Ridge, and so on. In winter, what is a summer scramble may well become a serious climb.

Note that the word was at one time used to indicate rock-climbing generally, or even climbing as a whole, cf. Whymper, *Scrambles in the Alps*.

SCREE (Am.: Talus; G.: Geröll; F.: Éboulis, Pierrier; It.: Ghiaioi, Grava)

Rock detritus from a crag covering the slopes below. In England the most spectacular scree slopes are those above Wastwater in the Lake District. Scree particles can vary from boulder size (sometimes called a boulder slope) to tiny pebbles – it seems to have an uncanny knack of grading itself. Large scree is always tiresome and can be dangerous if it lies at a steep angle. It can be crossed by scree-hopping (leaping lightly from boulder to boulder), but a certain skill is required to judge those boulders which will not turn over. Loose scree (i.e. small scree) is tiresome in ascent but often forms a quick way down from a crag by scree-running i.e. short hops downhill – again, good judgement is required. A long slope of loose scree is known as a scree-shoot or stone-shoot, for example, the Great Stone Shoot of Sgurr Alasdair in Skye.

Small slopes of scree can lie on ledges, particularly in gullies, and a climber must be careful not to knock them down on those people who may be below. Some gullies are filled with scree from top to bottom and are known as scree gullies.

SCRIVEN, George (1856-1931)
Irish doctor who was a companion of Conway (*qv*) and Penhall (*qv*) on some of their early Alpine climbs. After 1888 he climbed exclusively in the Eastern Alps, especially the Dolomites. Scriven was a rugby international: Captain of Ireland, 1882.

SEA-CLIFF CLIMBING
A branch of rock-climbing which has become increasingly popular in Britain over the last few years. Though most of the cliffs are easy to reach, the climbs are not always easy of access and to reach the foot of the cliff may involve difficult climbing or abseiling. Tides also present problems, as do occasional rollers (i.e. big waves) which seem to come in sequence. On some cliffs, the top tends to be very loose. Where cliffs are on private land there may be restricted access. Sea birds may be a nuisance because of their slime, or in Scotland, their aggressiveness. There are also problems of conservation and some cliffs are banned during the nesting season.

Sea-cliff climbing goes back to the early days of the sport when there were climbs done on Sark, St Kilda and Beachy Head. The latter had a certain vogue: Mummery, Crowley and others climbed on the chalk, sometimes cutting steps in it with their ice axes. This esoteric art seems to have disappeared.

The chief development was that in Cornwall, where Andrews (*qv*) started the cliff-climbing that has grown steadily ever since. The firm, rough granite of Cornwall was a major factor here. The cliffs were also used by the commandos for training, and some of the later explorers were commandos or ex-commandos.

Little seems to have been done on other sea-cliffs until after the last war, though mention might be made of A. W. Kelly's ascent of the Sugar Loaf, a sea-stack off the Isle of Man (1933). The vogue for sea-cliffs really began in the 1950s and gained momentum in the sixties. Mention might be made of Cullernose Point, the Gower, Swanage, St Bees, Torbay, Isle of Man, Lundy, Great and Little Ormes, Hoy, and, most significant of all, Craig Gogarth in Anglesey (*qv*).

Little seems to have been done on

Continental sea-cliffs with the exception of the Calanques, on the south coast of France, which have long been popular. (See *Sea-Cliff Climbing in Britain* by J. Cleare and R. Collomb.)

SELLA, Vittorio (1859-1943)
Member of the influential Sella family of Biella, Italy; nephew of Quintino Sella; founder of the Italian Alpine Club.

Sella was a distinguished climber, explorer and photographer. He made the first winter traverses of the following: Matterhorn (1882) Monte Rosa (1884), Grand Paradiso, Lyskamm (1885) and Mont Blanc (1888). In 1889 he was with Dent (*qv*) in the Caucasus, where he returned in 1890 and 1896, making a number of first ascents. In 1897 he was with the Abruzzi Expedition to Alaska and took part in the first ascent of Mt St Elias. He was with Abruzzi again on an expedition to Ruwenzori in 1906 where further first ascents were made (see ABRUZZI).

Sella paid two visits to the Himalaya. In 1899 he was with Freshfield (*qv*) on the famous tour of Kangchenjunga, and in 1909 he accompanied Abruzzi on the first real reconnaissance of K2, during which Chogolisa was climbed: a height record for the time (25,110 ft). Sella's photographs of the area played a big part in the successes of later expeditions.

As a mountain photographer, Sella must forever rank amongst the greatest. His expedition pictures contain a wealth of detail and information, are technically brilliant and of the highest artistic quality. They have frequently been reproduced. His Alpine studies too, are of the highest class; a collection of a hundred of them, *Among the Alps*, was published privately by Samuel Aitken.

SENTRY BOX
A large niche in a rock face, sometimes offering a stance and belay. There is a well-known one at the Black Rocks, Derbyshire. Term becoming obsolescent.

SÉRAC
A pinnacle or tower of ice. Séracs are found in ice-falls (*qv*) and at the edge of ice-cliffs (e.g. Route Major, Mont Blanc). They can attain an enormous size and because they are unstable are potentially dangerous.

SHAWANGUNKS, NEW YORK STATE
A series of quartzite conglomerate cliffs

Taulliraju in the Cordillera Blanca of Peru. This area is noted for its fine ice-fluted peaks and is very popular with climbers.

31 PATAGONIA. The Fortress (left) and the Shield, Paine Group. Some of the finest peaks in the world are in this region—and some of the worst weather. (*right*) 32 THE ANDES.

33 ANNAPURNA. The South Face of Annapurna in the Nepal Himalaya. The first ascent of this face in 1970 was a significant breakthrough in Himalayan climbing.

34 MOUNT EVEREST. The picture was taken from the Western Cwm and shows the SW Face, the goal of recent expeditions (left). In the background is Lhotse.

extending along a seven-mile ridge and forming the most important rock climbing area in the Eastern United States. The cliffs do not exceed 350 ft but are very steep and have many overhangs. The Trapps cliff has the greatest number of routes and is the most popular, partly because it is the most easily accessible, though the others are not difficult to reach.

The 'Gunks' are extremely popular, and there are climbs of all standards – the Stanage of America. The first climbs were made by F. Weissner and his friends in 1935.

Guidebook: *Shawangunk Guide*, by A. Gran.

SHERPAS

A race of people, Tibetan in origin, who settled in the Sola Khumbu area, south of Everest, and the Walungchung area near Kangchenjunga. They are Mayahana Bhuddists and revere the Dalai Lama. Their language is Tibetan and has no written form, though many speak Nepali and some English. Their villages are mostly between 7,000 ft and 14,000 ft above sea level and it is estimated that the Sherpa population is about 100,000. Unlike the Gurkhas, they are totally unwarlike.

It was primarily at the suggestion of Bruce (*qv*) that Sherpas were used as porters on the first Everest expeditions, and they have been used by every expedition since, except that after the partition of India, they were not allowed into Moslem territories such as the Karakorum. They quickly developed from being mere load carriers into climbers in their own right and several Sherpas have reached high summits, including Tenzing (*qv*) on the first ascent of Everest. However, it must not be forgotten that a Sherpa's prime duty is load-carrying, usually between the lower camps. If he goes higher and becomes a high-altitude Sherpa, he receives no extra pay, but regards this as promotion since it will ensure further expedition work and employment in the lucrative trekking business. The chief Sherpa on an expedition is the Sirdar. In 1972, a Sherpa's pay was 15 rupees per day, and a Sirdar 25 rupees–"all found" including climbing gear. A Sherpa often shares in the spoils left over after an expedition too.

Many Sherpas now find lucrative employment in the tourist industry, conducting treks.

SHIPROCK, NEW MEXICO

A spectacular volcanic core, 1,600 ft high,

rising like a group of spires from the Navajo Indian Reservation. It was climbed by Californians in 1939, using artificial techniques, a climb since repeated many times. There are several other routes.

The importance of the first ascent of Shiprock is that it showed the dominance of Yosemite-trained climbers for the first time. It was the first of the desert spires to be climbed and marked the first use of expansion bolts on American rock.

The canyon of the Brazos River, New Mexico, gives routes of more than 2,000 ft on good rock.

SHIPTON, Eric Earle (b. 1907)

One of the most significant explorer-climbers of the present century. A believer, like Tilman (*qv*), who was often his partner, in the small, light expedition.

Shipton lived in Kenya from 1929-32, where he met Tilman, and Wynn Harris. With the latter he climbed Mt Kenya, making the first ascent of Nelion and the second of Batian, 1929. The following year he made the first traverse of Nelion–Batian with Tilman.

In 1931 he joined Smythe's (*qv*) expedition to Kamet and was one of the four men to reach the top – the highest peak climbed at that time. He then took part in the following expeditions:

1933 Everest; reached about 27,700 ft
1934 The forcing of the Rishi Ganga, with Tilman
1935 Leader of a monsoon reconnaissance to Everest
1936 Everest; attempts ruined by weather
1937 With Tilman, explored the Shaksgam area of Karakorum
1938 Everest (Tilman's expedition); ruined by weather
1939 Second Karakorum expedition, Hispar, Biafo, Panmah, Chogo Lungma areas
1951 Everest reconnaissance; penetrated into the Western Cwm
1952 Leader of the Cho Oyu attempt
1957 Karakorum; third visit
1958-64. Six expeditions to Patagonia, included the N–S crossing of the South Patagonian Ice-cap, 1960-1.

Shipton was Consul General in Kashgar, 1940-2 and 1946-8. He held a similar post in Kunming 1949-51. During his second visit to Kashgar he attempted Bogdo Ola (see his *Mountains of Tartary*). He was President of the A.C., 1964-7. His books are: *Nanda Devi* (1936), *Blank on the Map* (1938), *Upon that Mountain* (1948),

The Mountains of Tartary (1951), *Mount Everest Reconnaissance Expedition, 1951* (1952), *Land of Tempest* (1963), *That Untravelled World* (1969).

SIEGE TACTICS
A method whereby a mountain or cliff is climbed by making repeated attempts, pushing the route a little further each time and retiring to base in between attempts. Fixed ropes (*qv*) are left in place so that the previous high point is quickly attainable each time.

The method is extensively used in the Himalaya and has been employed on the first winter ascent of the Eigerwand, the French route on the Troll Wall, Norway, and the ascent of the Nose of El Capitan, Yosemite, among others. The ethics of seiging are much discussed by climbers. It is now generally felt that pure rock-climbs should not be seiged, and there is support growing for the idea that no climbs anywhere should be seiged, though obviously there are severe practical difficulties in the Himalayas.

SIERRA AITANA
A range of limestone peaks inland from the resort of Benidorm, Spain. The highest point is Aitana itself, 1,558 m. Numerous rock-climbs of all grades.

SIERRA NEVADA (CALIFORNIA)
A range of high mountains, 400 miles long and 40 miles wide, which includes Mt Whitney (14,495 ft), the highest mountain in the U.S.A. outside of Alaska. There is a track to the summit, but the E Face offers good and popular climbs. Other good areas are the Palisades and the Minarets. Undoubtedly the most popular area of the Sierras is Yosemite valley (*qv*).

Guidebook: *A Climber's Guide to the High Sierra*, by A. Smatko.

SIERRA NEVADA (SPAIN)
A range of mountains east of Grenada, the highest of which is Mulhacen (3,481 m), the highest peak in Spain. The Pichacho de la Veleta (3,430 m) carries a permanent snow-patch, claimed as the most southerly glacier in Europe. The climbing is of little interest.

SIERRA NEVADA DE COCUY
A small section of the Andes some 300 miles NE of Bogota in Columbia and near the town of Cocuy. Heavy rain and mists hide the peaks for much of the time

(January is best month for climbing) and they were unknown until 1910. They have been compared with Ruwenzori (*qv*).

Most of the peaks are about 5,000 m, the highest being Alto Ritacuba at 17,926 ft (C. Cuénet, A. Gansser, 1942). The range extends for about 12 miles and all the important summits have been reached.

SIERRA NEVADA DE MÉRIDA
The highest part of the Venezuelan Andes, rising above the town of Merida from which there is a cable railway to the Pico Espejo (4,765 m). The climbs are short and many are easy. The highest is Pico Bolivar at 16,410 ft (F. Weiss, 1936. Claimed by H. Burgoin, 1934, but disputed). Only six peaks are above the snow line, which is approximately 15,000 ft.

SIERRA NEVADA DE SANTA MARTA
An isolated offshoot of the Eastern Cordillera of Colombia, and claimed to be the highest coastal range of mountains in the world. Opinion is divided as to whether they form part of the Andes, but they are usually counted as such. They were first explored by T. Cabot in 1930, but not visited by climbing parties until 1939.

The peaks run W–E and extend about 20 miles. There are three main groups: The Western Group, with the highest peaks; the Eastern Group with some fine ice mountains, and the rocky group near the head of the Cabaca Valley. All the main peaks have been climbed, but the group is very accessible and the climbing very good. The best season is January to March.

West Group
Pico Colon (18,947 ft) – A. Bakewell, W. A. Wood, A. Praolini, 1939
Pico Bolivar (18,947 ft) – G. Pichler, E. Praolini, E. Kraus, 1939
Pico Simmons (18,570 ft) – Mr and Mrs F. Marmillod, 1943
Pico Santander (18,175 ft) – A. Gansser, 1943

East Group
La Reina (18,158 ft) – P. Petzoldt, Mrs E. Cowles, Miss E. Knowlton, 1941
Pico Ojedo (18,012 ft) – Petzoldt party, 1941

Cabaca Group
El Guardian (17,340 ft) – Petzoldt party, 1941
There are numerous other peaks of over 17,000 ft in the area.

SIKKIM HIMALAYA

The smallest section of the Himalaya in area, lying between the Nepal Himalaya in the west and the Dongkya Ridge of Tibet in the east–the start of the Assam Himalaya (*qv*). Like its neighbours, Nepal and Bhutan, Sikkim is an independent native state.

Into this small area are concentrated some of the world's highest mountains, the literal centrepiece being the Kangchenjunga Group (*qv*), which forms a huge cross of ridges running N–S and E–W. Deep jungle valleys surround the group then around those again are high border ridges with peaks like Kangchenjau and Pauhunri. On the Lesser Himalayan range lies the hill station of Darjeeling, famous as the pre-war starting point for Everest and Kangchenjunga. There are no Siwaliks here (see HIMALAYA) and the whole region is one of the most easily accessible in the Himalaya, which accounts for its early exploration.

In 1883 Graham came to Sikkim to climb (the first expedition as such in the Himalaya) and claimed to have ascended Kabru (24,076 ft), but there is some doubt about this. In 1899 Freshfield made a classic high-level circuit of the Kanchenjunga massif and in 1905 came Guillarmod's attempt to climb the mountain (see CROWLEY). Two years later, Rubenson and Aas almost reached the summit of Kabru, and in 1910, Kellas climbed Pauhunri and Chomiomo. There was intense activity between the wars, with the Germans attempting Kangchenjunga three times (*qv*). Notable events include Cooke's first ascent of Kabru (the first 24,000 ft peak to be climbed in the post-monsoon period), the ascent of the beautiful Siniolchu (22,600 ft) by K. Wien and A. Gottner in 1936, and the ascent of Tent Peak (24,089 ft) by L. Schmaderer, H. Paidar and E. Grob in 1939. Kangchenjunga itself (28,207 ft) was climbed by J. Brown and G. C. Band in 1955.

8,000 m Peaks

Kangchenjunga I (28,207 ft, 8597 m) – 1955
Kangchenjunga II (28,146 ft, 8573 m) – 1973

Note: With the exception of Nanga Parbat in the Punjab, these summits are the only 8,000 m peaks not in Nepal or the Karakorum.

Other Important Peaks

Kangbachen (25,782 ft) – Unclimbed (1973)

Zemu Peak (25,526 ft) – Unclimbed
Jannu (25,296 ft) – 1962
Jonsong Peak (24,510 ft) – 1930
Tent Peak (24,162 ft) – 1939
Talung (24,111 ft) – 1964
Kabru NE (24,076 ft) – 1935
Sharpu (23,622 ft) – 1963
Nepal Peak SW (23,443 ft) – 1930
Pyramid NE (23,295 ft) – 1949

SILVRETTA ALPS

A range of mountains on the Austro-Swiss border, north of the Unter Engadine valley. The highest summit is the Fluchthorn (3,403 m). The climbing is mostly easy, but the peaks are shapely. The range continues NW to the Ratikon Group (Schesaplana, 2,967 m) and NE to the Samnaun Group (Vesispitze, 3,116 m) both of which offer considerable rock-climbing. (No English guidebook.)

SKI MOUNTAINEERING

A development of ski touring (as distinct from downhill ski running). The techniques and equipment are outside the scope of this book, but it is germane to say that the ski mountaineer, as in all ski touring, faces greater hazards than the man who keeps to a beaten piste. He must recognize the lie of the land, estimate the quality of the snow (which may change considerably during the course of the tour) and be aware of avalanche and crevasse dangers.

It may be possible for the ski mountaineer to make a complete ascent to the summit on his skis, with the possibility of a traverse, or the skis may be left at a convenient col and the final summit ridge ascended on foot.

Skis originated in Norway and the first Englishman to use them is claimed to be C. Slingsby (*qv*). They quickly spread to the Alps where their popularity was encouraged by Lunn (*qv*) who made the first ski ascents of many of the big peaks such as Dom, Eiger and Weisshorn. His guidebook to the Oberland was the first ski mountaineering guidebook to be produced (1920). In recent years the High Level Route (*qv*) from Chamonix to Zermatt has become a popular ski tour. In 1972 there was a British ski traverse of the Alps.

An extreme form of the sport has developed in the descent of steep faces on ski. The following are notable:

1933 F. Rieckh – East Face, Weisskugel; North Face, Zuckerhutl; East Face, Schrankogel (45°)

1935 Kugler and Schlager – North Face, Fuscherkarkopf (50°)
1941 E. Henrich – NE Face, Ruderhof-spitze
1960 L. Terray – North Face, Mont Blanc
1964 A. Hörtnagel and H. Wagner – North Face, Hochfernerspitze
1966 K. Lapuch and M. Oberegger – East Face, Göll
1968 Lapuch and Oberegger – North Face, Sonnblick (55°)
     S. Saudan – Whymper Couloir, Verte (55°); Gervasutti Couloir, Tacul (50°)
1969 S. Saudan – Marinelli Couloir, Monte Rosa (45-50°)
     Lapuch and Oberegger – NW Face, Gross Wiesbachhorn (60°); East Face integrale, Monte Rosa (55° plus)
1973 S. Cachat-Rosset–Couturier couloir, Aig. Verte
     H. Holzer–Brenva Face, Mont Blanc

Note: Down hill race courses average 15°.

May to July is the best time for this steep skiing, and soft snow is desirable, though it increases the chance of avalanches. Some descents are made roped, pitch by pitch, others solo (e.g. Saudan). Various safety devices are employed though their efficacy is open to doubt.

Another development has been the very short ski (60 cm) called "snow gliders" or "ski boards". These are light enough to be carried on summer ascents and are used to descend snow-fields and glaciers on the return, thus shortening the day. In 1961 the Austrians Winter and Zakarias used these short skis to descend the Pallavicini Couloir of the Gross Glockner (55°).

SKY HOOK (Am.: Bathook)

A chrome molly hook about 7 cm long to which an étrier can be attached. The hooked end has a diameter of about 2 cm and is finished with a squared chisel edge. It can be hooked on to miniscule projections and save the use of a bolt or peg and is secure.

SKYE

Most important of the Inner Hebrides, Scotland. Reached by ferry from Mallaig, Glenelg or (most usual) Kyle of Lochalsh. The principal mountains are the Black Cuillin (See CUILLIN OF SKYE). Other hills are the Quirang and the Storr, both noted for unusual pinnacles including the Old Man of Storr (first ascent, Whillans, 1955). The rock is bad. Macleod's Maidens are sea-stacks near Loch Bracadale.

Guidebook: *The Island of Skye*, by M. Slesser.

SLAB (G.: Platte; Fr.: Dalle, Plaque; It.: Placce)

A flat area of rock inclined approximately between 30° and 75°. May form a pitch of a climb, virtually a whole climb (e.g. Botterill's Slab, Scafell), or be large enough to hold several climbs (e.g. Idwal Slabs).

SLEEPING BAG

Only good-quality sleeping bags are suitable for mountain environments, especially at high altitudes or under winter conditions. The best are filled with down or a feather/down mix, and are box-quilted to avoid "cold spots". A "mummy" bag is one which is approximately shaped to the body and includes a headpiece. In very cold conditions two bags may be used, an inner and an outer.

For a large party on the hills, especially in winter, a sleeping bag should be carried as an emergency against exposure. (See also DUVET, PIED D'ELEPHANT.)

SLESSER, Malcolm (b. 1926)

Scottish author and university lecturer, noted for his ascents in Greenland, which he has visited seven times. In 1962 he visited the Pamirs and wrote a controversial book on his experiences (*Red Peak*, 1964). He was in the Andes in 1964 and 1966, when he climbed the NE Spur of Yerupaja (1964). He has also climbed in the Tombstone Range of the Yukon. In Greenland, Slesser has made 18 first ascents. In Scotland his most notable first ascent is the winter climb of the South Post, Coire Ardair (c. 1957). His books are: *Red Peak* (1964), *The Andes are Prickly* (1966), *Brazil* (1968), *The Discovery of South America* (1969), *The Mountains of Skye* (1971), *Scottish Mountains on Ski* (1971) and *Politics of the Environment* (1972).

SLIGACHAN

A lonely inn in Skye at the northern foot of the Cuillins. It was the great pioneering centre in the early days of climbing in the island but most people now prefer Glenbrittle. Prof. J. N. Collie (*qv*) spent the last years of his life here.

SLING (Fr.: Anneau de corde; It.: Cordino)

Loop of nylon rope or tape used for belays, runners, or abseiling (all *qv*) and an important part of a climber's equipment. Abseil slings are generally ready spliced but belay slings are usually tied by the climber. The strongest possible sling should be used for any situation–a No 4 rope (11 mm perlon) or tape at least 1 in. wide, but this is not always possible. Nylon rope should never run over a nylon sling because the nylon could melt with the friction – a karabiner should be interspersed between the two. Old slings should be conscientiously discarded for safety.

Hemp slings are not common today, but they do have a use in the Alps as loops from which abseils can be made the sling then being abandoned. Such loops are frequently found in place but should not be used, as they may be rotten.

SLINGSBY, William Cecil (1849-1924)

One of the great central figures of British mountaineering during the closing decades of the last century. A Yorkshire squire and textile manufacturer, Slingsby spent his boyhood in the limestone hills of the Craven area, which aroused in him a passionate interest in climbing and potholing that lasted throughout his long life. This was further enhanced by being related to other climbers of the times – the Hopkinsons, Tribes, and later, Winthrop Young, who was his son-in-law.

His greatest affection was for Norway; the mountains and the people. He first visited that country in 1872 and paid 15 subsequent visits, exploring and climbing what was then virtually unknown territory. He made many first ascents, including the formidable-looking Skagastolstind (Jotenheim Mountains) in 1876, which he completed solo when his Norwegian guides refused to continue. He was probably the first Englishman to learn the art of skiing. Wrote: *Norway, the Northern Playground* (1904).

Slingsby's first Alpine season was 1878 and was of little account, but in 1879 he climbed the Weissmies without guides and made traverses of Castor and Pollux, Mont Blanc and Dent d'Hérens. He also climbed the Matterhorn. From then on his summers were divided between the Alps and Norway. In 1887 he made the first ascent of Pt Barnes in the Bouquetins and the first S–N traverse of the Aig. Rouges of Arolla.

In 1892 and 1893 he was one of the élite climbing group centred around A. F. Mummery (*qv*) and took part in the famous attempt on the North Face of the Plan and the first ascent of the Requin. Slingsby's superb icemanship played a considerable part in both climbs.

He was a passionate propagandist of British rock-climbing and one of the leading pioneers. His many first ascents include Slingsby's Chimney on Scafell (1888) and Eagle's Nest Ridge Direct, Great Gable (1892) where he seconded Solly.

He was a member or honorary member of most British climbing and caving clubs. He died peacefully at his home in 1929.

SMITH, Albert (1816-60)

A journalist and showman who, after several previous attempts, succeeded in climbing Mont Blanc in 1851. The following year he made his ascent the subject of an "entertainment" in London, which ran for six years and made Smith a wealthy man. He also wrote an account of his adventures in *The Story of Mont Blanc* (1853)

Smith made no other ascents, but he was genuinely fond of the Alps and his show did much to influence public opinion favourably towards Alpinism. He was an Original Member of the Alpine Club and the first of that body to have climbed Mont Blanc.

SMITH, Eaglesfield Bradshaw (d 1881)

One of the Alpine pioneers who made some easy, but popular, first ascents: Dent du Midi (1855), Mittel Gipfel of Wildstrubel (1857) and Oldenhorn (1857)

SMITH, William (1827-99)

At the age of 15, with his brother and fellow pupils from Hofwyl School, made the first ascent of the popular Rifelhorn at Zermatt.

SMYTH BROTHERS

James Grenville Smyth (1825-1907) and Christopher Smyth (1827-1900) were parsons who, in 1854 and 1855, began the serious exploration of the higher Zermatt peaks. In 1854 they made the first ascent of Strahlhorn and the first English ascent of the Ostspitze of Monte Rosa. In the following year they were with Hudson and Ainslie (*qv*) in guideless ascents of Breithorn and Klein Matterhorn and finally, the first ascent of Monte Rosa.Later that season they were with Hudson again on the first guideless ascent of Mont Blanc.

They visited the Alps occasionally after this but did nothing else of note. In 1854 they were accompanied by their brother, Edmund Smyth, who, as an officer in the Indian army, did some early Himalayan exploration.

SMYTHE, Francis Sydney (1900-49)
A very popular mountaineering writer of the years immediately before the Second World War, and an accomplished mountaineer.

Smythe sprang to Alpine prominence in 1927 when he made the second ascent of the Ryan-Lochmatter route on the Plan (with J. H. B. Bell) and the first ascent, with Graham Brown (*qv*), of the Sentinelle Route on the Brenva Face of Mont Blanc. A year later he and Brown climbed Route Major on the same face. These two Brenva climbs were the most important contributions by British Alpinists to the inter-war Alpine scene.

In 1930, Smythe was a member of the unsuccessful International Kangchenjunga Expedition. In the following year he led his own expedition to Kamet (25,447 ft) with considerable success: Kamet was the highest summit attained at that time and the first summit over 25,000 ft ever reached.

On the 1933 Everest Expedition Smythe equalled the height record of 28,126 ft set by Norton in 1924. He was also a member of the 1936 and 1938 Everest Expeditions. He also climbed in Garwhal and the Canadian Rockies. During the War he acted as an instructor of mountain troops.

In 1927 Smythe abandoned his profession of engineer to become a full-time author. He wrote or edited numerous books on mountaineering which had great vogue at the time, though his somewhat romantic philosophy of climbing is little echoed today. He was a superb photographer.

He was taken ill in India while organizing an expedition in 1949, and though flown home, had a relapse and died.

SNOW BLINDNESS
A temporary but painful blindness caused by the glare of the sun from snow and ice over an extended period, for example, during an Alpine climb. Protection is afforded by sun-glasses or snow-goggles: but they should be of good quality. If the glasses are broken, protection may be afforded by an eye mask made from paper or card, with tiny slits to see through. An old remedy for snow blindness was to bathe the eyes in a solution of gunpowder!

SNOW BRIDGE
A blockage of snow spanning a crevasse (*qv*). Some are quite tenuous and if they have to be crossed require careful testing by the leader. He is securely belayed for this and he in turn belays the next man, and so on. Bridges may well collapse even after two or three people have crossed them. They are often much weaker in the afternoon after several hours of sunshine.

SNOW CAVE (SNOW HOLE)
An emergency shelter dug in snow. A bank of firm snow at least 30° and 8 ft thick is required, usually where the snow has drifted. Two tunnels are dug, five feet apart, into the bank to a depth of about 5 ft. They are then joined together inside and the cave suitably enlarged. Points to note are: the entrances should be as low as possible to conserve heat; one entrance should be permanently blocked after construction if possible; the other should be blocked with a rucksack as a "door"; ice axes should be taken into the cave for emergency; an air hole is needed.

The digging of a snow cave takes several hours and should only be undertaken in an extreme emergency.

SNOW-CLIMBING
A major part of mountaineering skill, both in the Alps and higher mountain ranges, as well as in Britain during winter conditions. Allied to, but different from, ice-climbing (*qv*).

The safe climbing of steep snow slopes depends upon experience, and particularly upon the recognition of the snow quality. This varies enormously: it can be extremely firm and compacted, wet and slushy, powdery, or crusty (when a thin layer of hard snow lies over softer snow). It might be lying over ice or hiding crevasses (*qv*). Snow which is quite safe in the early morning may become dangerous later in the day after the sun has been on it.

Steep faces of snow or snow gullies are subject to avalanche. Snow will avalanche at a very low angle given the conditions and there is no certain way of knowing what will and what will not avalanche. As a rule, however, steep slopes should be avoided for about three days after a heavy fall of new snow. (See AVALANCHE)

Crevasses (*qv*) are dealt with elsewhere. Where thin snow lies over ice, the climb should be treated as an ice-climb (*qv*), and crampons worn.

The best snow is compacted snow which allows the climber to kick steps in it. A short sharp kick is given, forming a step which points slightly downwards as it goes in. A steady rhythm is necessary or step-kicking becomes tiring. The second and third man improve the steps by kicking too, and it is possible to change leaders on a long climb and thus share the work. All the climbers move together. It may be necessary to cut the occasional step using the blade of the axe but this is not usual today: if the snow is that hard, it is better to use crampons and treat it as an ice-climb.

It is common practice now to wear crampons on all snow and ice-climbs, but there are times when the snow is so soft that it balls up the crampons and they become a nuisance, even dangerous.

When long axes were more common, they were used as "third legs": the axe was shoved into the slope ahead of the climber and used for balance when he stepped up. On normal slopes now, it is usual for the axe to be held across the chest in the position of braking, so as to be ready to hold a slip should one occur. For this, the right hand holds the head of the axe and the left the shaft (or vice versa). If the climber falls, he rolls on to his axe and gradually presses it into the snow. The axe then acts as a brake. This is possibly the most important use of the axe on snow-climbs and the technique should be practised beforehand on short, clear slopes so that it becomes automatic.

Where the climbers are moving together, it is normal to shorten the rope to about 20 ft between each man. The spare coils are wrapped round the body and tied off at the waist, and a couple of coils are usually carried in the hand. In the event of a slip the remaining climbers plunge their axes into the snow and whip the coils round to form an emergency belay.

If the snow is very steep, or has been interrupted by an ice pitch or rock pitch, then the rope is run out as in rock-climbing (*qv*). If possible, a rock peg provides the best belay, but failing that a dead man (*qv*) can be used, or the traditional axe shaft. For this the shaft is driven into the snow as far

as possible and above the belayer. He ties on to it as in rock-climbing and uses a waist belay to bring up the next man and so on. This method is invariably used in the Alps where the time taken to place a dead man is too great, though the dead man is safer.

Snow ridges can be very narrow and may be corniced (*qv*). In the latter case a line should be chosen well back from the edge, in case the cornice breaks off. If a climber falls from a ridge, his companion should immediately slide the other way as a counterbalance – a frightening but effective device.

In traversing steep snow slopes, the long axe has an advantage since it can be used as a prop against the snow, but balance and the proper kicking of steps is the real answer.

Very soft snow, or crusted snow, is extremely exhausting. On some expeditions to higher ranges, snow shoes (racquets) have been used to overcome this, but they are not common in the Alps or in Britain.

(See *Modern Snow & Ice Techniques* by W. March.)

SNOWDON (3,561 ft)

The highest summit in Britain south of the Scottish border. It rises as a complex of sharp ridges in the angle formed by the Llanberis and Nantgwynant vallies.

The summit, Yr Wyddfa, has a café and is connected to Llanberis by the only mountain railway in Britain. The other popular ways of ascent are: by track from Llanberis, the Watkin Path from Nantgwynant, the Snowdon Ranger path, the Pyg Track from Pen y Pass, and via the Crib Goch Ridge from Pen y Pass. All are extremely popular.

Important subsidiary summits of the massif are: Crib y ddysgl (3493 ft), Crib Goch (3023 ft) and Y Lliwedd (2947 ft). The Snowdon Horseshoe Walk embraces these as well as Yr Wyddfa: a classic walk.

The ridges enfold a number of small lakes (llyns) including: Llydaw, Glaslyn, Teryn, Glas and Arddu. All the ridges have important north-facing crags including Lliwedd, Llechog, Clogwyn du'r Arddu, Dinas Mot, Cyrn Las, Clogwyn y Person and Clogwyn y Ddysgl (all *qv*). Yr Wyddfa itself provides a number of gullies for winter climbing.

SNOWDONIA

The mountains of North Wales surrounding the principal massif of Snowdon (Yr Wyddfa, 3,561 ft). The area is bounded to the north by the coastal strip (Bangor,

Caernarvon), to the west by the Lleyn Peninsula, to the east by the Vale of Conway and to the south by the Vale of Ffestiniog. Most of this is a National Park.

Major roads penetrate the area, dividing it into easily accessible segments. In the south, the road from Bettws y Coed to Beddgelert cuts off the Moelwyns (Moelwyn Mawr, 2,527ft) and Moel Siabod (2,864ft). To the west of the Caernarvon-Beddgelert road lies Moel Hebog (2,566ft) and east of it lies Snowdon. Then comes the Llanberis Pass (*qv*), the Glyders (Glyder Fawr 3,279ft), the Vale of Ogwen (*qv*) and finally, the Carneddau (Carnedd Llywellyn 3,485ft). Despite this accessibility, the mountain groups are, within themselves, rugged and wild.

For climbers, the chief villages are Capel Curig, Llanberis, Nant Peris, Bethesda, Beddgelert, Bettws y Coed, and Rhyd Ddu – the first three of which are most popular, though there are climbing huts, camp sites, etc. throughout the area in great profusion.

Walking is more rugged than in the Lakes, often involving scrambles, for instance, Bristly Ridge, Crib Goch, Tryfan, Cnicht. Popular walks include the Snowdon Horseshoe, the Glyders, the Carneddau, Moel Siabod and the Moelwyns. The Welsh 3,000s (*qv*) is one of the most popular long-distance walks in Britain.

Rock-climbing is practised throughout the area, though the main centres are still the traditional ones of Ogwen and Llanberis (*qv*). The rock is nearly always sound and the climbs are of every length and grade. The first climb was the West Buttress of Lliwedd, done by Stocker and Wall in 1883. Developments since the last War, especially at Llanberis, Clogwyn du'r Arddu and Gogarth (though the last is not strictly Snowdonia) have put the area well to the front in British climbing. (See individual crags and areas.)

Guidebooks: *The Welsh Peaks*, by W. Poucher; the Climbers' Club Guides to Wales (11 vols); and *Rock Climbing in Wales*, by R. James.

SNOW PLOD

A term of disparagement, sometimes used to describe an ascent of an easy snow peak where little technique is called for, e.g. the Strahlhorn, Switzerland.

SOCIETY OF WELSH RABBITS

An informal club founded by C. E. Mathews (*qv*), Adams-Reilly and Morshead (*qv*) at Pen y Gwryd in January 1870. Its purpose was to explore Snowdonia in winter; most members were also A.C. members.

SOCKS OVER BOOTS

On wet, slimy rock better adhesion can often be obtained by wearing socks over P.A.s. A dying art.

SOLLEDER, Emil (1899-1931)

Bavarian climber and guide; one of the finest of the inter-war years, and a pioneer of GrVI routes in the Dolomites. His three greatest climbs were:

1925 Furchetta North Face (with F. Wiessner)
1925 Civetta North West Face (with G. Lettenbauer)
1926 Sass Maor East Face (with F. Kummer)

Solleder was killed whilst descending with a client from the Meije. They were unroped and the client was abseiling when the abseil block gave way. The client fell onto a ledge unhurt, but Solleder, perhaps trying to grab the rope, overbalanced and fell 2,000 ft to the Étançons Glacier.

SOLLY, Godfrey Allan (1858-1942)

A Birkenhead solicitor who had a long and distinguished career in climbing. He was present at, and took an active part in, some of the most significant events of the nineteenth and early twentieth centuries.

Solly began his Alpine career in 1885. He was a keen advocate of guideless climbs; a friend of Carr, Slingsby, Mummery *et al*. Was with Mummery on his first attempt at the Plan North Face (1892), but his only first ascents were minor ones. In 1893 and 1894 he visited the Caucasus and made a number of new ascents, and in 1909 he was in Canada, climbing in the Lake O'Hara region.

Solly was with Collie (*qv*) and Collier (*qv*) on the famous Easter Meet of the S.M.C. at Inveroran, when the first ascent of the crags of Buachaille Etive Mor was made, together with other ascents in Glencoe and the first ascent of Tower Ridge, Ben Nevis (1894). This is regarded as the start of rock-climbing on the Scottish mainland.

In the Lake District he was with Carr on the Hand Traverse of Pillar North Climb (1891) and made the first complete ascent of Arrowhead Ridge on Gable (1893). His most notable achievement, however, was the first ascent of Eagle's Nest Direct, Gable, in 1892.

Solly continued to climb to a great age. He made a guideless traverse of Grépon, aged 63, ascended Strahlhorn, aged 75 and climbed Pillar at 80. He was President of the S. M. C., 1910 and F. R. C. C., 1920.

SOLO CLIMBING
Climbing alone. A safety rope may or may not be used. The additional dangers of solo climbing are obvious, but many expert climbers find great satisfaction in this method of making ascents and indeed, the first solo ascent of a given route is recognized as a distinct achievement. Solo climbing has been common since the pioneer days when Lammer, O. G. Jones, Kirkus and others often soloed routes. Many first ascents were done solo, including Napes Needle (*qv*). Some of the hardest Alpine climbs of modern times were first done solo, e.g. Matterhorn Nordwand Direct and the Bonatti Pillar of the Dru. (See *On the Heights*, by W. Bonatti.)

SOLVAY, Ernest (1838-1922)
Belgian industrialist, inventor of the Solvay process for washing soda, who donated 20,000 fr. to the S.A.C. for the construction of a refuge at 4,000 m on the Hörnli Ridge of the Matterhorn (1906). Opened in 1916, it is known as the Solvay Hut and has played a considerable part in the Matterhorn story. The original structure has been replaced. Solvay himself climbed the Matterhorn at the age of 65.

SOUTH AFRICA, CLIMBING IN
The numerous mountains of South Africa provide a wide variety of climbs on rock, which ranges from the hard sandstone of Table Mountain to the basalts of the Drakensberg and the granites of the Spitskop in the deserts of SW Africa. The highest peak is in the Drakensberg: Thabantshonyana (11,425 ft). The better-known Champagne Castle (11,077 ft) was long regarded as the highest peak. There is no permanent snow or glaciers, though snow and ice-climbing is done during the winter months. Rock-climbs are more usual and include some of the highest difficulty. There are over 300 routes on Table Mountain alone.

The Mountain Club of South Africa was established in 1891. It has five sections: Capetown, Transvaal, Paarl, Wellington, Stellenbosch. It owns several huts. The Natal Mountain Club is independent and the West Province Mountain Club caters for non-white climbers, of which there are many.

SOUTH GEORGIA
An island, about 120 miles long and ave-

raging 15 miles wide, in the sub-Antarctic. A mountain range runs down the middle of the island, the highest point being Mt Paget, 9,625 ft, with many others of about 7,000 ft. D. Carse surveyed the island in the three seasons, 1951-2, 1953-4 and 1955-6, and G. Sutton investigated the climbing in the season 1954-5. The peaks are attractive and a number have been climbed, but the weather is usually very bad.

Expeditions have been made to other islands in the sub-Antarctic: Heard Island, Crozet Islands, Elephant Island, etc., but the weather is nearly always bad, and the attractions are limited.

SPACE BLANKET
An emergency blanket made out of a silvery foil and used to protect a climber suffering from exposure, or for benightment, etc. There is a heavier cellular model. A poly bag (*qv*) is probably just as effective.

SPENCER, Sydney (1862-1950)
A distinguished Alpinist at the turn of the century, Spencer made the first winter ascent of the Dom (1894), first ascent of the W Summit of Landstrandtinder (Lofoten, 1903) and, with Collie (*qv*) and Stutfield, several new ascents in the Rockies and Selkirks (1900). He is best known today for his route from the Nantillons Glacier to the Blaitière by the spectacular Spencer Couloir (with Ch. Jossi, 1898).

SPINDRIFT
Light powder snow blown about by the wind and often seen forming spumes from Alpine crests and summits. A superficial snow slide of powder snow is also called spindrift. It is very uncomfortable since it penetrates clothing by getting up sleeves and down necks.

SPITSBERGEN (SVALBARD)
A group of islands almost mid-way between the North Cape of Norway and the North Pole, and belonging to Norway. West Spitsbergen has mountains rising to just over 5,000 ft. The highest summits are: Newtontoppen and Perriertoppen, both 5,633 ft. The former was climbed by A. Vassiliev's party in 1900.

The first major expedition was that of Conway in 1896 when he made the first crossing of the island. He returned and climbed a number of peaks the following year. The island has attracted several expeditions since. The peaks, though low, are shapely. The chief difficulty is to reach the inland ice – two or three days through deep mud, dangerous crevasses and thick fog.

STACK
A free-standing pinnacle of rock left behind by the erosion of sea-cliffs. They can be of considerable height and may be difficult of access. They are numerous in Scotland, Ireland and elsewhere. Many have been climbed; the islanders of St Kilda once became expert stack-climbers in their search for gulls' eggs. Ball's Pyramid is an 1,800 ft stack, 400 miles off the Australian coast (first ascent 1965). Best-known British stack is The Old Man of Hoy (1966, Baillie, Patey, Bonington).

STANAGE EDGE
The most important gritstone crag in Britain. Though not continuous, the edge is about four miles long with climbs up to 75 ft or so, though many are only half this. There are almost 500 routes of all grades on excellent Rivelin grit and the crag is immensely popular. The nearest village is Hathersage, Derbyshire.

Climbing began here in 1890 with J. W. Puttrell (*qv*) and has since seen the development of many noted leaders including Kelly, Piggott Hargreaves, Linnell, Bridge, Brown and Whillans among many others. The influence of these rocks on the development of British climbing cannot be overestimated. (See *High Peak* by E. Byne.)

Guidebook: *The Sheffield Stanage Area* by E. Byne.

STANCE (G.: Standplatz; Fr.: Relais; It.: Punto di sosta
The top of a pitch (*qv*); the place where the climber halts to make a static belay. Usually a ledge, though possibly a very small one. Can be a chockstone (*qv*) or even a tree. In artificial climbing (*qv*) a stance may be taken in étriers. Note that the climber may not actually *stand* (though this is common); he may be sitting or even lying down.

STANIG, Valentin (1774-1847)
The earliest amateur mountaineer of the Eastern Alps who took part in the second ascent of Gross Glockner, 1800, the first ascent being made by local peasants the previous day. He also made the first ascent of Watzmann (1799 or 1801). Stanig was a cleric and amateur botanist.

STARR, Russell
A Yorkshire climber who made the first ascent of Fusstein, and first English ascent

of Olperer, two popular Zillertal peaks, in 1880.

STEPHEN, Sir Leslie (1832-1904)
Biographer, and one of the most eminent literary critics of his day. His first wife was the daughter of Thackeray and his own daughter was the novelist Virginia Woolf.

In his student days Stephen was a keen runner and walker and this stood him in good stead when he began his Alpine career. His first real season (though he visited the Alps previously as a tourist) was in 1858 when E. S. Kennedy, Hardy and Hinchcliff (*qv*) accompanied him on a six weeks' season which included the first traverse of Wildstrubel. It was the start of an astonishing career of first ascents, tabulated below (first ascents unless otherwise noted):

1858 Wildstrubel – first traverse
1859 Eigerjoch – first crossing
      Bietschhorn
      Weissmeis – first English ascent
      Dom – second ascent
      Rimpfischhorn
1860 Allalinhorn – second ascent
      Alphubel
      Oberaarhorn
      Blumlisalphorn
1861 Mont Blanc via Goûter – first complete ascent
1861 Shreckhorn
1862 Jungfraujoch – first crossing
      Fiescherjoch – first crossing
      Weisshorn – second ascent
      Pizzo Pioda
      Monte della Disgrazia
1864 Scherjoch – first crossing
      Winterlücke – first amateur's crossing
      Jungfrau from Rottal
      Lyskamm west summit
      Zinal Rothorn
1869 Cima di Ball – solo
1871 Mont Mallet
1873 Col des Hirondelles – first crossing
1877 Galenstock – first winter ascent

After his marriage in 1867, he curtailed his climbing at the wish of his wife. In 1871 he published *The Playground of Europe*, a collection of climbing pieces, mostly ones he had contributed to the *A. J.* It is one of the great classics of mountaineering literature.

He was President of the A.C. 1866–68.

STEPHENSON, Tom (b.1893)
A journalist who first proposed the Pennine Way in an article in the *Daily Herald* in 1935. The idea was inspired by the

Appalachian Trail of the United States, but the Pennine Way did not finally come into being until 1965. Stephenson became Secretary to the Ramblers' Association in 1948 and it was his persistent work which opened up long distance 'trails' in Britain.

STEPS
Holds cut or kicked in snow or ice. Steps should always be kicked in preference to cut with an axe because this saves a lot of time, but on very hard snow and on ice this is not possible. On hard snow, the adze of the ice axe is used to fashion the steps and on ice the pick is used. The ideal is to make a step which will take half a boot width and which slopes slightly inwards.

An expert step-cutter can fashion a step in three blows, even in ice. The weight of the axe head should do most of the work – step-cutting is very tiring. Large steps (usually in snow) are called "buckets" or "bucket steps". When snow lies over ice care should be taken to cut through to the ice.

The direction taken by a line of uphill steps varies according to the nature of the snow or ice and the steepness of the slope. The best and easiest line should be taken. On very steep slopes steps may be fashioned in zig-zag, with a turning step at the end of each line. In all cases it is usual to cut two or three steps ahead.

Step-cutting was an art for which numerous early guides were famous and prodigious numbers of steps were cut on some climbs. The art is less important today owing to the development of crampon techniques. (See ICE AXE, CRAMPONS, ICE-CLIMBING, SNOW-CLIMBING.)

STICHT PLATE
A device invented by Fritz Sticht to improve dynamic belaying. Instead of the rope passing round the climber's back for friction, it passes through a metal friction plate, which in the event of a fall by another climber applies a gradual brake to the rope.

STOGDON, John (1843-1919)
One of the guideless school of Alpinists of the early 1870s, but best known for his oft quoted account of a winter crossing of Bowfell in the Lake District, which almost ended in disaster (*A. J.* vol. V).

STONE, James Kent (Father Fidelis) (1840-1921)
Born in Boston, Massachussets, and edu-

cated at Harvard, Stone became a member of the A. C. in 1860 with the best list of qualifications entered up to that date. His only first ascent, however, was of Blumlisalphorn with Stephen and Liveing, 1860. In 1869 he became a priest and missionary.

STONEFALL
Natural stonefall is due to the processes of erosion and is consequently greatest where erosion is most pronounced. In Britain it is not a serious problem, but it is common in the Alps. Where stonefall is known to be serious, the area should be avoided or, if that is not possible, should be tackled at the time when the stonefall is minimal. This usually means before dawn. Guidebooks are often explicit in this matter. Stonefall occurs on open faces and especially in couloirs and gullies where the confined space makes the danger greater. Ridges are the safest from stonefall.

Though occasional large boulders come down, most stonefall is smaller, though large enough to do serious injury if it strikes a climber. It travels at great speed due to accelleration under gravity and its ominous whirring can often be heard even when the stones themselves cannot be seen.

Stonefall because of other people on the cliff or mountain is much more common in Britain, and gullies are again the black spots. Every care should be taken not to kick stones down accidentally and, of course, stones should never be thrown down cliffs. If a stone is dislodged a loud warning cry of "below!" should be shouted. The only protection against stonefall is a climbing helmet.

STONEY MIDDLETON
In Derbyshire. One of the most important limestone crags in the country with many fine routes, mostly in the upper grades. No climbs seem to have been done here before 1918-20 when Puttrell (*qv*) and his companions climbed in Fingal's Cave. The pre-war years also saw the remarkable ascent of Aurora in 1933 (F. Elliott). In 1950, J. Brown (*qv*) and his companions began the post-war surge with The Golden Gate and other climbs.

Guidebook: *The Northern Limestone Area*, by P. Nunn.

STOVE
There are four main types used by climbers:
(a) liquified butane (e.g. Gaz)
(b) paraffin (e.g. Primus)

(c) petrol

(d) methylated spirits or profol.

Type (a) uses disposible cartridges. Clean to handle and easy to light. Various sizes. As hot as (b) under laboratory conditions, but the flame seems readily affected by winds. Make sure a cartridge is empty before removing it from the stove.

Type (b). Very safe to use but can be fiddling. Needs pre-heating with meths. or profol. Cheap fuel.

Type (c). Probably the hottest type of stove, but the imflammable nature of the fuel and the possibility of leakage make it a little dangerous.

Type (d). Very small and easily portable stoves – "tommy cookers". Slow, but useful for bivouacs. Safe and simple.

STRATON, Mary Isabella (1838-1918)

One of the pioneer lady climbers, Miss Straton began her Alpine career in 1861 with a visit to the Grands Mulets. She went on to make the first ascent of the Aig. du Moine (1871), Punta Isabella (1875) and Aig. de la Persévérance (1875). In 1876 she made the first winter ascent of Mont Blanc. Miss Straton married her guide, Jean Charlet, and the family became Charlet-Straton. They lived in Argentière.

STREATHER, Harry Reginald Antony (b. 1926)

A British Army officer who has taken part in a number of important Himalayan expeditions. In 1950 he took part in the Norwegian first ascent of Tirich Mir as a member of the summit party and was with the Americans on K2 in 1953. In 1955, with Hardie, he made the second ascent of Kangchenjunga, following the initial success of Brown and Band.

In 1957, Streather accepted leadership of the Oxford University Haramosh Expedition. The expedition ended in tragedy, but was an epic of endurance and courage on the part of Streather: one of the great stories of modern mountaineering. (See *The Last Blue Mountain*, by R. Barker.)

In 1959 Streather led a British Army expedition to the Karakorum, and made the first ascent of Malubitang East.

Since 1961, Tony Streather has played a considerable part in endeavour training and has led various expeditions to Ethiopia, Kenya, Greenland and the Pindus Mountains of Greece, either for youth groups or the Army. Awarded the M.B.E. He is at present Lt.-Col. in charge of a jungle warfare unit.

STRONE ULLADALE

A huge crag at the northern end of Ullaval in Harris, Outer Hebrides. Reached by ferry from Uig, Skye. The place had a vogue in the late 1960s, culminating in the ascent of the great overhangs of the Nose. (The Scoop: Scott, Lee, Upton, Terry, 1969.)

STRUTT, Edward Lisle (1874-1948)

An accomplished climber and soldier, noted for his rescue of the Austrian Royal Family from a revolutionary mob in 1919. Second-in-command of the 1922 Everest Expedition, though he did not go high.

In the light of history, Strutt's career was blighted by his rigid conservatism over mountaineering detail which was highlighted during his editorship of the *Alpine Journal* in the 1930s and his presidency of the A. C. He undoubtedly weakened the Alpine Club in a changing world and perhaps retarded British (Alpine) climbing by more than a decade.

STUBAI ALPS

A popular area in Tyrol between the Otztal mountains in the west and the Zillertal mountains in the east. Penetrated by the long and beautiful Stubaital where Fulpmes and Neustift are centres. The factory at Fulpmes has given the district's name to a famous make of climbing equipment.

The mountains are mostly easy and hut-to-hut touring is popular. The highest summit is Zuckerhutl (3,505m). On the eastern fringes of the area there are some interesting rock peaks of which mention might be made: Pflerscher Tribulaun (3,096m), Serles (2,718m) and the Kalkogels.

Guidebook: *Stubai Alps*, by E. Roberts (excludes Kalkogels).

STUTFIELD, Hugh Edward Millington (1858-1929)

Traveller and game hunter who made a number of first ascents in the Canadian Rockies with Collie, Woolley and Spencer in 1898, 1900 and 1902. The 1898 party discovered the great Columbia Glacier and made the first ascents of: Survey Peak, Dome, Diadem, and Mt Thompson – all guideless. In 1902 the first ascents of: Mt Murchison, Mt Freshfield, Mt Forbes, Howse Peak, Mt Noyes and Mt Neptuak.

Joint author, with J. N. Collie, of *Climbs and Exploration in the Canadian Rockies* (?1910).

SUMMIT
The highest point of a mountain or hill. In Britain the summit is generally indicated by a cairn (*qv*) or a trig-block (*qv*). In the Alps a summit may be unmarked, or have a trig-pole, trig-triangle, cross or (very occasionally,) some other symbol – even a statue. Many Alpine summits have a book in which to record one's ascent. It is protected by a box. (See also MOUNTAINEERING.)

SUSTAINED
Meaning that the difficulty is sustained throughout the pitch or the climb, whichever is being described. Many climbs have a few pitches which are harder than the rest, and many pitches have a few moves which are harder than the rest, but the use of the word "sustained" means that the difficulty never relents.

SWANAGE
A series of limestone cliffs on the Dorset coast between Swanage town and St Alban's Head. Numerous climbs, some in excess of 100 ft and in all grades. Further along the same coast there are climbs at Lulworth and Portland. The area was developed in the 1960s.
    Guidebook: *Dorset,* by R. C. White.

SWEDEN, CLIMBING IN
Kebnekaise (6,965 ft) in Arctic Sweden is the highest summit, glaciated, but easy to climb and of little interest. In summer, the whole area is heavily infested with midges.

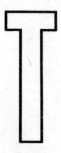

TAIWAN (FORMOSA)
An island off the coast of China occupied by the Chinese Nationalist Government. There are some fine mountains rising from the forests of the centre and north-east of the island, many of 11,000 ft to 12,000 ft. The highest is Niitaka (*c.* 12,950 ft).

TALBOT, Jeremy Owen (b. 1940)
Welsh climber noted for his development of the Gower area where he has made over 470 new climbs in the last few years. He has also (1963-6) made many first British ascents of difficult Alpine climbs, principally in the Oberland. His usual companion was the guide, Martin Epp. They made the first ascent of the NE Pillar of the Wetterhorn (1963).

Talbot has compiled five guidebooks: *Engelhorner and Salbitschijen* (1968), *Bernina Alps* (with R. Collomb) (1968), *Central Switzerland* (1969), *Gower Peninsula* (1970), *Kaisergebirge* (1971).

TAPE
Nylon tapes of various thicknesses are used by climbers for runners (*qv*) and étriers (*qv*). Three types of tape exist: soft, stiff and tubular – the names are self-explanatory. The breaking loads of tapes vary widely and they seem to be slightly lowered when wet (approx. 6½ per cent). The following are examples of breaking loads:

½ in. stiff	1,600 lb
1 in. stiff	3,000 lb
1 in. soft	4,000 lb
1½ in. stiff	4,750 lb
1 in. tubular	4,200 lb

There are other sizes available up to 2 in. wide. Tape is tied with special tape knot (see KNOTS).

TATRA
The highest mountains between the Alps and Caucasus, lying on the border between Czechoslovakia and Poland. The Tatra are part of the Carpathians, but the rest of that range is wooded and rounded. The best centre is Zakopane in Poland, a well-known ski resort.

The Tatra can be divided into the Low Tatra and High Tatra. The Low Tatra are in the west of the group and are mainly limestone. The High Tatra are granite peaks, shapely, with many fine faces and ridges. The highest summit is Gerlach (2,663 m). The rock faces are usually between 300 and 600 m high and among the hardest climbs are those on the Pulpit Rock, Maly Ganek N Face, Mnich E Face and Lemnica NW Face, though there are many more; the region boasts over two thousand climbs of all standards in an area only 30 miles long and 10 miles wide. The weather is often poor. There are no glaciers.

Most of the area is covered by the Polish and Czech National Parks, where walking and camping is strictly controlled, though members of alpine clubs have special privileges. There are good huts in all the valleys. Skiing is popular in winter and hard winter ascents are made frequently, too.

TAYLOR, Charles (1840-1908)
The Rev. Charles Taylor was a companion of the Pendleburys (*qv*) and with them on the first ascent of Marinelli Couloir.

TAYLOR, Sedley (1834-1920)
Cambridge don and social reformer who helped to found Girton College. A typical all-round Victorian man with interests in music, science and mathematics. He made a number of minor first ascents including that of the Klein Wannehorn (1866).

TEICHELMANN, Ebenezer (1859-1938)
"The little doctor", one of the famous pioneers of the New Zealand Alps and companion of the Graham brothers (*qv*). With Newton and others he made the first ascent of several important peaks including: Douglas, Glacier Peak, Torres, Spencer, Britol Top, Conway Peak, La Perouse, Tyndall, Malcolm (1902-11). A noted photographer.

TÉLÉPHÉRIQUE (E.: Cable car; G.: Seilbahn)
The French word is now in common usage among climbers, probably because of the influence of Chamonix where téléphériques are common and of considerable importance to the mountaineer. Though téléphériques are built for tourists

and skiers, they often help the climber by reducing the time taken to reach a hut, or in some cases a climb itself.

TENZING NORGAY (b. 1914)
The Sherpa who, with Edmund Hillary (*qv*), was the first man to reach the summit of Everest in 1953. Tenzing served as a porter with British expeditions in 1935, 1936 and 1938, and visited the Karakorum in 1950. In 1951 he was Sirdar to the French party which attempted the traverse between Nanda Devi and Nanda Devi East, when Duplat and Vignes were killed. Tenzing and L. Dubost reached the summit of Nanda Devi East (second ascent).

In the following year he was Sirdar and a full member of the Swiss teams to attempt Everest, and with R. Lambert reached a height of about 28,200 ft on the South Ridge.

Tenzing was awarded the George Medal in 1953. He is now Director of Field Training at the Himalayan Mountaineering Institute, Darjeeling. A biography, *Man of Everest* (In America: *Tiger of the Snows*), by J. R. Ullman appeared in 1955.

TERRAY, Lionel (1921-65)
One of the great French guides of the post-war era. With Lachenal he made the second ascent of the Eigerwand in 1947 and repeated many of the classic hard climbs of the immediate pre-war years. He had an outstanding record on expeditions (all first ascents):
1950 Annapurna
1952 FitzRoy*, Huantsan*, Nevado Pongos*
1954 Chomolonzo*, Makalu II*
1956 Nevado Soray*, Nevado Veronica*, Chacaraju West*, Taulliraju*
1962 Jannu*, Chacaraju East*, Nilgiri North*
1964 Alaska–leader of expedition which climbed Huntington
* indicates Terray reached summit
  Terray was killed in a climbing accident at the Vercors.

TETONS, THE, WYOMING
A superb range of granite mountains rising 6,000 to 7,000 ft above the flats of Jackson Hole and the Snake River, which are themselves almost the same height above sea level. The range is about 40 miles long and 15 miles wide. It is part of the Rocky Mountain system and the area forms the Grand Teton National Park, with fine forests of lodgepole pines, beautiful glacial lakes, and waterfalls.

The highest peaks are:
Grand Teton 13,766 ft
Mt Owen 12,922 ft
Middle Teton 12,798 ft
Mt Moran 12,594 ft
South Teton 12,505 ft
Teewinot Mt 12,317 ft
Cloudveil Dome 12,026 ft
Thor Peak 12,018 ft

The first ascent of Grand Teton was made by Spaulding and Owen in 1898, although it is possible that there were earlier ascents in 1872 and 1893. There are now some 20 routes, including:
North Ridge – R. Underhill, F. Fryxell, 1931
North Face – P. Petzold, J. Durrance, 1936

The most difficult summit to reach is that of Mt Owen, climbed in 1930 by Underhill, Henderson, Fryxell and Smith.

The Tetons are very popular and there are professional guides. Climbers in the Park must comply with certain regulations: for example, they must make notification of routes and times taken.

Guidebook: *Guide to the Wyoming Mountains and Wilderness Area*, by O. and L. Bonney.

THIN
A climber's expression meaning that the holds are small and scarce and therefore the climbing at that point is delicate and difficult.

THOMAS, Eustace (1869-1960)
Manchester engineer and designer of the mountain rescue stretcher which bears his name.

Thomas did not take up mountaineering until his late thirties, but went on to create some remarkable endurance records for mountain walks, including the first traverse of the Welsh 3,000s and the Derwent Watershed Walk (Peak District). He made three attempts on the Lake District Fell Record (1919, 1920, 1922) and was finally successful: 66½ miles, 25,500 ft of ascent and descent within the stipulated 24 hours. In 1924 he made the first traverse of the Scottish 4,000s, but used a car between Fort William and the Cairngorms which is no longer allowed.

At the age of 54 he took up Alpine climbing and with the guides Knubel and Lagger climbed 24 major peaks in five weeks. At Knubel's suggestion he later concentrated on peaks of 4,000 m or over and in six years he succeeded in climbing them all: 83 major peaks and 30 smaller ones. He later added minor pinnacles of 4,000 m, including the Aigs. du Diable.

In his sixties he took up gliding and held several records. He then learnt to fly powered aircraft and celebrated his 70th birthday by flying solo to Egypt.

THOMAS, Percy William (1854-94)

A climber who concentrated on new or difficult expeditions in the Alps during the 1870s. Made the first ascent of Cresta del Naso on Lyskamm (1878) and of the Aig. du Chardonnet W Ridge, now the usual finish to the traverse (1879). Made attempts on the Aig. du Géant and the Mittelegi Ridge of the Eiger (1880), but failed.

In 1890 he visited Colorado and made the first ascent of Mt Wilson, the highest peak of the San Juan Mountains.

THOMSON, James Merriman Archer (1863-1912)

The most noted pioneer of Welsh rock-climbing. He took a post as a teacher at Bangor in 1884, but his first climb seems to have been in the Lake District (Deep Ghyll, 1890). He did not begin climbing in Wales until 1894 when he quickly established a new school of climbing rivalling that of the Lakes. He raised gully-climbing to new standards and later, with Andrews and Eckenstein particularly, open-face climbing, especially on Lliwedd.

By 1896 Thomson had made 14 new climbs (there had previously been only 12 climbs in the whole of Snowdonia). These included the Second Pinnacle Rib (1894), Tryfan, and his famous ascent in March 1895 of the Devil's Kitchen, when it was iced up, using a hatchet from Ogwen Cottage to cut steps. During this period, too, he tackled the gullies of Glyder Fawr.

Two later gullies were also of importance: the Black Cleft of Dinas Mot (1897) – long thought one of the hardest climbs in Wales – and the Great Gully of Craig yr Ysfa (1900).

But it was Lliwedd that drew him most. His first route was the minor one called Intermediate Route (1894). Then came:

1894 Bilberry Terrace Route (the only one he did not lead)
1896 East Gully
1897 Craig yr Aderyn Route
1898 Elliptical Route
1903 Central Route
1904 Bracket Gully; Route II; Direct Route
1905 The Cracks; Horned Crag Route
1907 Girdle Traverse; Needle Traverse Climb; The Great Chimney; Avalanche Route; Red Wall Finish; West Wall of Great Chimney
1908 Rocker Route
1909 Three Pinnacle Route
1912 Child's Face

The Girdle Traverse was a new invention in 1907; since copied on almost every cliff. In their day, these Lliwedd climbs were regarded as suitable only for the most advanced experts.

Thomson "discovered" many of the Welsh cliffs: Idwal Slabs, Glyder Fawr, Craig yr Ysfa, Clogwyn y Person, Cyrn Las, Ysgolion Duon, Pillar of Elidyr. Perhaps because he had such a wide choice, and because his favourite cliff was Lliwedd, relatively few of his climbs are popular today. It is ironical that when the Abrahams and Jones (qv) visited Wales in 1899, the few routes they put up should remain much more popular than those of Thomson.

The Abrahams came to compile a guidebook, and it was this that convinced Thomson that guidebooks by local experts were needed, though he was originally against the idea. With Andrews he wrote *Climbs on Lliwedd* (1909) and, alone, *Climbing in the Ogwen District* (1910). He refused to use any classification (such as Jones had done), but here again, future events proved him wrong.

Thomson rose to be Headmaster of a Llandudno school. He died suddenly in 1912.

THREAD BELAY

Can be a runner or a static belay (qv). The belay loop is threaded behind a chockstone firmly embedded in a crack or some similar opening. For difficult threads a piece of bent wire, known as a threader, might be used to help matters.

THREE-POINT CONTACT

The basic rule of balance climbing. Of the four limbs, three should always be in contact with the rock, in other words, only one limb should be moved at a time.

THREE CLIFFS, THE

An obsolescent name for Clogwyn y Grochan, Carreg Wastad and Dinas Cromlech on the north side of Llanberis Pass, Snowdonia. The name seems to derive from a wartime guidebook published by the Climbers' Club: *Three Cliffs in Llanberis*, by J. E. Q. Barford (1944).

J. M. Edwards began climbing on Dinas Cromlech in 1931 and on the other cliffs in 1935, and all the early routes are his, notably:

1931 Spiral Stairs, Dinas Cromlech
      Flying Buttress, Dinas Cromlech
1935 Shadow Wall, Carreg Wastad
      Crackstone Rib, Carreg Wastad
      Hazel Groove, Grochan
1940 Brant, Grochan
      Slape, Grochan

It was Edwards's acceptance of the imperfect rock of these cliffs which helped to open the way for post-war developments. The cliffs played the most significant part in modern developments of anywhere in Britain, with the possible exception of Cloggy (*qv*), and Stanage (*qv*). Harding, Moulam, Brown and Whillans among others were responsible. Significant routes include:

1947 Spectre – Harding, Phillips
      Ivy Sepulchre – Harding
1948 Kaisergebirge Wall – Harding, Disley, Moulam
      Overlapping Wall, Carreg Wastad – Hughes, solo
1949 Phantom Rib, Grochan – Pigott, Miss Kennedy-Frazer, Stock
      Unicorn, Wastad – Harding, Hodgkinson, Hughes
      Lion, Wastad – Harding, Moulam
      Brant Direct, Grochan – Harding
1951 Hangover, Grochan – Brown, Greenall, Sorrel, Ashton
      Cemetary Gates, Dinas Cromlech – Brown, Whillans
1952 Cenotaph Corner, Dinas Cromlech – Brown, Belshaw
1953 Surplomb, Grochan – Brown, Whillans
      Sickle, Grochan – Brown, Cowan
      Erosion Groove, Carreg Wastad – Whillans, Allen, Cowan, White
1955 Erosion Groove Direct, Carreg Wastad – Whillans, Brown
1956 Cromlech Girdle, Dinas Cromlech – Brown, Whillans

Though a few "last problems" were climbed later, discovery moved away to other cliffs, leaving the Three Cliffs as a popular playground for Everyman. (See also LLANBERIS PASS and individual cliffs and climbers.)

Guidebook: *Llanberis North*, by D. T. Roscoe.

THROUGH ROUTE
If a chockstone in a gully or chimney leaves a hole through which a climber can pass, it is known as a through route.

THRUTCH
A north country expression meaning a hard push, and used to indicate strenuous body cracks or, loosely, any strenuous piece of climbing.

TIBESTI
A mountainous area in the middle of the Sahara Desert (Chad). The mountains are of volcanic origin, but the rock is said to be very poor for climbing. Visited by several post-war expeditions. The highest summit is Emi Koussi (11,204 ft).

TIEN SHAN
An important range of mountains north of the Pamirs (*qv*), lying on the border between the Kirgiz Republic of the U.S.S.R. and Sinkiang Province of China. Not as bleak as the Pamirs, the Tien Shan have some magnificent peaks, including many over 21,000 ft. The highest peak is Peak Pobeda (24,407 ft), not identified until 1946 and climbed in 1956 by V. Abalakov and others. It is the second highest peak of the U.S.S.R. The ascent has been repeated, but the mountain is remote and several climbers have been killed in attempts. Khan-Tengri (22,949 ft) was long thought to be the highest summit of the Tien Shan. It was climbed by M. T. Pogrebetsky's party in 1931.

TIERRA DEL FUEGO
"The Land of Fire" – an island at the southern tip of South America, the notorious Cape Horn. The principal peaks are the Darwin Range and the highest summit is Mt Darwin (8,700 ft), climbed by Shipton's expedition in 1962. Nearer the Magellan Strait is Mt Sarmiento (7,546 ft) "the Weisshorn of Chile", climbed by C. Mauri and C. Maffei in 1956. The weather in the area is notoriously bad.

TIGER
A complimentary name given to someone who is a good climber, though the term is becoming obsolescent.

The name originated from that given to the 15 Sherpas who were fit enough to go to the North Col and beyond in the 1924 Everest Expedition. Later, a register of Sherpas was formed and those who were particularly distinguished in their work were awarded a Tiger's Badge by the Himalayan Club.

TILMAN, Harold William (b. 1898)
Explorer, mountaineer, sailor and writer. Bill Tilman was a planter in Kenya between 1919 and 1933, when he visited the main East African mountains and also the Himalaya. His most notable ascent of the period was the first traverse of Nelion – Batian on Mt Kenya, with Shipton (*qv*) in 1930. In 1934 he and Shipton succeeded in forcing the entrance to the Nanda Devi basin through the Rishi Ganga – a problem which had defeated several strong parties. In 1936, with Odell (*qv*), Tilman reached the summit of Nanda Devi, the first ascent (25,645 ft).

Like Shipton, Tilman was a strong believer in the small expedition and he tried this out to a certain degree when he was given command of the 1938 Everest Expedition. Bad weather ruined the attempt and results were inconclusive.

During the Second World War Tilman fought with Balkan partisans, but 1947 found him exploring Sinkiang, where he returned the following year. On the opening of Nepal in 1949 Tilman was quickly on the scene, exploring the headwaters of the Trisuli Gandaki. The following year he led an attempt on Annapurna IV.

Tilman then turned his attention to combining sailing with mountain exploration, particularly in Greenland and Patagonia. In 1956 he made the first traverse of the Southern Patagonian Ice-cap. His converted fishing boat, *Mischief*, has become famous through his numerous books on her travels.

Tilman has always been one of the most popular travel writers. His books are: *Ascent of Nanda Devi* (1937), *Snow on the Equator* (1938), *Mount Everest 1938* (1948), *Two Mountains and a River* (1949), *China to Chitral* (1951), *Nepal Himalaya* (1952) and six *Mischief* books, 1957-72.

TODHUNTER, Ralph (1867-1926)
A fine rock-climber who made a number of first ascents in the Alps and was with H. O. Jones and G. W. Young on the first ascent of the Mer de Glace face of Grépon (1911). One of the first to explore Clogwyn du'r Arddu (East Gully, with Mallory, 1905).

TÖDI RANGE
a range of mountains extending from Göschenan in the west to Sargans in the east and forming the north flank of the upper Vorder Rhine. The highest point is Tödi (3,620 m), but other peaks of interest include Oberalpstock (3,328 m) and Bifertenstock (3,425 m). The peaks are generally easy but there is considerable rock-climbing of high quality. Several huts. The Glärnisch (2,914 m), further north, is a similar but lower area. (No English guidebook.)

TOPHAM BROTHERS
Harold Ward Topham (1857–1915) was a naturally gifted expert at "outdoor activities" before such a phrase was known. Sailing, skating, tobogganing (three times winner on the Cresta Run) and cyclist, he was also a fine climber with many first ascents of routes which have become classics. These include: Mittaghorn–Egginer Traverse, 1886 (but also accredited to Seymour King, 1882), SW arête of Fletschorn (1887), Cresta Signal of Monte Rosa (1887), E arête of Mont Blanc de Cheilon (1887) and traverse of the Aigs. Rouges d'Arolla (1887).

In 1888, with his brother Edwin, he made the first exploration of the Selkirks, and later, with Williams and Broke, went to Alaska to attempt Mt St Elias. The attempt failed at 11,375 ft on the S Ridge. Two years later (1890) he was back in the Selkirks making the first ascents of Mt Donkin, Mt Fox, Mt Selwyn, Mt Sugarloaf and Mt Purity. Some years later Mt Topham was named in his honour.

Alfred George Topham (1862-1920) made a number of first ascents in the Arolla district including the N Face of Pigne d'Arolla (1889) and the S Peak of the Bouquetins (1894). He also made the first direct ascent of the Arrowhead on Great Gable (1896).

TOPO
Short for "topographical picture". A photograph of a crag or mountain with the routes superimposed on it by means of lines. Used in many guidebooks.

TOP ROPE (Fr.: Aide extérieure)
A rope held from above. A second is naturally on a top rope but the term is reserved for special circumstances:
1. Short climbs where the rope is taken to the top by an easy way, belayed, and the free end lowered, i.e. the climb has not been led. Often used on outcrops for the training of novices since it saves time.
2. A leader in difficulty may call for a top rope from a party above to overcome some

pitch. Not common.

Some new climbs and difficult pitches are first led by top rope tactics (e.g. Flake Crack, Scafell), then led "clean". The old term was "inspection on a rope held from above".

On very short crags e.g. Harrisons Rocks (qv), it is possible to pass the rope round a belay such as a tree at the top and handle the rope from the ground.

TOTES GEBIRGE
A region of limestone mountains east of Bad Ischl in Austria. The highest peak is Grosser Priel (2,514m). Several huts, and the region is readily accessible. (No English guidebook.)

TRAGSITZ
A chair-like device used in mountain rescue for lowering injured climbers from a steep rock face. In certain cases of injury (e.g. the spine) a full stretcher will have to be used.

TRAVERSE (G.: Quergang, Überschreitung)
Literally, to cross. To traverse a mountain means to go up by one route and down by another, for example, to traverse the Matterhorn by going up the Hörnli Ridge and down the Italian Ridge. Frequently regarded as the most satisfying method of accomplishing a mountain ascent.

In the course of a climb, to traverse means to make moves leading to the left or right, rather than up. A girdle traverse is a climb which goes from one side of a crag to the other, rather than bottom to top. The first girdle traverse was Lliwedd, Wales (1907).

TRAVERS-JACKSON, George Francis (1880-1964)
One of the founders of climbing in South Africa with many first ascents on Table Mountain and elsewhere.

TREMADOC
A name used to denote a series of low-level cliffs close to the Welsh coast, above the village of the same name. Often enjoys better weather than the main Snowdon areas.

The cliffs are Craig y Gesail, Craig y Castell, Craig Pant Ifan and Craig Bwlch y Moch. Routes rarely exceed 300 ft and are mostly in the higher grades.

Tremadoc was one of the outstanding post-war discoveries. The first route was Hound's Head Buttress (Craig Pant Ifan) (Moulam and Sutton, 1951) and among many other good climbs, Vector (J. Brown and C. E. Davies, 1960) is perhaps most notable. The crag had tremendous vogue in the sixties and is still popular.

Guidebooks: Snowdon South, by T. Jones; and Tremadoc Area, by P. Crew and A. Harris.

TRIANGULATION POINT (TRIG POINT)
A summit used as a datum point by the Ordnance Survey. Shown on maps as a triangle and identified on the ground as a pillar of concrete or stone with brass fittings on top. In the Alps a similar point may be marked by a wooden pyramid, but this is not universal. (See SUMMIT.)

TRIBE, Wilberforce Newton (1855-1928)
One of the pioneers of British rock-climbing, friend of the Hopkinson's (qv). In 1870 he made the first ascent of Sgurr a' Ghreadaidh in Skye, with the 14 year old John Mackenzie (qv): one of the first to visit the island for climbing. In 1887 he was with the Hopkinsons on Scafell when they descended the face and erected Hopkinson's Cairn, and in 1893, with C. Hopkinson, he did Hopkinson's and Tribe's Route on the same crag. He also made the first British ascent of the Romsdalhorn. Tribe was President of the Bristol Stock Exchange.

TROG
Colloquialism for a walk – usually implies that it is long or arduous. One hears of "a hut trog" (the walk to an Alpine hut) and "just a trog" (an easy ascent). Walking boots are sometimes called trog boots.

TROTTER, Sir Henry (1841-1919)
While a captain attached to the Great Trigonometrical Survey of India of which he was Deputy Superintendent, Trotter accompanied Forsyth's Second Yarkand Mission of 1873-4. With others from the mission he helped to survey unknown territory in the Tien Shan and Pamir Mountains, crossing numerous high passes.

TRYFAN (3,010 ft)
A fine mountain in Snowdonia, overlooking Llyn Ogwen. Its rocky appearance makes it one of the most impressive peaks in Britain and accounts for its huge popularity. Some easy scrambling is almost essential for an ascent, even on the tourist

routes. The summit is marked by two upstanding fingers of rock known as Adam and Eve.

Tryfan is a popular rock-climbing mountain, the principal areas being the East Face and the Milestone Buttress (*qv*). Most of the routes are in the easier and middle grades of difficulty and are fairly long: a paradise for novices. The first rock-climb on the mountain was South Gully, climbed by R. Williams in 1887. Other notable ascents are:

1894 Second Pinnacle Rib – J. M. A. Thomson and H. Hughes
1899 North Buttress – O. G. Jones and Abraham brothers
Terrace Wall Variant – O.. G. Jones and Abraham brothers
Milestone Ordinary – O. G. Jones and Abraham brothers
1902 Gashed Crag – H. B. Buckle and G. Barlow
1911 Grooved Arête – Steeple, Woodhead, Barlow, Bowron, Doughty
1914 Overlapping Rib – Steeple, Barlow, Doughty
1927 Belle Vue Bastion – I. M. Waller and C. H. S. R. Palmer
1936 Munich Climb – Teufel, Seldmayr, Jenkins, Scheuhuber, Reiss, and Brandt.
Scars Climb – Noyce and Edwards
Soap Gut – Noyce and Edwards.

Guidebook: *Tryfan and Glyder Fach*, by A. J. J. Moulam.

TUCKER, Charles Comyns (1843-1922)
A companion of Freshfield (*qv*) with whom he made a number of first ascents, including Kasbek and Elbruz in the Caucasus (1868). Tucker later turned his attention to the Dolomites, making the first ascents of the Cima di Brenta (1871), Cima della Vezzana (1872) and the Rosengartenspitze (1874).

TUCKETT, Francis Fox (1834-1913)
A Bristol businessman who was one of the foremost explorers of the Alps, rivalling Ball (*qv*). He made the first ascent of the Aletschhorn (1859) and was with Stephen (*qv*) on the first complete ascent of the Goûter route up Mont Blanc (1861). His exploration of the Dauphiné in 1862 opened up this wild area and paved the way for Whymper and others.

He spent many seasons in the Eastern Alps where he made a number of first ascents and where his name is commemorated in the Rif. Tuckett of the Brenta Group.

Tuckett was an inveterate traveller and climbed in many (then) unknown places including Corsica, Greece, Norway, Pyrenees and Algeria. The *A.C.* Register credits him with 269 peaks and 687 passes.

He refused the presidency of the A.C. on business grounds. Though he wrote no books as such, a collection of his papers, entitled *Hochalpenstudien* was published in Germany in 1873, and his diaries and letters of 1856-74 were published in 1920 under the title, *A Pioneer in the High Alps*.

TURKEY CLIMBING IN
The principal mountains of Turkey are: the Taurus, bordering the Mediterranean; the Canik or Pontine Mountains, bordering the Black Sea; Erciyas Dag, near Kayseri; the Cilo Dag and Sat Dag of the Lake Van region; and Ararat, in the extreme east, near the Armenian border. Most of them offer prospects of discovery by modest expeditions, and the Cilo and Sat Dags in particular have a certain popularity in this respect. The heights are 12,000 to 13,000 ft and the rock is sometimes dubious. The highest peaks in each area are:

Cilo Dag, Geliasin (13,681 ft)
Sat Dag, Hendevade (12,500 ft)
Canik Mountains, Kackar (12,917 ft)
Erciyas Dag, Erciyas (12,850 ft)
Taurus, Kaldi Dag (12,,251 ft)
Ararat, Ararat (16,916 ft)

According to Genesis, the ascent of Ararat was made by Noah – it is certainly the earliest recorded ascent of a high peak, and unusual in that it was made by boat! Expeditions seeking the Ark have been made, and various claims put forward. Sceptics may prefer to believe that the ascent of J. J. F. W. Parrot in 1829, was the first ascent of the mountain.

TURNER, Samuel (1869-1929)
A Manchester man who climbed in various parts of the world and recorded his exploits in three books: *My Climbing Adventures in Four Continents, Siberia*, and *The Conquest of the N. Z. Alps*. His unconventional attitude, especially in ignoring the establishment, caused considerable antagonism and his books were heavily criticized. Turner died in New Zealand.

TYING ON
Using the main rope: (a) The waist tie. The rope is passed round the waist and tied with a bowline and two half hitches. Still frequently used by British climbers. (b)

The chest tie. The rope is passed round the chest, tucked under itself then over one shoulder, under the back of the chest loop and back over the other shoulder to be finished off with a bowline. Favoured by some Continentals, but rather awkward for rock-climbing. (c) Waistlength method. A length of stout hemp, made for the purpose is wrapped round the body and tied with a reef knot. A screwgate karabiner is clipped over all the strands of the waistlength. A loop is then made in the end of the rope and clipped on to the karabiner. The loop should be formed using a Tarbuck knot (see KNOTS), which employs the greatest elasticity of the rope in the event of a fall, but it is common practice to use a bowline or even two figure-of-eight knots. The Tarbuck is difficult to tie and sometimes has a tendency to come undone.

None of the above methods does much to reduce the impact of the rope in the event of a fall. This can cause severe bruising or even worse in extreme cases. Furthermore, it is not possible to hang from a rope for more than a few minutes without falling unconscious. Harnesses and baudriers (qv) are now becoming normal wear.

TYNDALE, Harry Edmund Guise (1888-1948)
A member of the Ice Club formed at Winchester School by Irving (qv), of which the best-known member was Mallory (qv). Tyndale features in the writings of both these men and was himself translator of several climbing books from German to English, and editor of a series of Alpine classics brought out by Blackwells, as well as the *Alpine Journal*.

TYNDALL, John (1820-93)
Rose from humble Irish origins to become one of the outstanding scientists of the Victorian age, working with Faraday and finally succeeding him at the Royal Institution. His early Alpine exploits were mostly concerned with glaciers and he was one of the protagonists of the great glacier controversy which raged throughout the latter half of the century. His *Glaciers of the Alps* (1860) was one of the highlights of the argument; his chief opponent was Forbes (qv).

From 1860, he turned to the more competitive element of climbing with an attempt on the Matterhorn, reaching the Great Tower on the Italian Ridge, then the highest point reached. In 1862 he made another attempt and reached the Shoulder, now called Pic Tyndall. Whymper saw in Tyndall a serious rival, but in fact Tyndall did not return to the mountain until 1868 (three years after the first ascent) when he made the first traverse from Breuil to Zermatt via the Italian and Hörnli Ridges.

Meanwhile, in 1861, he made the first ascent of Weisshorn; it was news of this success which made Whymper concentrate on the still unclimbed Matterhorn.

Tyndall was quick to take offence and rouse passions. He resigned from the A.C. (he was Vice-President at the time) over a joke made by Stephen about the place of science in climbing; fell out with Whymper over details of the Matterhorn; and, of course, with Forbes over glaciers. Later in his life he made some disastrous excursions into politics which tarnished his scientific reputation.

Tyndall described his Alpine experiences in *The Glaciers of the Alps* (1860) and *Hours of Exercise in the Alps* (1871).

TYROLEAN TRAVERSE
A sensational way of crossing a deep gap, usually to gain some otherwise inaccessible pinnacle. There are two methods, one for short gaps and one for longer gaps. In both cases the pinnacle has to be lassoed.
1. *Position assise*. A double rope is passed over the pinnacle and the climber sits astride both, pushing them apart. He pulls himself along by his hands.
2. *Position pendue*. For longer gaps. When the rope is secured to the pinnacle the climber hangs from it by his hands and one leg, crooked over the rope. He pulls himself along.

In both cases a safety rope is essential and it is usual for the climber to clip himself by a short line to the Tyrolean rope so that he won't swing if he comes off.

The name comes from the Dolomites (South Tyrol) where the method is used on the Guglia di Amacis, but the technique is uncommon. In Britain it has been used on some sea-stacks.

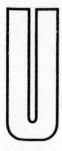

UNDERHILL, Miriam and Robert L. M. Two of the best-known American climbers of the pre-war era. As Miriam O'Brien, before her marriage to Bob Underhill, Mrs Underhill did notable climbs in the New England mountains, the Dolomites and at Chamonix: a number of first ascents and many first ascents by a woman. She was in the first all-women ascent of the Matterhorn and Grépon, and made the first ski traverse of Monte Rosa, Gressoney–Zermatt (1930). In Chamonix she made the first ascent of the Aig. du Roc (A. Couttet, G. Cachat, 1927) and the first traverse of the Aigs. du Diable (R. L. M. Underhill, A. Charlet, G. Cachat, 1928).

As man and wife they climbed together many times in Europe and America. Robert Underhill played a part in founding Yosemite climbing (*qv*). Miriam Underhill wrote *Give Me the Hills* (1956).

UNION INTERNATIONALE DES ASSOCIATIONS D'ALPINISM (U.I.A.A.)
An international body with representatives from the various countries which have mountaineering clubs. Lays down specifications for climbing equipment standards and discusses all matters of concern to climbers including conservation of mountain areas. Meets annually in various member countries in turn. The B. M. C. (*qv*) represents Britain.

UNITED STATES, CLIMBING IN
the mountains of the United States are so varied in character and so numerous, that they offer the climber a whole spectrum of climbing experience from expeditions of Himalayan size in the remote peaks of Alaska, through the Alpine-style ascents of the Tetons, to the hard rock-climbs of Yosemite and the eastern outcrops. These are dealt with under the relevant sections.

In 1876 the Appalachian Mountain Club was formed, followed by the Sierra Club in 1892 and the American Alpine Club in 1902. It is true to say that these mostly followed the pattern of climbing the easier routes up the higher peaks, many of which had been previously climbed by soldiers, surveyors, miners and general adventurers which the West had attracted. At the same time, many Americans went to the European Alps for climbing, including, of course, Coolidge and Miss Brevoort (*qv*). The standard began to rise after the First World War when climbers like R. Underhill and Miriam O'Brien began difficult ascents in the Tetons. In 1931 Underhill taught rock-climbing skills to some Californians who went on to develop the Yosemite. In the 1930s a further boost was added by the arrival of F. Wiessner from Europe, who developed the Shawangunks. Expeditional climbs to Alaska were done by F. Beckey, Bradford Washburn and others. In recent years American climbers have established themselves as equal to any in the world, whether at rock-climbing or expeditionary work.

See the following sections: ALASKA, CASCADES, COLORADO ROCKIES, NEW ENGLAND, SHAWANGUNKS, SHIPROCK, SIERRA NEVADA (CALIF.), TETONS, WHITE MOUNTAINS, WIND RIVER MOUNTAINS, YOSEMITE.

See also the following guidebooks:
A Climber's Guide to Tahquitz and Suicide Rocks, Calif., by C. Wilts
Climber's Guide to the High Sierra, by A. Smatko
A Climber's Guide to Joshua Tree National Monument, by J. Wolfe
A Climber's Guide to Yosemite Valley, by S. Roper
Climbers' and Hikers' Guide to Devil's Lake, by D. Smith
Adirondack Mountain Guide, – Adirondack Mountain Club
Monadock Guide, by H. I. Baldwin
Shawangunk Guide, by A. Gran
A Climber's Guide to Oregon, by N. A. Dodge
Maine Mountain Guide, – Appalachian Mountain Club
Guide to the Wyoming Mountains and Wilderness Areas, by O. and L. Bonney
Climber's Guide to the Cascade and Olympic Mts. of Washington, by F. Beckey
White Mountain Guide – Appalachian Mountain Club
Climber's Guide to Seneca Rocks, West Virginia, by F. R. Robinson
A Tourist's Guide to Mount McKinley, by B. Washburn

VALLOT BROTHERS

Joseph Vallot (1853-1925) and his brother, Henri, erected an observatory and refuge hut on Mont Blanc at their own expense. The hut figures in many accounts of climbing on Mont Blanc and is an essential part of the climbing there. It has probably saved more lives than any other hut, even the Solvay on the Matterhorn (qv). The brothers spent 40 years on a detailed survey of the region, culminating in the *Carte Vallot*, published posthumously.

VENEDIGER-GLOCKNER GROUPS

a group of mountains in East Tirol, which includes Gross Glockner (3,797 m), the highest peak in Austria. The highest of the Venediger group is the Gross Venediger (3,674 m). The peaks are mostly easy. (No English guidebook.)

VERCORS

An area of limestone peaks near Grenoble, offering very hard climbs on steep faces. The best-known peak is Mont Aiguille (qv). Further north, the Grand Chartreuse offers climbs of a similar kind.

Guidebook: *Selected Climbs in the Dauphiné and Vercors*, by E. Wrangham and J. Brailsford.

VERGLAS (Fr.) (It.: Vetrato)

Thin ice lying on rocks and making climbing difficult. May be general in cold conditions, but often, in the Alps, it is a local condition confined to some feature which gets no sun, e.g. a verglassed chimney might occur on an otherwise sunny rock face. Thick verglas can sometimes be tackled in crampons with advantage.

Mountain paths can also become icy and dangerous in cold conditions, even though there may be no snow about. On some crags and many Alpine peaks very cold conditions are an advantage because the ice binds together rock which might otherwise be loose. (See HOAR FROST.)

VIBRAM SOLES

sometimes called commando soles: both are trade names of well-known cleated moulded rubber soles; there are others. Obsolescent slang: vibs. Vibrams were introduced in Italy just prior to the war (1935) and were used in the first ascent of the Walker Spur and N Face of the Dru. They gained immediate favour in Britain in the post-1945 period. They have a number of advantages over nails (qv) and are now in universal use, except on certain lightweight rock boots where smooth rubber soles are preferred.

VISSER, Philips Christiaan (1882-1955)

Distinguished Dutch diplomat and mountain explorer who, with his wife, Jenny van't Visser-Hooft, made four journeys to the Karakorum in 1922, 1925, 1929-30, and 1935, which unravelled many of the glacier problems of the region. Mrs Visser Hooft wrote *Among the Kara-Korum Glaciers* (1926) in English and together they wrote (in German) *Karakorum* (2 vols), 1935, 1938.

VOLCANO

Any opening in the earth's surface through which magma flows, but here we take the common interpretation of the word to mean a mountain formed by such activity. They are built up of layers of lava and pyroclastic materials (i.e. material ejected by the volcano). The pyroclastic materials can vary in size from bombs or blocks (over $1\frac{1}{4}$ in. diameter) to fine ash.

The usual volcanic form is a symmetrical cone, well illustrated by Fujiyama, Japan. If we take their *true* heights, then some volcanoes are among the highest mountains in the world: Mauna Loa, Hawaii is 30,000 ft above its base on the sea bed.

Though there is a well-defined volcano belt around the Pacific, many volcanoes exist outside it, including such well-known mountains as Vesuvius and Kilimanjaro. These, and other volcanoes which are rarely active, such as Cotopaxi, are climbed quite frequently. Attempts are also made to climb active volcanoes (though not during eruptions!). A great many of the world's mountains are originally of volcanic origin.

WAGER, Lawrence Rickard (1904–65)

A member of the 1933 Everest Expedition, when, with Wyn Harris, he equalled the height record for that time of 28,126 ft. They also found the famous axe which must have belonged to Mallory or Irvine (qv). On the return, Wager climbed to the crest of the NE Ridge and looked over the E Face and into the Karma Valley, the only man known to have done so.

With the exception of 1933, Wager was in Greenland every season from 1930-6 and he returned there in 1953. As a professional geologist, he was in the great tradition of accomplished geologist-mountaineers and received many awards for his work. When he died, he was Professor of Geology at Oxford.

WAINEWRIGHT, Benjamin (1853-1910)

A London eye surgeon noted for his ascents in the Bernina, including the first ascent of Piz Prievalus (1882). A number of his routes on Roseg, Scerscen, Bernina were later added to or improved by other climbers who have subsequently been given the credit.

WAKEFIELD, Arthur William (1876-1949)

A Keswick doctor who established the Lakeland Fell Record in its present form. He set up a new record in 1904 and improved it a year later: 59 miles, 23,500 ft, 22 hr. 7 min. This stood until Thomas (qv) bettered it in 1920 – paced by Wakefield.

Wakefield began climbing with the Abrahams (qv) and took part in a number of first ascents. He left for the Grenfell Mission shortly afterwards, and did not recommence his climbing activities until his return after the 1914-18 War. In 1920 he took part with Bower and Masson in the first ascent of the popular Bower's Route on Esk Buttress, Scafell. He took part in the 1922 Everest Expedition and reached the North Col. He also made a number of ascents in the Alps and Canadian Rockies (1908, 1920).

WALKER, Francis (1808–72)

A Liverpool merchant and father of Horace and Lucy Walker (qv). Frank Walker did not begin climbing until he was 50. With his family in 1864 he made the first ascent of Balmhorn and the fourth ascent of the Eiger. In 1865, with Lucy, he made the second crossing of the Moming Pass, before joining his son, Moore and G. S. Mathews for their historic first ascent of the Brenva Face of Mont Blanc. In 1871, at the age of 63, he climbed the Matterhorn with Lucy but he was already a sick man and he died the following year.

WALKER Horace (1838-1908)

Son of Frank Walker and brother of Lucy (qv), Horace Walker was one of the most important climbers throughout the Victorian era. He always seemed to have the happy facility of being in the right place at the right time with the right people.

His first ascent was the Vélan at the age of 16 and his last the Pollux at the age of 67. In between he made numerous ascents – the list occupies six pages of the A.C. Register.

His first ascents include: Écrins (1864), Balmhorn (1864), Piz Roseg (1865), Gabelhorn (1865), Pigne d'Arolla (1865), Brenva Face of Mont Blanc (1865), Grandes Jorasses Point Walker, (1868), Elbruz (Caucasus 1874), and many new routes on peaks already climbed. He also made numerous second or third ascents and crossed many new cols. He ranged from the Dauphiné to the Tyrol and Dolomites.

Walker was an early advocate of winter climbing (1869, 1879) and, influenced by the Pilkingtons and their friends, began guideless climbing about 1894, including such peaks as Mont Blanc and Piz Bernina.

He was also one of the pioneers of climbing in Skye, where he made several first ascents, and he took enthusiastically to climbing in Snowdonia and the Lake District. In 1892 he made the second ascent of North Climb, Pillar Rock.

Walker was President of the A.C. from 1890-2. He was unmarried.

WALKER, Lucy (1835-1916)

Daughter of Frank Walker (qv) and sister of Horace (qv), Lucy Walker was one of the earliest women climbers. Though she climbed only with her family, guided by the famous Anderegg cousins (*qv*), she made several notable ascents including the first ascent of the Balmhorn (1864): the first time in which a woman had taken part in a major first ascent. She also took part in the fourth ascent of the Eiger (1864) and the second crossing of the Moming Pass (1865). In 1871, with her father, she climbed the Matterhorn – the first woman to do so and the nineteenth ascent.

After the death of her father in 1872, Lucy continued to climb with her brother for a few years, but then gave it up and confined herself to valley walks with her lifelong companion, Melchior Anderegg. She never married. Her portrait appears in Whymper's well-known engraving, *The Club Room at Zermatt in 1864*.

WALL (G.: Wand; Fr.: Face, Muraille, Paroi; It.: Muraglia, Parete)

The sheer face of a mountain, e.g. Eiger North Wall. English climbers interchange the word indescrimately with 'face' and either is correct – it would be pedantic to use different words for French and German-named mountains. Rarely used in connection with British mountains, though occasionally the term 'North Face of Ben Nevis' is used. Invariably used for Alpine and greater mountains. (See also NORTH FACE)

In English rock-climbing the word is more localized. It means rock above approximately 75°, that is steeper than a slab, and possibly overhanging.

WALLER, Ivan Mark (b. 1906)

A daring rock-climber of the inter-war years who took part in a number of first ascents of well-known climbs. In 1927 he made the first ascent of Belle View Bastion, Tryfan with C. H. S. R. Palmer, and a few weeks later made the second ascent, solo. Later that year he led Fallen Block Crack, Clogwyn y Ddisgl, when the second man failed to follow. In 1931 he seconded Kirkus (*qv*) on Mickledore Grooves, Scafell, and the West Rib, Dinas Mot. He also took part in the most notable ascents at the Black Rocks, Derbyshire: he was second to Longland on Birch Tree Wall (1928) and to Bridge on Lean Man's Superdirect (1930). In 1928 he made the first ascent, solo, of Lone Tree Groove.

During the Whitsun of 1951, Waller made a remarkable ski descent of the E Face of Helvellyn from the summit to Red Tarn.

WALTON, Elijah (1832-80)

A noted Alpine artist of his day. Illustrated many climbing books by T. G. Bonney (*qv*).

WARD, Michael Phelps (b.1925)

A consulting surgeon who took part in the Mount Everest expeditions of 1951 and 1953. In 1960-1 he climbed a number of peaks in the Everest region, including Ama Dablam (22,500ft). He 1964-5 he explored the little-known mountains of Bhutan and made a number of first ascents.

Ward also took part in the first ascent of the E Ridge of Bugaboo Spire (Canada) and in Britain was with Edwards on the first ascent of the Direct Finish to Longland's Climb, Clogwyn du'r Arddu (1947), and led the first ascent of Angle Groove, Ysfa (1944), Easter Eve, Nevis (1946) and Scimitar Gully, Ben Lui (1972).

He is a leading authority on high-altitude medicine and for this and his explorations has been awarded various distinctions by British and American societies. His books are: *Mountaineer's Companion* (Ed., 1969), *In This Short Span* (autobiography, 1972) and *Man at High Altitude* (1974).

WASDALE HEAD

A small hamlet with an inn, the Wastwater Hotel, in the heart of the Lake District. It was the most important centre of rock-climbing during the pioneer days and is still very popular. The principal crags are the Napes, Scafell and Pillar Rock.

WATKINS, George H. (1907-32)

Gino Watkins was the dynamic prodigy of Arctic exploration from 1927 until his accidental death in 1932. A good rock-climber he did a number of guideless Alpine climbs while still in his 'teens and on going up to Cambridge became interested in Artic exploration. In 1927 he led an expedition to Edge Island, Spitsbergen, and from 1928-9 explored the Quebec – Labrador border.

Watkins considered the possibility of an air route to Canada across the Arctic, learned to fly, and then organized a large-scale expedition to south-east Greenland to survey the route. Among his discoveries was a group of mountains which proved to be the highest in Greenland (Watkins Mountains). For this work Watkins was awarded the Gold Medal of the R.G.S. in 1932. He was then 25.

In 1932 he returned with a smaller

expedition to continue his work in Greenland, but was drowned while out hunting in a kayak.

WEDGE (Fr.: Coin de bois; It.: Cuneo)
Formerly used for protection in cracks which were too big for pegs, wooden wedges have largely been replaced by American hardware such as bongs (see PITONS). A wedge was of the shape suggested by its name and at the wide end it had a small hole through which a nylon loop was tied. A karabiner was attached to the loop when the wedge was in place and the climbing rope ran through the karabiner.

WELSH 3,000s
Name given to a walk embracing all the 14 peaks of 3,000 ft or more in Wales. They are all in Snowdonia (*qv*) and the walk involves about 30 miles and 18,000 ft of ascent and descent. The route is usually: Y Wyddfa, Crib y Ddysgl, Crib Goch (Snowdon massif), Elidyr Fawr, Y Garn, Glyder Fawr, Glyder Fach, Tryfan (Glyders massif), Pen yr Olewen, Carnedd Dafydd, Yr Elen, Carnedd Llewelyn, Foel Grach, Foel Fras (Carneddau). Time taken is reckoned from summit to summit.

The walk was first done by J. R. Corbett and E. Thomas (*qv*) in 1919 in a time of 20 hours. Now one of the most popular long-distance walks.

WELZENBACH, Willo (1900-34)
One of the great school of Munich climbers which arose in the 1920s and of which so many perished on the Alpine Nordwands and in the Himalaya. Welzenbach was the supreme prototype: he was the finest climber of his day and one of the best ice-climbers ever. The tragedy is that many of those who followed later did not have his supreme skill.

He began serious climbing in 1921 and between then and 1926, when a diseased elbow made rock-climbing difficult, he made a number of hard climbs in the Eastern Alps. He added 'Gr. VI' to the existing system, elaborated on how the scale should be used and is generally credited with the invention of it, though it originated with Dulfer. (See GRADES OF DIFFICULTY.)

It is for his ice-climbs that he is best remembered. They are still among the most difficult in the Alps:
1924 NW Face of Gross Wiesbachhorn
1925 N Face Direct, Dent d'Hérens
       N Face, Lyskamm E Peak

1926 NW Face of Glockerin
       N Face of Eiskogele
       N Face of Gross Glockner
       NW Face, Zermatt Breithorn
       Pt Welzenbach, S Ridge of Aig. Noire
1930 N Face Direct, Gross Fiescherhorn
1931 N Face, Grands Charmoz
1932 N Face, Grosshorn
       NE Face, Gspaltenhorn
       NW Face, Gletscherhorn
       N Face Direct, Lauterbrunner Breithorn
1933 N Face, Nesthorn

Ice pitons, invented by his partner F. Rigele, were used for the first time on the Gross Wiesbachhorn.

Welzenbach made plans for an expedition to Nanga Parbat in 1929, but these were frustrated and he did not go out until, against advice, he joined Merkl (*qv*) as second-in-command of the 1934 attempt on the mountain. In the terrible retreat (see NANGA PARBAT) he died in Camp 7.

WESMACOTT, Michael Horatio (b. 1925)
A statistician who was a member of the successful Everest team of 1953. Westmacott made the first ascent of Huagaruncho in Peru in 1956 and eight first ascents in the Arrigetch Range of Alaska, 1964. In 1968 he made the first ascent of Wakhikah Rah in the Hindu Kush.

Westmacott lives in the U.S.A.: he made Sam's Swansong on Cannon Mountain, New York State, in 1965.

WESTON, Walter (1861-1940)
A clergyman who lived in Japan on three occasions between 1888 and the First World War and who became known as the father of Japanese mountaineering. He made several first ascents in the Japanese Alps and aroused an interest in that country that led to the formation of the Japanese Alpine Club in 1905. He received the Order of the Sacred Treasure from the Emperor and in 1937 Japanese climbers erected a plaque in his honour. Weston also climbed in the Alps, particularly the Oberland, where he made the first unguided crossing of the Eigerjoch (1897). All his life Weston was blind in one eye. He had a commanding personality.

WETTERSTEIN GEBIRGE
A small but important group of limestone mountains on the Austro-German border,

235 WHITE GHYLL

immediately south of the ski resort of Garmisch-Partenkirchen. The highest summit is the Zugspitze (2,963 m), easily reached by cable car. Other interesting peaks include: Grosser Waxenstein (2,277 m), Alpspitze (2,628 m), and Partenkirchner Dreitorspitze (2,634 m). Several huts. (No English guidebook.)

THE WHANGIE
Popular local outcrop in the Kilpatrick Hills near Glasgow. Many climbs, mostly short.

WHARNCLIFFE CRAG
In the Don Valley, near Deepcar, Yorkshire. A gritstone crag with numerous climbs of all standards, and the traditional birthplace of gritstone climbing (J. W. Puttrell and W. J. Watson, early 1880s). Strangely enough, it is not true gritstone, but a coarse sandstone. Not very popular today.
Guidebook: *The Sheffield Area* (Rock Climbs in the Peak Vol. 1).

WHEELER, Sir Edward Oliver (1890-1962)
A Canadian from a surveying family who played an important part in the early ascents of the Rockies; climbed Oliver's Peak at age of 12. Joined the Indian Survey and accompanied the first Everest Expedition as surveyor (1921). Discovered the route to the North Col (see EVEREST). Became Surveyor-General of India 1941-7. Knighted 1943.

WHERRY, George Edward (1852-1928)
Surgeon and mountaineer, author of one of the strangest climbing books: *Alpine Notes and the Climbing Foot* (1896). Also wrote *Notes from a Knapsack* (1909) in which one chapter is entitled 'Why both Legs are of Equal Length'.

WHILLANS BOX
A metal-framed tent, box-like, designed for high-altitude camps by Don Whillans (qv). It has more room than a normal tent and is less likely to be crushed by powder snow. Used on several Himalayan expeditions.

WHILLANS, Donald Desbrow (b. 1933)
One of the finest mountaineers of post-war Britain, with ascents to his credit ranging from the gritstone outcrops of Derbyshire to the Himalaya. He began climbing at Shining Clough, Derbyshire, in 1950 and was soon leading the hardest climbs of the

day. In 1951 he met Joe Brown (qv) and they climbed the Direct Start to Valkyrie at the Roches. Later in the same year they climbed Cemetary Gates, Dinas Cromlech and Vember, Clogwyn du'r Arddu. It was the start of the most powerful partnership ever seen in British climbing (for other routes, see BROWN). Their last new climb together was Taurus, 1956.
Whillans also climbed with others during this period in Wales, Scotland and the Lakes. New routes include: Slanting Slab, Clogwyn du'r Arddu (V. Betts, 1955); Strapiombo, Tremadoc (G. J. Sutton, 1955); and the Old Man of Storr (G. J. Sutton, J. Barber, 1955).
In the Alps with Brown, Whillans made a first ascent of the West Face of the Blaitière (1954) and with Bonington, Clough and Dlugosz, the first ascent of the Central Pillar of Freney (1961). He took part in several early British ascents of classic routes, including the W Face of the Dru, with Brown (third ascent, first British ascent, 1954). They reduced the time taken from six days to 25 hours.
Whillans's interests veered away from rock-climbing around 1960. Unlike Brown, he has never returned to make concentrated attacks on other new cliffs. Instead he became a leading member of several high-altitude expeditions: Masherbrum, 1957; Trivor, 1960; Aig. Poincenot, 1962 (first ascent); Central Tower of Paine, 1962 (first ascent); Gauri Sankar, 1964; S Face of Huandoy, 1968; S Face of Annapurna, 1970 (first ascent); SW Face of Everest, 1971 and 1972; Roraima, 1973.
Whillans was at the centre of the controversy which was a feature of the Everest Expedition of 1971. He has reached the highest point yet attained on the SW Face (1973). He is a successful lecturer.
See: *Don Whillans-Portrait of a Mountaineer*, by D. Whillans and A. Ormerod, 1971.

WHITE GHYLL
A ravine on the flanks of Langdale, one side of which forms crags offering a large number of climbs, mostly in the middle and upper grades of difficulty. White Ghyll Chimney (Lyon, Herbert, Cain, 1923) was the first climb, but the Ghyll is particularly noted for its association with R. J. Birkett. The crag is very popular.
Guidebook: *Great Langdale*, by J. A. Austin.

WHITE MOUNTAINS, NEW HAMP-SHIRE

The three main cliffs of the White Mountains are Cannon (over 1,000 ft high), White Horse (800 ft) and Cathedral (500 ft). The rock is firm granite and there are climbs of all standards, many hard. They have been called 'the Yosemite of the North Eastern States'.

New Hampshire also offers the best winter climbing in the Eastern States. Best known is the Huntington Ravine on Mt Washington, where several gullies of 600 to 1,200 ft are frequently climbed, despite the appalling weather conditions for which the mountain is noted. Crawford Notch and Frankenstein Cliff also give good climbs, the former long and relatively easy, the latter short and hard.

Guidebooks: *White Mountain Guide*-Appalachian M. C.; *Cathedral and White Horse*, by J. Cote.

WHITE OUT

An unpleasant phenomenon of snow-scapes, where falling snow or even mist, can merge the land and sky together with complete loss of horizon. Eerie and dangerous, since it is possible to step over an edge unknowingly.

WHITWELL, Edward Robson (1843-1922)

A companion of Tuckett (*qv*) and making with him the first S–N traverse of Jungfrau and the second traverse of the Rothorn (1872). In 1874 he made the first ascent of the Aig. de Blaitière. Whitwell made a couple of attempts at the then unclimbed Dru, but failed.

WHYMPER, Edward (1840-1911)

One of the best-known names in mountaineering, forever associated with the tragic first ascent of the Matterhorn in which he took part (1865).

Whymper was born in London and became a wood-engraver, like his father. He showed considerable artistic skill and it was this that prompted W. Longman (*qv*), the publisher, to commission from him a series of Alpine sketches in 1860. It was Whymper's first visit to the Alps, and though he did little climbing that year, he saw in Alpine climbing a chance to make a name for himself and a possible chance to realize his ambition of becoming an Arctic explorer. It was this that led him to concentrate on unclimbed peaks right from the start (he served no apprenticeship at

climbing) and he had as a target either the Weisshorn or Matterhorn, since they were the highest unclimbed peaks of the time.

In 1861 he made the first English ascent of Mont Pelvoux in the Dauphiné. Hearing that Tyndall (*qv*) had climbed the Weisshorn, he decided to concentrate on the still unclimbed Matterhorn and went to Breuil in order to attempt the Italian Ridge, the Swiss or Hörnli Ridge being then considered unclimbable. At Breuil he met J. A. Carrel (*qv*), a local mason who was to figure prominently in subsequent attempts on the mountain.

Whymper's attempts on the Matterhorn can be summarized (all attempts on the Italian Ridge except where stated): (see table)

Carrel's part in these attempts cannot be overestimated. Whymper was fascinated by him, though he always did better when Carrel was not present, and the highest point reached before the final ascent (by Tyndall, 1862) was made by a party that only employed Carrel as a porter, not a guide. There seems little doubt that Carrel, a patriot, wanted the mountain climbed by Italians.

On 11 July 1865 began a series of events that were to end in tragedy. Carrel had made secret arrangements to attempt the mountain with an Italian party. Whymper, feeling angry and betrayed, joined Lord Francis Douglas in a return to Zermatt and there, by a series of coincidences, a large party assembled to attempt the Hörnli Ridge. The members were: Whymper, Douglas, Hudson (*qv*) and Hadow, with the guides Croz (*qv*), Old Peter Taugwalder and Young Peter Taugwalder. Joseph Taugwalder, a younger son of Old Peter, acted as porter for the first day.

The ascent was made without incident (summit reached 1.40 p.m. 14 July) but on the return Hadow, an inexperienced climber, slipped at a difficult passage, knocking over Croz. The two of them pulled Hudson and Douglas off, and though Old Peter and Whymper held the rope tightly, it snapped at the strain, and the four men plunged down the North Face to their deaths. Whymper and the two Taugwalders, shocked at the tragedy, made a dangerous return to Zermatt. The news of the accident stunned the entire civilized world.

More has been written about the Matterhorn tragedy than any other mountaineering event because of the unique circumstances surrounding it. (For details see the *Alpine Journal* and various books

Date		With	Height	Comments
29–30 August	1861	Unknown guide	12,650 ft	Camped on mountain
7–8 July	1862	Macdonald	12,000 ft	
9–10 July	1862	Macdonald Carrel	12,992 ft	
18–19 July	1862	solo	13,400 ft	Fell on descent
23–24 July	1862	Carrel	13,150 ft	
25–26 July	1862	Luc Meynet	13,460 ft	
10–11 August	1863	Carrel	13,280 ft	
21 June	1865	Croz Almer Biener	11,200 ft	On the South-East Face
13–15 July	1865	(see below)		First ascent. Hörnli Ridge from Zermatt

(The heights given are Whymper's own estimates.)

on the subject). The ascent of the Matterhorn is usually recognized as the end of the Golden Age of Alpine climbing.

Whymper made two further ascents of the Matterhorn in 1874 and 1895.

Though the Matterhorn is the central theme of Whymper's life, his other climbs, before and after, were considerable achievements. They were (all first ascents except where noted):

1861 Pelvoux (first English ascent)
1864 Aig de la Sausse (S Peak, first ascent)
Barre des Ecrins
Breche de la Meije
Col de Triolet
Mont Dolent
Aig de Trélatête
Aig d'Argentière
Moming Pass
1865 Grand Cornier
Dent Blanche (third ascent)
Grandes Jorasses (W Summit, now Pt Whymper)
Col Dolent
Aiguille Verte
Col de Talèfre
Ruinette

After 1865 he did no serious Alpine climbing but became interested in exploration, visiting Greenland in 1867 and 1872, the Andes 1879-80 and the Canadian Rockies 1901, 1904 and 1909. His first ascents include (in the Andes): Chimborazo, Sincholagua, Antisana, Cotopaxi; and (in the Rockies): Mt Mitchell, Mt Whymper, Mt White, Mt Kerr, Mt Marpole, Isolated Peak, Mt des Poilus, Mt Collie, Trolltinder (1901), Crowsnest Mountain (1904).

Besides his own books, Whymper helped to illustrate the following:

Mountaineering in 1861, J. Tyndall (1862)
Dolomite Mountains, Gilbert and Churchill (1864)
Regular Swiss Round, Rev. H. Jones (1865)
Alpine Regions, T. G. Bonney (1868)
Swiss Pictures Drawn with Pen and Pencil, S. Manning (1870)
Frosty Caucasus, F. C. Grove (1875)
Tent Life in Norway, H. Smith Stannier (1876)
Alpine Ascents and Adventures, S. Wilson, (frontispiece only, 1878)
Monte Rosa, the Epic of an Alp, S. H. Nichols (1886, U.S.A.)

After six years of meticulous revising and rewriting, Whymper published *Scrambles Amongst the Alps in the Years 1860-9* (1871). It is one of the great classics of climbing literature, universally known simply as *Scrambles*. An abridged version, entitled *The Ascent of the Matterhorn*, appeared in 1880. *Scrambles* has been translated into several languages and there have been several editions.

His second great work, *Travels among the Great Andes of the Equator*, appeared in 1891 with a second volume of scientific data in 1892. In 1891 he also published a pamphlet, *How to use the Aneroid Barometer* and, in 1896 and 1897 respectively, his tourist guidebooks to Chamonix and Zermatt. Whymper also wrote many articles for the popular press on mountain affairs, and with the decline of woodcuts in favour of photographs, his writings and lectures formed a substantial part of his income.

Whymper did not make friends easily and was not popular with most of his contemporaries. He figured in several long-standing quarrels over mountain matters and his general outlook was austere and severe; a forbidding personality. He married in 1906.

He died suddenly at Chamonix on 16

September 1911.

WICKS, John Herbert (1852-1919)

A member of the élite group which concentrated on Chamonix in the late 1880s and 1890s, Wicks made a number of new routes and variants. His usual companions were Bradby and Wilson (qv). Among his better-known exploits were: first guideless ascent of Charmoz (the Baton Wicks pinnacle is named after him) (1889); first ascent of SW arête of the Moine (1890); first ascent of the Pic Sans Nom (1890); first traverse S–N of Grépon (1893): and new routes on the Wetterhorn, Aletschhorn, Schreckhorn, Aig. de Talèfre, Aig. de la Brenva, and others of lesser note. In 1904 he made the second guideless ascent of the Old Brenva route.

WIDDOP

A series of gritstone buttresses on the moors between Burnley and Hebden Bridge, Yorkshire. Mystery Buttress is one of the biggest for this type of rock. At Hebden Bridge there is also Heptonstall Quarry, which has some long climbs, mostly hard.

Guidebook: *Yorkshire Gritstone*, by M. Bebbington.

WIEN, Karl (1906-37)

German scientist and leader of the disastrous Nanga Parbat Expedition of 1937 in which seven climbers (including Wien) and nine Sherpas were killed by an avalanche.

In 1924 he joined the Munich group that included notable climbers such as Welzenbach (qv) and Bauer (qv). He made three new routes in the Wetterstein in 1925 and in 1926 was with Welzenbach on the first ascents of the Glockerin NW Face, Eiskogele N Face, and Gross Glockner N Face. He then began some notable winter climbs (first ascents): Lyskamm, W Peak, and the traverse of Mont Blanc from Géant Glacier to Vallot Hut.

In 1928 he joined Rickmer's (qv) Pamirs Expedition, during which he climbed 26 summits. With Bauer's Kangchenjunga Expedition of 1931, he reached 25,263 ft – the highest reached on the expedition (with Hartmann). During 1933-4 he worked in Africa, climbing Mt Meru and attempting Mt Kenya, but in 1936 he returned to he Himlaya with Bauer's Sikkim Expedition, and climbed Siniolchu and Nepal Peak. Siniolchu (22,600 ft) is regarded by some authorities as the hardest Himalayan climb achieved before the War.

Wien edited *Willo Welzenbach's Bergfahrten* and Hartmann's *Kantschtagebuch* (Kangchenjunga, 1931).

WIESSNER, Fritz Hermann Ernst (b. 1900)

German-American chemist who had a considerable effect on the development of climbing in the U.S.A. Wiessner's early career was in the post-First World War arena of the Eastern Alps where he made numerous early ascents of the hardest routes at that time. Among his own first ascents are:

1919 Totenkirchl West Face (Piazwand) – first solo (but Preuss earlier?)
1925 Fleischbank SE Face with R. Rossi
      Furschetta N Face with E. Solleder
1926 Canali W Face with F. Simon
      Pala di San Martino, E Face Direct – with F. Simon
1927 Cima dei Lastei S Face – F. Simon, H. Kees
      Cima del Coro – Simon and Kees
1928 Sasso d'Ortiga, W Ridge – with H. Kees
      Civetta E Face – H. Kees
      Marmolada S Face – first solo (Original Route)

Weissner was a member of Merkl's 1932 Nanga Parbat Expedition and reached the ridge between Rakhiot Peak and Silbersattel; storms then forced the expedition to retreat. In 1939 he led the first American attempt on K2 and with Pasang Dawa reached a height of c. 27,500 ft, but lack of support caused his lines to be stretched and in a storm three Sherpas and D. Wolfe died. Wiessner was heavily criticized for his handling of the expedition.

Meanwhile he had gone to live in the U.S.A. and began climbing there. He opened up the Shawangunks in 1935 (qv) and by his example generally raised climbing standards, particularly in the east.

In 1935 he made the second ascent of the Grand Teton North Ridge, in 1937 the first ascent of the Devil's Tower, Wyoming (Coveney, House) and in 1939 the first ascent of Mt Waddington (with W. P. House). Numerous other ascents in the Rockies, etc.

Wiessner climbed in many parts of the world. He has completed all the 4000 m peaks of the Alps and made many ski ascents of the larger Alpine peaks. He still climbs regularly, though now in his seventies.

WILLIAMS, Alfred (1832-1905)

An Alpine artist whose pictures were much

in vogue at the close of the last century. 'Monte Rosa at sunrise from above Ulagna' is in the Victoria and Albert Museum.

WILLIAMS, William (1862-1947)
An American lawyer who made the first ascent of Piz Bernina by the SW arête (1885). Was with Broke and Topham (*qv*) on the attempt of the S Ridge of Mt St Elias in Alaska (1888) and lived to hear of the first American ascent 58 years later. Williams had the reputation of being a hard man on mountains.

WILLINK, George Henry (1851-1938)
An amateur artist whose sketches of 'climbers in action vividly illustrate climbing at the end of the last century. (See the Badminton volume, *Mountaineering*, illustrated by Willink and containing his chapter 'Sketching for Climbers'.)

WILLS, Sir Alfred (1828-1912)
High Court Judge and one of the best-known pioneers of the Alps. Though he made no notable first ascents it was his description of his ascent of the Wetterhorn in 1854 (fourth ascent), described two years later in his book, *Wanderings Among the High Alps*, that began the Golden Age (*qv*) (but see also SMITH, A.).

Wills was a protagonist in the glacier controversy that convulsed climbers and scientists in the latter part of the century, and a strong supporter of Forbes (*qv*).

An Original Member of the A.C. he was President from 1864-5.

He built a famous chalet in the valley of Sixt called 'The Eagle's Nest', where he spent the summer months and where Auguste Balmat (*qv*), his guide, was estate manager. He described the chalet and some of his expeditions in a book *The Eagle's Nest* (1860).

WILLS, William Alfred (1862-1924)
Son of Sir A. Wills (*qv*). Wills was associated with the élite party centred on Chamonix at the turn of the century, particularly Bradby, Wicks (*qv*) and Wilson (*qv*). He took part in most of their expeditions. His brother, J. T. Wills, also did some climbing, including a strange circular tour of the Matterhorn (1884).

WILSON, Claude (1860-1937)
One of the outstanding climbers of all time, with a long career beginning in the 1880s. He was one of the Chamonix élite at the end of the last century, contemporary of Mummery (*qv*), with whom he was in rivalry for the first ascent of the Requin, then unnamed (it had been provisionally christened Pic C. W. by Wilson's friends).

His first new route was the S Face of the Weissmies (1882), followed by some first ascents in Norway (1885), but from 1889, when he made the first guideless ascent of Charmoz, his record becomes one of continuous success. He made the first guideless ascent of Grépon (1892) and the first guideless traverse of it from S – N (1893). In 1904 he made the first traverse of Aig. de la Brenva. His new routes were numerous: ten major ascents other than those mentioned. In all he made 360 major ascents, 238 of which were guideless. His two brother, Francis Edward and Herbert, accompanied him on some of the early climbs, but his usual companions were Wicks, Bradby, Wills and Morse (*qv*).

Wilson was President of the A.C. 1929-

$$K = 91 \cdot 4 \text{-} T \ (4 \ \sqrt{v} + 5 - v/4) \text{ where } K = \text{wind-chill factor}$$
$$T = {}^\circ F$$
$$v = \text{mph of wind}$$

The sensation scale for K is:

50	hot	800	cold
100	warm	1000	very cold
200	pleasant	1200	bitterly cold
400	cool	1400	exposed flesh freezes
600	very cool	2000	exposed flesh freezes in 60 seconds
		2500	intolerable

The 1400 factor is reached by the following sample air temp./wind combinations: 20°F at 45 mph; 10°F at 18 mph; −10°F at 7 mph; −40°F at 2 mph. Temperatures of −30°F combined with winds of 30 mph have been experienced on Everest's South Col in winter.

31. He wrote *Mountaineering* (1893) and a privately printed account of his climbing career. As a doctor, he was one of the first to use electro-cardiographs.

WIND-CHILL FACTOR

The chilling effect of the wind can seriously effect a mountaineer and may ultimately lead to exposure (*qv*). On high-altitude expeditions and in winter climbing in the Alps the wind-chill factor needs to be carefully assessed. It is calculated from the simple formula on p. 239.

WIND RIVER MOUNTAINS, WYOMING

A range of fine granite peaks, north-west of the Great Divide basin. The range is some 75 miles long and 20 miles wide and is fairly difficult of access. The highest peaks are Gannett Peak (13,785 ft) and Fremont Peak (13,730 ft) ascended in 1833 (probably) and 1842, respectively.

Guidebook: *Guide to the Wyoming Mountains and Wilderness Areas*, by O and L. Bonney.

WINKLER, Georg (1869-88)

A Munich climber famous for his solo ascents, including the Winkler Turme in the Vajolet Towers (1887). In the following year he was overwhelmed by an avalanche while soloing the W Face of the Weisshorn. His body reappeared on the Weisshorn Glacier in 1955.

WINKWORTH, Stephen (1831-86)

A cotton spinner of Bolton who made a number of new passes including Col d'Argentière and Zwillingsjoch. Usually climbed with his wife, Emma, who became the first woman to ascend Aletschhorn and Jungfrau (1863).

WINTOUR'S LEAP

A limestone outcrop overlooking the Wye near Chepstow, Gloucestershire, with many fine lines of all standards. There are climbs also at Symonds Yat and Cleeve Hill.

Guidebook: *Rock Climbs in the Wye Valley and Cotswolds* – Gloucestershire M.C.

WOODMASS, Montagu (1834-1917)

In 1863 made the first ascent of Dent d'Hérens and first ascent of Parrotspitze with Hall, Grove and Macdonald (*qv*).

WOOLLEY, Hermann (1846-1920)

A Manchester climber of the school of exploration that included Collie, Freshfield and Dent (*qv*). He made the first ascent of the NW arête of the Gross Fiescherhorn (1887), but it is his climbs in the Caucasus (1888, 1889, 1895, 1896) Lofoten (1897, 1901, 1904) and the Canadian Rockies (1898 and 1902) for which he is remembered. He made first ascents in each of these districts, notably Katuintau, Mishirgitau, Koshtantau, Ailama, Tsitgeli, Sarumbashi and Gumachi (Caucasus) and Mount Athabasca, Dome, Mount Wilcox (solo), Diadem and Mount Thompson (Rockies).

With Hastings (*qv*), he made the first exploration of the Lyngen Peninsula (Norway) in 1897, and with Collie and Stutfield (*qv*) discovered the Columbia Glacier in the Rockies.

A fine photographer, he went to the Alps in winter mainly for the purposes of his hobby, but he made the first winter ascent of Rimpfischhorn (1893). Woolley was an all-round sportsman: champion oarsman, boxer, etc. President of the A.C. 1908-10.

THE WORKMANS

Dr William Hunter Workman (1847–1937) and Mrs Fanny Workman (1859-1925) were a remarkably adventurous couple noted for their explorations in the Karakorum. Both came from Massachusetts and Dr Workman had a practice there until 1889, when bad health forced him to retire. Meanwhile, in 1881, he had married Fanny Bullock (they sometimes used the name Bullock-Workman).

On his retirement they took up cycling and made remarkable journeys by cycle in Europe, N. Africa, the Middle East, Ceylon, Java, Siam and 14,000 miles in India. This took seven years and in the last of their voyages, in 1898, they first saw the Himalaya and were at once attracted.

In 1899 they made their first expedition, to the Biafo Glacier of the Karakorum. Then came:

1902-3 Chogo Lungma glacier and the ascent of Pyramis Peak (23,394 ft – a height record) by Dr Workman, then aged 56

1906 Nun Kun expedition. Mrs Workman reached about 23,000 ft – woman's height record – then aged 47

1908 Exploration of the Hispar-Biafo glaciers

1911 Siachen glacier exploration

1912 Siachen glacier and over Kaberi Pass to Baltistan

They alternated the leading of the expedition and the scientific work between them trip by trip. They wrote nine books, jointly, and those concerning their Himalayan visits had a certain vogue at the time. They were *In the Ice-World of Himalaya* (1900), *Ice-bound Heights of the Mustagh* (1908), *Peaks and Glaciers of Nun Kun* (1909), *The Call of the Snowy Hispar* (1910) and *Two Summers in the Ice Wilds of the Eastern Karakorum* (1917).

YELD, George (1845–1938)

A Yorkshire schoolmaster who became the great authority on the Graian Alps, where he made many first ascents. He collaborated with Coolidge (*qv*) on the guidebook to the area (*The Mountains of Cogne*, 1893) and wrote *Scrambles in the Eastern Graians 1878-1897* (1900). He visited the Eastern Caucasus in 1890 and made the first ascent of Basardjusi. On a visit to the Lipari Islands he climbed Vulcano, Vulcanello and Stromboli (1904). Editor of the *A. J.* from 1896-1919 and Joint Editor 1919-26: an unique record. Expert horticulturist and gold medalist of the R.H.S.

YOSEMITE VALLEY, CALIFORNIA

A valley in the Yosemite National Park of the Sierra Nevada. Though the peaks are fairly low (Half Dome 8,852ft), they rise in sheer walls and spires from the valley, immensely impressive to tourist and climber alike. The post-war climbs at Yosemite have had a profound effect on world rock-climbing, and it is arguably the most important rock-climbing centre in the world.

The rock is a compact granite, glacier-polished and with smooth cracks and flaring chimneys, which tends to give a muscular type of climbing, particularly on the big walls. All the routes tend to be hard, though they vary in length from short "outcrop" type cracks to major climbs lasting several days. Pegs and bolts are used, but the latter only where strictly necessary, and pegs are removed after use. (It was for use on the hard Yosemite granite that Chouinard developed his special steel pegs which have now become standard in America and Britain.) The ethics of climbing at Yosemite are high, and pitches previously bolted have in some cases been repeated with the tiny bat-hooks.

The long multi-day climbs have led to the development of webbing étriers, webbing belay seats, bivvy hammocks and an improvement in the techniques of sack-hauling and various rope manoeuvres.

The best seasons for climbing in Yosemite are spring and autumn when the storms are less frequent than they are in winter. In summer, with temperatures of 100°F plus, dehydration is a serious problem, particularly on the big walls. Even in spring and autumn plenty of water has to be carried.

The principal climbs of Yosemite are found on the Cathedral Spires, Sentinel Rock, Lost Arrow, Half Dome, El Capitan, Cathedral Rock, and Mt Watkins. El Capitan, with routes of 2,000 to 3,000 ft, all hard, is the most famous of these (*qv*).

Climbing in Yosemite began in 1933 and the following year the Cragmont Climbing Club, inspired by the Easterner R. Underhill, climbed Higher and Lower Cathedral Spires. The ascent of The Lost Arrow by J. Salathé and A. Nelson in 1947 brought this period of development to an end. In 1949 the Sierra Club rationalized gradings (*qv*).

The great modern breakthrough came with the first ascent of the Nose of El

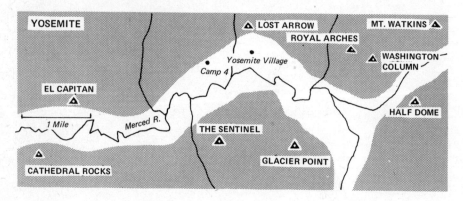

Capitan by W. Harding, G. Whitmore, W. Merry in 1958. The ascent was by siege tactics – 45 days spread over 18 months. 3,000 ft of fixed rope, 675 pegs and 125 bolts were used. Dihedral Wall of El Capitan (Baldwin, Cooper, Denny, 1962) also involved a 42-day siege, but climbers in the 1960s began to reject siege tactics as unethical As early as 1960, Fitschen, Robbins, Frost and Pratt repeated the Nose climb in a single push. Other outstanding climbs include:

1957 NW Face, Half Dome – Robbins' party
1960 W Face, Sentinel – Frost, Chouinard
1961 Salathé Wall, El Capitan – Pratt, Frost, Robbins
1964 S Face, Mt Watkins – Harding, Chouinard, Pratt
     North America Wall, El Capitan – Robbins, Pratt, Frost, Chouinard
     N Face, Half Dome – Robbins, McCracken
1966 Muir Wall, El Capitan – Chouinard, Herbert
1968 Muir Wall, El Capitan – Robbins (solo)
1970 S Face, Half Dome – Harding, Rowell
     Wall of Early Morning Light, El Capitan – Caldwell, Harding

(See also EL CAPITAN.)

Guidebook: *A Climber's Guide to Yosemite Valley*, by S. Roper.

YOUNG, Geoffrey Winthrop (1876–1958)

One of the most important figures in British mountaineering. Young was a son of Sir George Young who made the first ascent of the Jungfrau from Wengern Alp in 1865. In the following year, Sir George's brother was killed while climbing and all mention of mountaineering was forbidden in the Young household, though regular visits were made to Wales for hill walks. Young began rock-climbing in the Lakes as an undergraduate (and on the college spires; he wrote: *The Roof-Climber's Guide to Trinity*, 1900).

His first visit to the Alps was in 1897 (to the Tarentaise) and then followed years in the Oberland and Pennine Alps, making a number of good climbs. In 1905 he met Josef Knubel (*qv*), the guide with whom he formed a perfect team and with whom he did most (but not all) his great climbs. He usually climbed with a guide, but he did solo the Grand Cornier and he led an amateur rope on the first ascent of the Nesthorn NE Ridge (Young, Mallory,

Robertson, 1909). His best known routes are:

1905 Weisshorn, SE Face (improved 1906)
1906 Taschhorn, SW Face
     Breithorn. Younggrat
     Dom, SW Face
1907 Zinal Rothorn, E Face
     Weisshorn, Younggrat
1911 Gd. Jorasses, E Ridge (descent)
     Brouillard Ridge of Mt Blanc
     Gd. Jorasses, W Ridge
     Grépon, Mer de Glace Face
1914 Gspaltenhorn, Rote Zähn Ridge

He was a strong climber; he did all the tops of Monte Rosa, Lyskamm, Castor and back to Lyskamm in a day, and Charmoz, Grépon and Blaitière in a day.

During the 1914-18 War he served in an ambulance unit and lost his left leg in action. He invented an artificial limb and began climbing again achieving a number of summits including the Matterhorn. His last ascent was the Zinal Rothorn in 1935. (See his book; *Mountains with a Difference*, 1951.)

Young held climbing parties at the Pen y Pass, Snowdonia from 1900 until well after the War, and these were attended by most of the best climbers of the day. They did much to stimulate the exploration of the district. Young helped to persuade Thomson to publish the first climbers' guidebooks (*qv*). As early as 1907 he suggested an association of climbing clubs and in 1919 actually brought about such a thing, though it failed. In 1943 he tried again and the result was the establishment of the British Mountaineering Council in 1944 (*qv*).

By profession an educationist, Young was also a poet of merit and his poem, *The Cragsman*, is quoted in many anthologies. His textbook, *Mountain Craft* (1920), was for long the standard work. His book, *On High Hills* (1927), deals with his early adventures and is a classic of its type.

Young married Slingsby's (*qv*) daughter Eleanor. He was President of the A.C. 1941-4.

YOUNGHUSBAND, Sir Francis Edward (1863-1942)

Noted soldier-explorer. In 1887 he crossed the Gobi Desert from Peking and entered India over the Mustagh Pass, the first crossing by a European. Explored the Karakorum (*qv*) in 1889 and the Pamirs in 1890. Was head of the famous Mission to Tibet in 1903-4. Wrote *The Heart of a Continent* (1896).

Z

ZDARSKY, Matthäus (d. 1940)

One of the early ski-teachers of the Alps and an inveterate inventor of equipment, including the Zdarsky sleeping bag and the first reliable ski-binding. He made the first analysis of ski movements and invented the stem-turn. Zdarsky was badly crushed by an avalanche during the First World War and invented a device to enable him to overcome his disabilities. Zdarsky has been called the "Hermit of Lilienfeld" (cf. Coolidge) and the exponents of his ski method were once known as Lilienfelders. He was in his eighties when he died.

ZERMATT

The principal climbing centre of the Pennine Alps, Switzerland; an international ski resort and tourist village. The view of the Matterhorn from Zermatt is probably the best-known mountain scene in the world.

The village lies at the head of the Mattertal, a branch of the Visptal, and is reached by rail from the Rhône valley. The road is not open to tourist traffic beyond Täsch (1972), though this may alter.

It is the centre for many 4000 m peaks, including Matterhorn, Weisshorn, Monte Rosa and Dom.

In climbing history only Chamonix can seriously rival Zermatt as a pioneering centre. The Monte Rosa Hotel was practically a club house for the Alpine Club.

ZILLERTAL ALPS

A range of mountains on the Austro-Italian border between the Stubai and Venediger groups. Penetrated by the long valley of Zillertal where Mayrhofen is an international tourist centre. The peaks here are more difficult than in the neighbouring areas, and include rock-climbs as well as ice-climbs. The highest summit is Hochfeiler (3,510 m) which has a notable N Face. (No English guidebook.)

ZSIGMONDY BROTHERS

Three Austrian brothers, two of whom, Otto (1860-1918) and Emil (1861-85) were among the leading climbers of the day. With climbers such as Purtscheller (qv) and Schultz (qv) they made ascents which were regarded as outrageously dangerous at that time. They climbed without guides and often solo. Emil was the undoubted leader of the group. Dent said of him; "He was too dangerous to be imitated." In fact, the brothers and their friends were merely ahead of their time and the attitude they took to climbing eventually culminated in Welzenbach and others (qv) and ultimately led to the modern concept of Alpinism. Emil was killed trying a new route on the Meije. The Zsigmondyspitze in the Zillertal Alps is named after them.

ZURCHER, Alfred (b. 1889)

A Swiss mountaineer who started climbing in 1906 and made numerous Alpine ascents, many with Josef Knubel (qv). His greatest ascents were the first ascent of the North Ridge of Piz Badile (with W. Risch as guide, 1923) and the first ascent of the Lauper Route on the Eiger (qv), in 1932.

Index

The number before the stroke indicates the page, the number after the stroke the entry on that page. **Bold** figures indicate a complete entry.